MODERN MEDEA

ALSO BY STEVEN WEISENBURGER

A "Gravity's Rainbow" Companion: Sources and Contexts for Pynchon's Novel

Fables of Subversion: Satire and the American Novel

MODERN MEDEA

A Family Story of Slavery and Child-Murder
from the Old South

STEVEN WEISENBURGER

❧

📖 HILL AND WANG

A division of Farrar, Straus and Giroux

Hill and Wang
A division of Farrar, Straus and Giroux
19 Union Square West, New York 10003

Library of Congress Cataloging-in-Publication Data
Weisenburger, Steven.
    Modern Medea : a family story of slavery and child-murder from the
Old South / Steven Weisenburger.
        p.   cm.
    Includes bibliographical references (p.   ) and index.
    ISBN 0-8090-6953-9 (alk. paper)
      1. Garner, Margaret. 2. Fugitive slaves — Kentucky — Biography.
    3. Fugitive slaves — Legal status, laws, etc. — United States.
    4. Fugitive slaves — Legal status, laws, etc. — Ohio — Cincinnati.
    5. Garner, Margaret — Trials, litigation, etc. 6. Infanticide — Ohio —
    Cincinnati — Case studies. I. Title.
    E450.G225W45   1998
    306.3'62'092 — dc21
    [B]   98-15565

Grateful acknowledgment is made to the following for permission to reprint copyrighted material: The Oregon Historical Society, negatives 91889 and 91890, for the photographs that
appear on pages 22 and 29, The Cincinnati Historical Society, negatives A-81-188, B-98-025,
B-98-026, B-95-017, A-81-201, and B-86-041, for the photographs that appear on pages 63,
106, 113, 129, 196, and 211.

IN MEMORY OF MY FATHER

CONTENTS

❧

ILLUSTRATIONS

✥

ACKNOWLEDGMENTS

"... if I'd a knowed what a trouble it was to make a book I wouldn't a tackled it and ain't agoing to no more": Huck Finn's famous words, in farewell. But I suppose he didn't have the kinds of family, friends, and colleagues who have blessed my work with the support, encouragement, and helpful criticism needed to complete it. Here I have the honor of thanking them.

In 1989 I got the idea to research an essay on the Margaret Garner fugitive slave case as historical context for Toni Morrison's 1987 novel, *Beloved*. Soon the historical archive revealed unsuspected and complicated riches, the Garner case took shape for me as an alternate, parallel story to the one that Morrison imagined, and I realized the breadth of ground it was asking me to cover. I had spent my early career working on twentieth-century American literature. Now I had to retrain myself.

Fortunately, I have been able to learn from the work of historians whose research provides new views into the "domestic institution" of American slavery. Important to my own work were books on the telling complexities of slave culture, in particular those recent studies that have pushed inquiry into slavery's most intimate recesses. Thus I have learned much from and been inspired by the work of Jacqueline Jones, Elizabeth Fox-Genovese, Brenda Stevenson, John Blassingame, Sterling

Stuckey, Annette Gordon-Reed, Deborah Gray White, Marion B. Lucas, Jean Fagan Yellin, James Horton, and Henry Louis Taylor.

For advice and research assistance I am grateful to a host of wonderful librarians: the entire staff at the Cincinnati Historical Society, especially Ann Shepherd; Clark Evans, Joan Higbee, and Rosemary Plakas of the Rare Book Room at the Library of Congress; James Corsaro, of the Manuscripts and Special Collections Division of the New York State Library in Albany; Patricia Yannarella of the Boone County, Kentucky, Public Library; Chet Orloff and Cecil Housel of the Oregon Historical Society; Kenneth Hopkins of the Fort Worth Public Library; James Birchfield, in Special Collections at the University of Kentucky; Martha Severens of the Greenville County, South Carolina, Museum of Art; Tim Tingle, at the Kentucky Department for Libraries and Archives in Frankfort, Kentucky; Linda Mouchyn at the National Archives; and the staff at the Ohio Historical Society. Staff members in the Interlibrary Loan Department of the University of Kentucky Library responded promptly to my incessant requests.

For permission to reprint illustrations used in this book I am grateful to the Oregon Historical Society and the Cincinnati Historical Society.

Grants from the Southern Regional Education Board helped me to work in the Library of Congress. A sabbatical leave and grant from the University of Kentucky provided time and financial assistance at a crucial stage.

I am deeply grateful to Russ Castronovo, Carolyn Karcher, Charles Rowell, and Karen Sanchez-Eppler, who responded to my inquiries, suggested approaches, and encouraged this project in many ways. John Cawelti, Joe Gardner, Ellen Rosenman, and Mark Summers gave suggestions, at times a willing ear, and I thank them. I thank James Johnson for his encouragement and his example. At Hill and Wang, Lauren Osborne provided smart and meticulous editing that strengthened the manuscript by tightening the narrative and the prose, while always respecting my stylistic preferences.

I am well short of figuring out how to thank adequately William W. Freehling and Dana D. Nelson. Just having them as University of Kentucky colleagues has been a blessing. Yet Bill and Dana have supplied me with book lists, listened patiently to my brainstorming, encouraged the writing, read and critiqued chapters, and they've done it unstintingly, from the first that I told them about the Garner case. This book owes an immeasurable debt to their generous, wise counsel—in sum, to their friendship.

Finally, in writing of the Garners' tragic losses I have many times been thankful for the blessings of my own family: the in-laws who took an interest in this work, a brother and sister who encouraged it, my mother who read a draft of it, Rachel and James who have practically grown up with this story. The gratitude I owe my wife, Susan, for her moral, intellectual, and domestic support is, as ever, immeasurable.

De little baby gone home,
    De little baby gone home,
De little baby gone along,
    For to climb up Jacob's ladder.

And I wish I'd been dar,
    I wish I'd been dar,
I wish I'd been dar, my Lord,
    For to climb up Jacob's ladder.

Slaves' hymn for infant's funeral
(Traditional, ca. 1860)

MODERN MEDEA

PROLOGUE

❧✷❧

On a Saturday afternoon in late May 1857, Cincinnati lawyer John Jolliffe rode a ferry across the Ohio River to Kentucky. After a morning's work at his office, he was going to meet his wife for a midday dinner at the home of a Covington Presbyterian minister, Charles Sage, a fellow abolitionist. Also on Jolliffe's mind that day, perhaps as he walked up from the steamboat landing, past Covington's red-brick dry-goods shops and livery stables, was a recently concluded lawsuit against three Cincinnati election officials (Ward Judges) who refused the ballot of Jesse Beckley, Jr., "because he was a colored man." During the trial, defense witnesses testified that Beckley's mother was white and his natural father half Indian, half Portuguese. The boy's father died when his son was an infant, and several years later his mother married Jesse Beckley, a free black cabinetmaker who gave the boy his name and paid young Jesse's fees at Cincinnati's black secondary school, Hiram Gilmore High.

Judge Richard Spencer explained to the all-white jury that color should be determined either by pedigree (Ohio's constitution, he said, "used the term 'white' in contradistinction to the Indian or African races") or by inspection ("the word 'white,' when speaking in reference to color, means a color pure and unadulterated"). Anyone else was legally black or mulatto and automatically excluded from the polling booths, as Ohio law enfranchised only "white male citizens over twenty-one." Spencer told jurors how any evidence that Jesse Beckley was colored required a finding against the plaintiff and for those three Ward Judges. His instructions all but demanded such a verdict, for defense testimony had carefully detailed Beckley's pedigree, with its "Indian" tincture. Moreover, jurors could plainly see Beckley's relatively darker complexion and some may also have known he was active in the Convention of Colored Freemen of Ohio. They nevertheless deadlocked for ten hours before an astounded and frustrated Judge Spencer gave up and slated a retrial for Monday, the first of June, two days after the Jolliffes' dinner with the Reverend Sage.[1]

A quarter century's agitation against slavery and prejudice had schooled the conscientious white men who stood in solidarity with Cincinnati blacks and hung the Beckley jury. That Saturday, Jolliffe was hoping Monday's retrial would bring a more decisive victory against Ohio's exclusionary laws. As Jolliffe turned the corner of Third and Madison streets in Covington, a thin, bearded Kentucky planter called out to him by name. At first Jolliffe couldn't place the man, but then the planter strode up and bellowed: "My name is Gaines! I know you damned well, you damned rascal, you nigger thief! You came over here to steal our niggers!" A jeering crowd quickly gathered outside the Madison House hotel as Gaines continued cursing and pushing Jolliffe backward, obviously hoping the man would fight back. Instead, Jolliffe, who was raised a Quaker, ducked into a dry-goods store and asked owner William Timberlake for help.[2]

An unfortunate choice, Timberlake. For the last decade he'd been hiring out slaves from owners in Archibald Gaines's neighborhood, eighteen miles south at Richwood Station, Kentucky. Worse, Timberlake had been forced to use hirelings because in 1847 a number of his own slaves ran away to Michigan, where abolitionist lawyers just like John Jolliffe won the fugitives their freedom in a dramatic trial.[3] William Timberlake had never forgiven that loss, and that Saturday afternoon he "made some show of dissuading Gaines" but pushed Jolliffe back into the street.

Now risen to "a great passion," Gaines punched Jolliffe in the ribs and resumed working the crowd. "Here's a damned nigger thief," Gaines shouted, "and all those interested in niggers had better look out, for he's come over to steal their slaves!" Jolliffe also appealed to the crowd—for safe escort back to the ferry dock. He disavowed any intention of stealing slaves and promised never to return to Kentucky. One man in the crowd told Jolliffe to "Go to hell!" Another called out for someone to "Get a cowhide and let's cowhide him!" A few others suggested lynching. Finally help arrived. A deputy U.S. marshal drew his six-shooter, warned off the crowd, and guided Jolliffe back down Madison Street to the riverfront. An anonymous German man took Jolliffe's other flank. Following right behind was Archibald Gaines, himself now calling to onlookers for a cowhide whip. When somebody threw him one Gaines "struck Mr. Jolliffe with it over the shoulders." Another deputy marshal arrested Gaines and the crowd began dispersing.

Two days later Jolliffe lost the retrial of Jesse Beckley's lawsuit. Two days after that, the Mayor's Court of Covington tried Archibald Kinkead Gaines for assault. His attorney, longtime family friend John Menzies, admitted that Gaines punched and whipped Jolliffe (who did not attend) but also offered "as extenuation of the charge" facts "everyone well knew." Menzies was referring to the longest, most expensive and dramatic fugitive slave trial in United States history, a courtroom drama that had pitted Jolliffe against Gaines.

Sixteen months earlier, during the coldest Ohio Valley winter in recorded history, a twenty-two-year-old Kentucky slave named Margaret Garner gathered up her four children and fled Maplewood, Archibald Gaines's plantation. Leading the party was Margaret's husband, Robert, who brought along his parents, Simon and Mary, all three the slaves of Gaines's neighbor James Marshall. In a daring and well-planned escape, Robert drove a stolen horse-drawn sleigh eighteen miles up the turnpike to Covington. Abandoning the sleigh on a city street, the Garners walked across the frozen Ohio River and took sanctuary in the Cincinnati cabin of Margaret's free black cousin. Gaines tracked them to that place and soon had the cabin surrounded by deputy U.S. marshals from Covington and Cincinnati. Thinking all was lost, Margaret Garner seized a butcher knife and nearly decapitated her two-year-old daughter, Mary. She was turning on her other three children when slave catchers burst in and subdued her.

Margaret Garner's child-murder electrified the United States. "ARREST OF FUGITIVE SLAVES—A Slave Mother Murders her Child rather than see it Returned to Slavery!" cried Northern newspapers. The Garners' trial on a federal fugitive slave warrant lasted an unheard-of four weeks. It put Cincinnati at center stage in the national debate over slavery. Defending the Garners, John Jolliffe had orated to packed courtrooms and transformed the legal process into high political drama. Outside, crowds of pro- and antislavery partisans clashed and authorities met escalating threats of violence with four hundred federally authorized special deputies.

The ensuing public opinion battle raged for months, as Margaret Garner's story was told in churches and rented theaters by sympathetic preachers and outraged abolitionists. To them, no case more incisively revealed the pathology of slavery, and no deeds better symbolized the slave's tragic heroism. To proslavery writers her deeds demonstrated that slaves were subhuman. Only a beast would kill its offspring, they reasoned, so Margaret's child-murder proved the bond servant's need for Southern slavery's kindly paternal authority.

Both sides agreed that the Margaret Garner case posed crucial questions that divided the Union. For example, was the 1850 Fugitive Slave Act, which demanded that citizens assent to and assist with capturing fugitive blacks, constitutional? Then came key states' rights questions. How could the state of Ohio, having indicted the adult Garners for murder, accept the federal intervention that set aside the murder charge for Kentuckians' claims to their runaway chattels, a mere property suit? How could property outweigh persons in the scales of Justice? Finally, though, it all boiled down to slavery: Could Southerners count on national support for it? How much slavery must Northerners finally stomach? Could Southerners rely on Northerners to return their "property" when it ran away? Could Northerners be *forced* to assist Southerners, when helping was morally, spiritually repugnant? Both sides punctuated their rhetoric with images of fraternal strife and saw in their differences over Margaret Garner's case the roots of civil war.

During the June 1857 trial of Archibald Gaines on assault charges, John Menzies also recalled the Garner trial as an occasion when "lawyer Jolliffe grossly insulted and injured" the reputation of his client Archibald Gaines. The "abuse to Gaines and his family" included insinuations that Gaines was "inhuman" to Margaret Garner in ways too horrible to name before the court. One of Menzies's witnesses testified that, "in Kentucky, some of [Jolliffe's] remarks were thought a gross outrage" to any gentleman, and therefore required settlement "on the field of honor." Menzies claimed the chance meeting of 30 May 1857 had given Squire Gaines his first opportunity to do just that. Some Kentuckians on the twelve-man jury must have agreed that Archibald Gaines was only redressing a legitimate and long-standing assault on his honor and was therefore innocent. They deadlocked the jury's deliberations until the judge, refusing them any break for dinner, demanded a verdict of the twelve white men, five of whom owned slaves. Emerging from the jury room an hour later, the twelve Kentuckians reluctantly agreed to a guilty verdict but fined Gaines just twenty-two dollars and fifty cents. Menzies claimed a victory. Cincinnati papers claimed that Gaines's conduct and the paltry fine were an outrage to Ohio, another wedge gaveled into the rift between North and South.

The "Gaines-Jolliffe Affair" was only one among hundreds of interrelated clashes over slavery that erupted all through the states during the last antebellum decade. These were years when Southern demands that Northern jurisdictions return runaway slaves became an "acid test" of Union.[4] When Boston abolitionists "rescued" a fugitive named Shadrach before he could be remanded to the South. And when Boston Commons, hallowed ground where revolutionists joyously burned King George's coat of arms in 1776, in 1854 became the parade grounds where antislavery forces stood powerlessly, mournfully by as federal marshals marched fugitive Anthony Burns back to slavery. The Burns case was memorialized in the writings of Frederick Douglass, Walt Whitman, and Ralph Waldo Emerson, and it is still widely recounted in histories of the period.[5] In that decade, however, no antebellum fugitive case achieved the signal importance of Margaret Garner's.

Before Confederate troops fired on Fort Sumter, writers represented her infanticide in a spate of essays and poems, as well as two antislavery novels. One narrative appeared so soon afterward that modern publishers' swift "novelizations" of popular tragedies seem nothing new. During the Civil War, prominent politicians still squabbled over their handling of the Garner case. During Reconstruction, some of the principals in the Garner drama still debated their roles, and Margaret Garner took on mythic status. Kentucky artist Thomas Noble painted Margaret Garner as a heroic, defiant mother confronting slave catchers over the outstretched bodies of her children, and the renowned Mathew Brady produced a lithograph of Noble's infanticidal tableau, an image published in popular magazines such as *Harper's Weekly*.

Noble called his painting "The Modern Medea," a title with deeply troubling inferences. In Euripides' drama, a Medea already suspected of practicing the "black arts" of witchcraft kills her two children to spite their father, Jason. Jason had cut Medea to the heart by rejecting her for a racially "purer" wife; she countered by cutting off his royal lineage. Noble's title therefore implies that Margaret Garner destroyed Archibald Gaines's property—and the child of *their* illicit union—out of *jealous rage*. "The Modern Medea" thus plays on themes of miscegenation, sexual bondage, and the black woman as alluring and dangerous Other, themes nineteenth-century Americans typically spoke about in code.

Margaret Garner's translation into myth marked the beginning of a long amnesia. After Reconstruction and until 1987 she all but vanished from American cultural memory. But how could this have happened? Had the poems, fictions, and paintings—the whole range of artifacts meant to *memorialize* the Garner case—somehow failed to do their work? The lapse becomes doubly difficult for us to fathom because in its own epoch the Garner case became *the* most significant and controversial of all the antebellum fugitive stories. In fact, if sheer mass of reference and representation count for anything, then Margaret Garner was as compelling, perhaps even *more* compelling a figure of slavery than perennially famous fugitive slaves like Anthony Burns, Thomas Sims, and Dred Scott. But none of them ever disappeared from the histories.[6]

How then was the Garner case so different? Dred Scott came to symbolize the grand story of the clash over slavery's political and legal status under the Constitution. But even though it was never argued before the Supreme Court, the Garner case also turned on crucial issues in constitutional law. Therefore the difference must lie elsewhere. Gender was crucial. Margaret Garner's infanticide spotlighted the plight of women slaves and symbolized slavery's awful, violent power over and within slave families—issues once at the very heart of anti- and proslavery arguments but waylaid for generations in the grand narratives about slavery's constitutional challenges leading to disunion. The current generation of historians has returned to slavery's domestic drama, of the

Margaret Garner
DETAIL FROM THOMAS SATTERWHITE NOBLE, "THE MODERN MEDEA" (1867)

tense relations inside and around the "Big House" and the dissonant choruses of coercion, resistance, and violence echoing from it.

For over a century the Garner case surfaced only in the odd historical footnote. Then Toni Morrison's award-winning 1987 novel, *Beloved*, once more brought it before the public eye. Articles and interviews touted the novel's historical origins. Still, Morrison herself has always said that Margaret Garner's infanticide only provided the seed for *Beloved*, and that her sole nineteenth-century source was a reprinted journalistic article containing the "important things," such as the number and sex of Margaret's children and the barest facts about her child-murder. After that, Morrison deliberately avoided any further research. "The rest," she told reporters in 1987, "was novel writing."[7]

Morrison begins her story during Reconstruction, eighteen years after the infanticide, and unfolds her heroine's deeds in the briefest flashbacks. Few of the novel's events coincide with historical facts, though it is uncanny how once again—as it did for many nineteenth-century Americans—the Garner case symbolizes slavery's horror. But now in Morrison's novel the long-repressed memory of child-murder becomes a crisis that they and even a whole people must *work through*. In still broader terms *Beloved* insists that slavery as a whole constituted a historical trauma whose forgetting has put a people's collective sanity in chronic peril.

Among *Beloved*'s many gifts is the power to take what other generations could only regard as a tragedy and imagine out of it a fragile but happy ending. Another and equally powerful gift is that *Beloved* returns to us a slave mother who was always not only the subject of others' obscurely coded stories about her, but far more significantly herself a feeling and thinking subject. In Morrison's novel that long-forgotten past returns to trouble daily life in the form of a haint, or ghost, called "Beloved."[8] Ghostly yet physically hungry beyond satisfaction, haunting but herself haunted by slavery's disremembered horrors, the figure called Beloved well symbolizes the century-long amnesia about slaves' lived experiences. Perhaps Beloved also represents everything that cannot be *recaptured* through historical analysis, everything that cannot be summarized so that we can *claim* it as "our" history.

Perhaps, but I think Morrison's fictional return to this long-repressed historical subject challenges us with a host of questions. Who *was* the actual Margaret Garner? What brought her to draw a butcher knife across the throat of her two-year-old daughter? What happened to the Garner family and to other key players in the drama? How did the Garner infanticide become a *story*, and what kinds of social and cultural work did its tellers expect that story to *do*? Why, until 1987, did their stories mostly fail to inscribe Margaret Garner's deeds and desires in the nation's memory about slavery?

The following chapters tell the historical narrative that Toni Morrison's novelistic genius set aside. Being bound by rules of evidence, my book does not have her novel's imaginative freedom and keeps to the Garners' story, with its dramatic fugitive slave trial, their return to the South, and tragic finale. Unlike *Beloved*, these chapters do not lead to happy endings.

This is a story of slavery and child-murder, and it begins in northern Kentucky. There is a certain ease in reading (or writing) sentences like that. Sequenced in a narration, they wind meanings around a sense of determinable causes and effects. The Garner infanticide is, however, a historical instance that will always frustrate our need for unambiguous, finalized meanings. Margaret Garner was the slave of powerful and prominent Kentuckians, one of whom was a United States congressman and the second governor of Oregon Territory, the other a wealthy but star-crossed northern Kentucky "squire." We can know far more about these white people than we may ever know about Margaret. The sum of her own speech transcribed onto paper would fill little more than a page. Newspapermen's descriptions of her are discouragingly brief and sketchy.

Nonetheless, this project took shape as a book when my work in the archives uncovered historical evidence about Margaret Garner's white and black northern Kentucky families, evidence needed to reconstruct her experience in slavery. Evidence about conditions at Maplewood, her master's plantation, and at Margaret's Richwood Station neighborhood enabled me to piece together her life and struggles leading up to events of early 1856. As the Margaret Garner story thus emerged from archived letters, old newspapers, official records and documents, I understood that my first responsibility was to compose a work of narrative history about the Garner case. The first job was to tell Margaret Garner's story.

Inevitably, telling her story takes one away from the Garners. For me it compelled research into the lives of white people who owned the slaves, who fought in Cincinnati courts for their liberty, and who—in some instances—found their lives forever marked by Margaret Garner's child-murder, the tragedy's defining act. After that bloody deed, the Garners became captives, defendants, and then (once more) slaves. Throughout these closing acts in their drama all seven surviving Garners looked on impassively as whites struggled to decide their fate. In the following chapters these people, blacks and whites, must all take turns at center stage even while the story revolves around the main mystery: Why did Margaret take her daughter Mary's life? This book began as a search for answers to that ultimately unanswerable question.

Where *does* the Margaret Garner story begin? Perhaps with an abiding landscape. Today travelers driving south from Cincinnati on Interstate 75 speed past the Richwood Flea Market's tan warehouse. To the right, one mile farther west, beyond the green-and-yellow BP station at Exit 176, down State Route 338 and past the recently subdivided, gated country club community named Triple Crown, stands the same quaintly spired Presbyterian church where Margaret Garner's owners, their neighbors, and many neighborhood slaves (including Margaret) attended Sunday services.

As one turns right at the stop sign and bears west at Richwood Presbyterian Church, the America of interstates and eighteen-wheelers seems to tumble away. Here on the road's north side stretches the same estate Margaret's masters once farmed in gentlemanly style. There on the road's south side stretches the same estate of the Gaines family's best friend, Benjamin Franklin Bedinger. There, back down the road by the church, is where Margaret's husband and in-laws toiled for planter James Marshall. Subdivisions encroach on these lands from all sides but these old estates are still intact, still in the hands of Gaines and Bedinger and Marshall descendants. Mud Lick Creek still runs through this beautiful landscape as it did in Margaret's time, but now it is partly banked with expensive-looking stone masonry. A magnificent new mansion with high Palladian windows graces an eastern corner of the Bedinger place, Forrest Home, though Maplewood has changed remarkably little in a century and a half. Atop a knoll sits the same house that Archibald Gaines built after a November 1850 fire leveled the original dwelling. From the road one can see the rooms where Margaret Garner and her children did domestic labor and suffered whatever indignities or threats or assaults finally compelled her to run.

In *Beloved,* Toni Morrison calls this place "Sweet Home." Uncannily, here is the same land described in her novel as "rolling, rolling, rolling out before [one's] eyes . . . in shameless beauty," with its "lacy groves" of "the most beautiful sycamores in the world."[9] The sycamores still stand with clumps of tall oaks and squatting locusts. Outside Maplewood's front gate the Commonwealth of Kentucky has placed a historical marker commemorating it as the former residence of Major John Pollard Gaines, hero of the Mexican War and second territorial governor of Oregon.

Headstones of Gaines and Marshall family members dot Richwood Station graveyards, and their descendants still people this landscape because social and legal institutions privileged and protected their property. As for the Garners, who attempted to steal their selves in a daring resistance to antebellum slave law, the whereabouts of their graves or of any who descended from them were lost in the great diaspora of American slavery and Reconstruction. No markers or headstones for their kind in this place.

If one subscribes to an "organic" idea of character—that *what* one becomes follows from *where* one grows up—then the Margaret Garner story begins with this remarkable and haunted land. Here masters and slaves lived in tense relations that both confirm and disrupt myths about slavery. Theirs are human faces, enigmatic yet partly realizable from old, microfilmed newspapers and almost illegible, archived documents. Such pages can be just as vocal, or inscrutable, as this shamelessly beautiful land.

I begin here.

This book tells the story of Margaret Garner's journeys from this place.

1

FUGITIVE

❧

Summer 1840

The girl stood on the ferry dock, alert to each new sensation. A smell of tar rising off the piers. Acrid wisps from the glassworks and iron mills drifting westward with the Ohio River's rich, muddy dankness. A fetid odor from the stockyards and packing plants mixing with the redolence of grasses on a summer morning.

She faced north. Morning sun riding the horizon made a bright aura over her right shoulder, warmed her brown face, and cast long shadows over the limestone bluffs above Covington, behind her. Before her, sunlight glinting off Cincinnati's windowpanes blazed again off the river. The girl squinted into those dancing lights toward the chuff-chuff of a side-wheel ferryboat. Then it loomed red, white, and green and its gunnels nudged the piers as in a great clatter of chains the gangplank banged down.

The girl was seven years old and a slave. Four days had passed in Covington since she last saw her mother, eighteen miles south at Maplewood plantation, near Richwood Station, Kentucky. "Keep near, Peggy," warned Massa Gaines. Her given name was Margaret, after her grandmother, first in her family brought to this place from Virginia.

They called Margaret's mother Cilla, sometimes Cilly, but her given name was Priscilla.

His children gathered excitedly around this tall, noble-looking figure they called "Pa." John Pollard Gaines was a widely respected Kentucky planter, lawyer, and politician, and the only master Margaret had known. Four days before, he had hefted his wife, six children, and Margaret into a carriage and bounced them along the log-planked, "corduroy" Turnpike toward Covington, filling the passing hours with tales of his own father, Abner Gaines, who ran the first stagecoach line over that same road—Lexington to Covington, eighty miles in two days, winters and summers. Near Covington, Massa Gaines reined in at a house on the pike just south of town, where they would lodge with his youngest sister, Mrs. Bush. Her husband, Percival, was John Gaines's age (forty-five), called himself a manufacturer, and owned eight slaves. Nights, Margaret slept with Massa Bush's slaves, including two boys near her age. Days, the other slaves went about their chores while Margaret "nursed" (babysat) Mistress Gaines's youngest child, one-year-old Mary.[1]

Perhaps it seems strange that a slave child should have responsibility for a white baby. At Margaret's February 1856 fugitive slave trial her master's attorneys would call Southern witnesses to testify that slave owners would never consider such a usage. In turn her defense attorney would call to the witness stand a "free colored" woman who would assure doubters: "It's a common thing for colored children of 5 or 7 years old to nurse white children in the families they belong [sic]." She went on to say that it was how masters "train them up" to domestic service. Seven other defense witnesses would back her up, and eventually so would a range of twentieth-century historians, who have noted that by nursing white infants a slave girl like Margaret probably secured Maplewood plantation's few benefits: indoor work, leftovers from Massa's kitchen, better clothes.[2]

Disembarking from the ferry at Cincinnati, the West's self-styled "Queen City," Margaret walked on free soil for the first of only two times in her life. Fearing interference by the city's "damned abolitionists," John Gaines had cautioned his wife, Elizabeth, to keep a close watch on the girl, and sixteen years later Margaret would recall, "My mistress kept me very close to her all the time." On the ferry dock Margaret studied well-dressed black porters outvying each other's manners and hustling white Southerners headed to Queen City hotels.

White and black roustabouts loaded barrels of salt pork and whiskey and unloaded barrels of molasses and coffee. Everything seemed strange, and if it hadn't been for Southerners speaking a familiar lingo Margaret would have been overwhelmed by the dinning tongues: Irish brogues, Quaker thees and thous, thick-tongued German *ich*'s and *du*'s, the odd Connecticut Yankee.

John Gaines probably hired an omnibus and put Margaret atop it with the driver. We can imagine her looking back, gradually losing sight of Kentucky as they jostled away from the dock, up a wide thoroughfare like Broadway. All around her bustled the largest city west of the Alleghenies, a society of sharp contrasts. Despite its downtown of neat red-brick row houses and gleaming limestone mansions, well-paved streets and tiled sidewalks, Cincinnati was also a city where men, many of them black, drove stock right up Broadway to the slaughterhouse. The stench from manure and gutter slops rose everywhere with swarms of gnats and mosquitoes and flies. Perhaps Margaret glimpsed Bucktown, the mostly black neighborhood of dingy tenement houses and run-down shanties, whose residents nevertheless boasted of their schools and the Baptist and African Methodist Episcopal churches.[3]

She certainly saw a fair number of black people: hog butchers, brick masons, coopers, nattily dressed house servants, whitewashers—menials of all kinds, and all of them *free*. By 1840 Cincinnati's black residents amounted to 5.1 percent of its population, some 2,240 souls in a population of 44,000. Half of those black citizens had known slavery. Some had purchased their emancipation. Some Southern masters—rare ones —had brought other slaves to Cincinnati for legal manumission, sometimes calling on John Jolliffe to draw up the documents. The rest— probably half of the former slaves—were fugitives. Cincinnati in 1840 was also a very *young* town, where 80 percent of the people were under the age of thirty-six. The 1840 census reveals that Cincinnati's black residents were overwhelmingly young, and that almost half arrived during the 1830s, typically young men looking for work in the meatpacking plants.

Although it promised extraordinary opportunities to blacks, the Queen City was no sanctuary. Margaret Garner's 1840 sojourn there fell between two of its most vicious race riots, in which, in 1836 and again in 1841, Cincinnati whites leagued with Kentucky "rowdies" to unleash terror against the city's free blacks while police mostly turned their backs. Meantime the city's "Black Laws" required all free blacks to register and post a bond (as surety against any criminal or civil charges), denied them rights to sue whites, excluded them from jury service, and blocked access to public schools. Despite such blatant racism, Ohio Valley blacks still considered Cincinnati an "emporium of the West," a boomtown symbolizing the best and at times the worst of American democracy.

As the John Pollard Gaines family shopped and dined through that long summer's day in 1840, Margaret Garner might well have claimed her freedom. Once Gaines brought her across the Ohio River, Cincinnati's abolitionists might have whispered in Margaret's ear their willingness to spring her. With their good legal help she would have needed only to assert her desire for freedom before the right magistrate—one of the city's antislavery men. Histories of antebellum Cincinnati tell of some slaves who leaned toward the whispers and claimed their freedom. But they tell of equally many who failed. In the famed "Matilda case" of 1837 a teenage girl came with her master to Ohio, accepted abolitionist help, and lost despite the impassioned, brilliant arguments of antislavery lawyer Salmon Portland Chase, destined (as Ohio governor) to play a backstage role in the Garner drama.

John Gaines knew all of this but knew just as surely that no seven-year-old slave girl would stand up against her master, slavery, and American law to make a run at her inalienable right of liberty. Not with her mother held eighteen miles away in Kentucky.

John Gaines was a confident, commanding, and imperious Southerner who always knew what he was about. Beyond managing the day's shopping and dining, he of course kept close watch on his human property. One unforeseen result of his caution would be that Margaret's *not claiming her freedom* in 1840 would figure importantly at her fugitive hearing in 1856. Her lawyer would argue that her earlier sojourn automatically freed young Margaret; her master's lawyers, that Margaret could have fantasized the trip and that even if it did occur the law required a slave in transit on free soil to ask for her liberty before a court could grant it.

We are fast-forwarding the story. The record says that in 1840 Margaret "nursed" young Mary Gaines in Cincinnati, returned to Covington and the Bushes' house, then, several days later, to Maplewood and her parents. She'd come safely back, from the great Ohio River to tiny Mud

Lick Creek and the neighborhood where she was born. Still, Massa Gaines had taken little Peggy "over Jordan." The girl had lived one of the great metaphors of Southern slave culture: Margaret had "gone to Canaan-land," tasted freedom in Ohio.

Though everyone called Maplewood a "plantation," it had nothing of the Greek-columned grandeur out of slavery's storied past. Gaines's property was bordered south and east by dirt roads. Where they intersected, just below a knoll of pasture, stood Richwood Presbyterian Church, established in 1834, a year after Margaret's birth. Opposite, at Maplewood's northwest corner, atop a still higher knoll studded with oaks and sycamores, stood the master's house, a two-story brick and clapboard structure, probably aswarm with children, adults, and slaves. From Maplewood's porch John Gaines could survey nearly all three hundred of his rolling acres, his orchard, pond, barns, livestock, and black bondservants. When a Gaines slave plowed, watered cows and sheep, picked a pippin apple, walked to Sunday services, fished or gigged frogs in Mud Lick Creek, he or she did it under the watchful gaze of Maplewood's master or mistress.

As Southern slavery went, life at Maplewood probably imposed relatively few hardships on young Margaret. Maplewood was Boone County's thirteenth-wealthiest plantation and among its leaders in hog production. The work of Gaines's dozen or so slaves varied seasonally and never required of them the grinding gang labor of Cotton South plantations. They also lived in a neighborhood dense with other slaves. Just south of Mud Lick Creek, at Forrest Home plantation, John Gaines's closest friend, Benjamin Franklin Bedinger, oversaw nearly two dozen. To Bedinger's east and just south of Richwood Presbyterian Church, James Marshall worked his two hundred and twenty acres with the labor of eleven slaves. Smaller landowners in the neighborhood owned two to eight slaves each, and, while the figures are hard to come by and in any case were always shifting, we know that in any given year during the antebellum decades slaves in the immediate Maplewood neighborhood accounted for just under 50 percent of the total population, more than double the statewide percentage.[4]

In itself this fact is significant. Since this population remained fairly stable, it is clear that Maplewood blacks lived in a neighborhood with a well-developed slave culture. "Abroad" marriages knitted together slaves from neighboring plantations through ties of kinship. Slaves came together during all kinds of joint neighborhood tasks, seasonal jobs, and cyclical activities: in repairing roads, shoring up creek banks, mending fences, driving stock to markets and rail depots, hauling and weighing tobacco, milling grain, getting and hauling provisions, and attending services at Richwood Presbyterian. Historian Marion Lucas remarks that Kentucky slaves generally moved freely between plantations on Sundays and major holidays such as Christmas. And while the particular nature and extent of slaves' secret religious services in cabins and "hush harbors" remains enigmatic, it would be more remarkable if slaves around Maplewood did *not* attend them.[5]

After her birth on 4 June 1833, Peggy came to know Maplewood first from her parents' slave cabin, most likely situated behind and below an orchard running along the plantation's northern boundary, then from the kitchen of the Gaines house, where Cilla worked. From age five or six Margaret worked in her master's household and nursed his steadily burgeoning brood. When she escaped in 1856 Margaret and her children wore the coarse cotton clothing typical of slaves and lacked decent winter shoes. Otherwise, reporters observed, Margaret and her family appeared healthy and well fed. A neighboring doctor, Elijah Clarkson, took care of the Maplewood slaves' medical needs and claimed to have treated Margaret since her birth. He either attended or looked in on Margaret just after the births of her own four children, beginning in 1850.

Excepting her nominal father, Duke, who inexplicably disappeared from the print record when Margaret reached her early teens, the girl grew up with an intact nuclear family. She sometimes knew the fear, but probably until 1856 she never knew the actual fact, of loved ones being "sold south" by either of her two masters. In November 1849, when she was sixteen, John Pollard Gaines accepted a territorial governorship and sold Maplewood and all his slaves to his younger brother Archibald Kinkead Gaines, who passed Maplewood along to his descendants, who have held it intact until today. The principal themes of *their* story would be property, stability, prosperity, and tradition.

This is Margaret Garner's story, but telling it requires us to include the masters' lives, because their will dominated hers and became in a crucial way Margaret's "fate." For even though a slave might sustain kinds of psychological free agency, even at times resist or conspire to subvert a master's authority, Southern law denied her any biological, economical, social, political, or cultural agency except the master's. This means that in a profound sense slaves' ordinary lives are *not tellable*, for one of storytelling's most deep-seated conventions is that characters achieve their identity or "roundedness" precisely to the extent they behave as free agents. From saying "I am," from declaring independence, come both character and plot, the flesh and bone of stories. Thus Frederick Douglass's boyhood in slavery, though stuff for many memorable anecdotes, remains untellable until he fights the slave breaker and runs for New Bedford. Thereafter his life satisfies the terms culture requires for it to be memorialized as full-fledged narration.

Just so, Margaret Garner's life was nonnarratable until she escaped Kentucky and cut her two-year-old daughter's throat, practically in her massa's face, deeds that electrified her image against slavery's outer darkness. Then her story *had to be told.* Still, the restless demand of historical narration for the fixed stars of actual people and real events pushes inquiry into slavery's outer darkness, where memories that weren't committed to paper vaporized long ago and even those that were written down have become blurred inks on old newsprint and letter paper, sometimes preserved on microfilm. What those surviving texts say about her masters' lives, at times also the slaves' lives, reconstructs the texture of her life and thus points to reasons why Margaret Garner became a fugitive.

Masters and Slaves at Maplewood

What sort of men *were* her masters? What did it mean to be their slave at Maplewood?

To friends and allies John Gaines epitomized the handsome Kentucky squire. Six feet tall, "stout in person, with a fearless commanding presence, and limbs indicating great physical power," he impressed the discriminating ladies of Washington, D.C. One of them painted a word picture for her society column in a magazine called *The Huntress*:

> His face is partially round, partaking the old Saxon outline. His features are rather full, fair, regular, and manly, with a square forehead of moderate depth—firm and free, denoting ardor and strong mental powers. But no coward can meet his daring eye without

"The Major," John Pollard Gaines, ca. 1850
COURTESY THE OREGON HISTORICAL SOCIETY

shrinking—keen, clear and unblinking as the touring eagle's, it would penetrate a shield; it is a dark blue, and emits much fire and buoyancy. His warrior's brow, bold and vigorous, is tempered with gentleness and generosity, the true characteristic of the high-minded sons of Kentucky. His countenance is frank and free from alloy, open as day to the kindly charities of human nature. His manners are such as nobility of mind alone can boast, full of courtesy and polite attention.[6]

This sketch of John Gaines's patrician self-confidence colors in two surviving images: a daguerreotype of John and Elizabeth Gaines with eight of their eleven children, probably taken around 1848–50, and a formal portrait of Representative Gaines, probably done around 1849–50. Gaines's Democratic Party enemies, we should note, also saw behind that courteous nobility a man "tactless in action and overzealous in asserting his authority."[7]

His ancestors came out of Newton, in Breconshire, Wales. Knighted heirs, shareholders in the Virginia Company, they sailed to the colony in 1643, built a plantation on the Rappahannock River near Culpeper, used African slaves to start a tobacco crop, and rapidly prospered. In 1756 their descendant James Gaines fought with Colonel William Byrd against marauding Indians along the Virginia frontier. When the fighting was done he took his pay in land warrants and moved farther west, into the Shenandoah Valley, where he established a plantation in Augusta County. Himself one of twelve children, James Gaines also raised a dozen, and his fifth child, Abner, kept up the family traditions. He enlisted in a Virginia militia for the Revolutionary War, collected his pay in land warrants, set his sights still farther westward, on "Kentucke," and started another brood, eventually numbering twelve, six sons and six daughters.

Abner Gaines bided his time until 1797. That spring he and his brother Benjamin scouted the rolling hills south of Cincinnati, following the ancient buffalo trace as far as Big Bone Lick, already famous for its fossilized remains of mastodons. When Gaines set his gaze on the landscape now called Walton, whose rolling hills lush with knee-high grasses were studded with old-growth stands of oak, sycamore, and black walnut, it reminded him of his Shenandoah Valley birthplace. Abner and Benjamin Gaines purchased tracts and returned to Virginia for their wives, children, and slaves.

Some three thousand whites and three hundred slaves already lived in Boone County when Abner Gaines arrived.[8] Like other early settlers, Gaines planted Virginia tobacco, and at first he struggled. By the 1810 census Abner Gaines's household numbered seven children but still only four slaves, evidently the same who emigrated with him from Virginia.[9]

Margaret descended from these slaves through her mother's mother. Like neighboring Kentucky planters, Abner Gaines would have depended on his female slaves to assist Elizabeth Gaines with child care and other household chores. The job of his male slaves would have been, quite literally, to build his estate. Abner Gaines's slaves put up his first log dwelling, cleared and tilled his fields, and expanded his wealth in livestock. Their diet in those early years would have consisted mainly of cornmeal and pork—probably the least cuts of pork, such as ribs, jowls, and knuckles—plus whatever game, fish, or wild berries and nuts they could hunt, catch, trap, or forage.[10] *Not* the diet needed to bolster them against diseases, especially pellagra, or to strengthen them for the heavy labor of clearing fields and building homes and fences.[11] Perhaps this explains why the man's slave family grew so slowly during his first twenty years in Boone County.

Yet build his estate they did. The Gaines slaves probably inherited that first cabin after completing the master's plantation house, "a two-story home of more than fourteen rooms" constructed out of "solid brick on limestone foundation and all woodwork [of] solid walnut." Abner Gaines had moved his family into this commodious home by 1810.[12] He was rapidly prospering, as well as diversifying his holdings. In its 16 May 1818 edition the *Western Monitor* ran an advertisement proudly announcing commencement of the first "LEXINGTON & CINCIN-NATI MAIL STAGE, Abner Gaines—Proprietor." The ad boasted that Gaines himself lived on the road and owned a tavern at Williamstown, in Grant County, "for the accommodation of the passengers." He operated his stage line five years before selling out.[13]

Abner Gaines was determined that his sons should be gentlemen. He sent three of them, John Pollard, Abner Jr., and Richard, to read law at a private school in Cincinnati, though the studies of John, his eldest, were interrupted by the War of 1812. When he was nineteen John Pollard Gaines fought the British at Malden, opposite Detroit, in Ontario, Canada. Like his ancestors, he was paid in land warrants that he sold and swapped.[14]

Back at Boone County after the British war young John Gaines set up as a planter and (after eventually completing his legal training) as a lawyer. In 1824 he visited the family seat in Augusta County, Virginia, returning to Kentucky with a bride, Elizabeth Kinkead Gaines. By 1825 he moved with her to a newly purchased Richwood Station plantation that he named Maplewood. When Abner Gaines died in 1832, his widow, Eliza, moved to Maplewood and John Gaines inherited a sizable portion of his father's wealth and slaves, including Margaret's mother, Priscilla. The slaves' duties included serving old Eliza Gaines, nursing Elizabeth Gaines's growing brood, tending her house, and working the master's farm. With their help, John Gaines prospered. In 1842–43 several of his male slaves worked alongside hired hands in constructing a larger, more expensive residence for his rapidly expanding family.[15]

With neighbors Benjamin Franklin Bedinger and James Marshall, all Virginia gentlemen like himself, Gaines tried tobacco. He was still growing and shipping it as late as 1837, but, along with many other northern Kentuckians, soon came to depend largely on hog production for Cincinnati markets.[16] He also speculated in northern Kentucky and eastern Arkansas lands and in regional manufacturing ventures.[17]

John Gaines also speculated in slaves. From cash-strapped or bankrupted planters Gaines bought bondsmen at a discount, then demanded premium prices from itinerant traders. One such trade is notable because it involves names in the drama to come. Its details emerge from an 1843 business memo to Gaines from a fellow attorney:

> When Jas. M. Preston was here some 3 or 4 weeks since he informed me that he had levied an execution of mine for about three hundred dollars on four negroes of Dr. Clarkson's before he applied for the benefit of the bankrupt Law; which will hold good. These negroes, 2 men a boy & a girl, were previously mortgaged to Foster & Cave. The amount net principal and interest about $800. Preston can force a sale on those negroes, and if they are as valuable as Mr. P. thinks they are worth more than will satisfy. F & C claim will not have to be paid till they foreclose their mortgage and their bill for that purpose was not filed till last Nov. term. Aug't next is as soon as it is possible for them to get a judgment. My part would be for cash as it has been expensive. I propose for you to purchase the negroes if you think anything can be made on them and if you think and act so, you can take your time to pay me from the sale of them. Consult Preston and satisfy yourself.[18]

Here was a delicate case. Dr. Elijah Smith Clarkson was a lifelong friend and the physician who attended Gaines's family and slaves, and in 1843 John Gaines was Clarkson's attorney for a bankruptcy proceeding. Yet all of this about the slaves was going on under the table, which explains why Theobald admonished Gaines to silence: *"This is in confidence and I want your opinion."*

Clarkson had used his slaves as collateral in securing a home mortgage with the Foster & Cave firm in Covington; thus they wound up as listed property in the bankruptcy action. Those slaves' fate spells out in black and white the greatest insecurity Southern slaves knew: a constant danger of unexpected sale, perhaps to the Deep South, in consequence of their master's death or drunkenness or mere delinquency. Clarkson's wallet, it turned out, was simply overextended in 1843. Seven years later he owned an $11,000 home managed with the labor of seven slaves.[19] The bankruptcy was only a ditch that temporarily mired his wheels; he soon rolled on, but four of his slaves had been sold who knows where. Clarkson's friend and attorney John Gaines pulled Clarkson out of the mire, and helped himself to a little extra as well.

John Gaines's diverse agricultural and financial interests complemented one another. He combined the agrarian allegiances of a Jefferson, born of his commitment to Maplewood, with Hamiltonian allegiances to a national marketplace, where his fortunes were steadily building throughout the 1830s and 1840s. During these decades his politics were, however, wholly undivided. A die-hard member of the conservative Whig Party, Gaines further identified himself with the party's right-wing "Cotton Whig" membership. In his political speeches and correspondence, Gaines proudly proclaimed the "Southron" ideal, according to which slavery was the natural, constitutional, and spiritual right of whites. Unlike fellow Kentucky Whig Henry Clay, he never advocated gradual emancipation and recolonization in Africa for American slaves, and always claimed a right to own and trade them throughout the United States.

Gaines's hog production and speculative investments made Whig calls for tariffs, waterways, turnpikes, and railways natural to him. It probably seemed equally natural that he should begin a career in politics, for such had been his father's plan. When Margaret was an infant in the 1830s Gaines began serving the first of several terms as a Kentucky assemblyman. In 1845 he challenged a veteran of the Black Hawk War, Colonel John W. Tibbatts, for a U.S. congressional seat and barely lost, a surprisingly good showing for any Whig in northern Kentucky's predominantly Democratic Tenth District.

Gaines was fifty-one when war broke out with Mexico in 1846. He accepted the Kentucky governor's offer of a commission as major in charge of the 1st Regiment, Kentucky Volunteer Cavalry. The announcement surprised local Whigs, who were railing against the fighting as a bloody folly of the Democrats, and it angered family and friends, who thought Gaines was heedless of both his family and his age, which ought to have ruled out any more military campaigning. But the Mexican War promised grand patriotic adventures, perhaps the sort of fame that wins elections. In June, he took command of a regiment that included an audacious young captain named Cassius Clay (Henry Clay's nephew). By late July, Gaines was leading his troops nine hundred miles overland from Arkansas to Camargo, on the Rio Grande, and local Whigs had changed their tune and rallied to praise him.

At first Gaines's men saw little fighting. Then, in late January 1847, at the same time that Kentucky's Tenth District Whigs caucused at Burlington and unanimously nominated him, in absentia, for another congressional race, Mexican troops used the cover of a driving rain to surround Gaines and thirty of his enlisted men. The Mexicans were holding Gaines as a prisoner of war in Mexico City when northern Kentuckians handed Maplewood's squire a 124-vote victory over the Democratic challenger, their first ever and proof that Gaines's political instincts, in agreeing to fight President Polk's war, had been true. Shortly after, Gaines made a dramatic escape, fought at Montezuma, and— following stopovers with brothers scattered in New Orleans, Natchez, and southern Arkansas—finally returned to Maplewood in December 1847. He took a few weeks to tell neighbors his war stories, then once more kissed his wife and children goodbye and boarded a steamboat for Washington, where he was four weeks tardy.[20]

John Gaines was a congressman at an exciting moment. Revolutions rocked European empires, the Mexican War was successfully concluded, and the United States enjoyed a new coast-to-coast empire. Bills and resolutions on the western territories—New Mexico, California, and Oregon—preoccupied the members, and the issue of slavery in the new territories overrode all others. To these debates Gaines contributed not even a tittle. He missed the session's most crucial votes on new territorial governments and California statehood, and instead concentrated almost entirely on matters of patronage and preference.[21] He worked assiduously for Kentucky's veterans, securing here a widow's benefit and there a land warrant. Knowing of his family's long-standing use of military land warrants, we are hardly surprised by this emphasis, but with few exceptions it seems to have constituted Gaines's *only* legislative commitment.[22]

For the first session of the 30th Congress, John Gaines was in Washington for nine months. After an autumn at Maplewood he was back in Washington for the second, shorter session, returning home in the spring of 1849. These long absences tested his family's patience. Letters from the children continually revert to their longing to see him and, more importantly, to their mother's loneliness. "My dear Pa," wrote eighteen-year-old Florella in March 1848 during a visit to her uncle Benjamin's in Arkansas:

> I suppose you write home [to Maplewood] frequently, and I might hear of you through them, but I have received but a single letter since I left home, and that was from [younger sister] Harriet; she said that Ma was very careworn and I am afraid she is very lonesome, and that at times makes me very anxious to get back, not that I am home-sick, for I have spent my time very pleasantly indeed, but I am afraid that Ma needs us. Pa you said that maybe you would come home before the session ended. I do hope you will. I feel almost as anxious to see you now, as I did before you came home from Mexico.[23]

When Florella wrote this the Gaines children had seen her father for less than one month out of the previous twenty-four.

But Florella's mother, Elizabeth Kinkead Gaines, was more than just *emotionally* careworn. For two months after Gaines first departed for Washington in late December she was *physically* worn down, bedridden with pneumonia. She recovered, and in April 1848 journeyed to Washington, arriving late in the month and staying until the first session concluded on 14 August. The next autumn she again fell dangerously ill and her recovery this time took months and continued into the winter.

Despite his wife's illness John Gaines departed for Washington again in late November, "in company with Senator [Thomas Hart] Benton," after a gala send-off on the Covington dock. His children forwarded news from Maplewood: "Ma has been improving ever since you left," wrote young Harriet. "She walks through all the rooms above stairs and without the assistance of your cane and thinks of coming downstairs in a few days. She requests me to tell you because she knows you will be pleased at that."[24] This last comment is typical. During his absences Elizabeth Gaines seems to have communicated to her husband entirely through their children's letters.

She was left very much alone with the cares of plantation management, and what did that entail? Mrs. Gaines had to oversee her entire plantation household, especially the six female slaves whose daily labors—in gardening, cooking, cleaning, laundering, sewing and mending, spinning and weaving, as well as "nursing" the younger Gaines children—kept things going. She also had six young children at home, only one of whom, the teenaged Archibald (named for his uncle), was old enough to be useful as farm overseer. The rest of her eldest children were either attending schools or visiting Deep South relatives.

The John Pollard Gaines family, ca. 1850, probably just before they departed for Oregon. From left to right: Mary, Matilda, Archibald (named for his uncle), Harriet, John Pollard Gaines, LeGrand, Elizabeth Kinkead Gaines, Samuel, Florella, and Anna-Maria. Harriet and Florella would both die en route to Oregon. Not pictured: Gaines's eldest sons, Abner and Richard, and their infant, Elizabeth

PHOTO COURTESY THE OREGON HISTORICAL SOCIETY

Lonely she doubtless was for the company of white adults, and careworn from work, but surely this forty-six-year-old woman was also exhausted from childbearing. In fact she illustrates most poignantly a key aspect of nineteenth-century womanhood: a wife's lack of control over her own reproductive life, a lack profoundly analogous to what slave women experienced.

"Do you get as many children as ever?" one of the Major's business cronies once inquired.[25] In the Gaines tradition he did, but fell one

short of his forebears' patriarchal twelve. After her 1824 marriage Elizabeth Gaines gave birth about every eighteen months, beginning with
Abner (named after the child's grandfather). Toward the end, her births
were sandwiched between John Gaines's sojourns away from Maplewood. After she delivered their second-youngest, Matilda, he left on a
lengthy business tour to New York and Boston, and their youngest, Elizabeth ("Libby"), was born just months before he rode off with the 1st
Kentucky Volunteer Cavalry on 4 July 1846.

John Gaines was an extroverted, restless man, one hungry for success
and public honors, but also a man who, from our late-twentieth-century
perspective, epitomizes the male chauvinism of Victorian culture. During most of the 1840s Gaines nested at Maplewood only long enough
to "get" more children. By early 1849, childbearing had left his wife
frequently ill, with failing eyesight and teeth. In 1848 the children rejoiced when "mother had her teeth supplied, being eight in number,
which greatly improves her looks."[26] How did Elizabeth view her life at
Maplewood? We don't know, because none of her letters survive. She
may have considered herself too unlettered to write the worldly Major,
or she may simply have been too busy, like other plantation mistresses:
"Challenged daily by the limitless demands of her children, a husband
who believed in firm obedience from all of his dependents, and the
elusive wall of resistance that her house slaves formed."[27]

What about their slaves? In the surviving correspondence they are
hardly mentioned and even when they are it is rarely by name. Their
daily labors, their marriages, births, and deaths, even the facts of their
mere presence at Maplewood, seem to have been taken mostly for
granted. What we do find in archived papers—some pages almost illegible from bleed-through of the inks, many partially burned at the mar-
gins because of a 1911 fire at the New York State Library, which owns
them—are letters from Gaines's brothers and his son Archibald, wall-to-
wall with the routine of agricultural life of Maplewood and its cycles of
plowing, planting, harvesting. These letters tell us that John Gaines's
boys struggled at the adult work of running his plantation. Young Archibald fretted over how much acreage should be committed to oats,
rye, or grass, and worried that having the slaves plow Maplewood's high
ground might "destroy the beauty of the ridges by leaving it a sand
bank."[28] Their greatest headache was the Major's "pork concern."
Neighbor Benjamin Franklin Bedinger sometimes took young Archibald

under his wing for trips to Indiana, buying weanlings. (Bedinger would have been a good teacher: later in the decade he drove to Cincinnati four hundred hogs "of his own feeding, with corn of his own raising," and fetched a record price for them. He did equally well with sheep.[29]) The hog market, however, was always volatile. In November 1846, Bedinger warned Gaines (then soldiering in Mexico) of probable losses: "Your sons have made good crops better than mine I think; all your business is in pretty good condition save your pork concern . . . I am told there will be considerable loss there."[30] After the following year young Archibald wrote that the season's profit in hog raising would cover their indebtedness for seeds and weanlings, compensate Bedinger for the rental of some pasture land, pay his children's school tuitions, and leave them afterward with several hundred dollars free and clear—in all, not a bad year.[31] Meantime the congressman's salary and his other investments were adding to Gaines's steadily growing wealth.

What were his slaves' places during these years? We have just a few tantalizing mentions. For example, this: prefacing the political and economic news, young Archibald tells how, having brought home a photographic "likeness" of Representative Gaines, Dr. Bedinger showed it to the Major's slaves and "tried to make Lillian believe it was his [i.e., Bedinger's] but she insisted strongly that it was yours [and] Mother having lost her spectacles has not had the pleasure so far of giving it a fair inspection" and thereby settle the issue.[32] Lillian was a slave girl in her late teens and one of Mrs. Gaines's household servants. Here she was made the butt of a white man's joke.

But elsewhere in the correspondence, this: several years earlier, just after the Major's arrival in Mexico (in September 1846), his brother Abner wrote from New Orleans to tell about a proposition from their brother James, who desired "to purchase the negro girl daughter of your negro woman to prevent her [the mother] leaving the country,—and I said to him in answer that I . . . would not take [her] away without your sanction."[33]

During the Mexican War, Abner had final control of John Gaines's business affairs and probably resisted any such sale of a Maplewood slave girl because of concerns for her future. James Gaines was a consumptive man who moved at least twice in the 1840s, the second time to Covington, seeking a more hospitable climate for the tuberculosis then threatening to take his life.[34] If James suddenly died, could the girl be recovered from his estate? Abner refused that risk without Major Gaines's "sanction."

Who was the girl? Particularly telling is Abner Gaines's use of singular forms: "the negro girl daughter of your negro woman." He uses that precise phrasing because John Gaines then owned just one mother-daughter pair at Maplewood: Priscilla (Cilla) and her daughter Margaret (Peggy), then thirteen years old. But what made Cilla desperate to escape? Here is the key coincidence. About this time, a neighborhood planter named William Harper manumitted an elderly couple, Joseph and Sarah Kite. The Kites were related to Priscilla by marriage, and one may easily speculate that Priscilla's yearning for freedom grew out of her relatives' successful (legal) removal to free soil, and that she had the promise of a safe haven (or a way station on the Underground Railroad) at the Kites' Cincinnati house.

Probably her desire to escape was also driven by maternal protectiveness, for the "negro girl daughter" Abner Gaines wrote about was nearing that perilous age when slave girls became most vulnerable to the sexual demands of white masters. Women's slave narratives from the period all insist on that danger. Thus Harriet Jacobs's *Incidents in the Life of a Slave Girl* (1860): "I now entered on my fifteenth year—a sad epoch in the life of a slave girl. My master began to whisper foul words in my ear. Young as I was, I could not remain ignorant of their import." Like Jacobs, young Peggy was a household servant and therefore "compelled to live under the same roof" with her sickly mistress and her sons and their appetites. Jacobs's master "peopled [her] young mind with unclean images, such as only a vile monster could think of."[35] What were Margaret's circumstances? We have no evidence that Margaret was subjected to similar abuses at the hands of John Pollard Gaines. But Master Gaines's extramural adventures left his household under the guidance of two "ladies," one aged, the other chronically ill and careworn, and both of them probably confined for extended periods to the upper rooms while the rest of the estate was really run by a variety of young men and teenaged boys. George Davidson, the teenaged son of a family friend, came and went during the early 1840s; also present were the elder Gaines boys, Richard (until he left for school and business) and young Archibald. Priscilla, listed in the 1850 census as a black female, must have known the sexual subordination of slave women, as Peggy's mulatto status clearly indicates. It would therefore have been more extraordinary if Priscilla did not act to protect her adolescent daughter.

In any case the facts of John Gaines's long absences would have been worrisome enough for his slaves. They were subjected to constantly changing, differing regimes, and would have therefore known both the insecurities and the liberties typical of such a plantation household. Slave narratives constantly revert to the theme that unstable plantation regimes made slaves mindful of their own uncertain fate, as alienable properties liable at any day to be sold away on a master's whim. And as for the relative liberty that the Gaines slaves might have known because of the master's long absences, this too may have put them in mind of running. In 1855 Frederick Douglass concisely stated this recurrent theme: "Beat and cuff your slave, keep him hungry and spiritless, and he will follow the chain of his master like a dog; but, feed and clothe him well,—work him moderately—surround him with physical comfort,—and dreams of freedom intrude. Give him a *bad* master, and he aspires to a *good* master; give him a good master, and he wishes to become his *own* master."[36]

We have important corroborating information about Margaret from another source. In 1856, a decade after James Gaines offered to buy Margaret away from her rebellious mother and a few weeks after the Garner case was settled in Cincinnati courts, Maplewood neighbor Benjamin Franklin Bedinger wrote a *Covington Journal* editorial, "To the People of Cincinnati," a rambling, multipart polemic that comments on Duke, Cilla, and Margaret. Trying to account for Margaret's act of child-murder, Bedinger let go his racism with both barrels: "the truth is," he wrote in 1856, "Peggy is a very common, cross tempered, flat nosed, thick lipped negro woman, whose father was a very bad character." Margaret's meanspiritedness was her (putative) father's legacy to her, Bedinger suggested. Duke's meanness, in addition to the meddling of abolitionists who allegedly "taught her the beautiful morality found in the *higher law*, that it was noble to cut the throat of her offspring"— these were the beginnings of Peggy's fury, Bedinger argued.[37]

What had made Duke so hot-tempered? A generalized hatred of bondage? Cilla's sexual victimization? His wife's daughter's peril? We can never know. Archived letters and documents, published testimonies and news accounts, bring us this close to completing the puzzle but no further. Margaret Garner's story might well begin from this sketchy picture of her as an adolescent slave girl confronting, with Cilla and Duke, a dangerous and uncertain future. *And thinking of running. Thinking of it for years. Afraid and angry and waiting for the right chance to bolt.*

It developed that the Maplewood slaves had other good reasons to be worried, for Master Gaines was pondering a momentous change. When the second, short session of the 30th Congress was concluded in the late spring of 1849, Gaines returned to Maplewood, took to the hustings in a halfhearted campaign to hold his seat, and lost to Democrat Richard H. Stanton. Gaines must have been anticipating this defeat, for as early as December 1848 he had begun exchanging letters with his friend and political adviser, Covington lawyer and sometime newspaper publisher J. W. Menzies, about the prospect of an appointment to one of the western territorial governorships. Menzies noted that "old Zach" (President Taylor, Gaines's superior officer in Mexico) had to appoint governors in the new far western territories and that military and legal backgrounds would be highly desirable qualities in applicants for those posts. As a lawyer and decorated officer, Gaines would therefore be a natural, he argued. Menzies recommended California, but Gaines turned his eyes to Oregon because it seemed more suited to "Kentucky crops." In early October, Taylor offered Gaines the Oregon governorship, but only after his first choice, Illinois Whig congressman Abraham Lincoln, turned it down. Major Gaines immediately accepted and almost as quickly arranged a sale of Maplewood and its slaves to his brother Archibald, still a plantation owner in Arkansas. The Maplewood slaves had for years been disruptive and sometimes threatening escape. Now Gaines was shut of them. But their worst fears had assumed a palpable form.

So the only master Margaret had ever known lit out for the territories. At the time she had just given herself to James Marshall's young slave Robert Garner, their masters having consented to an abroad marriage. At fifteen he was a year younger than Margaret and that autumn these adolescents were expecting a child. Thomas would arrive in March 1850. Compared to the experience of Southern slaves in general Margaret's first birth marked a very early onset of childbearing, and we might well ask if she got pregnant in order to stave off the sexual advances of neighborhood whites, evidently a common strategy.[38] In any case, for Margaret the year 1849–50 marked the beginning of a great change and a period of deep uncertainty. Would she and Robert even be together for her baby's birth? Or in years after?

Robert Garner's insecurities under slavery were different from but equally disruptive as Margaret's. He was born at James Marshall's plantation, a quarter mile east-southeast from Maplewood. In 1856, Marshall's son Thomas would say that he "was raised with" Robert, an idyll (to him, at least) that was ended when James Marshall—obviously under some unknown financial duress—sold Robert to Boone County planter George Anderson, then residing a few miles north, near Florence. Robert was about nine years old and the elder Marshall "promised [his son Thomas] that when he got able he'd buy him back." Anderson farmed several hundred acres, and Robert Garner worked alternately for him and "a nephew of Anderson," another (unidentified) farmer with whom he apparently also lived for several years. Still worse, as Robert matured, Anderson regularly hired out his young slave. For several weeks every autumn he hired the boy out to James Marshall, to take droves of hogs up to Cincinnati. In 1847 he hired Robert out for longer periods to a Mrs. Poor in Covington, and then in 1848–49 hired him out to William Timberlake, a bit player in the drama ahead.[39]

A farmer, sometime merchant, and owner of seven slaves, Timberlake resided on the Turnpike six miles south of Covington in August 1847, when five of his slaves escaped, making it over the Ohio River with a party of seventeen others. They pushed hard, cutting northwest across Indiana until Timberlake and a large posse of whites surrounded them at a rural cabin outside Cassopolis, in Michigan's southwestern corner. There the armed fugitives resisted, local abolitionists broadcast a general alarm, and soon a "mob" of local whites and free blacks surrounded both parties and drove fugitives and slave catchers alike off to the county jail. The next day Timberlake pled for a return of his slaves under the 1793 Fugitive Slave Law, but the magistrate, a well-known antislavery activist named Ebenezer McDowell, freed the blacks after a brief habeas corpus hearing and then freed the whites from charges of attempted kidnaping, but on condition they either leave Michigan before sundown or face arrest. The case became a Southron cause célèbre in Covington's Whig paper, the *Licking Valley Register*. Months later a still outraged Timberlake wrote his friend and congressman, Major John Gaines, asking him to read the story of "The Cassopolis Slave-Kidnaping" and especially to read Judge McDowell's name into the *Congressional Record*, so that, "should he ever visit our district he can be treated accordingly, and that should be just the way we Kentuckians treat sheep killing dogs, shoot him down."[40]

Given Timberlake's long-simmering outrage over Cassopolis, we can well imagine the kind of possessive and ill-tempered master he probably was to Robert. In any case, Timberlake returned his hireling slave to George Anderson just before Robert and Margaret were married, in late 1849, and Robert continued in Anderson's service for five more years, apparently without being hired away. When George Anderson died in April 1855, James Marshall made good his old promise to young Thomas. He bought Robert back when the Anderson estate was settled — then straightaway hired him out again, this time for the entire autumn of 1855 to a Mr. Ellison of Covington.

Working for Anderson and Timberlake, Robert had lived within five and eleven miles of Margaret and her children, so that Saturday night through Sunday visits would have been possible. At Ellison's, though, he resided eighteen miles away from his wife and family and probably did not see them very much — if at all — during the entire autumn. When Ellison's contract was up in early December, Robert returned to James Marshall and took a drove of his hogs to Cincinnati just before Christmas. He had resided continuously at Richwood Station for just a month when the Garner party ran for their freedom on 27 January 1856.[41]

Rewind to the autumn of 1849, as John Gaines prepared to sell Maplewood and everything on it, a time when Margaret Garner had been studying some of slavery's hardest lessons. She had just turned sixteen and was pregnant by a young slave she had known from her childhood at Richwood Station, but who (just fifteen himself) had been sold and hired out and bought back, eventually to be hired out all over northern Kentucky. There was no telling where she, or Robert, might be living next month or next year. Margaret was learning her parents' anger by heart.

President Taylor formally announced John Gaines's appointment to the Oregon governorship on 4 October 1849. Neighbors and political cronies feted the Major throughout the month. As Gaines finished his packing on 19 November he commenced writing a journal: "Having sold my plantation in Kentucky and everything thereon to my brother Archibald K. Gaines, and paid every debt I owed so far as I know, I left

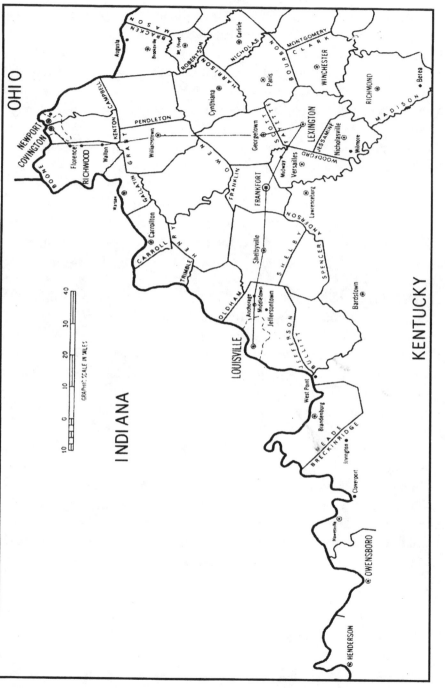

Northern and central Kentucky

with my family." From this archived document and from his correspondence we know that in New York Elizabeth Gaines outfitted their new Oregon home, from silver service to a spinet piano, while the Major ordered editions for a new territorial library and hired two white bondservants for a year's term. Two days into the new year, the U.S. Storeship *Supply* lifted anchor and the Gaines family began a voyage around Cape Horn.[42]

This change of owners took only a month and must have shocked the Maplewood slaves—persons included with the "everything thereon" at Maplewood, in the Major's vapid phrase. We know Archibald Gaines had assumed ownership of Maplewood by November 1849 because he took the year's drove of hogs to Cincinnati. Thereafter he seems to have settled down. By September 1850, the census taker passed through Walton precinct and at Maplewood tallied five white residents (three of them named Elizabeth!). Aside from Archibald himself there was John and Archibald's mother, Elizabeth ("Eliza"), his two children, Elizabeth ("Lizzie") and John (just returned to their father from his former mother-in-law), and his newly acquired second wife, Elizabeth (probably through common-law marriage, as no record survives).[43] The census taker counted twelve slaves, including Margaret Garner's five-and-a-half-month-old son, Thomas, listed as "black." In the slave trade these people, if sold all together, might have fetched $8,000 to $10,000; the census estimated Archibald Gaines's real estate at another $29,000.[44] He was the thirteenth-wealthiest property holder in Boone County. A Kentucky squire.

Margaret and other Maplewood slaves had known Archibald, "the Colonel," as a regular visitor to Richwood Station. He grew up with his eldest brother John at Abner Gaines's plantation in Walton, worked at his father's businesses while young, fought at San Jacinto during the Texas Revolution of 1836, and was mustered out at a colonel's rank. Afterward Archibald Gaines followed his forebears' examples, migrating westward with his brother Benjamin and parlaying bounty lands awarded for military service into a sizable estate in Chicot County, in the southeastern corner of Arkansas.

An uncle, William Henry Gaines, was already well established there. In fact, by processes of homesteading, land speculating, and canny purchases of tracts from Choctaws, William Gaines by 1850 had amassed the third-largest fortune in all of Arkansas. Under his tutelage, Archibald

From the 1850 Census: Slave Inhabitants of District 2,
Boone County, Kentucky, as recorded on 22 August 1850.
Here, the listing of Archibald K. Gaines's slaves is continued
from the previous page. Margaret Garner is number 5; her
five-month-old son Thomas is number 9

and Benjamin concentrated their efforts around Gaines Landing (named for their uncle William), at a C-shaped arc of the Mississippi called Cypress Bend. By 1843, when he returned to Kentucky for a wife, Archibald owned a section and a half of land and about forty slaves to clear it and raise his cotton, his brother Benjamin owned an equally large plantation, and both of them speculated in land sales. Throughout the 1840s Archibald traded tracts of Chicot County land as agent for George Theobald, John Gaines's friend and sometime partner. With his brother Benjamin, Archibald also ran a woodlot that supplied fuel to Mississippi steamboats.[45]

The Kentucky wife was Margaret Ann Dudley of Scott County, Kentucky (near Lexington). The Colonel married her in February 1843, and her parents soon moved to Richwood Station, where they became members of the neighborhood Presbyterian church.[46] In October 1844, Pastor George Bedinger of Richwood Presbyterian Church (B. F. Bedinger's son) noted in the parish's Session Books (a kind of weekly church log) that he had baptized Archibald and Margaret's firstborn. We don't know whether the couple was then living full-time in Arkansas and returned for the baptism, or whether Margaret Gaines stayed behind with her parents for the duration of her first pregnancy. The Gaines Papers tell us, though, that Archibald was in and out of Maplewood during this decade and that while his brother John fought in Mexico, Archibald was there to take a drove of his brother's hogs up the pike to Cincinnati, apparently making a bad deal of it.[47]

Archibald, who left behind only several letters, is conspicuous for his low profile. John was the gregarious, outgoing brother, the one their sister Elizabeth Gaines Hubbell would describe as "always the favorite" because of his sociable qualities.[48] In contrast, Archibald even looked the part of a melancholic:

Archibald K. Gaines . . . is not a large man, being but little above medium height, and quite slender. His head is small—his hair bushy, standing up, and gray. His face is thin, the lower part quite narrow, and marked with numerous lines. He has a small foot and hand; the latter looks rough, but more from exposure than labour. His dress is careless, but his general manner and appearance rather gentlemanly. There is nothing coarse, disagreeable or repulsive about his appearance, but on the contrary, he seems to be (and we have no doubt he is,) an agreeable and intelligent gentleman.[49]

Like all of his ancestors, Archibald "got" children quickly—a girl in 1844, a boy two years after that, and one year later another son—another Abner Gaines.

Then tragedy began stalking Archibald's life. First his son Abner died in infancy, probably a victim of the cholera then sweeping up the Mississippi. Next came a crippling blow, recorded in the *Covington Journal*:

Died. On the 7th day of January, 1849, at the residence of her husband, on Garden Lake, in Chicot County, Arkansas, Mrs. Margaret A. Gaines, wife of Archibald K. Gaines, Esq., aged 30 years.

Her death was caused by an accidental fall, in going down the steps some days before, which caused her to give birth prematurely to a female child (born dead). She died calmly and in the posses-

sion of her mental faculties, and like a Christian, in the full hope
of future happiness.

These blows knocked Archibald Gaines into a deep depression. Relatives
placed his children with their maternal grandmother, and it took six
months before neighbor Bedinger could assure John Gaines (then in
Washington): "We have authentic information of late date that his
health was much improved and still improving."[50] Archibald evidently
decided to leave Gaines Landing, site of his loss, but remained at Maplewood until late spring. When he returned to Gaines Landing in May,
Archibald had already spoken with John about buying Maplewood
should the Major get a territorial governorship. They agreed to the sale
in October 1849.

Owning Maplewood must have felt like a homecoming and a new
beginning. By the September 1850 census Archibald was already re-
married. But still the Gaines family was not through with sorrow. First
came news from afar: "Major Gaines—Melancholy!" reported the *Covington Journal* on 22 June 1850. On the way to Oregon, the Major's
daughters Harriet and Florella died of yellow fever at Santa Catarina,
Brazil. Crushed, Gaines wrote but a few more paragraphs in his preten-
tious journal about the voyage around Cape Horn.[51]

Disaster next struck at Maplewood in November 1850, when the
house built for John Gaines burned entirely to its foundation.[52] Archibald Gaines rebuilt immediately and the following summer moved into
the house that still stands at Maplewood. Summer brought more bad
news, however. In August 1851 outside Salem, Oregon, John Gaines's
wife, Elizabeth, was pitched from a runaway wagon whose wheels
crushed her skull.[53] She lay in a coma for three days before dying.

Then Death took his business elsewhere. Archibald and Elizabeth
Gaines began having children: first, in 1852, came Margaret Ann
Gaines; William LeGrand Gaines followed in 1854. When the Garner
case broke in late January 1856, Elizabeth was pregnant with her third
child, Jane, born in late March 1856.

By 1852, all seemed well, though trouble was brewing between Archibald and his slaves. In September 1851 brother Abner returned to
New Orleans after visiting Maplewood, his mother Eliza, and other relatives. On 12 September he wrote John in Oregon:

I have just returned from Ky. and left our mother in much better health than usual. James [the consumptive brother] is about the same as formerly and thinks he is not to die, has built him a fine house . . . on the Pike and is occupying it. Archibald has built a very comfortable house and is occupying it; is in fine health but poor spirits, says he is determined to sell all the negroes he bought of you, but will reserve the right in you to redeem them if you wish. Your son Richard has made him a proposition but I do not think Arch'd will accept it. Arch'd says how you must send him a title for the property you sold him and the money will be paid by one of his notes.[54]

Two key themes emerge from this document. The first involves Archibald Gaines's state of mind during the early 1850s. Here and elsewhere in the correspondence his "poor spirits" are a recurrent motif. A year later, for instance, another letter arrived for John from his son Archibald, then in Kentucky to purchase fresh livestock. In the letter young Archibald comments on the hair-trigger temper of his uncle and namesake, especially "the Col's" meanness toward young Archibald's little sister Anna-Maria, a sickly child left behind with the Bedingers at Forrest Home. (Itself an intriguing detail. Bedinger was John Gaines's closest friend, but custom and family ties would have dictated placing the little girl with her uncle Archibald at Maplewood. Yet Archibald K. Gaines was evidently deeply depressed after his wife's death and, for at least a few months, a bachelor whose own children were residing with grandparents. Hence leaving Anna Maria at Forrest Home made good sense.)

A second key theme involves the Maplewood slaves. For why would Archibald be interested to "sell all the negroes he bought of" John Gaines? Here again we must conjecture. One probability is that under John Gaines's absentee mastership the Maplewood slaves had gotten used to a revolving and perhaps even lax regime. The old obstinacy of Duke, Cilla, and Margaret that we have already noted might have further tried his patience. Add in the facts of Archibald's depressions and hot temper and, taken altogether, conditions at Maplewood must have become a dangerous mixture by 1851–52.

Letters to John Gaines from these years hint at other unstable circumstances at Maplewood. One surprise is that even the ownership of the land itself was unsettled. In November 1849, John Gaines wrote of selling his "plantation . . . and everything thereon." Things weren't so straightforward, however. Almost three years after writing these words John Gaines still had not transferred to his brother the deed to Maplewood, apparently because Archibald hadn't fully paid him and was still contesting some of John's financial claims from the hastily completed sale of the real estate, stocks, and slaves. In September 1852, almost three years after John Gaines's departure, the brothers at last worked out terms of a settlement and Archibald asked his brother to send him the properly notarized deed.[55]

As for the slaves, their lives were never more insecure. John's son Richard was constantly bargaining with his uncle Archibald over the slaves. One plan was to buy the lot of them, deal away several of the more valuable male slaves (thus to "realize about $2,200" for them and "invest that amt. in stock," young Archibald thought), then distribute several of the female slaves to John Gaines's children left behind in Kentucky. Anna-Maria, for example, was to "keep Hannah" for herself under this plan.[56]

While these negotiations were going forward, Archibald hired out some of his Maplewood slaves. Charlotte (then in her twenties) went off to a Florence, Kentucky, farmer named Hurston Perry, who evidently valued the woman's services very highly, for John Gaines's old political ally J. W. Menzies wrote to Oregon that Perry "desires to keep the girl, and she wishes to stay with him." If that did not suit, then (said Menzies, in 1851) Charlotte wished that John Gaines would return from Oregon and reclaim her: "she says she shall be ready for you whenever you wish the possession and hopes that you will signify your willingness [for her] to remain with him [Perry] until such time as you return to this place."[57]

Meantime at least one of the slaves remaining at Maplewood was resisting Archibald Gaines's sterner regime. In June 1852, Pastor George Bedinger made an entry in the Richwood Presbyterian Church Session Books telling of a deacon he had ordered to "converse with Sister Hannah a coloured woman [at Maplewood] touching a charge of insubordinate conduct as a servant and for the use of bad language unbefitting her profession." In all probability the deacon's conversation with Hannah occurred *after* she'd been given some form of corporal punishment, most likely a whipping—a terrifying prospect, for Archibald Gaines was a hot-tempered man who knew the uses of a cowhide, as his 1857 assault on John Jolliffe would prove. He may also have employed other means of corporal punishment common among Kentucky slaveholders, such as iron collars and leg bracelets.[58]

During the early 1850s, then, Maplewood slaves found themselves in highly volatile conditions. The master's house had burned to the ground. The slaves' new master, Colonel Gaines, was morose and mean-tempered after his train of tragedies and probably also a sterner disciplinarian than they'd ever known. Talk persisted that Major Gaines might return from Oregon, which was clearly (to Charlotte, for example) a sunnier prospect. Colonel Gaines had hired out some of the slaves, something the Major had never done. Worse still, rumor had the Colonel thinking of selling them all. Perhaps Gaines openly taunted his slaves with the common threat to "put them in his pocket"—that is, trade them for cash.

What was Margaret Garner's role in this unstable plantation "family"? Begin with plain genealogical facts. When Major Gaines left for Oregon she was pregnant with her eldest, Thomas, described in the September 1850 census pages as a black child of five and one-half months. In 1852 she had Samuel, a "mulatto" boy. Two years later came Mary, whose throat Margaret would cut and who was described in the Cincinnati newspapers after her death as "almost white." March 1855 brought Cilla, another "bright mulatto" (light-complected) child. At the time of her escape Margaret was again several months pregnant.

Put these facts alongside genealogical data for the Archibald K. Gaines family and several problems emerge. First, the births of Margaret's later children followed a pattern. Each time Archibald Gaines's second wife, Elizabeth, delivered a child a few months passed before Margaret also delivered another. This is why Margaret Garner's duties at Maplewood involved wet-nursing the Colonel's children; during this time she was Maplewood's only childbearing slave, and the closeness of their births would have allowed Elizabeth Gaines to soon hand off her child to a newly lactating Margaret. But consider Margaret's anguish at suckling the master's somewhat older brats while her own infants must be too early weaned. Then there were the constant demands on her time; her presence always expected in the big house while others—most likely her mother, Cilla—raised Margaret's children.

Then the real problem: Who fathered Margaret's children? That Robert was responsible for her first (Thomas) seems clear. But Margaret's subsequent light mulatto children raised damning questions, and it is

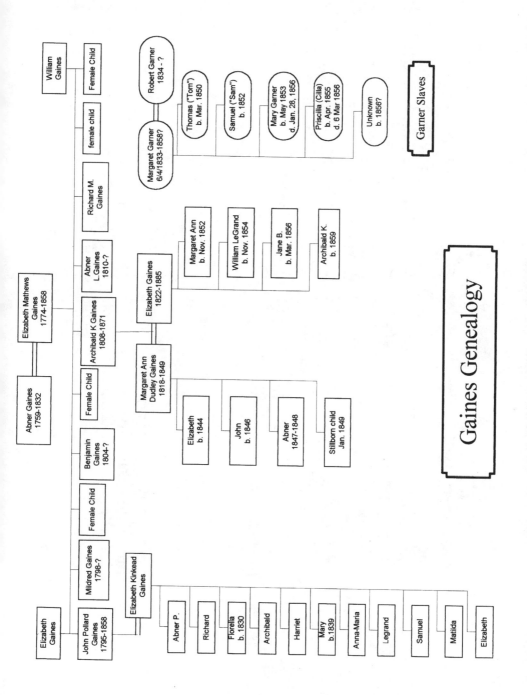

Gaines Genealogy

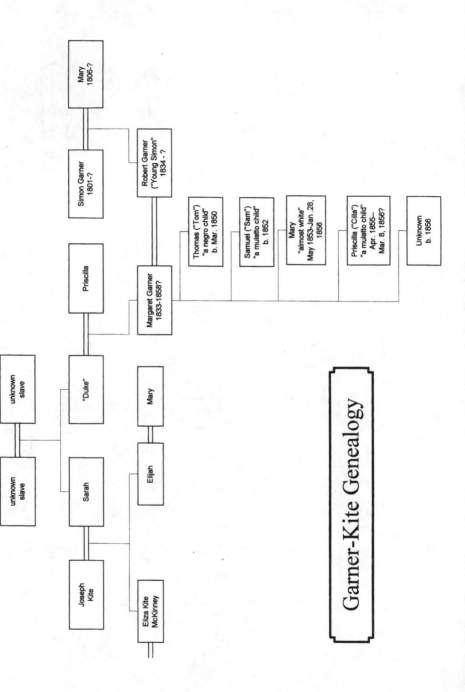

Garner-Kite Genealogy

hard to see how the child she was carrying at the time of her escape was Robert's, for he had been on a lengthy and distant hiring-out until just a month before the Garners fled. These signs pointed to a white father for most of Margaret's children. As Colonel Gaines was the only adult white male on Maplewood throughout these years, suspicion should quite naturally fall his way.

Here we step onto the most troubled ground in histories of American slavery, and we must start by giving Archibald Gaines the benefit of every doubt. For it is true that neither Margaret nor anyone else connected with the Garner case ever named him as the father of one or more of her slave children. It is also true that no one else in the Richwood Station neighborhood even so much as insinuated that he was. Gaines also never took any sort of formal step, such as legally agreeing to emancipate Margaret's children at adulthood, that would evidence a special relation to the children. Any evidence of this sort would of course be crucial testimony against Gaines. Nonetheless, it would be remarkable if any such evidence did exist, for Southerners accommodated to miscegenation by building "a wall of silence around the circumstance." White or black, they generally did not talk about it, especially not to outsiders.[59]

In Gaines's defense one might also argue that it is unfair to ask the record to prove a negative: that he was *not* the father. But working on the question of slave paternity, law professor and historian Annette Gordon-Reed demonstrates that this isn't so. In paternity cases it *is* possible for a defendant to show he was not the father simply by producing evidence that he had no access to the mother during the period when conception occurred. Such evidence has always been considered fully exculpatory, even before the advent of modern DNA testing.[60]

But Archibald Gaines *did* have access to Margaret Garner throughout the period in question, and the case for his paternity thus meets a threshold test. But there is more. Not only did Margaret begin having lighter-complected children *after* Archibald Gaines entered her life; those births also follow *a pattern* that lifts his paternity to the level of probability. Her births all followed just months after Elizabeth Gaines's. Why? One widely acknowledged rule of nineteenth-century sexual practices held that white women, who otherwise lacked reproductive control, could regulate a husband's sexual access during the last three to five months of pregnancy and for several months postpartum. Historian Bertram

Wyatt-Brown comments that Southerners commonly referred to this stretch as the "gander months" because that was when husbands traditionally sought their sexual "comfort" with other women. With slaves, if they happened to own them.[61]

In addition to the commonly accepted cultural logic behind the pattern of Margaret's births, at Margaret's 1856 trial there were carefully coded insinuations that Archibald Gaines must be the slave children's father. Antislavery activist Lucy Stone made those insinuations after interviewing Margaret at some length, and moreover she invited witnesses to look at the children's faces and see Gaines's features.

Did Archibald Gaines father Margaret Garner's mulatto children? With the kind of society represented by Maplewood, where white males exercised so much control over their dependents, in addition to rigorously controlling information about that society, the question will always fall far short of definitive proof one way or another. But if histories were constructed solely on foundations of definitive proof we could tell but few stories about the past. Pattern and probability and inference must also matter, and in answering the vexed historical question of white paternity of slave children they matter enormously. It seems reasonable to conclude that Archibald Gaines probably fathered one or more of Margaret's children. For further evidence, we will want to closely observe his actions after Margaret's escape.

One other question. Assuming that Archibald Gaines did father one or more of Margaret's children, what was the nature of their relationship? The possibilities range from rape to a somewhat coercive but consensual intimacy. The popular imagination commonly presumes rape, but that presumption overlooks all manner of contingencies and possibilities about which one cannot generalize. Of course, the power differential was always there, but it could be turned to a variety of advantages—for slave women as well as for masters. Perhaps the only way to answer the question in Margaret's case is to draw inferences from her actions during and after the escape.

What may we conclude about her life *before* the escape? By early 1856 Margaret Garner, daughter of resisting slaves who had once threatened running, had withstood six years of greater uncertainty and harsher treatment than she had formerly known. Rumors persisted that the Colonel might ship them all to the Deep South, perhaps to brother Benjamin's cotton fields in Arkansas. For practically all of their marriage her husband, Robert, had been hired out, often living miles away. Thus she had a slave's commonest motives for running: fear of sale and a desire to unite divided families.[62] Add in the likelihood of Margaret's sexual victimization, right down to her most recent pregnancy. Also, that in her uncle Joe and cousin Elijah she had invaluable contacts in Ohio. It's a wonder she hadn't run sooner.

Winter 1856

She had motives aplenty, and bad weather gave the Garners opportunity.

A heavy snow fell on the Ohio Valley over Thanksgiving and never melted, as daily high temperatures nudged up to just thirty-two or thirty-three degrees. By New Year's Eve the Ohio River was "choked with floating ice"; four days later, frozen solid. Then a still more punishing cold front roared down off the northern Plains. The nights of 9–10 January plunged thermometers to eighteen and twenty degrees below zero and, although there was much more of it to come, the *Cincinnati Gazette* proclaimed this winter "the coldest known in sixty years." By mid-January the Cincinnati–Covington ferries sat icebound at their landings and for the next six weeks residents with business on either side of the Ohio River freely crossed the "ice bridge" on foot. On 22 January it was so thick that the Licking Rolling Mill in Covington began hauling steel beams and bars over the ice to Cincinnati railheads by mule-drawn drays, and "large droves of hogs and cattle" were grunting and lowing their way from Kentucky to the Queen City's meatpacking plants. Evenings, the river came alive with horse-drawn sleighs, their "merry bells jingling past the long line of steamboats, ice-bound and silent."[63]

Commerce and culture continued. Also crime: as five more inches of snow fell during the morning of Saturday, 26 January, Cincinnati coroner John Menzies (the son of J. W. Menzies) held an inquest on the body of an infant white girl found dead in a culvert at the waterworks. His jury's verdict: "death from abandonment," the criminal neglect of a person or persons unknown. U.S. marshals were also vigilant that weekend. Rumors of the ice bridge had spread among northern Kentucky slaves and whole families began running for free soil. By mid-January abolitionists boasted of record numbers boarding Underground

Railroad "cars." Expecting more, and determined to enforce the 1850 fugitive law, Cincinnati's U.S. marshal, Hiram Robinson, put all his deputies on duty through Monday morning.

On Saturday evening at the People's Theater on Sixth and Vine a three-act comedy entitled A Lesson for Husbands concluded its local run. Several blocks away Smith and Nixon's Hall hosted a one-night stand of the Hutchinson Family Singers, well into their second decade of antislavery activism. The Hutchinsons had departed New England in September 1855, intending to sing their way to Kansas and buoy the spirits of embattled abolitionists at Lawrence. The group had reached Iowa City in late December but blizzards forced them back, and they stopped at Cincinnati, as Asa Hutchinson's wife was within days of childbirth. For Saturday night's concertgoers the Hutchinsons performed their most popular songs: an apolitical lyric like "The Snow Storm" suited the current weather, while "The Bereaved Slave Mother," with its images of a slave child torn from its mother at the auction block, moved local abolitionists to tears.

Imagine another audience. Same moment, but across the Ohio River in Kentucky, where the people of Covington were "delighted" as Warden's Troupe, an "excellent band of Ethiopian minstrels," mimicked the high jinks and work songs of mythically happy plantation slaves. This for twenty-five cents at the city's elegant, white-columned Magnolia Hall.[64]

Dawn on Sunday, 27 January, surprised everyone with the warmest temperatures in a month, although thirty-four degrees Fahrenheit also brought a dense, low-lying fog over the snowbound Ohio River valley. On their way to worship that Sabbath morning in Cincinnati, the black members of Allen Chapel on Sixth Street near Broadway fended off gangs of whites who emerged from the mist "to pelt them with snowballs and other missiles." Allen Chapel stood in a cluster of other black churches, schools, and businesses; for decades the area was called Bucktown and was repeatedly the target of racist violence, such as the September 1841 riot that one historian calls "the most severe urban outbreak against blacks in pre–Civil War America."[65] In comparison, this Sunday's outbreak was barely newsworthy. Tuesday's Gazette gave the story one column inch and complained of police bias. During the melee a young black named Soutall, "in defending himself, cut an Irishman, for which the colored man was arrested and no notice taken of the rowdies."

Sunday afternoon, as the fogs turned first to sleet and then into a steady, light snow, Catharine Beecher had returned to the city where, twenty years earlier, she and her sister Harriet Beecher Stowe ran the Western Female Institute. Beecher's lecture, for the American Women's Educational Association, promoted two of her forthcoming books on women's physical education and summoned her mostly female audience to a higher, healthier life of "better exercise, pure air and diet."[66] A very New England prescription for the good life.

Eighteen miles to the south, at Maplewood plantation, Archibald K. Gaines's family exemplified the good Southern life. Autumn 1855 had brought a bountiful harvest throughout the Ohio Valley, and Colonel Gaines's three hundred acres had blessed his extended family. His fifteen slaves had filled his granary with twelve hundred bushels of corn, two hundred and fifty of wheat, one hundred of rye, and fifty of oats; stocked his larder with four hundred pounds of butter, with preserves of pippin apples and peaches from his orchard; cut and stacked the firewood from his woodlot. Back in November and December they drove perhaps a hundred and fifty of Master Gaines's one hundred and seventy pigs, and thirty-five of his fifty beef cattle, to the Cincinnati markets. In his commodious barns and under his tall oaks and sycamores, Gaines's dozen horses, ten oxen, twenty-five sheep, and remaining pigs and cattle were as safely huddled against the winter cold as any farmer's livestock in the region.[67]

As at other Kentucky plantations, so the winter at Maplewood would have left Gaines's slaves with comparatively few chores, some of them critical, however. The livestock had to be fed, and watering them required pumping fresh water several times each day, for whatever was pumped and left unconsumed in the troughs soon froze. The cows needed milking. Wood had to be split, as Gaines's kitchen fires and the household coal grates demanded a religious attendance. Such were the tasks of his four male slaves: one aged eighteen, two others of thirty and thirty-one years, and another aged fifty-six. To his six slave women, ranging from twenty-two-year-old Lillian up to Charlotte, aged forty-six, fell a range of ordinary chores: grinding the week's supply of corn and wheat, mending and sewing the family's clothes, as well as washing, carding, spinning, and weaving the wool from Gaines's prize-winning merino sheep. It is also likely that, in addition to Margaret Garner, responsible for nursing the Colonel's infants as well as caring for his eighty-four-year-old mother, Eliza, several more of his female slaves (Hannah, perhaps another) were engaged in household service—cooking, as well as attending his four children and Elizabeth, his second wife, now seven months pregnant.[68]

To Colonel Gaines this weekend probably seemed to pass like any other. Once his slaves completed their Saturday afternoon chores he eased their bonds. By Sunday morning those in "abroad" marriages awakened next to spouses and breakfasted with families. Margaret's husband, Robert, was over from James Marshall's plantation, a quarter mile down the road. Margaret's freedoms, however, were probably somewhat restricted because of her duties as "nurse"—one of the mixed blessings of household service. Her master's aged mother and his pregnant wife both required care. Assuming, then, that Margaret did have to stay available this Sunday, her four children—Tom and Sam, ages six and four, and Mary and Cilla, ages two and a half and nine months—probably passed part of the day with Robert or with their grandmother Priscilla. Archibald Gaines may have allowed Margaret parts of Sunday afternoon and evening with her family. She too was expecting another addition to Master Gaines's slave property, her fifth child in seven years, a pregnancy now three or four months along and perhaps another reason for Gaines to go easy on her.

Some Maplewood slaves may have attended services with members of the Gaines and Marshall families at nearby Richwood Presbyterian Church. Its congregation numbered six slaves as baptized (but nonvoting) members, and its annual Session Books tell much about ordinary life in the neighborhood.[69] Among Maplewood slaves attending morning worship led by Pastor George Bedinger would be Hannah, chastised several years earlier for insubordination and cursing. Other Maplewood slaves doubtless attended, even if they were not (like Hannah) baptized members. Most planters preferred that their slaves receive authorized (white) versions of Christianity, emphasizing the duties of servants to their masters. Archibald Gaines and James Marshall were typical enough masters in other ways to have insisted on this observance. Then too, beyond Richwood Presbyterian the Gaines slaves would have had no other ready access to regular worship, white or black. Other Richwood

Station churches were a mile or two distant and, except for congregations in Cincinnati (out of the question), the nearest formally constituted black churches were fifty or more miles away—in Louisville, Georgetown, Lexington, and Maysville.[70] Alternatively, Richwood slaves probably gathered informally to worship through the "invisible institution," a network of unauthorized, secret services. Widely reported in the literature on slavery, these Sunday gatherings for singing and praying were constantly moving, to outdoor "hush harbors" when weather permitted and from slave cabin to slave cabin during winter months. Masters tried to suppress them because these meetings so obviously defied white authority, also because slaves' hymns were themselves subversive enough, with their yearnings for escape so thinly coded by images of crossing the "Jordan" to "Canaan-land."[71]

All available evidence depicts the Garners as strong-willed, adaptive, canny, resistant slaves. On this Sunday their desire to run *may* have been further strengthened by "two English ladies who were at that time guests in the home of Archibald K. Gaines"—or, we should say, *alleged* guests. In 1953, historian Julius Yanuck found a brief mention of these mystery women in a mid-February 1856 *New York Daily Times* story.[72] Yet they can be found in no other archival source, and the story, which appeared in a proslavery paper, clearly had political motives: to blame abolitionists, thus to "explain" why slaves would run from a mythically benevolent Kentucky bondage, thus finally to play out Southron stereotypes of weak and ineffective slave dependents.

The Garner family would soon be crossing over to "Canaan," but on Sunday their final preparations for flight had to be kept entirely out of sight. In this they evidently succeeded, for we know very little about their movements on that day. Subsequent testimonies indicate that the escape completely surprised Archibald Gaines and James Marshall but that Gaines's other slaves knew of the plan. These were therefore unimaginably stressful, emotion-packed hours. To her mother, Cilla, and to slaves she had known all of her life Margaret said farewell on that Sunday evening, perhaps over supper. Did she promise eventually to buy her mother out of slavery? Did they exchange keepsakes? James Marshall's son Thomas would later claim that he saw Robert and his parents, Simon and Mary, on Sunday evening, at his father's plantation. Later, around ten or eleven o'clock Sunday night, Robert Garner made his first move. At Marshall's barn he harnessed two of his master's finest standardbred horses and hitched them to a sleigh. His parents, Simon and Mary, left with him to pick up Margaret and the four children.

The next part we have to imagine. The incredible pall of a winter landscape. The hardly audible hiss of falling and drifting snow. The rustle of dried pin oak leaves like someone shuffling newspapers in another room. Plumes of mist rising from the nostrils of Marshall's horses and the rhythmic chunk-chunk-chunk of hooves in hard-packed snow. Then a crucial piece of Robert's plot: the rendezvous with Margaret and the children. But where? A walk over the terrain quickly tells us. Between the Gaines house, at the western end of Maplewood, and the Richwood Presbyterian Church, nestled just beyond its eastern boundary, a knoll of pasture land rises fifteen, maybe twenty feet above Richwood Church Road. Farther east and just behind the church rises another knoll, the Richwood Presbyterian Cemetery. Robert probably pulled the sleigh to a halt just in front of the church. Here in the roadbed the two knolls shielded the Garners from the view of anyone at Marshall's or at Maplewood. In all, a safe spot for their rendezvous. It didn't take long to bundle Margaret's four children and few belongings into the sleigh.

Antebellum paintings of fugitive slaves worked with a typology of figures: the frantic, scantily clad bondsman at full stride through wild bayous and streambeds, and always the slave catcher's leaping, baying dogs almost at his heels. John Huston's "The Fugitive Slave" (1852) and Thomas Moran's "The Slave Hunt" (1862) defined this genre for mid-nineteenth-century America.[73] But the Garners in that Christmas-card setting needed most of all to move with cool deliberation and utmost quiet, thus to let the neighborhood's literal sleeping dogs lie. Another detail: in this anxious silence someone—perhaps her mother—must have helped Margaret to the rendezvous with her children. Tom and Sam could walk the new snow but little Cilla and Mary would have to be carried. Margaret could not have managed all of them, plus her things, alone. She might have been waiting when Robert arrived with the sleigh. He was twenty-two and nearly six feet tall, "of mild and pleasant countenance," a young man "lithe and active" in his bearing who had worked with farm animals all his life. When he flicked the reins his master's sleigh slid northward and the passengers, with one hundred sixty-three years of cumulative experience under slavery, were bound for freedom.

Robert had lived in Covington, had many times taken hogs and cattle to Covington and Cincinnati markets, or walked the Pike for Sunday visits with Margaret, and he knew every inch of his route. He'd also formed a detailed plan. In March 1870, fourteen years after these events, Robert told a *Cincinnati Commercial* reporter that Margaret's Cincinnati cousin Elijah Kite had been previously "advised" of the Garners' plans and "requested to assist in their escape" by contacting Underground Railroad men. Kite would have the abolitionists ready for the Garners' arrival in Cincinnati. When did Robert and Elijah shape this plan? In an affidavit of 30 January 1856 Robert stated that "a few weeks" earlier—that is, early January 1856—James Marshall brought him to Cincinnati and then back to Richwood after "a few hours" in the city. But on the witness stand on Friday, 1 February, Elijah's sister, Eliza, told the court that Robert's last visit occurred "a little while before Christmas," or mid-December 1855. Elijah's father, Joseph Kite, testified that "sometime this winter" he saw Robert "driving hogs" on Broadway and that his niece's husband "took supper" with the family later that day. Elijah Kite might have blown the clouds from this hazy chronology during his trial testimony, but the Garners' lawyer, John Jolliffe, wisely avoided the whole issue, thus shielding Elijah from federal charges. Having been "requested to assist" his cousin's family, Elijah had also *conspired* in their escape. Should lawyers coax that kind of testimony from him Elijah would be charged under the 1850 Fugitive Slave Law; if convicted, jailed and fined up to one thousand dollars.[74]

In any case, Elijah Kite was supposed to make advance arrangements with the Underground Railroad, wait for the Garners' arrival at Joe Kite's house, then take the fugitives on to their first scheduled stopover. Probably this meant either taking the Garners to Levi Coffin's house, at Sixth and Broadway, or having one of Coffin's agents come to Kite's house, then get them swiftly on the Underground Railroad for Canada.

It was a good plan, and Sunday night provided the perfect opportunity. The Garners might expect no call from Massa Gaines until Monday morning. They had the cover of darkness and bad weather. The roads to Covington would be almost deserted, the toll stations unmanned, though masters Marshall and Gaines and northern Kentucky slave patrollers would be vigilant, for Sunday was the time when slaves most often ran.

A survey of Cincinnati and northern Kentucky newspapers from September 1850, when the new Fugitive Slave Bill was signed into law, until January 1856, when the Garners fled, shows that during this period six parties totaling twenty-eight slaves ranging in age from sixty down to one year made a break from Boone and Kenton counties for free soil. They included eleven adult males, nine adult females, and eight children, four boys and four girls. Of the six escapes, four occurred on Sunday evenings. Just four weeks before the Garners' attempt, in fact, a party of seven Kenton County slaves made their break at a still more opportune moment: in 1855 Christmas fell on a Sunday. Moreover, snow fell most of that day. This "Negro Stampede," as the *Covington Journal* called it, ended tragically. The Ohio River was still open, although clotted with floating ice, and the slaves, having stolen a skiff, were apparently struck by one of the floes and overturned in mid-river. Three of them were drowned, the other four captured downstream on the Kentucky side.[75]

Did the Garners know of these instances? It would be more remarkable if they did not. The Gaines and Marshall slaves had regular contact with Covington slaves—for example, when driving hogs up the Turnpike or when they accompanied masters to town for provisions. Robert, we know, worked for extended periods in the Covington area. Hireling slaves from all over northern Kentucky were in and out of Richwood Station during these years. Therefore the Garners *had* to know about prior escapes from the region. How might they have seen their chances, compared to those other cases? Of the twenty-eight slaves who made a run for it during those five years, three died trying (the 1855 drownings), one "voluntarily" returned to Covington after being captured in Cincinnati, fourteen were arrested and remanded back to slavery after fugitive slave hearings, and ten slaves apparently made their way safely to Canada. The Garners' chances of successfully escaping were therefore roughly one in three. We should also note how success bore little relation to gender or age. The ten who made it included six adults (two men and four women) and four children. One of the adults was the sixty-year-old man; three of the women were over thirty years old; the youngest child was a three-year-old girl.

Therefore, *if* the Garners could make it to the river without encountering "paddyrollers" (the dreaded slave patrols), and *if* they could pass undetected through Cincinnati, then their chances looked as good as any. They had the incalculable benefit of the ice bridge, relatives in Cincinnati, and Robert's experience of the route. Working against them were several factors: the stepped-up vigilance of patrols and sleigh tracks that would be easy to follow if their masters detected their escape before the night's snowstorm covered the road.

Leaving the crossroads in front of Richwood Presbyterian Church, Robert drove the horses due north, up Richwood Church Road, then cut east to the Lexington–Covington Turnpike just beyond Richwood Station, thereby avoiding a tollhouse in the village. From Richwood to Covington were four more toll stations, one every three or four miles, each manned by resident gatekeepers who ought to be asleep but still posed a hazard. By dodging the nearest one Robert cut their chances of early detection. After Richwood, if they stopped at all, Simon, Robert's father, would jump out and raise the tollgates.

They made good time. The Lexington–Covington Turnpike followed a ridgeline of limestone hills beginning north of Lexington and running to just south of Covington, where the hills abruptly fall away at the Ohio River basin. That night the road was snow-covered but wide and free. A buffalo trace, then an Indian path, then a "corduroy" log road over which Abner Gaines's passengers once jolted along for exorbitant fares, it was in 1856 a well-graveled pike with a brand-new railroad track running beside it.[76] The Turnpike would eventually become the Dixie Highway, U.S. 25, then be superseded by Interstate 75. It has turned into one of those funky late-twentieth-century byways flanked by mobile home parks with names like Deepwood Estates and old Flying-A gas stations converted to auto body shops.

After Florence, then a town of several hundred, the Turnpike commenced its long descent to Covington. Two more tollhouses remained: one at Erlanger Station, another a few miles outside Covington near what is now Fort Mitchell. In Covington, Robert drove the sleigh right down Pike Street, in a northeasterly direction, and at Washington Street turned left and reined the horses to a stop at the intersection of Washington and Sixth streets. There, outside the Washington House hotel, the Garners unloaded and made their way on foot. It was about three in the morning, the thermometer at twelve degrees Fahrenheit. Two hours later the Washington House landlord arose and discovered the sleigh, Marshall's prize horses still harnessed to it and "very much blown from the severe manner in which they had been driven."[77]

Why did Robert abandon the sleigh? He might very well have driven it another six blocks to Front Street and descended to the riverbank,

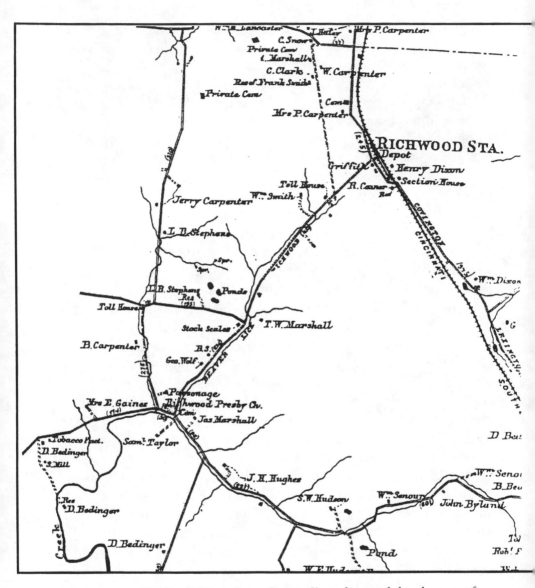

*From a map of Walton Precinct, Boone County, Kentucky, recorded twelve years after
A. K. Gaines's 1871 death, and showing the property of his widow "E. Gaines,"
opposite the "D. Bedinger" place (Forrest Home). A quarter mile to the east are
Richwood Presbyterian Church and, opposite it, the "Jas. Marshall" plantation*

SOURCE: ATLAS OF BOONE, KENTON, AND CAMPBELL COUNTIES, KENTUCKY (1883)

Looking east from Maplewood, winter 1996, toward Richwood Presbyterian Church and the cemetery behind it
AUTHOR'S PHOTOGRAPH

then simply sleighed them all across the Ohio. (Exactly what a party of five fugitives did two weeks later, on Sunday, 10 February; escaping from Mason County, Kentucky, they crossed at Maysville and "[n]either the sleigh, horses, or blacks have been heard of since."[78]) Probably Robert took them on foot because James Marshall's horses had simply given out. (One report has them "nearly dead from the hard drive."[79]) Also, Robert may have wanted to throw off any pursuers. Even with the gently falling snow, sleigh tracks would be traceable for hours after their passage, whereas footprints would soon disappear under the morning's pedestrian traffic. Interestingly, too, Robert abandoned the sleigh outside a livery stable just across Sixth Street from the Washington House. This says something more about the man: his spite was for the slave master, not the man's nonhuman chattels. Having sorely taxed Marshall's horses, Robert left the pair in the likeliest place for them to get much-needed care.

At this point in their journey each of the Garners had broken three, and Robert four, Kentucky statutes. They had gone "from the attendance

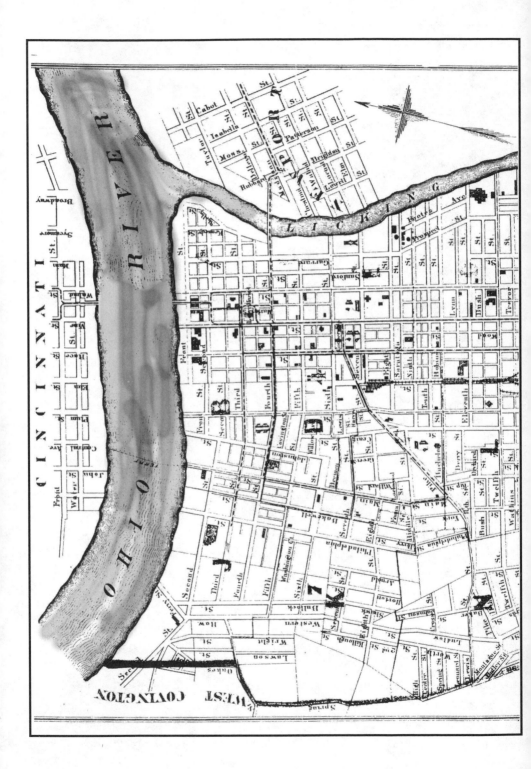

of [their] owner without a written permit," a felony punishable "by stripes, not exceeding thirty-nine." In stealing Marshall's horses and sleigh they had committed larceny, another felony punishable "by stripes, not exceeding thirty-nine." In not stopping to pay their tolls (and show their passes), they had committed a misdemeanor punishable by "stripes, not exceeding ten." Additionally Robert had evidently taken from his master a fully loaded six-shooter, another felony offense for which he could be "punished by stripes, not exceeding thirty-nine."[80] At the presiding judge's discretion these combinations of eighty-eight or, in Robert's case, one hundred and twenty-seven "stripes" could be administered in one whipping or over several sessions. Slaves were known to die from half that many.

In *Uncle Tom's Cabin*, Harriet Beecher Stowe's best-selling 1851 antislavery novel, Eliza Harris escapes over the Ohio River with her babe in arms as she skips precariously from one jagged ice floe to another, her feet leaving pathetically bloody kisses all the way. Long after the Garner case some who got the dates weirdly jumbled would claim that Margaret Garner's escape gave Stowe her model.

The real facts of early Monday morning, 28 January 1856, had none of Stowe's borrowed melodrama. These tightly bundled people descended the steep Ohio riverbank between icebound ferries. A family of eight slaves. Two grandparents and their son Robert, whom we may imagine carrying two-year-old Mary, the "beautiful child" also described as "practically white." Their daughter-in-law Margaret, carrying baby Cilla. The boys Tom and Sam walking beside them, surely wide-eyed with excitement and apprehension.

Sixteen years earlier, when she was just a year older than Tom was in 1856, Margaret had crossed in the summertime by riding a brightly painted ferry. Walking on water this time, she headed out into the darkness toward the dim aura of Cincinnati gas lamps shining through curtains of light, drifting snow. Halfway across was the Ohio state line. Stepping over that imaginary boundary, each Garner violated a federal statute. Now they were all "fugitives from labor and service."

2

CAPTIVE

ↄ⧉⫯ↄ

"A deed of horror"

In a light snowfall the Garner party crossed the Ohio River at Western Row, a major Cincinnati thorough-fare climbing uphill from the waterfront. With Robert guiding their two-mile walk, the family's quickest route would take them straight up Western Row to Eighth Street; turning left there and walking another three-quarters of a mile eastward would take them to Horn Street, where a right and two more long blocks would put them at Mill Creek Road. Just over a bridge, the Kites lived in "the third house beyond Millcreek." Safely inside, the Garners huddled around the Kites' wood stove, jubi-lant and warm but not yet safe.[1] The time: between five and six in the morning.

Today, the former site of Joe and Elijah Kite's cabin can be found several long blocks west of Interstate 75, off Gest Street, in a neighbor-hood of old warehouses, machine shops, and plating factories. The tur-bid, trash-strewn currents of Mill Creek flow into a stone dam. Spinney Park's baseball field supplies an alien patch of green inside a high chain link fence. And right where the Kites' cabin used to be stands the city's brown brick Mill Creek Wastewater Treatment Plant. The downtown skyscrapers glisten off in the distance, a fifty minute walk when I tried it on a hot autumn afternoon.

View of Cincinnati from above the Licking River
and Covington-Newport, Kentucky, ca. 1850
COURTESY THE CINCINNATI HISTORICAL SOCIETY

Elijah Kite soon left for Levi Coffin's Sixth and Elm Street store and directions to the Underground Railroad, a distance of three miles, round trip, through newly fallen snow. His long-lost cousin Margaret put her children down to sleep while Sarah and Mary Kite made breakfast. The group passed several hours over coffee, the Garners growing ever more anxious. By seven, Elijah had met with Coffin, who advised Kite to remove the Garners immediately. He wanted to meet them later, two miles farther up Mill Creek at a settlement of free blacks and white Quakers, a former home of the late John Van Zandt, made famous in *Uncle Tom's Cabin* as the Underground Railroad stationmaster named "Van Tromp." For decades the Mill Creek settlement had served fugitives as their first northbound way station. Coffin's concern, however, was that the Garners would have to make this crucial move in broad daylight, in full view of city constables and suspicious proslavery sympathizers.[2]

Census records and city directories from the period list Joseph and

Elijah Kite as laborers owning no real property, moving seemingly every year from one house or tenement to another. News reports say that Elijah rented the Mill Creek house and labored at nearby slaughter-houses during fall and winter and as a whitewasher during spring and summer. The Kite place, referred to as a "cabin" in some reports, had several rooms, a backyard privy, and a front porch. The Kites had shut-tered the front windows against the bitter cold. All four Garner children were sleeping in a back room as the adults kept vigil in front. They all had a great deal of news to share, and much catching-up to do. The Kites, Margaret's paternal aunt and uncle (Joe's wife, Sarah, was Duke's sister), had not seen Cilla's daughter for fourteen years, when Joe had purchased their freedom from Kentucky slave master William Harper.

What happened next, and why things unfolded as they did, remain unsolvable mysteries. We know that Elijah Kite returned to his family shortly after eight, at the same time a deputy U.S. marshal and a Cin-cinnati constable, on orders from the marshal's office, began a surveil-lance of the Mill Creek house. Why that coincidence? How did officers descend so swiftly on Kite's cabin? Elijah had been walking the mile and a half journey to Coffin's store between six and seven, exactly when Archibald Gaines, Thomas Marshall, and several deputy marshals had arrived in Cincinnati, en route to the U.S. Courthouse for the warrants and additional deputies needed to recover their fugitive property. Had Archibald Gaines's party crossed paths with Elijah and, having recog-nized the former Richwood Station slave, assigned a deputy to tail him? In turn, did Elijah spy the officers arriving to watch his house, and might that explain why the Garners remained at Mill Creek instead of departing immediately as Levi Coffin directed? Unanswerable ques-tions.

More important, how and when did the masters discover their slaves' escape in the first place? Here too the record is sketchy. Either old Eliza Gaines or the Colonel's pregnant wife Elizabeth awakened after mid-night, summoned Margaret, and then—getting no reply—roused Archi-bald. A short search, interrogations in the slave cabins, Margaret's mother, Priscilla, falling immediately under Gaines's suspicion because she had threatened running in the past, the hot-blooded Colonel calling for his cowhide to make Cilla tell all: something like this must have unfolded, and Massa Gaines soon had the details. We know that an alarm went out from Maplewood by two on Monday morning, so that

Gaines trailed his prey by several hours. Between two and three he cantered out of Maplewood on his best horse, armed with a rifle and pistol. Twenty years had passed since he had ridden in armed pursuit of other men, during the Texas Revolution, but family and neighbors still thought of the Colonel as a determined and fearless soldier.

Along the way Archibald Gaines enlisted help. For several weeks James Marshall had been laid up with "gravel" (gallstones), just now at its most acute stage. Unable to walk, much less sit a horse, Marshall sent along his nineteen-year-old son, Thomas (thus sending the young man in armed pursuit of the slave, Robert, whom Thomas would remember as his favorite boyhood playmate). Young Marshall and Gaines stopped just north of Richwood Station to rouse an old Gaines family friend, Major William B. Murphy, another veteran of the 1836 Texas Revolution.

The three men pushed hard, following the Garners' sleigh tracks right into Covington. In town they discovered the abandoned sleigh and horses under the care of the Washington House liveryman, proceeded several blocks farther to the U.S. marshal's office at the courthouse on Third and Scott, and there reported the fugitives before Marshal Clinton Butts, who gathered two deputies, John Patterson and another man named Robertson. About this time reports arrived of still other escapes. One group of six slaves had escaped from Covington shopkeeper Levi F. Daugherty, and three others appear to have made solo escapes, leaving masters in Covington and elsewhere in Kenton County.[3]

Clinton Butts therefore had a full slate of cases. He elected to take up that of Gaines and Marshall because the Boone County men had information about where to hunt for their slaves.[4] Either Gaines suspected that the Garners would take refuge with their relatives, the Kites, or he extracted that intelligence from Cilla. In either case, Butts's decision to assist Gaines gave the other nine fugitives a great advantage. The following day's *Cincinnati Gazette* reported that, willy-nilly, the other nine "were put upon the cars . . . by a director of the underground railway, and furnished with through tickets" to Canada. Five days later the proslavery *Covington Journal* angrily confirmed that they "made good their escape and have not since been heard of."[5] In effect, then, the Gaines and Marshall case enabled these other fugitives to realize their hope of liberty, and their success points up how awfully near Robert and Margaret had come to their own freedom. What if the Maplewood ladies had awakened later, putting Gaines into Covington another hour or two behind the fugitives? They might have found Butts out working the other cases. Everything would have been delayed, and the Garners might have made it up Mill Creek to the rendezvous with Levi Coffin.

Around seven, Gaines, Marshall, Murphy, and the three U.S. marshals crossed the frozen Ohio and made their way to the Hammond Street station house of the Cincinnati police. Someone there sent them on to Deputy U.S. Marshal George S. Bennet, who dispatched a man to summon John L. Pendery, federal Commissioner for the Southern District of Ohio. In federal judicial districts Commissioners were judges' hired subordinates, employed to take depositions or process bail applications—in short, to attend to a range of housekeeping tasks. Ordinarily they had no jurisprudential power to speak of, but the 1850 Fugitive Slave Law empowered Commissioners to issue warrants and, crucially, to try cases brought to the bar under that law. In Ohio's Southern District John Pendery served in that capacity for Justice John McLean; U.S. marshals therefore summoned him on Monday morning, and Pendery in turn sent a man to summon his court clerk, eating up still more time. Around seven-thirty Gaines and Marshall told Pendery what they knew and commenced the formal process of swearing out the fugitive slave warrant. About this time Pendery ordered a watch put on the Kite house, satisfying Gaines, who was apparently affecting an enormous frustration at the many official delays.

Around nine-thirty Pendery formally handed over the warrant. The original is lost but, as with surviving examples, that morning's document would have stated:

> The President of the United States to the Marshal of the United States, within and for the Southern District of Ohio, or any of his lawful deputies, Greeting:
>   Whereas, complaint has this day been made before me, John Pendery, a United States Commissioner, appointed by the Circuit Court of the United States, of the Seventh Judicial Circuit, and Southern District of Ohio, upon the oath of Archibald Gaines, and Thomas Marshall, agent for James Marshall, that on or about the 28th day of January, A.D. 1856:

And here in a central space the warrant would have named the eight slaves, identifying them as belonging to Marshall and Gaines and briefly stating the fact of their having "escaped from the service of the said" claimants. Then the conclusion:

> These are, therefore, to command you, in the name and by the authority aforesaid, to take the said *slaves*, if *they* be found within your District, or, if *they* shall have fled, that you pursue after *them* into any other District, and take and safely keep *them*, so that you have *their* bodies forthwith before me, to answer the said complaint and be further dealt with according to law.

Pendery entrusted the warrant to Deputy Bennet, presiding for U.S. Marshal Hiram Robinson, away on business at Columbus. Knowing from Thomas Marshall that Robert Garner was armed, Bennet took along three more deputies.[6]

Even before Pendery had commenced taking statements for the warrant, the three Covington deputies had already departed the courthouse and "made inquiries for the runaway slaves and traced them to Kite's house"—further evidence that Gaines had known the Garners' first destination. The Covington deputies returned to the courthouse with their "intelligence" just as Pendery dispatched Deputy Thomas Griffith to guard the Mill Creek house—no doubt gratifying the anxious Gaines. On his way Griffith enlisted another man identified in the newspapers only as "Snowfield, the watchman" or constable. Griffith and Snowfield (who has an apt name for such a day) both observed Elijah Kite entering the house, then waited several hours in bitter cold and occasional flurries before the remaining nine members of the party rode up. The six Kentuckians were first to arrive on horseback, and Griffith warned them against acting "until the authorities arrive"—his words from the next day's inquest. Following Griffith was Deputy Bennet, who pulled up shortly afterward with the warrant in his pocket and the other Cincinnati deputies in his wagon. Spying all this activity from inside the house, the Garners elected to stay put.

In an 1870 interview with a Cincinnati reporter, Robert Garner aired long-standing suspicions about events on that fateful day, for he believed that Elijah Kite sold them out to the slave catchers. This issue can never

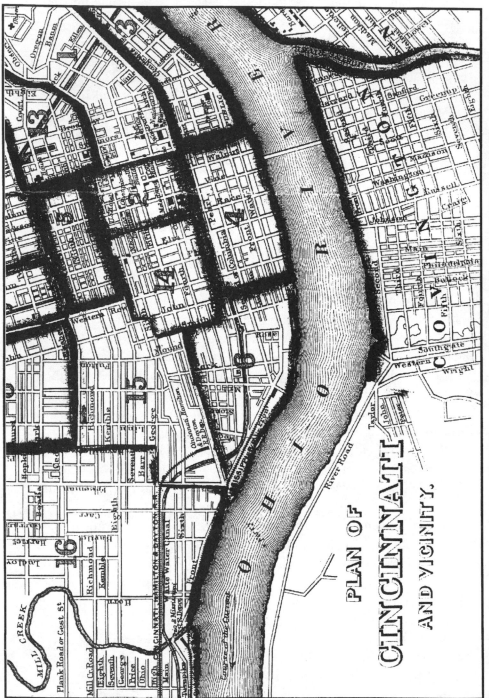

Map of Cincinnati, Ohio (1860). Note the projected suspension bridge connecting the city to Covington

be decisively settled, though Robert's suspicions deserve a hearing. Indeed, how *did* the Covington deputies so quickly learn for certain that the fugitives were stopping at the Kites'? It could have been blind luck. For example, they might simply have encountered Elijah Kite on the streets and interrogated him or, acting on Gaines's suspicions, recognized Elijah and tracked him, though on this snowy morning it may have been just as easy to track the Garners. More likely, though, Gaines's instinct and knowledge had led the way.[7]

Joe Kite was, in one Cincinnati reporter's words, "well known for years in this city."[8] Cincinnatians knew about his family's past as Boone County slaves and about Joe and Sarah's manumission in the 1840s (when the Gaineses also threatened to sell Margaret in order to stop Cilla from running). In 1849, having already purchased their daughter Eliza out of slavery, the Kites had drawn up a contract with William Harper of Richwood Station, agreeing to buy their son Elijah for $450, a generously low price, suggesting either that Harper was a man interested in his slaves' eventual freedom or that he had merely wearied of a troublesome, resisting slave and was glad to strike a deal for cash rather than lose all if Elijah ran.

In fact, before the deal was done Elijah *did* run, taking his wife and child and disappearing for several years, evidently lying low in central Ohio, then returning to Cincinnati in 1851, when he found employment as a whitewasher and hog butcher. Harper soon discovered his presence in Cincinnati and, interestingly, sued Joe Kite for the money instead of pursuing Elijah on a fugitive warrant. Harper's suit was tried before the Cincinnati Court of Common Pleas, whose judge sided with defense attorney John Jolliffe's argument that Harper's contract to sell Joseph Kite his own son Elijah was "null and void," having been illegally inscribed on Ohio soil where the statutes forbade *any* commerce in slaves. Cincinnati newspapers watched the trial closely, and the *Enquirer* complained of the judgment while the *Gazette* celebrated Jolliffe's victory. Boone County men were infuriated, and years later they still remembered the Kite case as another work of "the disorganizing, law breaking, meddling fanatics," those abolitionists who (they said) taught Kentuckians "that the *Union is no longer perfect*—that it is dissolved already."[9]

This is how old Joe Kite came to be known as a "notorious negro" in Cincinnati's relatively close society.[10] His widely remembered case might explain why the Mill Creek house was put under surveillance so swiftly. Nevertheless, only Elijah Kite had *exact* knowledge of the Garners' whereabouts and therefore *could* have given them up. In fact, relating how the fugitives were discovered, an *Enquirer* story says that Covington deputies "made inquiries," while the *Gazette* claims that they "obtained information" about the Garners, vaguely implying an informer. Yet these relatively more active and passive phrases do not say who, if anyone, was their source, or if the deputies simply "inquired" by following tracks in the snow. So it is *possible* that Elijah Kite conveyed, *as a fact* on the basis of which Pendery sent Deputy Griffith forward, information about the precise whereabouts of Margaret and her family.[11] Maybe this explains why Robert Garner long suspected Elijah Kite as a traitor. It might account for Elijah's long absence, and why he returned to the Mill Creek house just when Griffith and Snowfield put the place under surveillance.

It was possible that Elijah Kite turned in his own family, but *not probable*. Looking back, one suspects that the players in this drama converged on Mill Creek simply because they knew so much about each other, for Cincinnati-Covington was by any modern standard a small, close-knit pair of cities. Robert Garner's escape plans were rock-solid, but they could so obviously be foreseen and everything depended on speed. In any case, assuming Elijah *did* sell out his cousin and her family, why would he return to Mill Creek at all, knowing (as he must) that Robert had a pistol and the resolve to use it? On this view the sellout seems unlikely, though nothing explains why Elijah was mysteriously gone an extra hour either. That inexplicable delay in getting the Garners aboard the Underground Railroad doubtless cost them their freedom.

Months later another claim about the Garners' lengthy delay at Mill Creek surfaced in the *Covington Journal*, and it too needs airing. The occasion for this was an obsessively argued, serialized editorial devoted to "explaining and defending" Archibald Gaines, and subscribed by a writer claiming to be his "near neighbor" and calling himself "Justice" (B. F. Bedinger of Forrest Home, the *Journal*'s former editor/publisher and still, in 1856, a part owner). In his first installment Justice satirized an abolitionist story that apparently had been circulating, about how Robert "had to stop on the way [to the Kites'] to buy shoes for his poor bare-footed children, and the delay, consequent on this merciful and fatherly act, made him *a little late for the underground cars*, and the result was his master caught him." His sarcasm mounting, Justice wondered who among Cincinnati merchants would have "got out of his bed at that hour of the night [at six in the morning], to shoe these children?"[12]

But Justice derided a story enclosing a palpable truth, if seen from another side. Cincinnati newspapermen who saw the Garners on the day of their escape all pointed out the fugitives' inadequate clothing and poor winter shoes, needs that would in fact have been swiftly answered had they moved on to Levi Coffin's recommended stopover. Cincinnati's underground resisters commonly provided everything from clothing and shoes, food, money, clandestine jobs, transportation, and, as a last resort, legal aid to runaways. After the 1850 Fugitive Slave Law many of the city's black leaders volunteered for the Life Guards, a resistance league known for meeting fugitives' practical needs, a group that sponsored annual clothing drives for that purpose.[13] Had the Garners made it to the Mill Creek "station" on the Underground Railroad, this network would have jumped to assist them; and Justice either misunderstood or did not know the extent and practical focus of local resistance work. He misread how the Garners, fleeing into the worst winter on record with little more than they could carry, eagerly anticipated how the whole machinery of support—complex machinery that Elijah Kite had gone to Coffin's store to set into motion—would spring to meet their needs.

In fact the Life Guards were probably busy assisting the nine Kenton County fugitives who successfully fled north. By one estimate, some 175 fugitives passed through Cincinnati during the eleven-week stretch when the Ohio was frozen. This averages sixteen each week, and most of them (as we have noted) on Sunday nights.[14] Thus the Garners' long delay probably had much less to do with buying shoes, or even with a traitorous Elijah Kite, than with underground volunteers scrambling to answer their calls that frantic Monday morning.

From here on, the record becomes no less cloudy. We must deal with the natural variation in witnesses' accounts filtered through the unabashedly political penny papers in a nineteenth-century American border city. By 1856 the Democratic, proslavery *Enquirer* and the Republican, antislavery *Gazette* had been at loggerheads over slavery for years, while the *Commercial* and the *Columbian* elbowed each other for middle ground. Taken together, their writers leaned heavily toward paraphrase and summation, using few direct quotations. Reporters provided invaluable summaries and transcriptions of court proceedings, crucial in a case like this one, for which court records have vanished. Their records of courtroom testimonies are, however, selective, concentrating on dramatic moments. Some reporters transcribed speakers' dialects; others translated dialects into standard English. Their articles vividly sketch people and scenes yet show frustratingly scant investigative skill. Where modern readers would expect close interviews with perpetrators and victims and their extended families and co-workers, concentrating on backgrounds and contexts, antebellum newspapermen accepted a much higher barrier around the private domain and never considered vaulting over it for a story. Their racism also held them in check. Only in 1870, seven years *after* Emancipation, did it occur to a reporter that the recollections and views of a principal actor in "The Garner Slave Tragedy," a black man, might be worthy of record.

We do know the following: At ten Monday morning, after twelve hours as fugitives and perhaps only six or seven on free soil, the Garners found themselves surrounded by an armed posse of eleven men. Gaines and Marshall stood with Deputy George Bennet in front of Kite's house, the others at the sides and back. Bennet repeatedly called on the slaves to surrender, identifying himself and his authority to take them before a United States court. For some minutes he received no answer. The doors and windows remained closed and shuttered. Bennet called again for their surrender. Then Major Murphy tried his hand and evidently communicated briefly though unsuccessfully with Robert, who shouted defiance from behind a window.

Responding to all this commotion, the Kites' neighbors began gathering. A crowd of twenty or thirty interested blacks and whites eventually swelled (by one account) to a "mob" numbering several hundred. Robert surely took heart from this growing, angry crowd and probably hoped antislavery activists would mount a "rescue." But the slave catchers determined to wait no longer. The *Enquirer* has Deputy Bennet "thundering" at Kite's door, and Joe Kite eventually peering out a window, agreeing "to admit them," then refusing. The *Gazette* adds that "two of the Kentucky officers," Butts and Robertson, finally determined to "force an entrance."

They assailed the front of the house. Robert fired three shots from his revolver as Bennet, Butts, Robertson, Gaines, and Patterson used chunks of firewood to smash open the door and shuttered window. All five men scrambled inside, Patterson evidently entering through the window just as Robert fired another round. The pistol ball tore off Patterson's finger and "lodged in his upper lip, leaving the finger hanging by a mere thread." Patterson staggered out the door and collapsed on the front porch, his jaw and several teeth shattered, as Archibald Gaines wrestled with Robert for the six-shooter and managed at last to wrench "the pistol from his hand before he could shoot the other two barrels off."[15] About the same time Patterson had staggered out the front, Elijah's wife, Mary, had fled out the back.

Subduing Robert, the posse found him uninjured but heavily and inexplicably bloodied. Then their eyes took in the interior tableau:

> a deed of horror had been consummated, for weltering in its blood, the throat being cut from ear to ear and the head almost severed from the body, upon the floor lay one of the children of the younger couple, a girl three years old, while in a back room, crouched beneath the bed, two more of the children, boys, of two and five years, were moaning, the one having received two gashes in its throat, the other a cut upon the head. As the party entered the room the mother was wielding a heavy shovel, and before she could be secured she inflicted a heavy blow with it upon the face of the infant, which was lying upon the floor.[16]

This from the *Cincinnati Enquirer*. The *Covington Journal* adds that when the posse burst into the Kites' cabin the infant's "blood was spouting out profusely, showing that the deed was but recently committed." Several of the posse leapt past Mary Garner's body to wrest the coal shovel from Margaret. The *Cincinnati Commercial* adds that when deputies subdued Margaret, little Cilla was "bleeding quite freely at the nose" from shovel blows that also left her "much swollen" about the forehead. Deputy Bennet shouted for one of the posse to go hail a doctor. The Garner boys, Thomas and Samuel, were bleeding and crying inconsolably while, having herself emerged from under one of the beds in a back room, old Mary Garner continued a high wailing.

This version, synthesizing testimonies from members of the marshals' posse, gives us an outside-in perspective. Yet we want to know what was happening *inside* the Mill Creek house as officers called on the Garners to surrender. That version can be similarly constructed from testimonies of the Kites and the Garner adults, who were interrogated during the coroner's inquest. Reporters also interviewed Margaret after the slaves' capture.[17]

Margaret would later tell a *Commercial* reporter how the Kites and Garners were still lingering over their breakfast when "she heard someone cry out, 'They are coming, they are coming!' " The fugitives hesitated for a lengthy period, debating what to do. When Bennet demanded their surrender everyone inside began to scatter.[18] Bennet's "thundering" at Elijah Kite's door sent them into a final panic.

Robert began brandishing his pistol as Margaret discovered a large carving knife—one of Elijah's slaughterhouse tools—and (in the coroner's standardized grammar) pled with her mother-in-law, Mary: "Mother, before my children shall be taken back to Kentucky I will kill every one of them!" She ran to little Mary and with "a single stroke of the knife" nearly decapitated the child. Margaret then once again pled with her mother-in-law for help. In the *Enquirer's* recounting, old Mary replied: "I cannot help you to kill them." Then she claimed to have run from the room and taken refuge under the bed until discovered by Bennet's posse. From her hideout Mary Garner saw nothing further.

A "single stroke of the knife": this phrase says so much but not nearly enough. Obviously Margaret Garner had struck with great force, if she nearly decapitated little Mary. But did that indicate reasoned premeditation, or mad fury? There is so much more that we do not know: Why did Margaret begin with Mary? Did she say anything to the little girl before drawing the knife across her throat? Look into her eyes? Do it from the front or from the child's back side? Margaret Garner had lived all her life on a farm: she knew how lambs were dispatched swiftly and relatively painlessly.

Differing accounts from Joe and Sarah Kite indicate that after Margaret killed little Mary, either she gave Robert, or Robert rushed to take up, the child's body. Thus his bloody clothes. Robert soon laid the girl's dying body on the floor, and Sarah Kite saw him momentarily "pacing the room wringing his hands and screaming, as if bereft of reason, while the elder man [Simon Garner] was also pacing the room and groaning." Then Robert began waving the revolver about. During these moments of despair, murderous anger, grief, and violent mania, he apparently did not see Margaret continuing her bloody work on Thomas and Samuel, who must have struggled fiercely against their mother, for their wounds about the scalp and neck were mostly superficial.

Sarah Kite did intervene, however, and somehow either talked the knife out of Margaret's hand or wrested it from her just as the posse crashed through the front door and window and Robert began firing. Sarah gave the knife to Elijah's wife and told her to get rid of it. The boys were wailing all this time as Robert, overwhelmed, yielded the revolver to Gaines while Patterson, bleeding heavily and groaning, staggered out the front as Mary Kite ran out the back door to the privy and threw in the knife, from where it was never recovered, and Margaret, undeterred by her aunt Sarah and still wholly bent on keeping her babies from Kentucky slavery, took up a coal shovel and dealt her youngest, Cilla, a "blow to the face."

The *Commercial* reporter heard that "Robert and Margaret fought with the ferocity of tigers." The posse restrained them at last. Robert and Margaret Garner's resistance and rage against slavery was ended, at least for the time being.

Arrest and Inquest

Noon. 28 January 1856. A bloodied John Patterson was lying in the marshals' wagon when a surgeon arrived, examined him, and ordered the man carried away for hospital care. He then dressed the children's wounds. Thomas had "two gashes" on his neck, one nearly "four inches long" that miraculously missed opening a carotid artery. Samuel had a superficial scalp wound behind an ear, and Cilla a facial contusion noticeable throughout the coming weeks' court proceedings.

Marshal Bennet bundled the Garners into another wagon ordered up for the purpose and sent them to the U.S. Courthouse. He also sent ahead for the city coroner, Dr. John Menzies, who soon reined up at the Mill Creek house to hold a preliminary inquest over little Mary Garner's body. Before Menzies arrived, however, a strange scene unfolded. One of Kite's neighbors, a white laborer named Sutton, saw Archibald Gaines appear on the front porch of the house carrying little Mary's body and sobbing uncontrollably over her corpse. From his almost incoherent phrases, deputies realized that Gaines meant to leave Cincinnati on horseback with the corpse. They had a difficult time persuading the distraught man to put down the child's body and stay at the Kites' house.

Did his behavior indicate that Archibald Gaines's relationship to the murdered child went beyond that of master and slave? Again we should give him the benefit of our doubt, for during the course of her domestic labor at Maplewood's "big house" Margaret might have often brought little Mary with her, when Gaines might have come to know and care for the child. Yet the extremity of his grieving, and especially his clinging to the corpse, suggested then and now a still dearer relation to the little girl.

When the coroner arrived Gaines still refused to release Mary Garner's body and insisted on carrying it inside by himself. Probably the Colonel got his way because John Menzies, the eldest son of John Pollard Gaines's longtime friend and political adviser, John W. Menzies, was able to put the hair-triggered Gaines at ease. Another tie in the network of Cincinnati-Covington affiliations.

When the hastily arranged coroner's jury of six men arrived on the scene, Dr. Menzies opened a preliminary inquest. He began by interrogating the slave catchers who had come to Mill Creek that morning, including Gaines and Deputies Butts and Robertson, the first into the Kites' house. None of them "could throw any light as to whether the father or the mother of the child had committed the bloody deed," and their testimony confused Coroner Menzies and his jury. Robert's bloodied condition and proximity to Mary's body all pointed to him as the child-murderer, yet before marshals took them off to town, the adult Garners had evidently described Margaret's child-murder to bystanders —hearsay of questionable use. Meanwhile Gaines and Butts could only testify to having seen Margaret wielding the coal shovel on Priscilla, and no one else seemed to know how young Tom and Sam were cut; by this time all of the Kites had been taken away to the courthouse. Menzies lacked key witnesses and didn't even have the murder weapon. He was forced to adjourn the inquest.

The coroner's people and the marshals, along with Murphy, Thomas Marshall, and Archibald Gaines, all departed the Mill Creek house in a procession headed for the courthouse on Fourth Street, between Main and Walnut. Gaines rode with the body of Mary Garner, and was still visibly crying over her shrouded form. The procession struggled to open a way through an angry crowd numbering several hundred, many of whom followed the procession into town. News of the Garner infanticide flashed through Cincinnati streets. Once they reached the courthouse, Gaines and Marshall expected Commissioner Pendery immediately to commence a hearing on the fugitive slave warrant. This was normal "usage" and Gaines acted as if he thought Pendery would award him custody of his slaves by that afternoon. He was hugely mistaken.

With news reporters hovering, Archibald Gaines and Thomas Marshall found their slaves at the U.S. Courthouse on Fourth Street. There *Cincinnati Commercial* reporter George J. Guilford observed the fugitives seated "around the stove with dejected countenances" keeping "a moody silence, answering all questions propounded to them in monosyllables, or refusing to answer at all." Describing Robert and Margaret as "mild and pleasant" slaves "partially stultified" by the day's "exciting trials," Guilford characterized their silence as a pathetic symptom of their downtroddenness—as if they were just too naturally shy, or habitually cowardly, to speak or act in the presence of whites. But why should we think so? Guilford himself wrote that before being taken at the Kites' both Robert and Margaret had "fought with the ferocity of tigers."

Can silence speak? Of course, and by their "moody" refusal to answer the questions of white newsmen the Garners should be seen acting within a broader historical context. Captured rebel slaves typically responded to their oppression just as the Garners did. When they were retaken after bloody uprisings, insurrectionists Gabriel Prosser (in 1800) and Nat Turner (in 1831) both declined to speak or even, later, to enter pleas at their trials. They declined, in other words, to acknowledge their revolutionary deeds as actionable "crimes" because they had already rejected as tyrannical the entire legal machinery that whites had used first to oppress and then to indict them.[19]

But were the Garners' deeds rebellious? Certainly their troubled relations with Boone County masters tells of a continuing resistance. But was their escape and infanticide a rebellious act? Certainly, again. By 1856, for masters as well as slaves, "simple escape from slavery had come to seem a potential revolutionary act, with its suppression guaranteed by the [1850] Fugitive Slave Act."[20] As for the infanticide, what *had* Margaret Garner done? Destroyed her master's *property* with the same knife stroke that destroyed his *progeny* (if Gaines fathered Mary Garner). On this view of things, Margaret's child-murder was a masterstroke of rebellion against the whole patriarchal system of American slavery.

In *Cannibals All!* (1857), perhaps the most powerful statement for the Southron ideal of a benevolent but all-powerful master class of slaveholders, polemicist George Fitzhugh argued that natural law should regulate slavery according to reciprocal roles. In Fitzhugh's view, dependent slaves have as much control of their masters as masters exercise over them: Massa needs the slaves' labor, just as they need his benevolent protection. Thus "the interests of master and slave are bound up together, and each in his appropriate sphere naturally endeavors to promote the happiness of the other."[21] The model for this reciprocal benevolence, to Fitzhugh as to the myriad of Southrons for whom he spoke, was the extended patriarchal family, within which slaves and their offspring became Massa's metaphorical "children." And how could a patriarch not act benevolently toward his own children, or they in turn to him? This formula lay at the heart of proslavery writers' defense of their peculiar institution.[22] Without kindly patriarchy, men in their selfish grasping were destined to fall, to become "cannibals all," a condition prevailing (argued Fitzhugh) throughout the industrialized North and its free-labor masses. But behind Fitzhugh's metaphors were disruptive, literal facts; and not least among those facts, as antislavery writers kept insisting, was that too often Massa's slaves *were* his children. In the words of antislavery writers such as Harriet Jacobs or Lydia Maria Child, the much-vaunted plantation household was instead a "brothel" for gratifying the master's lust, the tortured results of which were the South's burgeoning population of mulatto children.[23]

Margaret Garner's child-murder had the effect of making visible these otherwise invisible roles and realities, exposing the whole "Southron" social and cultural system to subversion and attack. Occurring literally under the gun of "the patriarchal family," her infanticide was as horrible to contemplate as Fitzhugh's fantasied "cannibals." Everyone soon grasped its incisive effect; reporters sprang to attention, and were quickly followed by pro- and antislavery activists. All sought to control the meaning of Margaret's infanticide. Recognizing this, however "stunned" they were, the Garners chose silence, and our image of their "moody" forms hunkered around the jailhouse stove, news reporters fluttering around this grieved family circle, therefore remains one of the most powerful from that day's events.

From then on, reporters' fleeting, two-dimensional images of Margaret and her family are practically all that we have, and often those images tell us mainly of the Garners' passivity amidst arguments and actions swirling all around them, as prominent whites stepped onto center stage and sought control over the fugitives' fate. Margaret's child-murder also became *their story,* and tracing these other strands necessitates leaving the Garners aside at times.

When Commissioner Pendery opened his courtroom at three that afternoon, Archibald Gaines and Thomas Marshall appeared as claimants on the federal warrant. Deputies brought in the Garners and their masters formally identified them, but Pendery was clearly wary about the looming jurisdictional dispute. His contemporaries described the Commissioner as a tall, lean man and "a good-natured, easy lawyer, of moderate abilities and kind heart," who would "rather see all the negroes set free than sent back to slavery." Formerly a Whig, Pendery was an "opponent of the Pierce Administration" on his way toward eventual Republican Party membership. Rumor had it that nepotism got him the Commissioner's job; his sister-in-law was the wife of his employer, U.S. Supreme Court Justice John McLean, whose Seventh Judicial Circuit included Southern Ohio.[24]

Pendery presided over a hearing that lasted barely more than half an hour, as first Gaines and then Marshall stated their claims to the Garners. Soon the Commissioner found the lapse that he clearly wanted: Thomas Marshall had left Richwood Station without getting a power of attorney from his father, a crucial detail because the Commissioner's warrant clearly listed *James* Marshall as the rightful owner of Simon, Mary, and Robert. Without a power of attorney Thomas Marshall had no legal claim before the bar. Pendery therefore decided to continue the hearing at nine the next morning.

Lacking a cell for them in the U.S. Courthouse, Pendery ordered the slaves taken away for a night at the Hammond Street station house—a barracks with one cramped holding cell. Outside the courthouse "a wild and excited scene presented itself—the sidewalks and the middle of the streets were thronged with people."[25] The fugitives emerged on the steps, ringed by an armed guard and beyond them an angry mob. Deputy

Marshal Bennet called for a city hack, but no driver would agree to transport the Garners because of the dangerous crowd. Instead, "the prisoners were accordingly walked under the conduct of a strong escort. Some threats were made by a portion of the mob, but no violence or attempt at rescue made." Safely inside the station house, all seven Garners, exhausted and still wearing their bloodied clothes, huddled around a large potbellied stove. As before, they still refused to speak with officers or reporters about themselves or their roles in the infanticide.

Around three o'clock, shortly after the Garners' transfer, John Jolliffe appeared before Cincinnati Probate Court Judge John Burgoyne. Jolliffe related details of the Garner tragedy that had doubtless already seared the judge's ears, and expressed fears that Kentucky "rowdies" would attempt a kidnaping. He petitioned Burgoyne for a writ of habeas corpus ordering those persons holding the slaves to produce them immediately; for the Garners were, he reminded Burgoyne, suspects in or witnesses to a murder that he depicted as a fatal consequence of the slave catchers' violent assault on the Kites' private property. It was a smart, but broadly anticipated move. Habeas corpus writs are designed to protect the rights of persons illegally detained. They force officials not only to show that they "have the body" of a person but to show cause for the person's imprisonment; thus they force officials either to indict or to release a suspect. But Jolliffe was in effect reversing things: the adult Garners had not yet been charged with murder; he wanted them released from federal authority *so that they could be.* In effect, he was challenging the authority of federal marshals to hold fugitive slaves in the first place, challenging the Fugitive Slave Law's legitimacy. If granted, Burgoyne's writ would force federal authorities to relinquish custody of the Garners and further prevent any removal of them to Kentucky without a prior hearing before Burgoyne's court. Recognizing Jolliffe's gambit, but knowing how such writs usually proved futile in fugitive cases, Burgoyne (known as "a staunch abolitionist") had the writ inscribed and put in the hands of a Hamilton County deputy sheriff, Jeffrey Buckingham. Buckingham gathered a posse and led them the several blocks to the Hammond Street station house.[26]

Hammond Street had become a very crowded scene. When Buckingham arrived, more than two hundred men, a number of them black, were milling around it in the snow and ice. Shouts—some demanding that the poor slaves be set free, others that the child-murderers be hanged that night—echoed down the streets. Security was tight. Federal marshals denied entrance to Deputy Sheriff Buckingham with his writ of habeas corpus and his small posse. They also turned aside John Jolliffe and his assistant counsel, James Gitchell. Jolliffe left to consult again with Judge Burgoyne and left Gitchell at Hammond Street, where he was said to have "remonstrated with" Marshal Bennet about possible lawsuits for refusing the lawyers access to their clients. Bennet eventually allowed Gitchell to stand in a kind of foyer. When Archibald Gaines arrived shortly before 4 p.m. he was "freely admitted" while the *Gazette* reporter, trailing him, was "seized" and "put out" summarily. All of this, of course, amounted to pure political partisanship.

Waiting in an open area on the first floor of the Hammond Street building, George Guilford of the *Commercial*, known for its moderate stand on slavery, got a scoop. He "called [Thomas] Marshall from the stove to the window, and took out [his] note book and put down what he said at the time." In company with Major Murphy, young Marshall said pretty much what one would expect: that the Garners were always well treated and "never evinced any inclination to be free." But then Marshall made a crucial slip: "these people," he said of the Garners in general, "had been on this side of the river frequently."[27] Jolliffe would make much of that claim in days to come.

Meantime federal marshals admitted no one else to the Hammond Street station. Gaines may have met with the Garners, but we have no record of it. He exited out a back door, from which Thomas Marshall had been watching their horses. In a light snowfall, sometime after four o'clock, Gaines passed through the darkening streets of Cincinnati. Riding on his horse's flank behind the saddle was tied a long bundle swathed in white cloths—"the dead body of the murdered child. He was taking it to Covington [he said] that it might rest in ground consecrated to slavery."[28]

Thomas Marshall remained inside at Hammond Street, probably on orders from Gaines to continue shadowing the Garners. The young man gave another interview, this time to a reporter from the *Enquirer*, an ardently Democratic, proslavery paper. The young Marshall claimed that he had always treated Robert Garner "more as a companion than as a slave," and went on to relate how they were "playmates in childhood" and grew up together. He also made what seems a very formal statement, well calculated for attribution: "And now, if money can save him [Robert] from the effect of the rash act he has committed I am willing to give it to any amount." During this time the *Enquirer*'s man also got a look at the Garners. "The old couple are mild and rather intelligent in their appearance," he would write for Tuesday morning's readers, and "the mother of the children is a good-looking, hearty negress, while her husband bears the appearance of having been well cared for."[29]

As darkness approached, a tense contest began. Federal marshals still refused to admit Deputy Sheriff Jeffrey Buckingham with his habeas corpus. In fact, they began trying to "decoy him out" of the building so that "they might lock the doors against him. They invited him to go and take a drink at the St. Charles [Hotel], but Jeff was not to be caught in any such traps." When the marshals claimed they were holding the Garners on orders from Cincinnati mayor James J. Farran, Buckingham called their bluff and sent for Farran. Fifteen minutes later the mayor told Buckingham that "the [county] jail was the place for the slaves" and departed, ordering Buckingham along for protection. Gathering reinforcements, Buckingham returned to the jail around five, and again "Lieut. Hazen, who [had] charge of the Hammond street Station House, refused to admit the gentleman." After a heated debate, Hazen finally admitted Buckingham and his posse, who emerged triumphantly after fifteen minutes and hustled the Garners through the crowd and into a waiting omnibus. Buckingham's men directed the driver to take them to the county jail, but as they pulled away Deputy U.S. Marshal Bennet leapt into the omnibus and, pulling his gun, ordered the hackman to drive them all to the U.S. Courthouse.

Deputy sheriffs and marshals trailed the omnibus to Fourth Street, where "another fuss" began, one that put the Garners in a very precarious spot. Guns were drawn everywhere, and any attempted abolitionist "rescue" might have sparked a full-scale battle. Yet here was precisely that eventuality which Gaines had ordered Thomas Marshall to watch for. Because *if* the Garners could be detained at the U.S. Courthouse until Gaines returned the next morning with a power of attorney from Marshall's father, and *if* Commissioner Pendery could then be persuaded to reopen his proceeding, just like that the Garners might be remanded back to slavery—perhaps even by the next day, Tuesday.

Deputy U.S. Marshal Bennet, still faced with the lack of a cell at the courthouse, made a snap decision and ordered the fugitives upstairs to his office. Deputy Sheriff Buckingham, counterpunching, followed them up and threw open a window, from which he brandished a revolver and called "to the crowd, directing some to inform Sheriff Brashears of the situation" and to request of him still more reinforcements. At seven o'clock came a "large force" of armed deputies commanded by the Hamilton County sheriff, a tall bearded man with an unusual name—Gazoway Brashears. His arguments were not recorded for us, but they (or perhaps his superior force) finally prevailed. By eight, Hamilton County sheriff's deputies took the Garners back into custody and sent them to the county jail, accompanied by federal deputies Bennet and Ellis, as well as Thomas Marshall.

At last Deputy Sheriff Buckingham could formally serve Judge Burgoyne's writ of habeas corpus, but when Brashears examined the document he discovered yet another problem. Judge Burgoyne had specified that "the negroes were in the custody of one Bennet and Ellis, without naming the latter as Deputy Marshals of the United States," instead assuming (apparently) that they were the slaves' owners. Brashears therefore declined to serve the writ, believing it was invalidated because of Burgoyne's factual error.

Leaving aside the question of how the exhausted and frightened Garners understood these punch-counterpunch tactics of U.S. marshals and Hamilton County sheriffs, what did these things mean to the whites who had, incredibly, taken up arms against each other over the fugitives? By the time of the Garner case, the struggle over slavery in Cincinnati —and especially the struggle over the Fugitive Slave Law—had evolved into pitched battles with skillful tacticians operating amidst clearly identifiable factions. Remember, too: even though the Queen City prided itself on being the nation's sixth largest, its 1856 population (around 110,000) was still small by current standards. Its principal citizens, its abolitionists and proslavery men, all tended to know each other; indeed the same familiarity existed between Cincinnatians and Kentuckians across the river. Recall the family relationship between Coroner Menzies and Colonel Gaines. Then too, the record tells us that Deputy Marshal Bennet and Deputy Sheriff Buckingham were performing more than just the duties of their respective offices; both were acting out their politics and were even willing to spill the blood of longtime acquaintances over slavery.

Within Cincinnati alone, lines were sharply drawn. One study of census records (showing place of birth) found that in 1850 nearly *half* of Cincinnati's population had immigrated from slaveholding states, especially Virginia and Kentucky.[30] Add to these sectional allegiances the city's ethnic and racial tensions—especially Irish immigrants competing for manual labor against blacks (many of whom had lived there longer)—and it's obvious why these tensions often boiled over. Irish "roughs" were in the forefront of the city's antiblack riots against residents of Bucktown.[31]

Additionally, Cincinnati's civic institutions commanded highly partisan allegiances. At least since passage of the 1850 Fugitive Slave Law, Hamilton County sheriffs drew members from the ranks of the various liberal splinter parties that were coalescing into the new Republican Party. These splinter parties included former Conscience (or antislavery) Whigs, Liberty Party men, Free-Soilers, and liberal members of the American (or Know-Nothing) Party, who in the fall of 1855 had shocked the state by electing the Republican candidate for governor, longtime Cincinnati antislavery attorney Salmon Portland Chase. Throughout the last antebellum decade, these men continually battled Cincinnati's mayoral leadership and area federal officials, who all owed allegiance (and often their appointments) to proslavery Democrats, the so-called Doughfaces (Northern proslavery Democrats, including the city's many Irish and its former Southerners), who had long dominated antebellum Cincinnati politics. In 1856, all deputies serving under U.S. Marshal Hiram H. Robinson were ardent proslavery Democrats.

When John Jolliffe petitioned Probate Court Judge Burgoyne for a habeas corpus writ on the afternoon of 28 January he was acting with a speed learned from years of experience. Burgoyne he well knew as someone sympathetic to antislavery goals; otherwise Jolliffe's petition to the Probate Court—little more than a glorified justice of the peace—made no sense in a case involving both capital murder and federal statutes. But Jolliffe knew Burgoyne was empowered to issue writs of habeas corpus, and this afternoon one writ was all he needed to buy some time to organize the Garners' defense. He probably even smiled inwardly as Burgoyne instructed his clerk to make out a writ erroneously naming Marshals Bennet and Ellis as owners of the slaves, for Jolliffe knew that the error made it impossible for the writ to be formally received and that it might thus protract the legal process. Perhaps Burgoyne himself recognized Jolliffe's game and played along, for *he* certainly knew who Bennet and Ellis were.

Consider also the drama unfolding late Monday afternoon and evening at the Hammond Street station house. Denying the *Gazette* reporter entrance but admitting another from the *Enquirer* was straight party politics: the *Enquirer* was guided by Doughface principles while the *Gazette* was long noted for its antislavery stance. People not only recognized this rift in general terms; they well knew the principal players. Edmond Babb, for the *Gazette*, had been roughed up some when the federal marshals ejected him from the Hammond Street station house, but that was trivial compared to the treatment he would receive a month later, across the Ohio River in Covington. Cincinnati's political polarization was evident also in clashes between the antislavery, Republican leadership in the sheriff's office and the Democratic U.S. marshal's. It was a border city in the literal and the metaphorical sense, a microcosm of the soon to be divided Union.

As Cincinnati went to bed, these factions had reached an evening's truce. The Garners were lodged in two cells at the Hamilton County jail, guarded throughout the night by U.S. marshals in addition to county sheriffs. The habeas corpus had been served, but turned back on a technicality that would lead to its being resubmitted the next day. The U.S. marshal, Hiram H. Robinson, away on business this day, was hastening back to the city from Columbus after receiving telegraphic news of the Garner case. Hamilton County Probate Court Judge John Burgoyne was hastening to Columbus to consult on strategy with Governor Salmon Portland Chase.

An epilogue to this incredible day: Sometime that evening, members of the Ladies Anti-Slavery Sewing Circle brought fresh clothes for the Garners. Among them was Synthelia Jolliffe, wife of attorney John Jolliffe. The ladies found the Garners occupying two adjoining cells, males in one, females in another. As the night passed, the prisoners scarcely ate, but their jailers did engage them in conversation and sent along to eager reporters a few nuggets. Margaret, they said, acknowledged killing little Mary, "and her determination was to have killed all the children, and then destroyed herself, rather than return to slavery," because of "cruel treatment on the part of their master," Archibald Gaines.[32]

Late Monday evening the men guarding the fugitives heard "low and plaintive notes of Negro song" echoing from the Garners' cell. A spiritual? Maybe a funeral dirge? We are indebted to diligent antislavery witnesses like Thomas Wentworth Higginson for transcriptions, made in the 1860s, of slave songs prevalent throughout the South. The *Enquirer* reporter did not set down for us the fugitives' plaintive words. Perhaps it was this traditional lyric, reported to have been commonly sung at the funerals of slave infants:

> *De little baby gone home,*
> *De little baby gone home,*
> *De little baby gone along,*
> *For to climb up Jacob's ladder.*

> *And I wish I'd been dar,*
> *I wish I'd been dar,*
> *I wish I'd been dar, my Lord,*
> *For to climb up Jacob's ladder.*[33]

"The damned abolitionist"

Tuesday brought light snow. Over their morning coffee and cakes Cincinnatians read the first published news of the previous day's infanticide. The *Gazette* and *Commercial* kept to the main facts; the proslavery *Enquirer* editorialized:

> there is much excitement existing, the bloody episode having invested the affair with a tinge of fearful, although romantic interest. The Abolitionists regard the parents of the murdered child as a hero and heroine, teeming with lofty and holy emotions, who, Virginius like, would rather imbue their hands in the blood of their white offspring than allow them to wear the shackles of slavery.[34]

That classical allusion is significant—the first of many attempts to define and regulate the meaning of Margaret's "deed of horror."

Antebellum readers knew about the infanticide of Roman centurion Lucius Virginius through passages from Cicero and popular English texts. British playwright James Sheridan Knowles dramatized the story

CITY-NEWS

AMUSEMENTS, ETC., TO-DAY.

PEOPLE'S THEATRE.—*Corner of Sixth and Vine streets*—Open every evening.

LECTURE BY THE REV. OLSNETT M. BUTLER, D. D., at *Smith & Mason's Hall.*

Arrest of Fugitive Slaves.

A Slave Mother Murders her Child rather than see it Returned to Slavery.

Great excitement existed throughout the city the whole of yesterday, in consequence of the arrest of a party of slaves, and the murder of her child by a slave mother, while the officers were in the act of making the arrest. A party of seventeen slaves escaped from Boone and Kenton counties, in Kentucky, (about sixteen miles from the Ohio,) on Sunday night last, and taking with them two horses and a sled, drove that night to the Ohio river, opposite to Western Row, in this city. Leaving the horses and sled standing there, they crossed the river on foot on the ice.

Five of them were the slaves of Archibald K. Gaines, three of John Marshall, both living in Boone county, a short distance beyond Florence, and six of Levi F. Daugherty, of Kenton county. We have not learned who claims the other three.

About 7 o'clock this morning the masters and their agents arrived in pursuit of their property. They swore out a warrant before J. L. Pendery, Esq., U. S. Commissioner, which was put into the hands of Deputy U. S. Marshal Geo. S. Bennet, who obtained information that they were in a house belonging to a son of Jo. Kite, the third house beyond Millcreek. The son was formerly owned in the neighborhood from which they had escaped and was bought from slavery by his father.

About 10 o'clock the Deputy U. S. Marshal proceeded there with his posse, including the slave owners and their agent and Major Murphy, a Kentuckian, and a large slave holder. Kite was called out and agreed to open the door, but afterwards refused, when two Kentucky officers, assisted by some of the Deputy Marshals forced it, whereupon the young negro man Simon, the father of the children, fired a revolver three times before he was overpowered. By one of these shots special Marshal John Patterson, who raised his arm to reach the pistol, had two of his fingers of his right hand shot off, the ball afterwards striking his lip.

In the house were found four adults, viz: old Simon and his wife, and young Simon and his wife and four children of the latter, the oldest near six years and the youngest a babe of about nine months. One of these, however, was lying on the floor dying its head cut almost entirely off. There was also a gash about four inches long in the throat of the oldest, and a wound on the head of the other boy. The officers state that when they questioned the boys about their wounds they said the folks threw them down and tried to kill them.

The young woman, Peggy, and her four children belonged to Marshall, and her husband and the old man Simon and the old woman Mary to Gaines. Old Simon and Mary are the parents of young Simon.

The news breaks: headlines and opening paragraphs from the Cincinnati Gazette *of Tuesday, 29 January 1856* in a five-act play of 1820, a text published in the United States six years later and, if reports in the *New York Tribune* are accurate, performed on American stages as "one of the most touching and effective of recent tragedies."[35] Still, the most widely known retelling of the tragedy was Thomas Babington Macaulay's *Lays of Ancient Rome* (1842), reprinted in a best-selling American edition of 1853.[36]

Legend had it that Virginia was the maiden daughter of Roman patrician Virginius, whose rival Marcus Claudius seized the girl and claimed her as the daughter of a slave woman he owned, and claimed moreover that Virginius' wife, embarrassed at her childlessness, had taken Virginia from the slave woman and passed the infant as her own. At trial Virginius vouched for his daughter's genealogy. Opposing him, a large body of armed patricians also appeared, ready to enforce what everyone else saw as a rigged verdict, for Marcus Claudius brought suit merely as the agent (everyone knew) of another man frustrated in his lustful pursuit of the maiden child. When the court ruled for Marcus Claudius, Virginius, seeing his daughter would be debauched, plunged a butcher knife into Virginia's breast while exclaiming, "There is no way but this to keep thee free!"[37]

Thus the *Enquirer* took first crack at setting the terms for understanding Margaret's infanticide. Or, more accurately, they attempted a preemptive strike against abolitionists, who, they knew, would also mythologize it. Incredibly, in the same breath the *Enquirer* cautioned readers about the political uses of stories, the ways plots drawn from the culture's encyclopedia of well-known histories, legends, and myths never are value-neutral. This turned out to be a quite hypocritical warning, given the *Enquirer*'s own manipulations of the Garner "tragedy" in weeks to come.

Why Virginius instead of Medea? Remember: Coroner Menzies adjourned his inquest on Monday afternoon with Robert Garner's bloodied clothes pointing to him as chief suspect in Mary Garner's death. Then Monday night Margaret Garner confessed her guilt to officers at the county jail, but too late for reporters to work that detail into the next day's editions. Tuesday's *Enquirer* therefore predicts abolitionist "Black Republicans" will cast Robert as Virginius because they still think that *he* killed Mary Garner, who would therefore be (as Virginius insisted) *his* daughter. If it held, this version would effectively shove into the wings ugly questions about paternity and Southern miscegenation, questions that would always haunt the Garner tragedy but that proslavery polemicists wanted to mute.

On Monday afternoon Commissioner Pendery had slated the Garner fugitive slave hearing for the next morning. But on Tuesday he had to postpone because of the incomplete inquest, which resumed at nine in Coroner Menzies's downtown office, with onlookers spilling outside as the "excitement . . . [was] intense to unravel the bloody mystery, as to whether the father or the mother committed the fearful deed." Deputy U.S. Marshal Robertson, of Covington, picked up his testimony from Monday but added nothing new. At midmorning Menzies called Mary Kite and interrogated her (after a break for the midday meal) into the afternoon, then he called her husband, Elijah, and grilled him almost until it was time to break for supper. Both testified to seeing Margaret Garner wielding the butcher knife on her two sons, Tom and Sam; but they didn't witness little Mary's murder. Frustrated, the six-man coroner's jury proposed holding all four adults "as accessories to murder, but this was overruled by the Coroner." Doubtless aware of Margaret Garner's (unofficial) confession Monday night, Menzies decided to interview several Garners at the jail and adjourned the hearing until six in the evening.[38]

At the county jail Tuesday evening Mary Garner provided the formal testimony Menzies wanted. Moreover, although not formally called to testify, Margaret voluntarily confessed to killing her daughter, adding "that her determination was to have killed all the children and then destroy herself rather than return to slavery." She also complained to the coroner's jury and attending newspapermen "of cruel treatment on the part of their master," Archibald Gaines, and named him "as the cause of their attempt to escape."[39] To Menzies's jury, though, such explanations were beside the point. Their verdict: "We do find that the said child, Mary Garner, was killed by its mother, Margaret Garner, with a butcher's knife, with which she cut its throat." Two of the six jurors also released what amounted to a dissenting opinion—that Simon, Robert, and Mary Garner should be held as accessories to murder.

Before Coroner Menzies and his jury arrived at the jail on Tuesday evening, the Garners had another visitor. Shortly after noon, John Jolliffe had accompanied two sheriffs from Judge Burgoyne's court to serve an amended habeas corpus. That done, Jolliffe used the rest of the afternoon to interview his clients and begin plotting strategy. His questions focused on reports circulating among sheriffs and reporters that some of the Garners claimed to have been previously brought onto free soil by their masters. Robert, Mary, and Margaret confirmed those rumors, but Jolliffe needed dates, places, circumstances, and witnesses to call. He was betting a long shot. Here might be the stuff to at least delay, perhaps even win the Garners' fugitive slave hearing.

From his office above the *Cincinnati Gazette*, at 120 Main Street, John Jolliffe could hear the steam presses churning out the news he sometimes made, and he could look down Main to the icebound Ohio River. Beyond it: Covington, Kentucky, and the Slave Power (as he would say). Antislavery work had consumed half of Jolliffe's fifty-two years when the Garner case broke. He stood five feet eight inches and weighed a "stout" one hundred and eighty pounds. A lapsed son of devout Quakers, he dressed modestly, preferring a black frock coat and vest, simple cravat, and plain boots, but without the flat, broad-brimmed hat worn indoors or out by other Quaker abolitionists such as Levi Coffin. In surviving pictures Jolliffe is clean-shaven (in an age when beards and elaborate mustaches were taken as signs of manliness), and in his broad-featured face one notices most of all the eyes, large and penetrating.[40]

The *Gazette* building rarely closed, giving Jolliffe's clients ready access to his law office. This is how he wanted it. If clients didn't find him there they could walk three blocks west, to 248 Race Street, the rental house he and his wife, Synthelia, occupied for several years during the mid-1850s. John and Synthelia Jolliffe never had children but had, perhaps in their stead, widespread philanthropic commitments. In addition to her work as an officer in the Ladies Anti-Slavery Sewing Circle, she was active in a number of other organizations serving unwed mothers and orphans. John was a trustee of the Colored Orphans Home (a Quaker charity) and a sometime officer in a half dozen or more antislavery causes.[41]

In 1856 it was understood in Cincinnati's abolitionist and free black communities that "lawyer Jolliffe" was *always* available for legal aid in any matter touching antislavery. When Southern masters strode down steamboat ramps leading slaves (often young mulatto women, sometimes with their children) brought North for emancipation, dockmen and passersby sent them to Jolliffe. Jolliffe drew up the documents and guided the masters and their former slaves through the city's Probate Court.[42]

He took the money of slaveholders only in those cases. Otherwise he reviled them and ran a very modest legal practice on fees from the usual run of wills, minor lawsuits, divorces, and low-profile criminal cases. In the city's legal circles Jolliffe was a lesser light compared to other Cincinnati attorneys, such as future President Rutherford B. Hayes or Thomas Spooner, both active in forming the new Republican Party, or compared to another prominent Republican with the marvelous name of Flamen Ball.[43] But among antislavery activists Jolliffe was an outstanding figure. Throughout southern Ohio he did the great majority of antislavery lawyering, did it pro bono, and continued doing it despite constant threats and several physical assaults.[44] Yet Jolliffe himself was Southern-born, a proud native of Virginia, and seemingly a turncoat—until we look closely at his background.

Jolliffe descended from Quaker dissidents who fled England as civil war threatened. Merchants and millers, they settled on Virginia's Elizabeth River in 1650, then kept moving westward. Jolliffes were among the first settlers in Winchester, Virginia, and built Hopewell, its Quaker meetinghouse. Jolliffe's grandfather William kept slaves, bet on horses, and soldiered for General Washington, practices that put him at odds with the pacifist, antigambling, antislavery Friends of Hopewell.[45] John Jolliffe's father, another William and another backslider, inherited his father's "slave woman called Phillis" and acquired on his own several others before he was compelled to emancipate all of them as a condition of his 1799 marriage to Rebecca Neill, a devout Quaker. Pennsylvania Quakers began purging congregations of slaveholders during the 1760s, and after the Revolution they redoubled their efforts throughout the former middle colonies. By the time of William's marriage to Rebecca, Quakers in northern Virginia had virtually eliminated slave owners from their ranks.[46]

When John Jolliffe was a boy his father managed a large shipping business at Alexandria, sending boats out of Chesapeake Bay laden with flour, flaxseed, beeswax, and dried fruits, and welcoming them back from Liverpool laden with sugar, coffee, and tea. After war broke out in 1812, William Jolliffe lost a small fortune, sold his vessels, and returned his family to Winchester, where he bought Swarthmore, a gristmill and five-hundred-acre farm. His son John was educated at a private academy (Pierpont's), then at Henry Tucker's Winchester law school, an unorthodox choice and a sign that John would follow his ancestors' slide

away from the Friends. Quakers frowned on "pharisaical" lawyers, preferring to settle disputes in the dialogue of Friends' meetings, and John
Jolliffe had undoubtedly grown up hearing family and neighbors fondly
quoting Paul's scriptural injunctions against the law in 1 Corinthians 6
("Go not to law one with another"; "dare any of you go to law, against
the unjust?").

Jolliffe's law school teacher Henry Tucker was a Unionist who argued
that Northern dependence on Southern goods would bulwark the
United States against calls for the abolition of slavery. But Tucker also
regarded slavery as a blight and (like his more famous father, St. George
Tucker, who in 1795 argued for emancipation in his *Dissertation on
Slavery*) he favored the gradual emancipation of slaves by eliminating
the institution's keystone, *partus sequitur ventrem*, the legal doctrine according to which the child inherited the enslavement of its mother.[47]

John Jolliffe graduated in 1827 and moved to Ohio.[48] Through an
aunt, he secured a position with Batavia lawyer Thomas L. Hamer, a
man so well known for his courtroom eloquence it was later said that
future President Ulysses Grant (along with other boys) used "to sit in
the court-house windows and hear Mr. Jolliffe and Mr. Hamer make
speeches."[49] At first, though, Jolliffe struggled financially and worried his
relatives with thoughts of moving to the Deep South, perhaps New Orleans. Within two years Jolliffe had turned the corner. News from traveling Friends reached the Winchester Jolliffes that their son was "ranked
as high as any candidate for honors and promotion in the State [of
Ohio]," and that he could "go to the Legislature if [he chose] and
perhaps might go to Congress." His father's advice during this early
period: "Keep thy hands out of thy pockets; do not read novels, they
will disorder thy mind. Keep thy coat brushed clean. Often read the
scriptures."[50]

Jolliffe must have kept on reading novels, because thirty years later
he would be an author of two. His first, *Belle Scott; or, Liberty Overthrown! A Tale for the Crisis* (1856), was nearing completion as the
Garner case broke in late January 1856. *Chattanooga* (1858) pivots
around a slave mother's infanticide and was obviously inspired by his
feelings for Margaret Garner. Wholly forgotten in our time, these novels'
courtroom scenes and arguments, their representations of antebellum
strife over slavery, say much about Jolliffe's views on antebellum politics
and culture.[51]

In 1833 Hamer and Jolliffe parted ways: Hamer to a U.S. congressional seat, Jolliffe to the first of several terms as Clermont County, Ohio, prosecuting attorney. He also became increasingly active in Ohio abolitionism. By 1840 he was chair of the county's American Anti-Slavery Society committee, organizing and fund-raising in the district alongside Gamaliel Bailey, then the society's chair at Cincinnati.[52] He had also married Synthelia McClure, a woman whose Scotch parents were among Batavia's original settlers. Also he was in political difficulties. For years a Democrat, "a flaming Jackson man" in a district dominated by Whigs, Jolliffe ran successfully for county prosecutor until his antislavery work caught up with him and angered Clermont County's Cotton Whigs, who put a higher premium on doing business with slaveholding Kentuckians. They ousted him from office in the fall of 1840.[53] Within months Jolliffe closed his Batavia law practice and moved twenty miles west to Cincinnati.

The Jolliffes moved into the first of several houses they rented on Race Street and found John an office several blocks away, on Third. He advertised a law practice "For Hamilton, Clermont, and Brown Counties," an area stretching from Cincinnati to Ripley along the Ohio River.[54] Jolliffe quickly took up the steady stream of wills, minor suits, and criminal cases, plus the occasional emancipation; all of it supporting his pro bono work for fugitives and his unending work for reform causes: temperance (a favorite of Synthelia), poor relief, and antislavery. When Joe Kite's Boone County master William Harper decided to let his slaves purchase their freedom, in 1846, Jolliffe had the documents recorded in Probate Court. In subsequent years he defended the Kites against Harper's lawsuits growing out of an (illegal) contract drawn up for the purchase of Elijah.

After a decade John Jolliffe had become one of Cincinnati's most prominent abolitionists. An elected officer in the American Anti-Slavery Society convention held at Cincinnati in April 1851, he drafted a resolution calling up volunteers against the 1850 Fugitive Slave Law: "it is time to do and suffer, and if need be, die," Jolliffe urged. Then, using a rhetoric of martyrdom and sacrifice that would become powerful and even literal in both the Garner case and his own later writings, he threw down the gauntlet: "It is the time for every one who claims to be a friend of the slave to lay his *all* upon the altar." He foresaw war: the abolitionist needed immediately "to harness himself anew for the con-

John Jolliffe, ca. 1850
FROM *HISTORICAL, GENEALOGICAL, AND BIOGRAPHICAL ACCOUNT*
OF THE JOLLIFFE FAMILY OF VIRGINIA, 1652–1893 (1893)

flict; to throw himself into the thickest of the fight . . . to do still more and more, neither giving nor taking quarter, till slavery shall be—not circumscribed in its limits—not defeated in its demands with regard to the Fugitive Slave Law—not divorced from the General Government—*but actually and wholly abolished from the land.*"[55]

Jolliffe served as an officer at the next two Anti-Slavery Society conventions, in 1852 and 1853. In the summer of 1852 he also ran for Congress, not as a Democrat—having left them in disgust some years earlier—but as a candidate for the newly formed Free Democracy Party, one of many spun off from the rapidly disintegrating two-party system. Free Democrats tried (unsuccessfully) to enlist Salmon Portland Chase, then ran a slate of abolitionist candidates led by Jolliffe and James Birney. In his southern Ohio congressional district Jolliffe polled just 82 out of 6,383 votes, a mere six in his own ward.[56]

Even so, Jolliffe's running on a straight abolitionist ticket defies another generalization of historians. They usually define a split between Garrisonian or "moral" abolitionists on the one hand and on the other hand those "political" antislavery activists like Salmon Chase. They see moral suasionists as entirely rejecting party politics, elections, indeed any conventional political action as inherently tainted and therefore futile, while political activists like Chase supposedly made hay and eventually claimed victory in Lincoln's 1860 election.[57] Yet the career of John Jolliffe is evidence not that such generalizations are wrong but that actual people tend to defy categories. Jolliffe was a lawyer and politician who throughout his career employed the rhetoric of moral suasionists like William Lloyd Garrison—a rhetoric of uncompromising principles, zealotry, even martyrdom. Still Jolliffe was a pragmatist, an impassioned speaker who didn't flinch from taking his politics onto the hustings where he could face the unpersuaded, win a few votes, perhaps even sign up a convert. His courtroom practices reflect the same melding of higher law appeals and practical action.

Jolliffe's kind of notoriety reaped a varied harvest. A Delaware paper once published an erroneous obituary eulogizing "John Jolliffe, Esq., of Cincinnati" as "an able and devoted advocate of the cause of the slave." Encountering Jolliffe on the street, an amazed *Gazette* reporter handed over the story and thereby gave the abolitionist a unique "chance of reading his obituary in advance."[58]

But things were not always so laughable. On the morning of Friday, 2 September 1853, Jolliffe and his wife took their young niece shopping for produce in the open-air market along Cincinnati's Fifth Street when, crossing the avenue while holding the little girl's hand, Jolliffe was struck a blow from behind "that felled him at once." Jolliffe came to with the "impression that he was knocked down by an express or meat wagon," but further stunned to see a man kicking and calling him a "damned abolitionist." It was Judge Jacob Flinn of the Cincinnati Criminal Court, another bit player in the drama ahead.

Flinn was elsewhere remembered as a "great double-fisted giant" of a man, a hard-drinking Irishman and diehard Democrat.[59] His size explains why no one stepped into the fray, leaving Synthelia Jolliffe and her niece to scream for help until a friend of Flinn's, U.S. Marshal William Ruffin, coaxed the judge away. By nine o'clock that morning Ruffin had Flinn arraigned on a charge of assault and battery before another magistrate of Flinn's own Criminal Court. Flinn volunteered a guilty plea, the magistrate accepted it, required Flinn to post a $500 bond, and set sentencing for the next day, Saturday.[60]

By then all Cincinnati was in an uproar and split into familiar factions: proslavery Democrats versus abolitionists drawn from upstart parties like the Free-Soilers, Know-Nothings, and Free Democrats. Moreover, everyone in Cincinnati recognized why Flinn—"a Judge!" exclaimed the Gazette—had assaulted "lawyer Jolliffe." During the previous week low waters brought on by drought had forced a New Orleans–bound steamboat, the Tropic, to dock at Cincinnati rather than Covington, where slaveholders always demanded stopovers in order to avoid abolitionists. That day (Friday, 26 August) the Tropic carried three slaves: Edward, a "young mulatto man," Hannah, a young woman, and Susan, a four-year-old black child who was no relation to Edward or Hannah. Just days earlier, the child had been sold away from her mother by a Virginia master, John Ambrose; now all three were traveling to a new Mississippi master in custody of the steamboat captain, a man named Lipsey. While the Tropic was docked, a free black stevedore named William Troy learned of the slaves' plight and contacted Jolliffe, who had Lipsey served with a writ of habeas corpus. Jolliffe's strategy: get the case before a sympathetic judge, show how the slaves' master or agent had brought them onto free soil, and have the slaves assert their desire for freedom. The court would be compelled to emancipate them.[61]

Edward, Hannah, and Susan were legally defined as slaves in transit, not fugitives. This meant any hearing on William Troy's habeas corpus needn't follow procedures set up in the 1850 Fugitive Slave Law and any state magistrate (such as a District Court judge) could rule on the case—presumably in accord with state laws forbidding the keeping of slaves anywhere on Ohio soil. Nonetheless, despite his having no jurisdiction in what was technically an Ohio matter, U.S. Marshal Ruffin intervened and demanded a hearing on the Tropic slaves before Judge Flinn of the city's Criminal Court. Whether Flinn had any legal jurisdiction was doubtful, but Ruffin chose the Irishman for his reputation as a proslavery Democrat, and Flinn gave them a swift trial. Bailiffs led a very frightened and manacled Hannah into a courtroom packed with white "rowdies" who barred William Troy and any other blacks from entering. Responding as expected to the scene's coercive force, the terrified Hannah "expressed a wish to be allowed to return to her master on the boat"; Flinn immediately remanded her to Lipsey's custody. When Flinn asked Hannah if she had "charge of the child Susan," the woman responded that, yes, she did, "whereupon the judge also ordered [Susan] back into the custody of the claimants without examination." Jolliffe repeatedly rose in protest and Flinn as often gaveled him down. Next up was Edward, manacled like Hannah. Flinn quickly heard testimony from Lipsey about his capacity as agent for the Mississippi owner and about his reasons for docking on the Ohio side. Once again Jolliffe repeatedly protested and Flinn just as often gaveled him silent.

During a lengthy, impassioned summation Jolliffe suddenly doubled over, staggered to his seat, and asked for a continuance due to illness. Flinn thought Jolliffe was faking and issued a summary judgment for Lipsey, who just as summarily led the slaves back to the *Tropic*, cheered the whole way by a proslavery crowd.

The next day's *Gazette* ran charges from antislavery forces that Flinn had not only misconstrued the law, he had also been inebriated. On Thursday, 1 September 1853, the day before Flinn's assault on Jolliffe, a mass meeting convened at the city's Masonic Hall, "where a large number of citizens" (including Jolliffe) called for Jacob Flinn's impeachment. Next morning when Flinn assaulted Jolliffe he was apparently drunk and most certainly acting from an outraged honor. The "Flinn-Jolliffe Affair" (as newsmen called it) thus boiled down to another local skirmish over Southern slavery. At his trial on the assault charge—a process punctuated by several fistfights—a sobbing Flinn had pled guilty but protested that he was "driven to desperation" by attacks on his character. The unsympathetic judge fined him seventy dollars and court costs.[62]

The "Flinn-Jolliffe Affair" illustrates again Cincinnati's sharply divided and highly volatile political culture, whenever slavery was at stake in the courts. When seats on the bench came open, loyal party men always stood first in line, and the Franklin Pierce administration continued the dominance of Democrats Fillmore, Taylor, and Polk by packing the federal bench. In Ohio, federal judges reflected Democratic commitments to strict enforcement of the Fugitive Slave Law. Locally, too, Cincinnati's Democratic mayors had for years succeeded in getting their people on the Criminal Court bench. By contrast, other courts (such as Probate and Police) tended to reflect Free-Soil priorities. Ethnicity fur-

ther divided Queen City institutions. A member of Cincinnati's powerful immigrant Irish population, Judge Jacob Flinn stood with other
party allies such as Mayor James J. Farran, a former editor at Robinson's
Cincinnati Enquirer. This powerful Democratic bloc regarded the city's
blacks, radical German immigrants, and abolitionists as a patchwork
liberal opposition threatening the Queen City's commercial links to the
slaveholding South. Such ethnic divisions were starkly visible in the list
of those arrested for fighting during Flinn's trial: a Thomas Carnahan
or Michael Murray on the one side and on the other a Josef Schweitzer
or Jacob Zimmermann.[63] Such battles made Flinn, Farran, and proslavery Democrats deeply fearful of the "Black" (antislavery) Republicans.
They even began amassing an arsenal.

During the months before Margaret's infanticide city newspapers
broke open a scandal that centered on Farran, charged with securing
from Ohio's Democratic governor William Medill a number of crates
of Sharps rifles for distribution to the city's Sarsefield Guards and Shield
Guards, two Irish-American militias. Republicans charged that Medill
supplied the guns to a Cincinnati barracks of a legitimate, state-
authorized group, the Ohio Militia, knowing full well the crates would
be diverted to the unauthorized Irish groups. Republicans also charged
that Medill and Farran wanted guns available in case of public disturbances during the October 1855 gubernatorial elections; also, and more
significantly, in case the city experienced any future disturbances while
enforcing the Fugitive Slave Law. Farran denied the charges. Medill
lost the gubernatorial race to the Republican Salmon Chase; some said
he lost it primarily *because* of problems like the "Irish Filibuster Case."[64]

When the Garners escaped to Cincinnati several months later, a
newly inaugurated Governor Chase had launched an investigation into
Mayor Farran's alleged diversion of weapons, but the Sarsefield Guards
and Shield Guards still had their rifles. During the Garner case, with
Farran's tacit approval, Irish militia members broke out their guns and
paraded up and down city streets. Hired temporarily as deputy marshals,
they would escort the Garners back and forth from the jail to the U.S.
Courthouse.

Following passage of the Fugitive Slave Law in 1850 John Jolliffe
argued practically every fugitive case tried before federal judges and
commissioners in southern Ohio. These cases made him see, with fellow
abolitionists of long standing, that moral resistance to the fugitive law

had to be transformed into an active political force against slavery. Jol-liffe agreed with abolitionist Wendell Phillips's remarks to a Boston au-dience early in 1852 that despite the movement's precious few courtroom victories the cases had galvanized fourteen months of con-tinual "agitation" against the fugitive law and thus produced beneficial results. The new battleground was "Public Opinion," the title of Phil-lips's speech. "What gunpowder did for war," he proclaimed, "the printing-press has done for the mind" and nothing had turned the tide of battle more than newspapers: "The penny papers," he proclaimed, "do more to govern the country than the White House at Washington." To Phillips and other movement leaders, outraged public opinion had at last begun to crest. For twenty-five years abolitionists had been arguing that the first step had to be a widespread "feeling" or sentiment against slavery, followed by the second step, "thought" in the form of a moral discourse about its evils, so that at last (in Phillips's wording) "the world acts out the thought."[65] By the early 1850s many abolitionists agreed with Phillips that the movement had reached the threshold of the third and final step. Penny papers like Horace Greeley's *New York Tribune*, Gamaliel Bailey's *National Era* in Washington, and the *Cincinnati Ga-zette* had brought them there. The South kept throwing up "great scoun-drels for texts," whose stories were quite obviously moving the battle into city streets.[66]

In fact, while many historians claim that Northern resistance to the Fugitive Slave Law tailed off into the mid-1850s, Cincinnati defied that generalization. There, on the front lines against slavery, action often came in wave after wave, each vigorously reported. In September 1853, only one week after the "Flinn-Jolliffe Affair" and the *Tropic* case that triggered it, two white men swore out a warrant against a young black named John Watkins for "having committed an outrage upon the person of a young woman." When brought before the bar, however, it turned out the whites not only couldn't produce the outraged young woman, their whole charge diminished to mere hearsay. Recognizing a ruse slave catchers commonly tried in their efforts to have authorities detain "sus-picious" blacks, Judge Thomas Spooner threw out the warrant. But while exiting the courthouse Watkins was arrested yet again, this time by a Constable Hardin for allegedly stealing a watch. Aided by the two Kentuckians, Hardin forced Watkins into a carriage; then, "seeing that his direction was towards the [Ohio] River, and suspecting he was being kidnaped, [Watkins] tried to run." In plain sight of outraged bystanders Hardin pistol-whipped young Watkins into submission. A crowd gathered, shouts rising on either side as some hollered for help in stopping the fugitive and others incited the crowd to "Stone the kidnapers!" Sheriffs arrived and escorted Hardin, the Kentuckians, and a bleeding Watkins back toward the courthouse, the whole way meeting a hail of stones "by which several [officers] were injured." Midway up Broadway three U.S. marshals arrived on the scene to (again) force Watkins back toward the dock where his farmer master was said to be waiting. "Pistols were drawn, and fired into the air," as sheriffs and marshals found themselves once again at a standoff. During this ruckus Watkins made good his escape. Next day, the *Gazette* exulted while the *Enquirer* blamed Watkins's disappearance on an "infamous riot" damaging to the city's commerce with the South.[67]

During the 1850s, John Jolliffe represented slaves in seventeen different fugitive cases, all of them highly publicized. In two, the slaves relented under fear or pressure and voluntarily returned to their masters. In three other cases the slaves were illegally returned to Kentucky without due process. In one case, a slave escaped during trial (more on that, directly). In eleven cases decided before the bar Jolliffe succeeded *only once*, an open-and-shut case on behalf of a mulatto slave woman abandoned in the city by her drunken master. By any measure Jolliffe's was therefore an extremely frustrating dedication. Those eleven unsuccessful cases involved twenty-six adults and seven children, all remanded back to Southern slavery.[68]

Knowing he was so likely to fail, why did Jolliffe keep arguing these cases? Certainly he believed that no matter what happened, fugitives deserved the best legal representation. By all accounts John Jolliffe was the best in Ohio. He also knew that these battles had an immense effect on public opinion.

Strategies

By 1852 Jolliffe had developed an intriguing brief against the Fugitive Slave Law. His argument was simple, unique in the annals of abolitionism, and one that he kept refining and redeploying right up until the war. In court, Jolliffe's argument used to run two or three hours. He adapted it for his novel *Belle Scott*, where it runs twenty-eight pages of text and even at that length is "given as extracts only, from the speech."[69] His essential point: that slavery is a sin. Jolliffe claimed that for believing Christians slavery violated a rock-bottom precept summed up in the maxim from Matthew 19:18, "Thou shalt love thy neighbor as thyself"; or Matthew 25:40, "inasmuch as ye have done unto one of the least of these my brethren, ye have done it unto me." Jolliffe believed in the equality of whites and blacks (warranted, he thought, in Matthew 19). Whatever conditions had made African-Americans the "least of [God's] brethren" (in the sense of Matthew 25) were irrelevant, for slavery meant "stealing" the products of people's labor and, equally evil, hunting them down in support of thieves.

Article IV, section 2 of the Constitution affirmed the right of a master to reclaim a fugitive "from service or labor," and compelled citizens to assist in hunting down fugitives. But Jolliffe argued on First Amendment grounds that Christians did not have to obey the constitutional injunction. If Christians were required to help return slaves, then that requirement interfered with their right of religious liberty—a right (he said) "to avoid sin." The Fugitive Slave Laws of 1793 and 1850 also interfered with that right, according to Jolliffe, and were therefore unconstitutional. To him, the problem was not that section 2 was contradicted by the First Amendment; they might coexist as long as slavery continued. But the First Amendment severely limited what government could *do* about fugitives. A slaveholder might himself go after a runaway slave, but the government could never require citizens (even federal marshals) to help that slaveholder.[70]

"If this theory is true," Jolliffe claimed, then "Congress has no right, and never can have, until the First Amendment of the Constitution shall be repealed, to pass any law, by which any man shall be required to aid in the surrender of a fugitive slave." *Belle Scott's* hero, a lawyer named Ives (clearly Jolliffe), takes that theory into court, whence its antislavery influence spreads through neighboring communities but without final success. Jolliffe well knew the monumental job of ultimately overthrowing the Slave Power. He imagined that the political and legal victory would finally have to develop out of a greater cultural and moral struggle waged on the porches and in the parlors of ordinary Americans. These at least are the settings for that struggle in *Belle Scott*, where Northerners see the reforming power of novels with their "effect on the morals of the young" and Southerners complain that "all this fuss [over abolitionism] would be put an end to" if everybody would just quit reading the novels and newspapers that spread it like a contagion.[71] For Jolliffe as for Wendell Phillips the crucial work was in changing "public opinion." An activist lawyer writing a novel centered on a fugitive hearing, Jolliffe understood how the drama of Margaret's fugitive trial might, like a novel, powerfully influence the war against slavery.

For almost three years after Millard Fillmore signed the Fugitive Slave Law in September 1850 no fugitive cases were tried in Ohio's Southern District, not because slaves weren't escaping North but because circumstances had simply prevented a test of the law. The vehemence of local proslavery forces crowding the streets and courtrooms probably scared several fugitives into voluntarily returning to the South (as happened with Hannah in the *Tropic* case). In several other cases those same crowds simply spirited alleged fugitives back over the river, evidently thinking the new law authorized them to do so.

In 1853, newly inaugurated President Franklin Pierce made enforcing the fugitive law a priority and instructed his Attorney General, Caleb Cushing, to vigorously prosecute all cases under it. Indeed the new administration's goals went further. Thus Cushing in a September 1853 warning to Boston abolitionists: "If there be any purpose more fixed than another in the mind of the President and those with whom he is accustomed to consult, it is that the dangerous element of Abolitionism, under whatever guise or form it may present itself, shall be crushed out, so far as his administration is concerned."[72] With that kind of support, Ohio's federal commissioners swiftly caught up with other jurisdictions like southeastern Pennsylvania, whose Commissioners had decided dozens of fugitive cases during the years just after passage of the new law.

At all events it was August 1853 before John Jolliffe got a case he could take to trial. His defendant was George Washington ("Wash") McQuerry, a twenty-eight-year-old intelligent and "rather good-looking, bright [i.e., light-complected] mulatto man."[73] Wash's claimant, Henry Miller of Washington County, in central Kentucky, filed affidavits alleging that McQuerry and four other slaves escaped from his plantation one night in 1849 by stealing horses and racing the fifty miles north into Ohio. McQuerry was living near Dayton when slave catchers captured him and brought the frightened young man down to Cincinnati's Galt House hotel, apparently intending to circumvent a fugitive hearing.

A hotel porter told well-known black schoolteacher Peter Clark of the young man's plight, Clark awakened Jolliffe at two in the morning and together they took steps to force a formal hearing before Supreme Court Justice John McLean, then at his summer residence in Cincinnati. The trial unfolded with startling speed. Jolliffe argued the constitutional issue but was gaveled silent; co-counsel James Birney asked for a continuance but was denied. Twelve hours after Wash was taken into federal custody, McLean ruled that "the sacred duties of [his] office" commanded one judgment: fifteen minutes later deputy marshals transported Wash by ferry to Covington.[74] No doubt McLean's talk of "sacred duties" set Jolliffe's blood boiling.

Still he kept arguing these cases. In June 1854 there was the family of nine slaves who paddled a stolen skiff over the Ohio River, took refuge on a farm, and were sold out by a neighbor pretending to be a "friend of the slave." Opposing Jolliffe that time was a Cincinnati attorney with the remarkably appropriate name of Ketchum, who called the owners to testify, made a brief summation, and after a morning's work had the slaves back with their Boone County masters that same afternoon. Among the three masters was one John Gaines, cousin to Archibald K. Gaines.

Despite his many courtroom losses, when Robert, Mary, and Margaret Garner told Jolliffe their masters had previously brought them into Ohio, Jolliffe had some grounds for hope. Simon Garner might be a lost cause, but if Pendery could be persuaded by evidence of prior Ohio visits, then all the others might go free, including Margaret's three children—on the principle of *partus sequitur ventrem*, for all were born after her Cincinnati sojourn of June 1840.

But this strategy faced huge practical and legal obstacles. In the first place Jolliffe had to find a way of getting testimony about the Garners' Ohio sojourns before Pendery. He couldn't call the Garners themselves, because Fugitive Slave Law provisions denied defendants any right to speak in their own defense. Jolliffe had to find the witnesses whom the Garners said would corroborate their claims of having been in Ohio. For that he needed time, but cases like McQuerry had demonstrated the swiftness—really, the impatience—of Justice McLean and his Commissioners in bringing fugitive hearings to a conclusion. Pendery would deny any request for a continuance. Finally, Jolliffe had to confront a roadblock built into laws treating slaves in transit, laws stipulating that while still on free soil the slave had to *assert* his or her will to be free. But the Garners had come to Ohio and *voluntarily returned* to Kentucky, in tacit agreement to their status as slaves.

Jolliffe knew the unlikelihood of winning the Garners' liberty from Commissioner Pendery, given these difficulties. Nevertheless, he pressed on. Already by Tuesday evening he had his legal assistant, James Gitchell, and other antislavery friends out hunting up those witnesses that the Garners had named. Yet Jolliffe probably realized from experience that they hadn't enough time. Past cases led him to expect a trial lasting two days at most.

Certainly Jolliffe hoped to prolong that trial as much as possible, and this effort might be aided by features wholly unique to the Garner case. Margaret's child-murder had made her and the other three adults indictable under Ohio statutes, and murder was arguably preeminent compared to issues of property handled under the federal fugitive law. In fact, nothing like this had ever been tried, and here then was one potential for blocking claimants Marshall and Gaines, if only for a time. Moreover, the value of this states' rights clash in shaping public opinion—as a drama revealing slavery's evils and as a podium for antislavery polemics—was simply unparalleled. Jolliffe couldn't neglect that greater cause even as he gave the Garner case his utmost attention, and for both efforts he needed to buy time. Then, too, prolonging the trial might have another, unforeseeable benefit: it increased the possibilities for a rescue.

That was not at all a far-fetched hope. In October 1853, Jolliffe and Rutherford B. Hayes defended a young Kentucky fugitive named Louis who had escaped over the river and made his way to Columbus. After arresting him there U.S. marshals returned with Louis to Cincinnati for a hearing before Commissioner Samuel Carpenter. Jolliffe's opposing attorneys produced affidavits from Louis's claimant, Alexander Marshall of Fleming County, and brought in two of Marshall's neighbors who affirmed both Marshall's long ownership and the facts of his slave's escape. Aside from the (by now) usual arguments against the law's constitutionality, Hayes and Jolliffe's only defense was that Louis had previously brought a drove of horses into Ohio for his master. A surprisingly sympathetic Carpenter indulged this argument, granted an adjournment while Jolliffe hunted up witnesses supporting Louis's claims of having been in Ohio, and sat patiently while Jolliffe and Hayes offered closing statements lasting three hours *each*.

Carpenter recessed the hearing to deliberate and next day when he brought the courtroom back to order it was packed wall to wall with angry blacks and whites on either side of the issue. Obviously frightened by the excited crowd, Carpenter began reading his verdict in a low, almost incomprehensible tone that told everyone the result: However reluctantly, he would rule against Louis. Spectators in the gallery "expected every moment to hear the negro consigned to slavery," as did the antislavery forces gathered around Louis and his attorneys at the defendant's table. Then came a surprise. But here let the Quaker abolitionist Levi Coffin tell it:

> Louis was very crowded, and to gain more room, slipped his chair back a little way. Neither his master nor the marshal noticed the movement, as they were intently listening to the judge, and he slipped his chair again, until he was back of them. I was standing close behind him and saw every movement. Next he rose quietly to his feet and took a step backward. Some abolitionist, friendly to his cause, gave him an encouraging touch on the foot, and he stepped farther back. Then a good hat was placed on his head by someone behind, and he quietly and cautiously made his way around the south end of the room, into the crowd of colored people on the west side, and, through it, toward the door. I and several other abolitionists had our eyes on him, and our hearts throbbed with suppressed excitement and anxiety lest he should be discovered. The door and passage were crowded with Germans, through whom Louis made his way, and passing downstairs gained the street.

Carpenter ordered U.S. Marshal Hiram Robinson to hunt up Louis "at any cost," and a "vigorous search" commenced, eventually extending to the city's northernmost outskirts and lasting most of a week. The whole time Louis was "lodged in the house of one of his colored friends, on Broadway near Sixth Street," a few doors down from Coffin's store. After another week Coffin and two unnamed fellow abolitionists first brought Louis to Coffin's, then sneaked him out of town to the next station on

Cincinnati attorney and Probate Court Judge John Burgoyne, ca. 1855
COURTESY THE CINCINNATI HISTORICAL SOCIETY

the Underground Railroad for Canada. Later it was rumored that Jolliffe had instigated Louis's dramatic escape by a whispered suggestion in his ear. Jolliffe never denied the charge.[75]

Beyond his legal training and his experience arguing fugitive cases, John Jolliffe had the temperament for a fugitive case certain to revolve around a rebellious slave mother's infanticide. In his novels the white women characters are strong, politically astute citizens who complain of being denied the vote. Some, especially his self-reliant widows, smoke; all hate slavery. An especially intriguing feature of *Belle Scott* is the way its men and women characters differently respond to slavery. The men witness slavery's horrors, such as whippings, and visions of slaves' blood infect their dreams like "a contagion" that spreads, only slowly, to their consciousness, but even then their thinking about slavery forms a too lengthy prologue to belated action against the "peculiar institution." In contrast Jolliffe's women see slavery's horrors and immediately speak in clear and forthright language against it. They slice through abstractions and lose patience with men's reluctance to act. They take ineffectual men to task, stating simply that any man who supports the fugitive law "does not support the Constitution of this country."[76] The "widow Johnston" who makes that claim could well have been John Jolliffe before a U.S. Commissioner.

Jolliffe's heroines in *Belle Scott* and *Chattanooga* are both women of mixed heritage who battle laws linking lifelong bondage to the vagaries of race. Echoing Patrick Henry, both proclaim their determination to have "Liberty or Death," and each tragically dies. Others of his slave women confess a willingness for their children to die rather than continue in slavery. "I knew she had gone where no tyranny could crush— no cruelty oppress her," one slave mother says over her dead daughter's grave in *Belle Scott*.[77] We don't know exactly when Jolliffe added these lines to the manuscript draft of his first novel, but the strong likelihood is that he had already written them by 28 January 1856. Still, when news of Margaret Garner's infanticide first broke, it must have seemed as if John Jolliffe were providentially placed to argue her case.

Wednesday, 30 January 1856. The morning dawned clear and bright yet bitter cold, with a morning low at zero Fahrenheit. The Garners awakened in their cells and looked about: "There was no window and the door was made of thick iron bars; these crossed each other, and left small openings of about an inch and a half square."[78] The hearing before Commissioner Pendery was scheduled for nine.

Others were making their way uptown. From Covington, where they probably spent the night at the Magnolia House, Archibald Gaines and James Marshall crossed the icebound Ohio River with their Kentucky lawyers, John W. Finnell and Samuel T. Wall. Finnell was a Cotton Whig of long standing, once a close political associate of John Pollard Gaines, an ardent proslavery advocate, a former editor of the *Covington Journal* and, more recently, Kentucky's Secretary of State. Wall was his Covington law partner. Representing Marshall and Gaines from Cincinnati was Colonel Francis T. Chambers, formerly of Mason County, Kentucky, and an old friend of John Pollard Gaines who in 1847 had formally nominated his fellow Whig for the Tenth District congressional seat.[79] Now a successful Cincinnati lawyer and newly pledged member of the Democratic Party, Chambers had represented clients in many high-profile lawsuits and in several fugitive cases.

Before formally opening the hearing Pendery gathered John Jolliffe and his assistant, James Gitchell, for a pretrial conference with Chambers, Finnell, and Wall. The Commissioner laid down some ground rules and announced a key decision: he would sever the case of Simon, Mary and Robert Garner, claimed by Marshall, from that of Gaines for Margaret and her children; moreover, he had decided to try the two cases in that order—first Marshall, then Gaines. Pendery probably set this order because he remained uncertain what effect (if any) the murder warrant for Margaret Garner would have on the fugitive hearing. He thought the federal case had priority, but they had no precedent for a case like Margaret Garner's, with its compelling states' rights issues. As for Jolliffe, he would have preferred not to sever the two claims, but acceded to Pendery's decision because it gave him several advantages. He already knew from interviewing him that Robert's claims of being previously taken into Ohio by his masters were the strongest, and Jolliffe would want to lead with arguments for Robert. If he could win there, Margaret and the children might have a chance. Tackling Marshall's claim first would also give James Gitchell more time to hunt witnesses and research the states' rights issues that Margaret's case would raise.

By eight-thirty Wednesday morning the Garners were escorted out of the county jail for a brief ride to the U.S. Courthouse, "conducted in an omnibus, attended by a strong posse of officers," many of them members of the Sarsefield and Shield Guards, specially deputized for the occasion, and each of them shouldering one of those disputed Sharps rifles. Reporters noted that the Queen City seemed to have prepared for a war.

The Garner trial was ready to begin.

3

DEFENDANT

❦

Around nine Wednesday morning Deputy U.S. Marshal John Ellis led the Garners down the back steps of the Hamilton County jail and through a double gauntlet of newly sworn, rifle-toting deputies. Most had been recruited Tuesday evening from Cincinnati's Irish militias and from Covington's taverns. Overnight another snow flurry had bleached Cincinnati white and the day was "cold and cloudy." Residents and shopkeepers were out sprinkling coal ashes over walkways and streets left once again "in a most dangerous state."[1]

A *Gazette* reporter observing the Garners emerge from jail thought the fugitives were "comfortably clothed for the season," wearing coats and hats donated by the Life Guards and other abolitionist societies. Margaret carried Cilla to a waiting omnibus. Robert lifted Tom and Sam inside, took his mother's arm as she climbed up, then followed his father into the carriage. Ellis climbed up next to the 'bus driver. Then the marshal's "strong posse" surrounded the carriage, and as it emerged onto Hammond Street the men put on resolute faces for the hundreds of agitated spectators.[2]

The old Federal Courthouse, Cincinnati, from Kenny's Illustrated Cincinnati *(1875),*
after it had been converted for use as a post office

At the courthouse a larger and angrier crowd confronted the procession. The Garner fugitive slave trial was slated to begin at nine and inside the courthouse Commissioner Pendery's hearing room was already "jammed with eager spectators." All were (apparently) white, as deputies had obeyed orders to turn away from the courtroom door anyone who looked "colored." Now those excluded blacks, perhaps three hundred strong, their numbers swelled by several hundred more antislavery activists, spilled down the courthouse steps and into Fourth Street. Piercing through this shivering, outraged "mob" (said the *Enquirer*), deputies met volleys of snowballs and shouted curses. After marching into an alley the marshal's men halted to re-form their double-walled gauntlet; Ellis led the Garners through it and into the courthouse. With slight variations, everyone repeated this ritual every day of the trial.

Margaret and Robert Garner had fled North, *as a family*, because they were determined to stay together and to never again be treated as human chattels, as objects. Yet they had become objects in ways that must have seemed totally strange and outrageous—prizes in a great political and legal struggle, "topics" for gregarious news reporters to "write up," objects of pity and scorn to total strangers, and targets for idle spectators' curious gazes. For hours each day they would sit silent, as decreed by federal law, while attorneys pointed them out and talked about them in elaborately phrased sentences. These whites took center stage. But the Garners would shadow their every action.

Shortly after nine, a black-robed John Pendery entered his courtroom to call the Garner case. On his right sat claimants Archibald Gaines and James Marshall, sufficiently recovered from his bout with gallstones to make the journey; next to the Boone County masters sat their attorneys Wall, Finnell, and Chambers. It was Pendery's first glimpse of Marshall, a bewhiskered and broad-shouldered planter "of medium height." Gaunt-looking Squire Gaines he recalled from early Monday morning, when the Kentuckian had the Commissioner called into court to swear out the fugitive slave warrant. On Pendery's left sat the seven Garners with Jolliffe and Gitchell. Behind them rose a double wall of U.S. marshals; behind them, a wooden settee and a railing; behind that, the spectators.

Front and center among the crowd huddled a contingent of newspaper reporters, including Edmond Babb and Thomas Shinkwin of the *Gazette*, George Guilford of the *Commercial*, and James Hendrie of the *Enquirer*. Each had an eye or ear for different details—the *Gazette*'s Shinkwin, for example, was particularly attentive to dialects—and each was biased by his own anti- or proslavery views. Taken together, their reports comprise an invaluable record for a case whose official transcripts appear to have long ago disappeared during a history of Cincinnati courthouse fires, moves, and reorganizations.

After Pendery brought the room to order and announced his decision to split the trial in two, Jolliffe immediately rose and moved for a continuance—exactly as the claimants' attorneys knew he would. Fugitive slave hearings were designed to be the jurisprudential soul of brevity. The 1850 law restricted testimony to witnesses who could identify the fugitives and warrant the master's claim on their labor and service, and to defense witnesses who could impeach either the identification or the claim of bondage. It denied fugitives the right to testify in their own defense and empowered the Commissioner to render a summary judgment; then, if he ruled against the fugitives, to remand them immediately to their master or his agent. Typically the whole process unfolded during one day and scarcely ever consumed more than two or three. Until the Garner case.

Until the Garners there had never been a case involving a capital crime committed while fugitives were on free soil, and now Margaret's infanticide posed profound constitutional questions.[3] Could federal law force Ohio to give up alleged felons because Kentucky law said they were also property? Even when Ohio law expressly prohibited property in human beings? More generally, did constitutional protections of property take precedence over human rights? On such issues the 1850 Fugitive Slave Law said nothing; it had been expressly written to speed a claimant *around* them.

But John Jolliffe needed time to prepare such a complex and crucial case—hence his motion for continuance, the first move in a strategy well calculated to stall Pendery's decision. He asked Commissioner Pendery for time to gather evidence that some of his clients had "often been permitted to visit this city." Colonel Chambers objected that Jolliffe hadn't used "due diligence" to "obtain his evidence in the two days already passed," and Jolliffe countered that, the coroner's inquest having run most of Tuesday, he hadn't even been given time to interview his clients "till yesterday afternoon," when he first learned of their Ohio sojourns. Also, Jolliffe said, he'd been preparing to argue the habeas corpus writ that Probate Court Judge John Burgoyne had issued in response to Margaret Garner's child-murder. Thus he invoked by implication the complex of constitutional, states' rights issues behind this case; but Chambers, rising with a show of great frustration at this widely anticipated tack, asked why in any case Jolliffe had failed to submit "a written statement of facts he expected to prove and the names of the witnesses he expected to prove them by." Jolliffe said he hadn't the means to take down defendants' written statements properly and formally. He was representing wholly destitute persons. At that Pendery appointed his official court reporter, a well-known officer in Cincinnati's Know-Nothing Party named J. Bell Pollock, to transcribe the Garners' statements. Pendery then recessed till early afternoon.[4]

When the hearing resumed Jolliffe read into the record the affidavit Pollock had taken down from Mary Garner. In it she told of being hired from James Marshall by Cass Warrington of Covington, who, when he bought her labor in 1850, "asked said Marshall if he was afraid the said Mary would run away, to which said Marshall replied, in the hearing

Colonel Francis "Frank" Chambers,
the Cincinnati attorney who led the team
that argued Gaines and Marshall's claims
for the Garner fugitives
COURTESY THE CINCINNATI HISTORICAL SOCIETY

of this deponent, that deponent might pass and re-pass to Cincinnati whenever she pleased." Mary also stated that during her twelve months of service in Covington she regularly attended church in Cincinnati and often went there "to market" with Warrington's wife, Polly, Polly's sister Sally and brother Ben. She further stated that the ferryboat pilot knew that "she came over frequently." Like Robert and Margaret, Mary Garner marked her "X" at the bottom of this affidavit. None of the Garners could write their names.

When Jolliffe finished reading, Chambers asked Pendery to rule on the defense motion for a continuance, but the Commissioner wanted to hear all three defendants' statements. So Jolliffe read into the record Robert Garner's affidavit, relating his claims of a Christmas 1855 visit to Cincinnati with Thomas Marshall and of being variously hired out to William Timberlake and James Poor, each of whom brought him to Ohio on errands and business. In what would become the most hotly contested claim, Robert also stated that James Marshall himself took

Robert to Cincinnati with a drove of hogs in autumn 1849, and that while they were being slaughtered Marshall and young Garner lodged for five nights with a "Mr. Rice, a Dutch butcher."

Here Jolliffe paused before turning to Margaret's affidavit, and repeated his request for time to subpoena these witnesses. There were just so many of them. And what of those in Kentucky, who might resist a summons . . . ? But Chambers interrupted, arguing that there was "not a word in the affidavit which has been read by Mr. Jolliffe giving sufficient reason" for a continuance. Jolliffe countered: "Why should these persons not be entitled to have their witnesses present, that every word they may have to say may be heard? The court should grant a continuance of a day, a week, a month, aye, a year, if necessary, to give these people a chance to bring their witnesses and establish their right to freedom." Pendery cut them off and told Jolliffe to read Margaret Garner's deposition. Here he set a basic rhythm for days to come—defuse an argument by delaying judgment.

Margaret Garner's statement hinged on one claim, regarding her only visit to Cincinnati: the 1840 journey there with John and Elizabeth Gaines, when she served as "nurse" to the infant Mary Gaines. In the deposition Jolliffe read to the court, Margaret "pray[ed] that her case may be continued until she [could] obtain the testimony of John Gaines on her behalf."

The record doesn't tell us but we can well imagine Archibald Gaines's reaction to Margaret's "prayer." In 1840 he had been down in Arkansas carving a plantation out of the swampy lands around Gaines Landing. He'd certainly never *heard* of such a visit, a relatively trivial event in whites' daily lives. This claim was a desperate maneuver, perhaps patched together only yesterday when this "damned abolitionist" interviewed the slaves. Anyway, now his brother, the Major, was nearly three thousand miles and a month's journey removed, in Oregon, and this slave woman was before a white man's court, "praying" for relief that would be insanely expensive and its result unpredictable. This showed exactly why abolitionists had to be run out of the district. Because what if John Gaines's testimony seemed to corroborate Margaret's claim? Her deposition craftily pointed out that all three of her (surviving) children were "born since the time when deponent was brought into the state of Ohio." If the unforeseen consequence of his brother's 1840 sojourn over the Ohio River was Margaret's freedom, then so were her children free.

Partus sequitur ventrem: that was the law. Archibald Gaines was boiling. Chambers immediately renewed his attack:

> [Col. Chambers] Your honor, the case has its painful aspects. It has its reasons for an appeal to the sympathies of every one, with which the Commissioner has nothing to do. It has been ably argued by the members of Congress which enacted the law, and the responsibility, though a great and painful one, rests upon your honor. Into the moral view of the question it is not your province to inquire; it is for you to decide upon the facts.

Of course, those "painful aspects" involved Margaret's infanticide, and brushing them aside along with the "moral view" of slavery that they commanded surely galled Jolliffe. Still, Chambers had opened the issue of Congress's enactment of the fugitive law, and Jolliffe meant to zero in on the question of its authority over state law in this case:

> [Mr. Jolliffe] The fact of the defendant's coming to Ohio, if proved, does free the party. The Constitution of this state—the Constitution of 1802, which rules this case—does not acknowledge slavery. The moment the party touched our soil the slave fell, and the free woman stood. The term "summary" does not mean the Judge should hear one side only, but that the case should not be docketed and continued from term to term, [and] that it should be heard as soon as ready. Bringing the woman [Margaret] into this state made her free, and once free always free.

These arguments, quoted here only in snippets, consumed Wednesday afternoon. As the day wore on, Margaret's bandaged boys played under the defense table. Cilla alternately slept and fussed in her mother's or her grandmother's lap, as Simon and Robert watched attentively. Occasionally one of the Garners leaned low and whispered comments and questions to Jolliffe or Gitchell, or one of the lawyers explained the process to them.

At four-thirty, with attorneys on both sides repeating themselves, Pendery cut off debate. Everyone had looked for this clash of views, including Pendery. Determined to keep a tight rein, he closed the day with only a partial ruling on Jolliffe's motion for a continuance. Feeling "constrained by a sense of right and justice," Pendery granted a brief continuance for Mary Garner but noted (ominously, as it turned out) that even if testimony supported her claim about numerous trips to Ohio, that still might not sway his final ruling on James Marshall's claim on her "labor and service." Jolliffe's motions for a further continuance based on the affidavits of Robert and Margaret he set aside until next morning, though it was obvious Pendery would rule in favor of the defense on those too. Later, walking from Fourth Street back down to his office on Broadway, Jolliffe felt good about the first day's skirmishes.

Meantime a large crowd continued to mill around the courthouse, where many had kept vigil all day, braving twenty-degree temperatures and a stiff northwesterly wind, at times catching bits of news relayed from white abolitionists inside. From the *Enquirer* we have a brief anecdote about their "considerable excitement." As the cavalcade of deputies led the Garners' omnibus out an alleyway toward the county jail, the "mob" surged around. Let reporter Hendrie's bigoted outlook take it from there:

> The principal promoters of the fuss were some mulatto women, who were extremely lavish of opprobrious epithets to the officers that guarded the way leading to the vehicle. "D-n you!" shouted one of these saddle-colored ladies, who, by the way, was dressed in the extreme of fashion, in answer to a request by one of the officers to stand back, "D-n you! I'm free born, half white, and as good as any white-livered b-h in Ohio!" The officer took no notice of her or her companions, but not so with a pair of masculine darkies who undertook to express their disapprobation of the proceedings in a noisy manner, and who were in consequence pounced upon and, in spite of their struggles and some little demonstration of a rescue, hurried to the Hammond street Stationhouse and locked up.

With variations, this scene was repeated each day of the trial.

Elsewhere in Cincinnati the Garner case was item number one. For U.S. Marshal Robinson the large, unruly street crowds posed worrisome threats of race riots or an abolitionist rescue; he responded with a call for still more deputies, a call distributed on handbills printed that afternoon with his own *Enquirer* presses. An important detail, for Robinson was not only the district's U.S. marshal, but also co-owner of the city's most widely distributed paper. He had enormous influence. Throughout southern Ohio this ardent proslavery Democrat enforced federal laws and shaped public opinion about them. He would soon command a force of deputies operating at battalion strength.

That afternoon at the county courthouse Judge Burgoyne received Sheriff Gazoway Brashears's return on Tuesday's amended habeas corpus writ, this one accurately naming the Garners' alleged owners. Brashears warranted that, though the fugitives were being detained at the county jail, he found them in the custody of Deputy U.S. Marshal Bennet, who promised to produce them for any murder warrant. A seemingly minor matter, this process nonetheless ensured that the Garners could not be remanded back to slavery without an Ohio court's prior release, exactly what Jolliffe wanted.

At the jail, Hamilton County prosecuting attorney Joseph Cox interviewed the Garners, verifying testimony they had offered before Coroner Menzies's jury. An antislavery Republican who had stumped the district for Salmon Chase's gubernatorial campaign, Cox was deeply moved at Margaret's forthrightness. "My own feelings were intensely enlisted on her behalf," he later recalled. "She had no concealment to make of her attempt to kill her children, but told me freely that it was her firm determination to destroy them all, and herself also." Listening to her with Jolliffe also present, Cox knew that while it was his "duty to prosecute" Margaret, it was also improbable that "any jury, in admiring the heroic spirit of that mother," would ever vote a guilty verdict on a first-degree murder charge.

Thus a coordinated legal strategy was starting to emerge. First Jolliffe had to hold off the Kentuckians' attempt to reclaim the fugitives. Then at the state's trial Cox might win a conviction of Margaret, perhaps the others, on a lesser homicide charge that would send them to an Ohio penitentiary, safely out of their masters' reach. As Cox put it: "I felt it my duty to shield her as much as possible from a fate [slavery] which she dreaded much more than the punishment of the [Ohio] law." It all hinged on delicate, untested matters of law, as well as on timing.[5]

Wednesday evening at Smith and Nixon's Hall the Hutchinson Family Singers performed at a concert that was "tolerably well attended" despite another snowstorm. Local abolitionists made short speeches on behalf of the Garners and the troupe performed a repertoire "pretty strongly tinctured with antislavery sentiment." At concert's end a "Mr. James Elliott stated that by arrangement with the Hutchinsons, the room [Thursday] evening would be occupied by a meeting of those desirous of expressing sympathy with the fugitives now under arrest, at which the Hutchinsons would sing." Next morning's *Gazette* advertised the event.

Thursday, 31 January. On their way to court the seven Garners again rode among Robinson's augmented force of deputies, "tall fellows and strong, fully capable of maintaining the supremacy of the law against misguided sympathizers, who allow their passions and prejudices to run riot, and who, if triumphant, would alike swamp the Constitution and make a chaos of society." Again the view of Robinson's *Enquirer*. And again those "misguided sympathizers" rained snowballs and "opprobrious epithets" on the deputies.

Pendery opened the day by granting Jolliffe some time to find his witnesses, but ruled out any lengthy continuance to subpoena testimony from John Gaines in Oregon. With that partial victory Jolliffe immediately rose to make his next motion. He knew that earlier that morning Sheriff Brashears had visited Pendery's chambers bearing subpoenas summoning the fugitives to appear before an Ohio grand jury, expected soon to name Margaret Garner on a murder charge and Simon, Mary, and Robert as accessories. He also knew Pendery had struck "an arrangement" so that state officers wouldn't formally serve these subpoenas until the federal fugitive slave hearing concluded. But subpoenas were subpoenas, Jolliffe argued. The law required officers of the court to serve them with all deliberate speed, and here before man and God were the persons named in those documents. Pendery should allow—"nay, encourage"—those officers to fulfill their duty, Jolliffe argued.

> [Col. Chambers] I am not surprised at this motion, or to see the gentleman, the champion of the sovereignty of the State of Ohio, using all his endeavors to bring the people under her laws, but the sovereignty of the Union he had entirely set aside.
> [Mr. Jolliffe] No, sir, not me.
> [Col. Chambers] I know not what may be the sentiment of the immense multitude here assembled, whether they love the Union better than anything else, or love a nigger better than ten white men, but I know I do not.

How did the Garners take *that* "sentiment"? No matter to Chambers, for whom they might have been invisible. He was playing to an all-white gallery, U.S. marshals having once more excluded Cincinnati's free blacks from the courtroom.

Still, Chambers's uncertainty about "the sentiment" prevailing among that "multitude" inside and outside the courthouse opens on a wider historical perspective. In 1856 Cincinnati was a Northern border city divided in two, armed to the teeth, at times even battling in the streets over slavery. Its citizens had already pressed beyond just acknowledging the possibility of disunion and civil strife over slavery. They could fill out the muster rolls for regiments on either side, and the Garner case was their bugle call to arms. Each day's face-off between deputies and antislavery forces in the streets, as inside the court neighbors and co-workers erupted in cheers or jeers, threatened wider strife.

As if to embody the very genius of violence, there arose suddenly from a back seat of Pendery's court the great bulk of John Jolliffe's former assailant, the same hard-drinking, hot-tempered Jacob Flinn who had knocked the "damned abolitionist" cold in the middle of Cincinnati's Fifth Street market. What next? He too wished to make a motion. Now returned to private practice by angry voters and serving as legal counsel for Marshals Robinson and Bennet, Flinn would be willing, if Pendery desired, to "look into the matters so as to give proper advice to the court." Yet the notorious Flinn wasn't an attorney for the claimants or the defendants, and thus offering his services as a friend of the court was a wholly uninvited and self-serving gesture. Things were verging on absurdity, or chaos. Pendery knew it and "declined" Flinn's services as amicus curiae.

Pendery did allow Jolliffe and Chambers to battle on for another hour, and their cross fire produced some of the trial's most widely quoted rhetoric. Jolliffe, for example, took the imagery of disunion and impending warfare to its logical consequence—human sacrifice on slavery's altar:

> [Mr. Jolliffe] It might seem strange that as attorney for these people I should demand that they be given up on a charge of murder, but each and all of them has assured me that *they would go singing to the gallows rather than be returned to slavery.*

At that the audience broke into loud, sustained cheering, and Chambers, startled by the intense antislavery feeling, mellowed his rhetoric with a remarkable caveat:

> [Col. Chambers] As to these people going to the gallows singing, I would rather go there myself than go into slavery. But I would rather take a chance of a slide on the Underground Railroad than consent, just at this particular time, to go singing or any other way to the gallows.

In closing Chambers argued that since they were first slated to hear the claim of Marshall for his slaves, and the murdered child belonged to Gaines, "the question was irrelevant as to this case." Pendery agreed and asked for Chambers to call his first witness supporting Marshall's claim.

Once more Jolliffe rose with a motion. He wanted to know why "the Marshal is excluding a certain class of people from the room." Had someone issued an order to bar the door against free blacks? If so, who issued it? And anyway was such an order legal? Jolliffe pointed out that the same principle might have been used to exclude "the foreign born population" during the recently opened "trial of the Irish filibuster cases," involving those mysteriously distributed and still prominent Sharps rifles. He asked Pendery to rescind his order or, if someone else had ordered the blacks' exclusion, to countermand that person's order. Pendery immediately pinned the blame on Marshal Robinson. The court erupted in jeers and catcalls. Just who was in charge?

Having pricked him from one side, Jolliffe, still standing, thrust at the heart of his problem:

> [Mr. Jolliffe] Then I guess I must go and hunt up my own witnesses. For as many of them are colored people, they have not been permitted in the courtroom.

Angry over being scoffed at, Pendery turned on Jolliffe. There was no provision of the fugitive law, he said, requiring the court to subpoena defense witnesses. Therefore those subpoenas Jolliffe had requested on the previous afternoon were hereby refused, "the U.S. Marshal being under no obligation to serve them." Pendery lectured Jolliffe: "the Comptroller at Washington City had refused to allow" payments for the serving of warrants in previous fugitive cases. This was how he knew that the court had no obligation to help the Garners' defense. Suddenly Pendery's bailiff interrupted his recitation, calling the Commissioner into chambers for what became a fifteen-minute recess. Returning, Pendery told them that Marshal Robinson (somewhere in the building, but avoiding the courtroom) still "did not like to admit the colored people [to the courtroom] so they were still excluded." With that, Pendery curtly handed the subpoenas back to Jolliffe.

Jolliffe then moved for appointment of "a special deputy" in the person of "a light colored mulatto" named William Beckley. *He* would subpoena defense witnesses and not even charge a fee for his services. After another objection from Chambers, and another recess to confer with Robinson, an exasperated Pendery caved in: "to prevent trouble the Marshal will serve these subpoenas, and I will pay the fees out of my own pocket," he announced.

[Mr. Jolliffe] Oh no, you shan't do that.

Disregarding Jolliffe, U.S. Marshal Robinson dutifully approached the defense table to take the subpoenas. He wanted a quick exit.

Still Jolliffe wasn't through. First he raised an issue that I have set aside. Robert, Jolliffe noted, was named in the subpoenas as "young Simon" and this was erroneous: "His name is not Simon, but Robert Garner."

It was common practice among slave owners to impose names on their chattels, for naming symbolized the owner's power—that of a deity to bring his creatures under the authority of his word, his *logos*. Until John Jolliffe's objection, all official documents as well as every journalistic account of the Garner case had called Robert "young Simon," his name under slavery. By insisting on his Christian name Jolliffe asserted Robert's identity *on free soil*, and made this point with Robinson standing there, the marshal's attempt to take and serve Jolliffe's subpoenas arrested in midair by this demand for the cultural integrity of black people. The point was lost on Robinson; Pendery too, it seemed. In a frustrated desire to begin hearing testimony, he ordered Robinson simply to amend the documents.

But Jolliffe raised yet another objection. Now that he'd gotten Pendery to accept and have his marshal serve defense subpoenas, he took up one of the documents and pointed out another lapse:

> [Mr. Jolliffe] It has in its place simply a scroll, made with a pen, and the word "seal" written there. That such might be sufficient on a deed or bond, in the State of Ohio, I do not deny, but on a process issued from a United States Court it is not sufficient. This is not the Commissioner's fault. The Congress that passed the Fugitive Slave Law had failed to provide a seal for the Commissioner, and it was a hiatus in the proceeding that is, thank God, so much the better for the cause of human freedom. In processes between different States, the seal is the only evidence to authenticate them.

Jolliffe was casting Commissioner Pendery as inauthentic, as lacking official power. For did not Congress's failure to give him a proper seal evidence the Commissioner's unconstitutional status? Behind Jolliffe's objection stretched a corpus of debates on the authority of Petty Commissioners in fugitive slave cases. Pendery knew it and refused to open that debate too. He simply told Jolliffe an anecdote: When Supreme Court Justice McLean appointed him to the office, the justice had detailed the Commissioner's duties and assured him "that a seal was not necessary." End of discussion. With that, Jolliffe's delays were exhausted. Shortly after two o'clock, Pendery ordered James Marshall's attorneys to call their first witness.

In a criminal trial the defense attorney might open with such an array of motions not only to test key procedural or legal issues but to prepare grounds for later appeals to higher tribunals. For Jolliffe and the Garners nothing of that sort lay ahead; there was no appealing a Commissioner's decision in a fugitive case. Their only higher tribunal was that of American public opinion, and to that body Jolliffe had been taking his case throughout the previous hours of debate. His motions brought before the bar every critical issue: Was the Commissioners' authority constitutional? Under the 1850 law, could Commissioners grant assistance to claimants but not to the defense in the summoning of witnesses? Especially when the fugitive law provided for Commissioners to be paid twice as much—ten dollars instead of five—when they remanded alleged fugitives back to slavery? Too, had Congress really intended for the 1850 law to have absolute priority relative to state processes, especially over

capital crimes such as murder? Newspapers in Cincinnati and Columbus as well as other Northern cities, from Chicago to Boston, would be
editorializing on these questions for weeks to come. Thus Jolliffe's first
two days had dramatically succeeded. People could see obvious problems with the 1850 law. Also, while greatly assisted by Pendery himself,
Jolliffe had exposed the Commissioner's discomfort and ineffectuality.
Finally there was this: Jolliffe's strategies were winning the Garners
priceless time together on free soil.

Act II: "the seething Hell of American slavery"

The parade of claimant's witnesses began testifying on Thursday afternoon and quickly followed each other. First James Corbin, a "near
neighbor" of Marshall's, who knew "old Simon" for twenty-five or
more years and "young Simon [Robert] ever since he was born." Then
Thomas Marshall, who testified to his father's ownership of all three and
to being "raised with young Simon." Next, George Washington Marshall, a nephew of the claimant, who also stated that his uncle "was not
in the habit of bringing his boys over to this side [of the Ohio River]
when he brought hogs" to market. Finally Chambers called Major
W. B. Murphy, who affirmed that the elder Garners and their son
were "Marshall's property by the laws of Kentucky."

George Washington Marshall's testimony brought snickers from every
white man used to seeing Kentucky slaves driving hogs up Broadway,
running their masters' errands, or attending Sunday church services.
Such scenes were commonplaces in Northern cities along the border
zone.[6] Everyone knew that young Master Marshall was reciting from his
script.

Until they called Murphy, Jolliffe didn't cross-examine any of Marshall's witnesses. And why would he? He wasn't contesting the Kentuckian's claim that the Garners had been his slaves. With Murphy,
though, Jolliffe wanted to know if he had been "present at the arrest."
Answering, the major volunteered, in fact ventured pretty well into, a
detailed narrative about the presence there of Elijah Kite ("whom I
knew," Murphy noted, further evidence that he and Gaines knew where
to hunt up the Garners on Monday morning). The major also told of
his wanting Kite to coax the Garners outside for a peaceful surrender

and return to Richwood Station. Chambers finally cut off his story with an objection: this testimony was irrelevant to the case. Pendery sustained him.

> [Mr. Jolliffe] Was anyone murdered during the arrest?
> [Col. Chambers] We do not wish to go into all these fancy matters.
> [Mr. Jolliffe] The fact I intend to bring out is that the mother of these children, frantic at the time of the arrest, had murdered one of her children (a little girl) rather than have it taken back into slavery. I do not regard that as a "fancy matter."

Again Pendery sustained Chambers, because the child-murder involved "a slave of Mr. Gaines's and not one of Mr. Marshall's," whose claim they were trying. Jolliffe defiantly rephrased his previous question, bringing another objection from Chambers, who thought "this was trifling with the dignity of the Court."

> [Commissioner Pendery] The court understands how to maintain its own dignity, and asks Mr. Jolliffe: What object does he have in proving the fact of the death of the child?
> [Mr. Jolliffe] I intend, on the final argument of this case, not only to allege but to demonstrate conclusively to the Court, that the Fugitive Slave Law is unconstitutional and, as part and parcel of that argument, I wish to show the effect of carrying it out: that it had driven a frantic mother to murder her own child, rather than see it carried back to the seething Hell of American slavery.

Here, the *Gazette* tells of loud "bursts of applause" drowning out calls from the bench for "Order! Order!" But Jolliffe was rolling and Pendery let him go. For nearly a half hour Jolliffe recapped his argument from *Belle Scott*, that the Fugitive Slave Law violated First Amendment guarantees of religious freedom. He concluded with an ominous warning:

> The Commissioner is here as the guardian of religious liberty in the United States, and if he acts wisely he will bring happiness to thousands and tens of thousands, but if he follows evil counsel the consequences can not easily be foretold. In a brief time, perhaps in less than six months, the Union may be severed. The Stars and

Stripes may float over separate nations and blood flow between them. I desire to introduce this evidence simply to show the illegitimate effects of the law.

"For a few moments after Mr. Jolliffe sat down," notes the *Gazette*'s Mr. Babb, "shouts of applause and cries of order filled the Court Rooms."

With its images of slavery's "seething Hell" Jolliffe's speech offended the honor of Kentucky. The duty of responding fell to Gaines and Marshall's attorney John W. Finnell, John Pollard Gaines's close friend and political adviser:

> [Mr. Finnell] Your honor, the Court should have nothing to do with the case in a moral sense. What are we here for? Is it to determine the moral question of slavery? Upon that point I have to say that I am a Kentuckian and a slaveholder. I was reared by an old negro woman, who, next to my wife and children and my own mother, I loved as dearly as any white person on earth and I wish most sincerely that there would not be a slave in the universe. But we are not here to discuss that point. My client has not the means to spare to pay me, nor am I here for that purpose. But if at any time the gentleman [Mr. Jolliffe] wishes to discuss the moral view of slavery I shall cheerfully meet him when and where he pleases.

That last remark has the ring of a duelist's challenge, to settle their difference "on the field of honor." Paying tribute to the memory of the mammy who "reared" him was another classic Southron strategy, yet Finnell wasn't done. In closing he turned toward a spectator in the courtroom, James Elliott, the antislavery activist who had spoken on behalf of the Garners at Wednesday night's Hutchinson Singers benefit concert:

> There are other systems of slavery beside ours. The Irish are enslaved by England and that man, fresh from the bog, had better stayed there and removed the shackles from his own enslaved brethren than come here to meddle with our institutions.

Defending American slavery by pointing at foreign bond servants was a cliché of the proslavery, "Southron" argument.

But why attack Elliott? The man had emigrated to America twenty-five years earlier, grown up in Louisville, Kentucky, with his school-teacher father, and made his way to Ohio around 1845. In the region Elliott was fairly well known as a sometime *Cincinnati Commercial* correspondent at Columbus and as an abolitionist of long standing, the *Enquirer*, for example, naming him "an Old-line Abolitionist of the blackest hue" who also "strongly opposed" the Know-Nothings' bigoted nativism.[7] More recently a hardworking Republican during Salmon Chase's successful gubernatorial campaign, Elliott was rewarded with a nomination (just then under discussion at Columbus) for the post of Cincinnati Canal Commissioner—a minor plum. Excepting Elliott's antinativist politics, though, we don't know why Finnell, a Cotton Whig turned Know-Nothing, singled him out. Elliott himself thought it was a random shot.[8] It was a symptom, though, of how the Garner case continued to vibrate a taut web of political, social, and cultural relations.

With that odor of anti-immigrant bigotry hanging in the air Pendery adjourned for the day. Outside the "snow fell fast" and the previous day's scene repeated itself but with an added twist that would recur over the coming weeks. A "crowd" of black women followed the Garners' omnibus, "waving their handkerchiefs and uttering cries of encouragement" to Margaret. They did not know it, but this was the last they would see of her or the three children for a week. With testimony begun on James Marshall's claim to Robert, Simon, and Mary Garner, neither Margaret nor her children—nor, for that matter, her claimant, Archibald Gaines—were required in court. Gaines returned to Maplewood and his pregnant wife, while a pregnant Margaret and her children remained at the county jail.

Thursday evening, the owners of Smith and Nixon's Hall canceled the Hutchinsons' benefit concert because of rising concerns about civil disturbances. Otherwise the city's social and cultural life continued, including (somewhat ironically) a performance of *Othello* at the National Theater.

Meanwhile, U.S. Marshal Hiram H. Robinson departed on the last eastbound train. He was headed to Washington, D.C., desiring there an audience with Attorney General Caleb Cushing and, if possible, President Pierce. No longer would abolitionists like Jolliffe mock him in court, for if Cushing and Pierce would grant him powers to call up a sizable enough posse, perhaps even give him authority to impose martial law, Robinson would take charge of the city and ensure a speedy trial and the return of the Garners. Robinson expected to arrive in the capital by Friday evening and get back to Cincinnati by Monday, he hoped with incontrovertible orders in his pocket.

That day at Richwood Station, the Maplewood slaves assessed their situation. By now they knew all the facts about Margaret's recapture, little Mary's death, and the chance that all four adult Garners would be tried for murder. They had seen Master Gaines but momentarily on Monday night when he rode in with the shrouded body of Mary Garner. After arranging for its burial in a frozen grave somewhere in the neighborhood (a site lost in time's drift), on Tuesday he had gathered some legal papers and a change of clothes, left to consult with James Marshall (nearly over his bout of "gravel"), and journeyed with him to Covington. Gaines's slaves hadn't seen their master since. Certainly they were desperately anxious about his mood when all this was over. If Gaines threatened them on Tuesday, as other performances suggest that he would have, they were even more fearful, Cilla especially.

In any case, sometime Thursday, with light snow falling and the continuing promise of a firm ice bridge, four more Gaines slaves ran for freedom. They made their break around midnight, says the *Covington Journal*, and so successful was their flight that nothing further was ever heard of them. Drifting snow covered their tracks. Where did they cross? How did they connect with the Underground Railroad? What was their fate? The historical record does not say. From scanty reports and archived documents we can be relatively certain Margaret's mother, Cilla, was among them, probably with Hannah—for both had histories of resistance. We know, also, from a report appearing several days later in the *Cincinnati Commercial*, that their "tickets" had been "punched through" to Canada.[9]

We may well imagine Archibald Gaines's rage at such a loss. Of the fifteen slaves formerly numbered among his "stocks," four more adults —several of prime age and condition—were now irrecoverably lost. Margaret and her children made nine, total. He probably felt that the chances of reclaiming the four remaining Garners were good, but the price—in blood as well as money—would be terrible. The awful march of devastations had resumed its way through the life of this ill-fated

Kentucky planter but he would bear it with a gentleman's honor and all of his fiscal resources.

Friday, 1 February. This morning Jolliffe began calling defense witnesses but had difficulty getting them into court. Pendery called several recesses while deputies hunted up people named in the Garners' affidavits (and during Jolliffe's Tuesday afternoon interview), but at times he had to push Jolliffe along to his next available witness. And the witnesses, once found, were often ineffective. Some may have given vague testimony because they were fugitives fearing discovery; others may have been scared at finding themselves at the center of such a formal spectacle; others doubtless feared calling white men liars, a dangerous business in antebellum Cincinnati.

Early in Friday's session a "rowdy" young man stood up amidst the spectators and poured a stream of abuse at Commissioner Pendery. The young fellow shouted that they ought to send these slaves back to Kentucky without any more foofaraw. This whole process was just a dodge and Jolliffe a "damned abolitionist" who ought to be tarred and feathered, or worse. The "rowdy" was quite "evidently inebriated" (at ten o'clock in the morning) and Pendery had him ejected. As deputies hustled the young man outside, Jolliffe quipped that "the cool air might have a beneficial effect on his system." Overnight it had turned bitterly cold once again, the temperature reaching only fifteen degrees Friday afternoon and plunging still further over the weekend.

Another disruption quickly followed. Cincinnati's unofficial "head" of the Underground Railroad, Levi Coffin, had slipped into the room and stationed himself between the defendants' table and the courtroom wall. There, in a silent show of solidarity with the Garners, he "stood, as Quakers were accustomed to do, with his hat on." One of the deputy marshals ordered him to remove the hat in deference to Commissioner Pendery's authority. Coffin declined, explaining that he "meant no disrespect, but it is the custom of my people." At that the deputy raised a cane and "knocked the offending broad brim on the floor." Stone-faced throughout, Coffin stood ramrod straight, heedless of the absurd deputy and of his hat, which lay on the floor for some time before the deputy picked it up and put it on the end of the table. Still the outraged spectators glared at the deputy. At last he gave in, "returned, took the hat, and placed it very gently on Levi's head."[10]

Little morality plays-within-the-play, episodes like these punctuated

Quaker abolitionist Levi Coffin, ca. 1855
COURTESY THE CINCINNATI HISTORICAL SOCIETY

the Garner hearing until its end. Friday, however, the spotlight was on defense witnesses. Jolliffe led with Charlotte Armstrong, a black woman who testified to seeing Mary Garner at the Bethel Methodist Episcopal Church in 1852, and twice after that: once again at church, another time at the Fifth Street market, "between eight and nine o'clock. I said to her, you over to market very often? She replied yes." Moreover, she recalled Mary Garner saying that the marketing "was for her owners." Immediately Chambers objected. This was only Jolliffe's way of weaseling into the hearing some testimony by the defendant, just what the Fugitive Slave Law disallowed. Pendery sustained him, but the woman had proved a solid witness, clear on dates and details. When Jolliffe asked her to identify Mary Garner she didn't hesitate: "Yes, sir," Charlotte Armstrong declared, "that's the same woman, if I was qualified to death."

She contrasted sharply with Jolliffe's next witness. John Wilson was an elderly free black who recollected seeing Robert Garner walking on Broadway near Bethel Church one Sunday. Robert asked him for directions to Elijah Kite's dwelling, where he (Robert) wanted to spend the night. But Wilson couldn't recall when this was and his identification of Robert was vague:

> [John Wilson] It is very hard for me to draw these old intellects of mine on that pint. I think it is near two years ago, as near as I can come at it. I know him by his complexion and by his feet, he turns them a little out. I have no doubt in my own mind that it is the same man but I can't explain myself any better, as I'm not much in court business. But his face is too plain to be mistaken. There was a white man with him; I think it was that man.

Here Wilson pointed to James Marshall, a fairly good identification. But when did these events occur? In his affidavit Robert stated that James Marshall took him to Cincinnati in 1849, but John Wilson's vague recollection put the two men on Broadway just two years ago, in 1854. In his cross-examination Chambers pressed this point and a jittery Wilson caved in: "Ah, that's where you got me. When a white man asks me a question, I'm out and gone again." The lengthy representations of his dialect, quoted in Saturday's *Gazette*, show that even the antislavery reporters thought Wilson comical—a mere Jim Crow. Jolliffe needed better.

He called George J. Guilford, the *Commercial* reporter who had interviewed Thomas Marshall on Monday afternoon, right after the Garners were arrested, and Guilford was superb. He recalled young Marshall as saying in the presence of Major W. B. Murphy that "these people"—by whom Guilford understood the young man to mean *all* the slaves, those of Marshall as well as Gaines—had "frequently" been allowed "on this side of the river." Guilford could not produce his notebook, because he had not anticipated testifying and so had already thrown it out. Still he was absolutely clear about words and other details which, in any case, his newspaper had published from those unrecoverable notes. Jolliffe next called Joseph Kite, who testified that Robert had been over to stay with them around Christmas. After Kite came James Elliott, who corroborated Guilford's testimony. On Monday afternoon Elliott had gone to the U.S. marshal's office to ensure the Garners would have an attorney should slave catchers try to speed the case before a Commissioner. He testified that when Guilford asked the Garners, in the presence of Thomas Marshall, "if they had ever been in

Ohio" and the fugitives said, "yes, they had," young Marshall never contradicted them.

There Jolliffe's defense stalled. With deputies unable to find witnesses he'd subpoenaed, he was reluctant to proceed. Pendery called a noon-time recess but when they returned around one o'clock the witnesses still weren't available. Gitchell left to see what he might do, and it turned out that during Thursday's disturbances outside the courthouse U.S. marshals had arrested one of their witnesses, a black man named William Alexander. Here was a consequence of their excluding blacks from the hearing, Jolliffe pointed out. Pendery ignored him and ordered deputies to go get the jailed witness. Jolliffe used the delay to petition Pendery on behalf of nine-month-old Cilla Garner, for whom he thought the court should appoint a legal guardian, a common practice in criminal cases whenever defendants were jailed with nursing infants. Pendery refused. At two-thirty deputies finally produced Alexander, who testified to seeing Robert driving hogs up Broadway with a white man, who "appeared to be doing more [work] than him [Robert]." This brought laughter and seemed to corroborate the otherwise less than cred-ible testimony of John Wilson, but Alexander failed to identify James Marshall as the white man. His identification of Robert also faltered during Chambers's cross-examination. "I know that man by his hat," Alexander said, and many in the courtroom (including Pendery) broke into an "almost incessant and universal laughter" because Robert hadn't a hat on his head or even near him. On redirect Jolliffe had another try at him and the embarrassed but determined Alexander stood firm: "That," he said, pointing out Robert, "is the man I saw on Broadway; I am willing to swear it before my God."

After another short delay deputies produced Jolliffe's next witness, "a light-colored mulatto woman" named Betsey Ann Bates, who helped the Garners even less than Alexander. She recalled seeing Mary and Simon Garner marketing in Covington, "but never on this side of the river." The *Enquirer* remarked that Jolliffe "dropped her like a hot muffin" and that when he turned to the claimants' side to ask if they would "take the witness," Chambers huffed, "We don't want her."

With that Jolliffe had run out of options. Deputies still hadn't located key witnesses, in particular the Cincinnati butcher named Rice with whom Robert claimed to have briefly lodged some years before. Jolliffe's case was stalled, and a frustrated Pendery recessed at three-thirty Friday afternoon. Once again "amid great excitement" in the streets, deputies returned the Garners to the county jail. Each day the crowds grew larger.

Saturday, 2 February. U.S. Marshal Hiram Robinson had made his train connections despite winter storms and reached Washington on Friday night. Saturday morning he was first rebuffed at the offices of Attorney General Caleb Cushing, who was probably too busy working for President Pierce on affairs in Kansas, where civil strife over slavery still threatened. An undaunted Robinson next tried the White House. Two months later Robinson would claim that President Pierce had received him and agreed that the Garners must be returned to Kentucky at all costs. To that end, Robinson claimed, Pierce promised not only to pay any special deputies from his own "secret service money" but to instruct Secretary of War Jefferson Davis to empower Robinson to call on the U.S. Army commander at the Covington garrison for federal troops, if needed. None of these claims can be verified.

More probably, a twice-rebuffed Robinson sat down sometime Saturday and penned an appeal to Cushing. This document was dutifully filed with Cushing's incoming correspondence, where it had lain unnoticed until I found it at the Library of Congress. Robinson's plea for advice reveals how he and other proslavery Democrats viewed the Garner case.[11]

A man looking to shore up public support, Robinson in his cover sheet asks Cushing for a reply that could be published in the *Enquirer* —probably the reason Cushing never did oblige.[12] "Sir," Robinson began. "Late events in Cincinnati not yet settled and others of like character at former periods growing out of an attempted execution of the fugitive slave act, have inclined me at this time to ask Counsel of you." After summarizing an earlier, 1855 fugitive trial (the "Rosetta Case" of March 1855), Robinson launched into his main request:

> Within the last week . . . [s]even slaves were arrested by my deputies, during my absence, on a U.S. Comm.'s warrant. Connected with the arrest was a tragic event, shocking in its features, but the responsibility of which cannot be laid at our door. I mean the murder of one of her young children by one of the Slave women, and the mutilation of two others, while the officers were forcing their way into the premises where the slaves were secreted.
>
> Soon after these arrests my deputies were waited upon by a

deputy Sheriff and served with a writ of *habeas corpus* emanating
from a Probate Judge,—a kind of exaggerated Justice of the Peace
in Ohio. An attempt was made, when my deputies refused to obey,
so far as producing the slaves in Court, to *compel* obedience, and
also to *rescue* the slaves from our possession by the power of numbers. The matter had not been settled when I was last despatched,
and involved a high excitement, threatening seriously the peace of
the city and as seriously a conflict between the authorities of the
State and General government.

That "high excitement" was the armed standoff between federal marshals and county sheriffs, first at the Hammond Street station house,
then the U.S. Courthouse, on Monday afternoon and evening, events
Robinson hadn't witnessed because he'd "despatched" himself to the
state capitol at Columbus. His naming Sheriff Buckingham's effort to
serve Burgoyne's writ of habeas corpus a "rescue" attempt was erroneous
and self-serving. Cincinnati abolitionists had only put their state courts
to work protecting the Garners' rights, should they eventually be ruled
free blacks. But Robinson regarded it differently and wondered:

what are my powers, rights, and duties, in cases of this character?
Am I justified in resisting the *Habeas Corpus* writ in so far as to
hold possession of an alleged fugitive until he is heard on the
warrant by which he is arrested? Is the interference of a State tribunal, to rescue out of my possession the fugitive, by compelling
me to produce the body before it, while I am also required by
warrant to produce him before a tribunal of the General Government, a lawful procedure and one which I am hereafter to be
governed by? If not, then, in the event of a conflict of jurisdictions,
violence being threatened or used to interfere with my duties and
powers, *at what point* of this resistance of the local authorities, or,
of the community (which latter need not be seriously apprehended
in Cincinnati) will I be fully justified in invoking the people or
calling on the military to aid me in executing my duties and up-
holding the laws of the General Government? Have I, under my
own discretion, the power to call out the military? Should a fugitive
be received into a county jail, placed there by a Marshal, and,
when once in, there held by the Sheriff, who refused to give him

back to the keeping of the Marshal, is such an act on the part of
the Sheriff not a clear *resistance* of the laws and authorities of the
United States, and indictable by a U.S. Grand Jury and punishable
by a U.S. Court?

Robinson wanted Cushing to order federal judges to override and even
punish officers of state courts. Moreover, he wanted Cushing's blessing
on a declaration of martial law. A man girding himself for battle, Robinson pledged to act "without fear, favor, or affection"—a phrase from
the marshal's oath.

Hiram Robinson was not a man to doubt his "course in such trying
times," but he wanted an official, public authorization in his pocket,
despite (or in addition to) the fact that Attorney General Cushing had
already spoken to his questions.[13] As a publisher, Robinson also desired
a far-reaching social and *cultural* control, beginning with power to impose his own proslavery reading on "late events." Representing the Garner case as a drama (just as his own newspaper had already done, on
Tuesday, in comparing the Garner infanticide to the Roman tragedy
Virginius) was subtle but incisive. According to commonplace conventions of the dramatic stage, a "tragic" Margaret Garner would be defined
by the pathos of her *own* overreaching, excessive violence, so "shocking
in its features." Marshal Robinson's reading would exonerate the deputies who arrested Margaret and foreclose an agitated public's questions
about his men's complicity with Southern slavery, seen as forcing Margaret's hand during the capture and causing her infanticide.

Margaret Garner was rapidly becoming a symbolic property, as op-
ponents in the slavery struggle hastened into the contest over her meaning. Yet Attorney General Caleb Cushing didn't need a narrative of the
Garner infanticide from Marshal Hiram Robinson. Brief telegraphic accounts of the fugitives' desperate capture had appeared in major United
States newspapers just a day or two after Monday morning's events.[14] By
Friday and Saturday, copies of the *Gazette, Commercial*, and *Enquirer*
had traveled via railway express to cities like St. Louis, Chicago, Cleveland, Boston, New York, Philadelphia, and Washington, whose papers
reprinted copy from the Cincinnati accounts of Tuesday and Wednesday.[15] Weeklies began their coverage beginning with the next available
issues.[16] Nearly all followed news of the Garners until the slaves' fugitive
hearing concluded. Excepting the Deep South, where editors practically

imposed a news blackout on it, the Kentucky slave mother's infanticide was already nationally famous.[17]

Queen City residents were also reading the first reports of national opinion. It would take a few more days for antislavery papers from New York and Boston to arrive in Cincinnati, meanwhile Wednesday's Cleveland *Plain Dealer* had featured the Garner case as its chief story, reprinting in full Tuesday's Cincinnati *Enquirer* text. Ardently Democratic, Thursday's *Plain Dealer* editorialized to Cincinnatians: put aside sentiment, enforce the fugitive law, keep civic order. On Friday, Robinson's *Enquirer* approvingly quoted their advice.

The antislavery *Gazette* devoted two full columns to a two-day eruption of debates in the Ohio Senate. First thing Thursday morning a Senator Brown of Wood County (south of Toledo) introduced a resolution telling how "certain quiet, peaceable persons" in Cincinnati, "guilty of no offence known to our laws," were surrounded and "attacked" by Kentucky slave catchers aided by U.S. marshals. Brown called on the Judiciary Committee to draft a bill "to prevent the recurrence of such scenes in our State." After divisive arguments lasting all day, the resolution passed on a vote of 24–7. Senators representing southern Ohio counties along the Ohio River cast all but one nay.[18] Heated discussion continued on Friday, as one senator argued for the Garners' "natural right to defend themselves against their pursuing owners," even to kill them for liberty's sake. He would do so, just as he "would kill a rattle snake." Other denunciations of the slaveholding gentry rose to such a pitch that all seven Doughfaces sat silenced.[19] Cincinnatians studied such reports in Saturday's papers and realized the extent of national interest. Comprehending how such stories had been crackling over telegraph wires and riding the rails back and forth across the North, they began to see themselves moving upon a brightly spotlighted stage.

Arriving in court Saturday morning, Jolliffe was surprised by a still larger force of newly deputized marshals, another one hundred, augmented this time by representatives of the Covington police force. Inside the courthouse, another spectacle: As Pendery entered, one of these Kentuckians—a "tall, bony, gaunt" man "with a small, red, sunken eye, hollow cheeks, and a sharp chin"—broke from the ranks of his fellows, stood before the Commissioner's bench, and began swinging a shillelagh above his head. Reporter Babb, of the *Gazette*, observed how the man occasionally paced the courtroom and during his "perambulations" took special delight in mounting the wooden settee (placed just before the railing) and swinging his "huge club" over spectators' heads, singling out free blacks allowed in to testify.

Despite these diversions Jolliffe staged his best day of testimony, summoning ten witnesses who supported the Garners' claims that their masters permitted them to travel freely into Cincinnati. Alfred Gilmore, a free black working as a laborer in Cincinnati, testified to having seen Robert Garner at the People's Theater over Christmas. Gilmore also stated that Deputy Marshal John Ellis—one of the party surrounding Kite's house on Monday morning and now one of the deputies escorting them every day from jail to courthouse—could verify this claim, as he (Ellis) had worked as an usher at the People's Theater that night and had even seated Robert Garner. Joseph Kite's wife, Sarah, testified that Robert had visited them over Christmas. She was followed by William Marshall (no relation to the Boone County clan), who stated that when he formerly worked as a Cincinnati policeman he had often seen young Robert in the city. Vincent Hayes was a freed black and a former Boone County slave who testified to knowing Robert Garner for years in Kentucky and having seen him in Cincinnati over Christmas. Fildin Corbin, described as a "very light colored mulatto," said that Elijah Kite brought Robert and Simon to his Bucktown house during the holidays. Elijah Kite confirmed Corbin's testimony, but also said that the Christmas 1855 visit was the first time that he, at any rate, had seen his cousin-in-law visiting Cincinnati. Spencer Cash, a "copper colored" mulatto, described seeing Robert "driving hogs" up Broadway just before Christmas.

Then Jolliffe's train of witnesses stalled, as Gitchell still hadn't appeared with the stars. During the wait, once more Jacob Flinn rose with an amicus curiae motion designed (he said) to "correct" factual "errors." On behalf of Marshals Robinson and Bennet, Flinn asked Pendery to stipulate that in excluding black spectators they only "acted in strict conformity with the instructions laid down by the Commissioner." Pendery let him finish, refused comment, and adjourned for the noon hour.

Resuming at one o'clock, Jolliffe quickly interviewed a "light colored mulatto," John Farrar, who saw Robert and Simon Garner near "Lower Market [Street] before Christmas." Then came the man they had sought for two days—Jacob Rice (or Riis), the German who butchered James Marshall's hogs back in the mid-1840s. Rice described several transactions. At one Marshall had brought along "two black boys ('nagurs')"; at another sale, in 1847 or 1848, only young Robert had accompanied Marshall and the two had lodged for two nights with Rice at his Hamer Street house. The old man recalled their stay:

[Jacob Rice] In the night I tell Mr. Marshall, "Mr. Marshall, where we lay the boy" and den he say, "Very well, lay 'em on the ground—makes no difference where he lays." My old woman tell me, "now, old man, take the boy over to the childers, and put 'em over to the childers bed." In the morning Mr. Marshall tell me, "Where is the boy?" He say to my old woman, "What is the reason you give him a bed?" Well, then, my old woman say to Mr. Marshall, she said how, "These people like us." He said he no call them people. They same like anoder ting—he wouldn't say a dog. And then next morning he take 'em, and he goes 'long home. Dat's all I knowed.[20]

In the trial's most dramatic moment so far, Rice—having not seen them for almost a decade—unhesitatingly identified Simon and Robert Garner, then just as clearly pointed out James Marshall from the group of white men at the claimants' table: "Yes," Jacob Rice noted, "he is in the court like a gentleman. . . . He comes to my house with hogs, looking like his nagur, and now he is dressed like a gentleman." Antislavery partisans roared.

Jolliffe wasn't through. He called Rice's daughter, Margaret Fisher, whom his agents were still out seeking. Another half hour's delay. During it, Rice—his testimony completed—sat and talked familiarly with Robert and Simon Garner until Gitchell entered with Margaret Fisher, who paused to greet her father, took the stand, and confidently answered Jolliffe's first question. Had she ever seen any of these defendants?

[Margaret Fisher] I've seen that young man before. I think he is the very boy that staid at our house years ago, but he's grown very much. He stayed all night at Mister Rice's—my father's, at the corner of Hamer and Black streets, about ten years ago. I believe the boy slept with the journeyman. . . . I have no doubt of it at all. He was brought there by a gentleman whom father had

hogs of. I can't recollect his name just now, but would know it if
I heard it.
[Mr. Jolliffe] Was it Marshall?
[Margaret Fisher] Yes, it was.

Jolliffe asked her to point him out and Colonel Chambers objected.
Pendery overruled him and himself asked Margaret Fisher if she could
identify Mr. Marshall. Let the *Gazette*'s Edmond Babb take it from
there:

> The witness [Mrs. Fisher] stood up and looked around for some
> time. It was a moment of intense interest, for the identity of Mar-
> shall with the man who stayed with the negroes at the butcher's
> was all that was wanting to make the evidence complete. A brother
> of Mr. Marshall, who resembles him strongly, rose, and [Mrs.
> Fisher] looked at him eagerly as though about to recognize him
> as the man, but did not speak. Next to him was a man crouched
> down, with the head of his cane to his lips and looking stealthily
> out of the corner of his eyes. At length the witness said: "THAT
> MAN WITH THE STICK TO HIS MOUTH IS HIM." It was
> Marshall.

Again the court erupted in cheers and jeers, and Jolliffe sat down.
    Cross-examining the twenty-seven-year-old Margaret Fisher, Cham-
bers tried hard to rattle the woman's recollections but failed entirely.
She recognized James Marshall even despite the man's beard, which
(she recalled) the Kentuckian hadn't been wearing eight or ten years
ago. Marshall's reactions confirmed that this was so. To another of
Chambers's questions she volunteered (before Chambers cut her off)
that "the little boy [Robert] behaved fust rate; everything his master told
him to do he done." Mrs. Fisher also vehemently denied being coached
on her testimony; in fact, she hadn't seen her father for several days,
until Gitchell and the others found her and brought her down to the
courthouse. Jolliffe was delighted. When Chambers gave up at four-
thirty Saturday afternoon, Jolliffe rested his defense. Pendery scheduled
rebuttal witnesses and closing arguments for Monday, beginning at nine-
thirty, and adjourned.
    Outside the weather had turned bitterly cold, as temperatures

plunged to twelve below zero Saturday night and Sunday morning. By midday Saturday, slush on the streets and sidewalks had turned treacherously slick. That evening, a while after the day's testimony concluded, as the marshal's posse led the Garners out the courthouse's back door to the waiting omnibus, a man leading them pitched headlong downstairs and "broke two of his ribs." It was Deputy John Ellis, the People's Theater usher who once seated Robert Garner.

That night, several miles north of Maplewood, six slaves belonging to a planter named Thomas Bowen "were taken with a sudden leaving." The 1850 census lists Bowen as a Kentucky-born farmer. In 1856 he was sixty-two, his Virginia-born wife, Sophia, fifty-four; residing with them were seven children, ages eight to twenty-seven. The family of slaves probably included a twenty-six-year-old black male, his thirty-one-year-old mate, and four of the five juvenile slaves counted by the census taker.[21] They fled "over the ice bridge" into southeastern Indiana and apparently their freedom, as nothing further was ever recorded about them. Monday's *Gazette* sarcastically called for investigations: "Since everything that facilitates the escape of slaves has been pronounced unconstitutional," the editors demanded Congress investigate "the moral character of Jack Frost" for aiding and abetting fugitives.[22]

On Sunday, their first Sabbath in captivity, the Garners were visited by Dr. W. H. Brisbane, a former South Carolina planter who had emancipated all his slaves and moved to Ohio, where he pastored a large congregation in Cheviot, a community ten miles west of Cincinnati. Known all over southern Ohio and Indiana as an "old-line abolitionist," Brisbane prayed with the fugitives for about a half hour.[23] Otherwise they appear to have had no other visitors. The whole region, in fact, was battened against the cold. Tuesday's *Enquirer* reported low temperatures of twenty-five and twenty-nine below zero on the mornings of Sunday and Monday, "the severest [temperatures] ever experienced in this locality."

Monday, 4 February. Despite the killing cold the Garner trial drew another "immense crowd of spectators to the Court-room." Most were turned away, many adjourned to neighborhood taverns, some actually bundled themselves against the cold to stand vigil on the courthouse steps. Inside, Finnell and Chambers quickly summoned three rebuttal witnesses. Recalled to the stand, George Washington Marshall testified that his uncle James typically drove about one hundred hogs to Cincinnati markets, and that it was a common and (in his view) legal practice for masters to employ their slaves in that work. He also said the slaves always voluntarily returned to Kentucky—a crucial point. Chambers's next two witnesses seconded young Marshall's testimony. None of this bothered Jolliffe, who counterpunched with James Rebold, a free black butcher who had apprenticed for Jacob Rice and recollected a teenaged Robert staying at Rice's house with Marshall, who (Rebold noted) called his slave "Little Sammy" or "Sambo."

With that, Pendery called a noon-hour recess and slated closing arguments for one o'clock that afternoon.

Act III: "wrap this land in flame and drench it in blood"

At one o'clock Monday afternoon Kentuckian John Finnell rose to summarize his case for claimant James Marshall. Finnell promised not "to wear the patience of the court, already tired out by the protracted length of the case." He set aside questions about "the moral aspect of slavery," saying he could not know if "it were a crime" in the likes of Abner Gaines or anyone else's "forefathers to introduce in this fair country the institution of slavery." It had come to Kentucky nevertheless, and "the Federal Constitution" secured for Kentuckians a right to "this species of property." Then he thrust at the North: "Whence did we derive our institution of slavery?" Finnell asked the court, and just as quickly answered: slavery resulted "from the cupidity of Yankee slave dealers." He turned his back on the chorus of hisses.

Despite promising brevity Finnell wasn't through sermonizing. He continued a lengthy introduction depicting himself as a centrist, accepting on one hand states' rights doctrine but rejecting on another "the ultra Southern doctrine of nullification" should federal law ever interfere with slaveholding. Indeed, federal statutes protecting his claimants' rights to human property were clear and must be respected, just as a child respects benevolent parental authority. A provocative analogy, uttered in context with Margaret Garner's infanticide, and Finnell wasn't done with it:

> [Finnell] What are we without the doctrine of the supremacy of the Federal government, leaving to the states their peculiar prov-

ince? It is only the care of a mother for her children, only the superintending of their general progress, and never insisting on more than their provisional and educational care. The Constitution of the United States covers this whole ground: Whatever ultra men may say at the South, or ultra men may say at the North, there is but one interpretation, which is that property in slaves shall be held sacred.

Finnell's analogy thus developed into an extraordinary metaphor. According to it, Columbia, the Union's alma mater, superintends only the "general progress" of her children, the states, and never meddles in "the particulars" of their growth. What, then, if one of those states, such as Kentucky back in 1792 or perhaps Kansas now in 1856, should look for admission to the Union as a slave state? Should Mother intervene, or not? In short, does she treat slavery as a "general" or a "peculiar," a federal or a local, matter? Of course, to John Finnell as to all Southrons slavery was "peculiar" to the states and therefore beyond parental—that is, federal—disciplinary authority. But then Finnell pushed his metaphor still further. Should the federal government or any authority treat slavery as a "general" matter and intervene against it, then the effect would be to kill the Union. In short, to wipe out her children as if during an infanticidal mania. Thus smearing the bloody blame for little Mary Garner's death on those abolitionist Northerners who, according to this metaphor, virtually inspired Margaret's infanticide, Finnell politicizes her tragedy as never before.

With Margaret away at the county jail with her children, Finnell's parable of national infanticide may be variously understood. On the one hand, her absence from the courtroom denied Finnell the added benefit of gesturing toward her for rhetorical effect. On the other, Margaret's not being there was precisely what enabled Finnell or any others in the coming weeks and months, whether pro- or antislavery, to make a symbol out of her. For this is just how thought works: it compensates for absence, especially the absence of definitive meaning, by filling it with symbolic presence, a plenitude of meanings. But Finnell's symbolizing also divided his audience. News writers tell how long gales of cheers and jeers erupted at this point in his two-and-a-half-hour oration.

Still Finnell wasn't through with his metaphor. Turning to Jolliffe ("my friend"), he referred to their sharp exchange during Thursday's session, when Finnell met Jolliffe's image of Kentucky slavery as a "seething Hell" with sentimental allusions to his "own mother" and her "old negro woman," Finnell's mammy. "Sir!" the Kentuckian exclaimed. "I am not a Christian; would to God I were! But I am the son of a Christian mother and I know of no higher law in civil matters than the Constitution." Then, turning to Pendery, he wrapped up this phase of his argument. Jolliffe's "admiration of divine law" was itself admirable but beside the point; his honor's court should instead be concerned solely with civil matters. To Finnell the issue was clear: Would the childlike states be obedient to a good mother who reciprocally indulged some of their "peculiar" tastes, such as for property in slaves? If not, the consequence would be disunion and slaughter of the mother's offspring. The Kentuckian had made his metaphor into a prophecy. Now Margaret Garner's infanticide symbolized impending civil war.

Next Finnell set forward the basis of Marshall's claim for Simon, Mary, and Robert Garner, pursuant (he said) to the Constitution, the 1793 fugitive law, the 1850 compromise, and case law, all of which formed (he thought) a tight package. For here was the legal heart of his argument. He reviewed in detail the testimony supporting Marshall's claim of ownership and proving the slaves' escape, then came to the hypothesis that he knew Jolliffe would urge: "that these persons have been in the state of Ohio, and having stepped upon free soil became free men." After Jolliffe's parade of witnesses Finnell wisely decided not to dispute the slaves' claim of having previously been taken on free soil. Granting that they had sojourned there, he claimed those facts were irrelevant because of legal precedent, found specifically in the well-known case *Strader v. Graham*, one of the most crucial U.S. Supreme Court opinions leading up to *Dred Scott* in 1857.

Jacob Strader and three others co-owned and operated the steamboat *Pike*, out of Louisville. In January 1841, the *Pike* boarded three black "scientific musicians" (minstrel performers), but without any written or other consent of their master, Graham. At a stopover in Cincinnati the slaves absconded North, allegedly making it to Canada. Graham filed suit before a Louisville Chancery Court, seeking a judgment against Strader for the full value of his lost "property" (at a steep rate of $1,500 per slave). His grounds were that the ship captain violated a Kentucky statute that prohibited the transporting of slaves without an accompanying master, or agent, or the master's written consent. Complicating facts came out at trial, however. During the mid-1830s Graham had employed a free black Louisville musician named Williams to train his three slaves, Reuben, Henry, and George. For four years until their escape Graham had also paid Williams to tour his slaves up and down the Mississippi and Ohio rivers, including lengthy sojourns through the free states of Indiana and Ohio. Evidence at trial included a letter from Graham to Williams mentioning two of the minstrels by name and discussing the slaves' trips through Ohio. During those four years steamboat captain Strader had become familiar with the blacks' far-flung travels, and knowing that Williams was manumitted, he mistakenly assumed that Reuben, Henry, and George were also free.

Graham's attorneys argued that in negligently disregarding Kentucky law Strader and the co-owners were liable for the slave owner's loss. Strader's attorney claimed Graham couldn't have it both ways: couldn't tour his slaves on free soil without proper supervision, then sue unwitting parties to the slaves' escape. The Chancery Court's divided opinion mostly favored Strader.[24] Unhappy with that result, both parties took it to the Kentucky Court of Appeals. In a reversal entirely favoring Graham, the Appellate Court rejected the defense's claim that Reuben, Henry, and George were freedmen by virtue of having previously sojourned on free soil. Judge Thomas A. Marshall's 1844 decision for the Kentucky court accepted that Graham's slaves, *whenever* they set foot on free soil, were liberated by the Northwest Ordinance, which in 1787 had laid the foundation of Ohio law. But Marshall also ruled that in voluntarily returning to Kentucky the slaves had renounced any freedom that prior sojourns may have conferred on them. He held that in January 1841 they left Kentucky as fugitives, abetted by Strader, who was therefore liable to Graham for money damages.

Strader appealed to the U.S. Supreme Court, then waited until 1851 for their twofold ruling. The most important but least well understood result in *Strader v. Graham* was this: representing a unanimous bench, Chief Justice Roger Taney simply decided that federal courts had no jurisdiction in the case. He held that the slaves' status, however affected by their having sojourned on free soil, was solely for state courts to adjudicate. In 1851 this was unexceptionable legal doctrine for proponents of states' rights on either side of the slavery question.

That was the Court's straightforward *decision*, which let stand the Kentucky Appellate Court ruling. Another matter entirely was an accompanying *opinion* that Taney, acting wholly separate from the other eight justices, recorded with the Supreme Court's decision. Writing it, Taney argued that whatever may have been the effect of Ohio law on the blacks while sojourning there, in returning to Kentucky (voluntarily or not) they reverted to slavery. Taney claimed "the condition of the negroes as to freedom or slavery after their return depended altogether upon the laws of Kentucky, and could not be influenced by the laws of Ohio; that it was exclusively the power of Kentucky to determine for itself whether their employment in another State should or should not make them free on their return." Then he went even further, dismissing the Northwest Ordinance, which, "*if* still in force, could have no more operation than the laws of Ohio in the State of Kentucky."[25]

Strader cast a dark shadow over Jolliffe's defense. In declining federal jurisdiction the Taney Court affirmed only the finality of Kentucky's decision and not its legal soundness, a matter the whole Court might have reviewed had it accepted jurisdiction. But the Court had declined jurisdiction and *Strader* therefore ought to have carried minimal weight, except for Taney's written opinion. Technically he only offered obiter dicta ("remarks in passing"), but in the last antebellum decade proslavery thinkers seized on Taney's text and erroneously elevated its opinions to legal doctrine. They thought it meant that the Northwest Ordinance was a dead letter and that, in effect, Kentucky law flew like an eagle over the heads of slaves wherever they went, with or without their masters, thus overruling any law of another state or territory regarding slaves—such as Ohio's "free soil" provisions in its 1802 constitution.

In 1857 Taney's opinion would have a powerful effect on *Dred Scott v. Sandford*, but in 1856 its meaning was arguable at every crucial point. Finnell knew it yet still read into the record large portions of Judge Marshall's ruling for the Kentucky Appellate Court, then Chief Justice Taney's Supreme Court opinion. The formality of his recitation, however, scarcely masked the decisive problem. How in the world could a federal Circuit Court Commissioner, a functionary whose ordinary job entailed taking depositions and bonds on behalf of real judges, a functionary whose appointment Congress never ratified (as it must with judge appointees), be given authority to adjudicate a paramount legal question of his time, and do it on the basis of a complex and highly ambiguous instance? Finnell never said how. But the Garners' case had come down to this: either Finnell was right and Justice Taney's obiter dicta in *Strader* meant the Garners' sojourns were immaterial or Jolliffe was right in arguing that once their masters allowed them over the Ohio River the slaves' chains forever fell.

Before sitting down Finnell fired one more shot at Ohio's "fanatics in morals, bigots in religion, and demagogues in politics" by holding up for scorn copies of the Ohio legislature's Margaret Garner resolution of Thursday, 31 January ("one of the most injudicious acts that has ever been enacted by a sovereign state of the Union"). Still he saved a last, vitriolic attack for Jolliffe, epitome of "the political abolitionist"—that "most loathsome thing upon the face of the earth." But here Finnell contradicted himself: "What concern is it of yours what the domestic institutions of Kentucky are?" he asked Jolliffe, "For you cannot stretch the arm of your legislation across to me in Kentucky!" Yet *Strader*, he had just claimed, empowered Kentuckians to project *their* statutes over the river into Ohio. The court erupted in jeers and hisses.

Pendery adjourned until two o'clock Tuesday afternoon, the first break in his methodical schedule. The reason: Judge Leavitt had booked the courtroom that morning for testimony in the "Irish Filibuster Case." Cincinnatians were about to learn how those Sharps rifles came into the hands of Sarsefield Guard members now patrolling the streets as "special deputies" of Marshal Robinson.

Tuesday afternoon, 5 February. As spectators made their way into the courthouse on Tuesday afternoon a black woman confronted "one of the Special Marshals at the Door." The *Gazette*'s Edmond Babb reports their exchange:

> "Why, John!" said she, "is you a officer here?"
> "Yes," said he, with an important air.
> "Why law," said old Aunt Dinah, "how times is changed. Don't you 'member the last time I saw you?"
> "No," said he.
> "Why yes you do—you was on the chain gang."

Inside, James Gitchell carefully reviewed the facts offered in witnesses' testimony, made a brief foray into arguing the unconstitutionality of the 1850 fugitive law, and then concentrated on proving the indecisiveness of *Strader v. Graham*. Evidently Gitchell's was low-grade oratory; none of the papers provide even a single quotation from it, though we would very much like to know specifically how he attacked Taney's obiter dicta on the Strader case.

Wednesday, 6 February. This morning finally brought a slight warming but four inches of new snow, most of it from a squall that rolled in off the river as marshals transported Robert, Simon, and Mary Garner, this time wholly without incident. Now U.S. Marshal Hiram Robinson and Deputy Bennet had in their employ some four hundred special deputies.[26] Robinson, who had returned by express train on Monday, ordered them to line the fugitives' route from jail cell to courtroom, so that from now on incidents of "mob" reaction almost disappeared. Practically speaking, Cincinnati was under martial law, and the legal process could roll mechanically toward its inevitable end.

At nine-thirty Wednesday, John Jolliffe began a three-hour summation, the same argument he had already rehearsed (but not yet published) in his novel *Belle Scott*. He meticulously laid out his argument that the Fugitive Slave Law violated constitutional guarantees of religious freedom, probably knowing in advance that Pendery would reject it. Yet Jolliffe stood rock-solid in making that argument. Indeed he refused to refute Finnell on the applicability of *Strader v. Graham*. Was he simply conceding that legal argument? The fact that he had (at Tuesday afternoon's session) given to Gitchell the job of refuting Finnell on *Strader* indicates that Jolliffe (like many others) considered *Strader* still so indecisive that Pendery would have to fall back on commonsense morality. Therefore Jolliffe built his summation on New Testament scriptures and quotations from English poetry, especially Shakespeare. On that humanistic foundation, he believed, "moral abolitionism" received the warrant for its most urgent work: claiming a Northern sanctuary for fugitive souls.

Jolliffe knew this work required people to feel with and think about slaves as persons, not as property, and that he should enact his commitment to their fellowship with him, as equals. He took care to speak from a position behind the defendants' table, symbolically putting the Garners *before* him, at center court, and forcing Pendery—as well as James Marshall and his lawyers—to look at the slaves in attending to his speech. Jolliffe also made it a point frequently to touch the Garners, placing his hand on a head or grasping a shoulder.[27] He was not patronizing them but suggesting instead something like a clergyman's pastoral care or, for that matter, just a man's loving humanity toward others.

Jolliffe led by turning to the claimants' table, dismissing Finnell's attacks on Ohio abolitionists as an "ill-advised" cannonade using "grape and cannister" to mow down the very "Union-savers" all Kentuckians should regard as brothers. As for Finnell's charge that Ohio was acting the ungrateful neighbor in not promptly returning the Garners, Jolliffe turned to address the audience:

[Mr. Jolliffe] When a poor Kentuckian comes here naked, we clothe him; hungry, we feed him; oppressed, we relieve him; bound on a journey, we put him on a certain railroad and have him through in lightning speed. If Kentucky feels aggrieved, let her ladies retaliate. Let them set up sewing societies for the poor Ohioans.

He was interrupted by "Applause and cries of order," then continued:

No, poor Kentuckians, even the most destitute, find friends and counsel here. For all these people, on both sides of this case, are Kentuckians. The only difference between them is that while they (looking towards the slaves) are heroically struggling for freedom, that man (looking at Mr. Marshall) comes into court, his hands all dripping with warm blood, and asks to take the father of that murdered infant back into interminable slavery and the grandfather back into everlasting bondage.

Again, more "Applause and cries of order."

When Pendery gaveled his court back to order Jolliffe got to the heart of his summation. He was "not here as a theologian to discuss difficult points" but only "a civilian asserting rights," among them his liberty from any government's demands that he do evil. He surveyed a long history of struggle: Daniel's praying despite Persia's refusing him the right, Apostles martyred by the Roman Empire, Protestant "saints" refusing observances required by the Holy Roman Empire. Had the United States become an imperial behemoth? Would they compel one of their members, Ohio, to commit a sin? If so, the Union would fall like imperial Rome.

As for their "right and duty" as Christian people, Jolliffe continued, scripture simply commanded Commissioner Pendery to "love your God with all your heart, and your neighbor as yourself" (Matthew 19:19). It was the right for which Revolutionary fathers "poured out their blood like water," a simple right (he noted) "to love that old man (putting his hand on the head of old Simon) as you love yourself, and to do to him as you would have him do to you, and it is your duty, sitting here in the temple of Justice, to exercise that right." The Commissioner, Jolliffe argued, was under an oath to support "not only the 2nd section of the 4th article but the whole Constitution," especially the First Amendment protection of religious freedom. Perhaps Pendery knew about previous cases, when Jolliffe tried parts of this argument. It was nonetheless the first time an abolitionist had fully tried this novel argument in a U.S. court.[28]

For well over an hour Jolliffe hammered out his key points. Abolitionists, he said, had "for the last twenty-five years been asserting these rights, bearing upon their own shoulders the rights of the whole American people," all the while "hated" and "despised" for their sacrifices. The current case, however, transcended even that sacred political struggle. He stepped over and put his hand on Robert Garner's shoulder:

[Mr. Jolliffe] This man is here a prisoner, guilty of no crime, his wife in jail in a delicate situation, needing her husband's aid, and Mr. Marshall asks you to tear him from his wife's arms. His three children, one an infant at the breast, demand his care, and you are asked to tear him from both wife and children that this man (pointing to Marshall) may take him into Kentucky, to sell his flesh, blood, bones and soul, on the auction block. Do your duties as a Christian interfere with that? Can you do it and keep your conscience void of offense? Can you do it and maintain for the people of the United States the right of religious freedom? Never in the history of jurisprudence has a question of such importance been submitted to the decision of a single man. If you sustain these rights, you sustain religious freedom for us all; if not, you betray humanity.

Again Pendery had to gavel down an eruption of cheers and applause.

Having come back around to basic human rights, where he began, Jolliffe then repeated the cycle. Again he critiqued the constitutional crux, focusing this time on the 1850 fugitive law and its interference with people's First Amendment rights. Again he stepped behind the Garners, this time "putting his hand on Mary's head" and appealing to their sympathy for her as "an old woman" with long membership "in the Church of Christ." Then he invoked the image of Margaret and her children, jailed several blocks away, and turned to Finnell and Chambers:

[Mr. Jolliffe] My friends, what would you have? Just so sure as you tear that suckling babe from its mother, the very stones will rise against you. Not in mob violence, but in six months time the Union will be at an end. And better far that it should end, than to sanction such violence. The Constitution does not require you to do an act which shall wrap this land in flame and drench it in blood.

Acknowledging that "this argument has not been used by any of our great men in the Congress," Jolliffe moved toward his conclusion.

He recapped testimony about the Garners' masters permitting the slaves visits to Ohio. Then, without (again) taking up the challenge posed by *Strader*, Jolliffe simply claimed that "the maxim of the law was, 'once free always free.'" Clearly, he was placing all his bets on the untried constitutional argument for religious liberty. And betting, moreover, on the powerful emotional, humanitarian appeal of this case. Slavery, he argued, was a form of cannibalism, a "roaring, seething, hissing Hell" of sins symbolized by Margaret Garner's child-murder, itself practically beyond comprehension but still a consequence of the claimants' desire to hold property in slaves. Shakespeare, he noted, had tried to show a similarly incomprehensible resolve in Lady Macbeth. But even the Bard could go no further than to have her voice a willingness to kill one of her own children: "I would, while it was smiling at my face/ Have plucked the nipple from its boneless gums/ And dash'd its brains out."[29] If "the poet's imagination could go no farther" than this, Jolliffe wondered, then could James Marshall or Commissioner Pendery do so? Could they further that horror of which the slave mother's infanticide was a symptom by sending the Garners back to the South? To Pendery he said: "I now leave the religious liberty of the United States in your hands. Such a case has never before arisen, and if you separate these

people it will be such a judgment as has never been given since Pontius
Pilate sat upon the judgment seat."

Jolliffe took his own seat next to the Garners, and spectators applauded his effort for some minutes. It was twelve-thirty. Colonel
Chambers, scheduled to deliver the rebuttal summation, begged a continuance to address "the new course of argument"—Jolliffe's First
Amendment defense of the fugitives. Pendery agreed, and adjourned
until nine Thursday morning.

While John Jolliffe was speaking, a Hamilton County grand jury formally received Coroner Menzies's inquest on Margaret Garner's child-
murder and returned four indictments: against Margaret Garner for
murder and against Robert, Mary, and Simon Garner as accessories.
The states' rights showdown had formally commenced. Hamilton
County prosecuting attorney Joseph Cox immediately asked a Criminal
Court judge for a *capias*, a writ commanding officers formally to take
an accused into custody. When it was served at the jail, Sheriff Brashears
summarily "turned the Marshal and the special deputies [who were
guarding the Garners] out" of his building.[30]

Thursday, 7 February. This morning Brashears refused to release the
fugitives to deputy U.S. marshals and so, at nine o'clock, with Chambers
ready to commence his rebuttal, John Jolliffe found himself sitting beside three empty chairs, no doubt delighted at this latest standoff. Hearing that the county sheriff was resisting federal deputies, Mayor James
Farran dashed off an order to his chief of police, Richard Hopkins.
Desiring to preserve "the comity that should exist among the States of
the Union," he ordered Cincinnati police to both assist "the claimants
of the fugitives" *and* to "prevent all molestation" of the Garners. Thus
he ordered Hopkins smack into the middle of a cross fire. No one
seemed to know where events were headed.

At the same moment, in Washington, attorney Montgomery Blair
filed a brief on behalf of Dred Scott, the Missouri slave whose appeal
before Chief Justice Taney's U.S. Supreme Court would bring forth
antebellum America's definitive legal judgment on slavery. That event
passed with scarcely a glance from newspaper reporters, who took
months to realize *Dred Scott*'s importance. In Commissioner John Pendery's crowded court this morning everything remained on hold for an
hour.

We don't know how he managed—by threat, compromise, or cajoling—to have Brashears release Robert, Mary, and Simon Garner, yet by ten o'clock Pendery produced them and Colonel Chambers commenced his rebuttal. Finnell had orated for two hours and a half, Jolliffe for just over three; but with only a half-hour break at noon Chambers addressed the court for nearly five hours. The newspapers agree it was mostly a tedious recitation of precedent-setting decisions in the history of slave laws. For interested souls the *Gazette* merely ticked off his sources: "among them 3 Marshall, 228; 8 Pickering, 136; 6 Connecticut Reports, 493; 5 Monroe, 458 . . . Story's Commentaries Sec. 1802, 3, 4, 5, 6." Chambers's quotations went on and on. When he tried to cite the Revised Statutes of Kentucky both Jolliffe and Gitchell objected on grounds that Kentucky law had no authority in Ohio, but Pendery— minding how proslavery forces interpreted Taney's opinion in *Strader v. Graham*—overruled them and so Chambers rolled methodically forward. He also recited whole sections of the 1850 Fugitive Slave Law.

The only notable moments of Chambers's summation were at its beginning. Some cheered his claim that Jolliffe had rehearsed those white witnesses who testified on behalf of Robert Garner; as for the blacks, he said none "were worthy of credibility." He also took offense at Jolliffe's image of James Marshall's "hands all dripping with warm blood" as being very "unkind":

[Col. Chambers] I know my client to be a man of pure, unblemished character. He will hold up his hands in the sight of God and men, with Mr. Jolliffe or any of his Abolition friends, and let God and the world look upon them and see which has the deepest stain. If there is guilt anywhere except in the heart of that mother it is not with my client, but with those who had incited her to the deed. It was a deed of horror calculated to excite the public mind against slavery—but only to a limited extent and for a brief period.

Thus blaming abolitionists for having "incited" Margaret Garner to child-murder, Chambers denied the woman any free will. He was fantasizing a conspiracy of "fanatics" using her as their tool or *slave*—an outrageous charge for which Chambers was loudly hissed. But there was more to his fantasy:

There is a good time ahead—life to the nation if people will only be quiet. We have the Union yet, and let those who would dissolve it for the sake of the slave remember that in achieving the liberty for three millions of blacks they are periling those of twenty-four millions of the white race.

Here it was: the specter of race war, of "three millions" of bloodthirsty Margaret Garners unleashed and even directed by fanatic Northerners. It was pure demagoguery.

Chambers's decision to follow this paranoid fantasy with a four-hour recitation of statutes and case law symbolized much. It demonstrated his belief, and that of others like him, that the only thing guarding whites from racial bloodbath was the monolith of laws protecting property in slaves.[31] He also argued the position Chief Justice Taney would soon affirm in *Dred Scott v. Sandford*—that slaves weren't citizens with constitutional protections:

[Col. Chambers] I hold that they have no rights, except such as their master chooses to give them. And now, knowing that your Honor's mind must be with me, and believing that justice—only justice—stern justice will be done, I submit the case of my client.

That concluded the trial of James Marshall's claim to Simon, Mary, and Robert Garner. Pendery ordered the Garners back to the county jail, announced he would render a decision on Marshall's claim after hearing Gaines's claim to Margaret and her children, and set the beginning of that trial for ten the next morning.

Robert, Mary, and Simon Garner were taken out to the omnibus under brilliant skies. Temperatures had warmed into the low thirties. Down at the river, crews using dynamite were attempting to bomb holes in the eight-inch sheet of ice so that Covington–Cincinnati ferries might resume service. Blasts thundered off buildings and hillsides like a titanic downbeat to the marshals' solemn parade through a double wall of deputies.

Act IV: "We have proved the property to be A. K. Gaines's"

On Thursday afternoon southern breezes pushed heavy, dark clouds into the Ohio River valley. At dusk a cold rain lashed Covington and Cincinnati. In city taverns dynamiters calculated dawn attacks on the ice bridge and "steamboatmen rubbed their hands in gleeful expectation of a speedy escape from their icy lock." But it was only a tease. The downpour turned first to freezing rain, then heavy snow. Again thermometers fell and all night long it snowed, piling and drifting "to fantastic depths." Beneath lay a thick glaze of ice. Thus "the 'Fugitive-Slave Bridge' added to its solidity" by dawn Friday, 8 February, first scheduled day of hearings on Archibald Gaines's claim to the "labor and service" of Margaret, Tom, Sam, and Cilla Garner.[32]

The Garners were absent from Commissioner John Pendery's courtroom on Friday morning, however. So were Gaines and his attorneys, Finnell, Wall, and Chambers. John Jolliffe was present but stood along a side wall and stepped forward only to tell Pendery that he took "no part in this latest controversy" and had "begged of the Sheriff not to bring [Margaret and her children] in Court" until it was settled.[33] This "latest controversy" was the jurisdictional clash between state and federal authorities. Pendery had staved it off, but now, with all four adult Garners indicted for child-murder, he had to hear arguments and rule on it.

Representing Hamilton County sheriff Gazoway Brashears, attorney George Mills asked Pendery formally to transfer custody of the four Garner adults from U.S. Marshal Robinson to the sheriff.[34] Noting that Brashears already held them "as a courtesy," he remarked that a legal transfer would release Marshal Robinson from "all unpleasant results in pecuniary losses," namely those accrued in payrolls for a force of deputies now swollen to over four hundred and costing Washington, by one estimate, $800 per day.[35] Yet those sums were only a gratuity. The real item on Mills's bill was comity, the legal principle of courtesy or consideration one jurisdiction pays to another by enforcing its laws—a more abstract but, some then said, priceless foundation stone of the Union. Looking back, modern historians have described the fugitive slave question as "the acid test for comity provisions" written into the Constitution's fourth article.[36] The Garner case proves the accuracy of that view.

Still hanging around as amicus curiae was the burly Irishman Jacob Flinn, who claimed he was "astonished at the proposition of Mr. Mills" because it threatened to overthrow the entire Union. An indulgent Pendery let their argument rage all morning and into the afternoon, though it boiled down simply to this: Mills argued that the alleged masters' claims on the Garners involved a suit in replevin (a suit to recover property held by another), in short that it was a civil trial subordinate to any criminal matter, such as the defendants' indictment for murder. Flinn argued that the fugitive slave hearing involved federal statutes with precedence over any state process; he called Mills's motion "a contempt of [Pendery's] court." Mills countered with a warning that, if allowed, Flinn's way would "demolish the gentle bonds preventing civil strife." Each side quoted extensively from statutes and case law, and Jolliffe was probably delighted to see them run on like that. A further delay only blessed the Garners with more time outside the slaveholding South.

The day's most significant exchange, however, unfolded as Pendery queried Mills and Flinn. What would happen, he wondered, if the court should decide to remand the fugitives? On their way to Kentucky, Pendery asked, couldn't Ohio sheriffs empowered by a habeas corpus writ seek to "wrest" the fugitives away from marshals? Moreover, if a claimant from one state made out an affidavit stating his "fear" of such intervention by authorities from another state, couldn't the Commissioner order "a sufficient force to assist the Marshal in carrying the slaves to Kentucky, from whence they escaped?" Didn't the 1850 fugitive law authorize him to call up a *posse comitatus* in such a case? As he listened to him, Jolliffe's heart must have sunk, for the Commissioner was so obviously tipping his hand. Clearly Pendery had already decided the Garner "slaves" had "escaped" from Kentucky on Sunday night, 27 January. Therefore the Commissioner had already decided against Jolliffe's claim that the slaves' prior sojourns on Ohio soil had dropped their chains before they ever departed Kentucky over this winter's ice bridge. Now Jolliffe's whole defense rested on the question of religious freedom.

That explained why Pendery was asking how the court could best ensure the Garners' safe return to Kentucky—he was planning to remand them. But even the question of how best to return the fugitives was already settled, for Pendery, like Hiram Robinson, well knew that U.S. Attorney General Cushing authorized them to call out the militia or a *posse comitatus*. The Commissioner was only using the court to mold public opinion. Late Friday afternoon, when Pendery cut off Mills and Flinn, saying he would "take the question under advisement" and issue a ruling later, it was one more attempt to stage-manage an explosive situation.

The day ended, however, with a fateful question hanging in the air. George Mills asked Pendery: What would happen if the Garners were "delivered up by the Marshal to the master, and taken back to Kentucky?" Was there "any means of bringing them here to answer this crime?" After all, they could not then "be demanded of the Governor of Kentucky as *fugitives from justice* because being taken away [from Ohio] by legal process was not fleeing." Flinn avoided the substance of Mills's question and lamely contended that as property slaves could "not be held to answer for a crime," but Mills deftly countered with a reading of Kentucky statutes holding slaves punishable for capital offenses such as murder.[37] Then he drove at the real issue: "By deciding that a man can hold, as property [in Kentucky], one who has outlawed himself by crime in Ohio," then the consequence of such a decision, he warned Pendery, would "be to render impotent the whole State of Ohio." None of the journalistic accounts represents Pendery as responding to this claim although Mills had cannily circled right back to the vexing issue of comity and Pendery's dilemma with it. Events would soon give George Mills's questions prophetic power.

Saturday, 9 February. Fifteen minutes before nine deputy marshals opened the courthouse doors to spectators. A majority were women who had waited out the cold and light flurries for their chance at a seat. Among them reporters noted prominent abolitionist Lucy Stone, just in from Indiana, where she had been giving antislavery speeches. Probably she had met with Jolliffe to discuss guardianship of the Garner children, should abolitionists succeed in either winning their liberty or purchasing them.[38] Reporters also noted the presence of some free blacks, now admitted for the duration of this trial. To the *Gazette*'s Edmond Babb it was a "curious" sight: "the great variety of complexion, embracing every conceivable shade."[39]

At nine o'clock Archibald K. Gaines was seated with Wall, Finnell, and Chambers; behind him, waiting to testify, were his Boone County neighbors. Jolliffe and Gitchell sat alone. After a quarter-hour wait Pendery sent a deputy marshal with orders to bring on the fugitives but

Sheriff Brashears refused to release them until Pendery decided Mills's motion. Incensed, Pendery brusquely denied the motion to transfer custody and demanded that marshals bring on the defendants or face a contempt citation.

"A little after 10 o'clock, Margaret and her children were brought in." It was their first public appearance in nine days, and spectators fixed their gazes on the fugitives. Ensuing moments produced our most complete word picture of Margaret Garner as the *Gazette*'s Babb, unlike his less sympathetic and more businesslike *Enquirer* and *Commercial* colleagues, took down the scene. He judged she was a mulatto of one-fourth to one-half "white blood," estimated her height at about "five foot three inches," and noted her "delicate" and "intelligent" eyes and forehead. "The African," he thought, appeared mainly in her "broad nose and thick lips." As she crossed the courtroom he began to note her clothes: "She was dressed in dark calico, with a small handkerchief on her shoulders, pinned closely about her neck, and a yellow cotton handkerchief was wrapped turban like or *a la ole Virginy* around her head." Then Babb turned his gaze on the children: "The child in her arms is a little girl about nine months old, and is much lighter in color than herself—light enough to show a red tinge in its cheeks."

Seated at the defense table, Margaret seemed to shy from spectators' gazes. Babb noted that her eyes

> were generally cast down. She would look up occasionally for an instant with a timid, apprehensive glance at the strange faces around her. The babe, with its little hands, was continually fondling her face, but she rarely noticed it, and her general expression was one of extreme sadness. Only once when it put its hand to her mouth we observed her smile upon it, and playfully bite its little fingers with her lips.

Then Babb noted something else, an "old scar" on the left side of her forehead, "just above the outer extremity of her eye brow . . . and on the cheek bone of the same side, another." Sometime on this first day Babb found a moment to ask Margaret "how these scars came there" and she told him, "White man struck me."

Who maltreated her so brutally? Archibald Gaines? He was the only "white man" with authority to strike her that hard. His moodiness and hair-trigger temper, motifs running throughout Margaret Garner's story, make him the likeliest suspect because, by contrast, nothing of the sort ever appeared in the print record on John Pollard Gaines, her master until Margaret was seventeen. Babb seems to have accepted that she meant Archibald Gaines, the most obvious "white man" in court with her, and so he turned his attention to Margaret's children:

> The boys are four and six years old, respectively, and are bright-eyed, wooly-headed, cunning looking little fellows, as almost all little black boys are. Their fat cheeks dimple when they laugh, and they amused themselves most of the time during the trial, by sitting on the floor and playing with the table legs.
> The murdered child was almost white—and was a little girl of rare beauty.

Typical of nineteenth-century white Americans, Babb focused on racial characteristics and, having listed them, seemed to think no more about it.

Oh, but he had. Why that closing memento of the absent yet unforgettable "murdered child," Mary Garner? It sends one back through Babb's paragraphs to observe how racial identity was a key theme. He speculates on Margaret's mixed heritage (was it her father, or a grandparent, who was white?), reads contrasting signs of white and black identity typed on her face, remarks Cilla's still more pronounced white features ("much lighter" and with red cheeks), and contrasts Cilla with the boys' typically African features, counterpointed at the last with the memory of Mary, a "rare beauty" who was "almost white." One mother but different fathers, one black and the other (or others) white: that was the unspoken message in Babb's description of Margaret's children. Racial identity was thus his apparent theme and miscegenation the story, told in code. Importantly, Babb's tacit inquiry into the paternity of Margaret's children tallies with my own inquiry, based on a range of evidence. Moreover, testimony in the just concluded hearing on Marshall's claim had disclosed that Robert was hired out and therefore many miles distant from Richwood Station during much of the previous four-year span. Any attentive persons in the audience would have been wondering about whether Robert fathered all of Margaret's children, and in hours to come Jolliffe would try to probe Gaines's witnesses about just that issue. These developments tell us that some had begun to see paternity as an underlying issue—perhaps a motive—in the Garner infanticide.

With the Garners now in court Pendery dispensed with a reading of the 1850 fugitive law and ordered Gaines's attorneys to call their first witness. Jolliffe objected: the court knew he had a motion for a continuance, which it was obliged to consider. Jolliffe wanted time, he explained, not to round up scattered defense witnesses but to secure a deposition from just one: Margaret's former master, John Pollard Gaines, "now in Oregon." Jolliffe then read into the record Margaret's deposition of Wednesday, 30 January, detailing facts of her 1840 sojourn to Cincinnati. Objecting, Chambers claimed the 1850 law granted Commissioner Pendery no authority to depose a former master, either by subpoena ordering him to Cincinnati or by anyone interrogating Governor Gaines in Oregon. Jolliffe countered that his testimony was important enough that Pendery should either grant the motion to depose him or "compel the claimant to admit the fact that this woman had been in Ohio with her owner's consent." Pendery denied his motion and again called for the claimant's witnesses.

Jolliffe rose again, this time moving that the court sever the trial of Gaines's claim to the children from that of his claim to their mother. He said this would allow Margaret to be sworn as a witness for the children and "to state the facts given in her deposition." Samuel T. Wall objected "most strenuously."

[Mr. Wall] These people [Margaret and the children] are all claimed together as slaves under one warrant, and what the mother might swear to after the frenzy she has exhibited, we do not know, and will not risk.

Again Pendery swiftly cut off debate, denied Jolliffe's motion, and called for the claimant's witnesses.

But Jolliffe had a third motion: he begged the court to appoint for the infant Cilla a guardian *ad litem* (that is, for the purpose of this trial). Evidently Jolliffe had been working hard on possible guardianship of the children, having earlier written to Lucy Stone to inquire about her willingness to take Cilla. Stone had declined because (she said), "my [speaking] arrangements would keep me for some time absent."[40] To Pendery, Jolliffe suggested as an appropriate choice a local Baptist min-

ister, the Reverend A. A. Livermore. Why Jolliffe would ask this only
for Cilla is unclear. Was it because of her infancy? Or because of her
more obviously questionable paternity? This time Francis Chambers
objected:

[Col. Chambers] This proposition is too absurd for argument. It
brings the case where the gentleman [Jolliffe] has all along tried
to put it: that is, within the humanities.

Exactly right, Jolliffe probably said to himself, for, with Pendery having
so obviously decided every legal question, the moral, humanistic arguments were all that remained of Jolliffe's case. But no matter. Pendery
denied Jolliffe's third motion and again called for witnesses.

An afternoon session lasting until four o'clock brought testimony from
two prominent citizens of Boone County, Dr. Elijah Smith Clarkson
and Major William B. Murphy. Clarkson, unwittingly finagled out of
two slaves by his attorney, John Pollard Gaines in 1843, described himself as Archibald Gaines's longtime friend and family doctor. He testified
to knowing the fugitive, "Peggy," and her mother, "Cilly," as Gaines
family slaves of twenty years and more. He told of attending the births
of Margaret's eldest children, Tom and Sam, but (interestingly) not her
two youngest, Mary and Cilla—the lighter mulattoes of more questionable paternity. At Wall's prompting Clarkson also told how John Gaines
transferred all of his real estate, domestic stock, and slaves to his brother
Archibald in the autumn of 1849, then departed for Oregon.

Major Murphy testified to a similarly lengthy friendship with the Maplewood squires. Of the defendant he said, "I know Peggy, there; have
known her for some time, I declare I can't say how long." Like Clarkson,
he affirmed that first Major Gaines and then "the Colonel" claimed her
as their slave and she "served them as such." That was all. From the
record it appears Wall was finished with Clarkson and Murphy in short
order—perhaps fifteen or twenty minutes each.

Cross-examining them, however, Jolliffe was determined to bore in
at two vital points: John Gaines's 1849 sale of the slaves to Archibald,
and the paternity of Margaret's children. Probing both witnesses on the
alleged sale, Jolliffe asked far-ranging questions about the Gaines family,
now scattered in Natchez, New Orleans, southeastern Arkansas, and
Oregon. He asked about Mary Gaines, whom "Peggy" had nursed dur-

ing the 1840 sojourn to Cincinnati. Neither witness recollected that event. They also couldn't recall if they'd ever seen her "nursing" any of John Gaines's infants. Next Jolliffe wanted to know about the family matriarch, Eliza Gaines. Did she claim ownership of Margaret? (Clarkson's answer came in a weird double negative: "I do not know whether Mrs. Elizabeth Gaines does not claim to be the owner of Peggy during her life.") Jolliffe also wanted to know about the formal transfer of these slaves to Archibald. Was there a bill of sale? Clarkson couldn't say and Murphy stated that he wasn't there when the transfer took place; he simply "knew her as Mr. Gaines's woman"—an arresting locution. All of this left the legal fact of ownership in doubt, at best a matter of hearsay or assumption based on custom.

Jolliffe's questions remind us that from 1850 until 1853, when archived letters reveal Archibald and John Gaines finally settling up, legal ownership of the Maplewood slaves was very much in dispute; also, that the slaves themselves experienced anxious years of doubt about their fate; and finally that even by January 1856 they still may have wondered exactly who was their owner. Probably Jolliffe was exploring this material because Margaret herself had confided doubts to him on that score. Moreover, if testimony should reveal that John Pollard Gaines had the only provable title to Margaret, then Jolliffe really would have reason for that continuance to secure testimony from Oregon. It was a long shot and momentarily successful in casting a shadow of uncertainty over the trial.

Jolliffe also tried Gaines's witnesses on the issue of paternity. Questioning Clarkson and Murphy, he first concentrated on whether Robert (whom they persisted in calling "young Simon") was "this woman's husband." Both said he was "known to be" Margaret's husband but neither could supply the how or when of it. Jolliffe elicited testimony about Robert's long absences from Richwood, when James Marshall hired him out. Then he asked Clarkson: "Is he [Robert] the father of these children?" Chambers cut off an answer by quickly rising to say, "We admit that." However, Jolliffe was asking the family friend and doctor for testimony, not about fathering in a general sense, but legal, biological *paternity* of the fugitive children, things otherwise in doubt and therefore not "admissible" *as facts*. Jolliffe rephrased the question but Chambers again blocked him and finally demanded that Pendery move Jolliffe along. Not wanting to trifle over an apparent matter of semantics, the

Commissioner sustained him. Later, Jolliffe met the same cul-de-sac during his cross of Major Murphy, and again Pendery sustained Chambers. Jolliffe, frustrated, quietly announced he was done with Murphy.

Pendery adjourned them until Monday morning, the courtroom cleared, and deputy marshals carried out all three Garner children as Margaret, "taking the proffered arm of the polite deputy U.S. marshal, Mr. Brown, was escorted to the omnibus" under a brilliant sun.[41] A large crowd of sympathetic women waved scarves and called encouragements. Gaines departed immediately for Maplewood, where, his attorneys surely advised him, he had to find something documenting his ownership of Margaret.

That night the People's Theater at Sixth and Vine streets staged "a benefit drama, *The Fugitive Slave*," written and directed by and featuring a Mr. George W. Jamison, billed in two starring roles: in blackface as "Uncle Jerry (an old Negro)" and as "Alonzo, a White Slave." Evidently no playscript of *The Fugitive Slave* survives, but enthusiastic accounts in the *Cincinnati Enquirer* indicate that the drama conveyed no antislavery message. In fact, its depictions of slaveholder benevolence marked the play as having, instead, an obvious Southron allegiance—the reason why some playgoers cried fraud and booed the performance.[42] And just whom was the play supposed to "benefit"? Mainly George W. Jamison himself, for the man appears to have cynically sped his troupe North to stage it during the Queen City's uproar over his nominal subject and then, by Sunday, just as quickly hustled his "high histrionic talent" back South.

Sunday, 10 February. On this, the Garners' second Sabbath in captivity, they worshiped in their cells with Baptist minister P. S. Bassett, a professor at Cincinnati's Fairmont Theological Seminary and apparently, like W. H. Brisbane from the week before, one of several area pastors who preached at the jail on a rotating basis. He too found the Garner males and females still occupying separate cells. Two days later, Bassett, an antislavery man, wrote up his jailhouse encounter for the *American Baptist* newspaper. Other Northern papers such as *The Liberator* reprinted his account as "A Visit to the Slave Mother who Killed her Child."[43] Though it tells us nothing new, it stands as one of the few extant testimonies of Margaret and her mother-in-law Mary. It did, however, cause an extraordinary, though distant, echo: Bassett's text would become the single seed of Toni Morrison's 1987 novel *Beloved*.

Monday, 11 February. At nine in Washington, D.C., in a barely occupied Supreme Court, lawyers commenced oral arguments in the Dred
Scott case.[44] In Cincinnati, overflow crowds once more packed Pendery's court for the last day of testimony in the Margaret Garner fugitive
slave hearings. As he entered the building and brushed off the morning's
lightly drifting snow, the *Gazette's* Edmond Babb noted something new.
All the deputy marshals "appointed to guard this negro woman and her
children" wore "the badge of the Legion of Honor (a red ribbon in the
button hole)." A prideful display of pseudo-military solidarity, he
thought.

At ten o'clock John Finnell called Peter Nolan. For years a part-time
laborer in Richwood Station, Nolan, his wife, and two children lived
just off Richwood Church Road, near James Marshall's plantation. He
had "an understanding that she [Margaret] belonged to" Squire Gaines
but under cross-examination Nolan, like Clarkson and Murphy on Saturday, could not say that old Eliza Gaines *did not* own Margaret. Here
Archibald Gaines produced his bill of sale:

> . . . and on Mr. Finnell's stating that he knew it to be J. P. Gaines's
> handwriting—that he corresponded with him, etc.—it was admitted
> without being legally proven. It read as follows: "I have sold and
> delivered to A K Gaines five slaves: Sam, Harry, Peggy, Hannah,
> and Charlotte, and all my right and interest thereto, for the sum
> of $2,500, which sum I acknowledge the receipt of. Given under
> my hand this 17th day of November, 1849.

This paper laid to rest the issue of ownership.

After Nolan came two more Richwood farmers, John Ashbrook and
James Marshall. Both testified to knowing "Peggy" for fifteen or twenty
years, and to "understanding" that Squire Gaines "owned her labor and
service." As to the children, first Ashbrook said that he knew "the two
eldest children," Tom and Sam, but not "the youngest." Marshall also
said he knew "Peggy and the two eldest boys," but not her youngest. It
looked suspiciously like Gaines's neighbors had either decided or been
counseled to stonewall discussions of Margaret's "almost white" girls. If
Jolliffe wanted to question the Garner girls' paternity he would get no
help from Boone County's loyal planter aristocracy. With that show of

white fraternity Finnell closed his case by entering as evidence the entire portion of *The Revised Statutes of Kentucky* pertaining to slaves.[45]

Jolliffe immediately began calling defense witnesses and focused on the practice of slave girls employed to "nurse" (or mind) masters' children. Gaines's witnesses had said they never heard of such a thing; Jolliffe called five black women, all former slaves now in their twenties and thirties, who began "nursing" white infants when only five to seven years old. Jolliffe then put before Pendery a copy of the murder indictment against Margaret Garner, and Chambers vigorously protested. "It cannot possibly make *any* difference as to the *status* of this woman, as to whether she owes labor and service to Archibald K. Gaines or not," Chambers argued. He said the state of Ohio would have to wait until after the federal process was completed. Pendery must do so, "lest the Union be severed."

The trial had circled back to the issue of comity and now Jolliffe countered with an argument he might have used on Friday, had he been given the job instead of Mills. Beyond asserting Ohio's right to claim persons indicted for capital crimes, Jolliffe (correctly) pointed out that federal courts never had ruled on such a conflict of jurisdictions; Pendery, who therefore had absolutely no precedent, was honor-bound to remand "these persons" over to Hamilton County sheriffs and let claimants Marshall and Gaines file an appeal before the federal courts. This made good sense. After all, should Pendery rule against them, the Fugitive Slave Law denied the Garners any right of further appeal, whereas the claimants *did* have that right. Thus everyone might be satisfied, and a complex question in constitutional law properly settled. As an added point, Jolliffe argued that the 1850 law was superseded by a Tenth Amendment clause reserving to states all rights not expressly assigned to federal jurisdiction: for example, the right to execute its own criminal laws.

Pendery let arguments run for nearly an hour, then refused to receive Jolliffe's copy of the Hamilton County murder indictment. "The Court," he said, "already has a motion pending on this question." It was becoming increasingly clear that Pendery would ultimately rule for the Kentuckians, but he did give Jolliffe a small victory: permission (over Chambers's objection) to call Margaret Garner as witness for her children. Perhaps Pendery's way of balancing the slate, it provided an incredible moment. Margaret Garner's testimony was quite possibly the only time after passage of the 1850 law that an alleged fugitive slave was allowed to speak before a U.S. court in his or her own defense.

[Mr. Jolliffe] Were you ever in Ohio before?
[Margaret Garner] Yes, sir.
[Mr. Jolliffe] When?
[Margaret Garner] I came here when I was about seven years old. I came here with John Gaines and his wife; her name was Eliza Gaines. They came on a visit to Mr. Bush's, who lived in Covington, and stayed there a week. During that time they spent one day over here, and they brought me over to nurse the baby; that was Mary Gaines. Mary wasn't quite as large then as my baby [Cilla]. They brought me across the river to Cincinnati. We came over pretty soon in the morning, and stayed tolerable late in the evening.
[Mr. Jolliffe] Where did you stay while in the city?
[Margaret Garner] I don't know whether it was a tavern or a private house they stopped at, and I don't remember the name of the people where they stayed.
[Mr. Jolliffe] Do you remember anything else from your visit to Cincinnati?
[Margaret Garner] I don't recollect anything particular on that day I was over here, except that my mistress was very particular in keeping me close by her. She kept me sitting by her all the time. I don't know what they came over here for.

Margaret testified to a number of other details: that on 4 June 1856, she would be twenty-three years old; that "Mr. John P. Gaines was my master at that time [of the 1840 visit to Cincinnati]"; and that Mary Gaines, now aged seventeen, was presently living at Maplewood. This was surprising new information that raised an obvious question: if Mary Gaines was available, and just eighteen miles away, then why hadn't Gaines offered her as a witness? Not that she would recall an event from her infancy, but she might well know something about this and other important questions, such as the prior ownership of her father John Gaines. Looking back, though, one is struck by the fact that while the defense had called a range of witnesses, blacks and whites, women and men, the claimants' witnesses had, to the last one, been white males. Except-

ing day laborer Peter Nolan they were, to a man, patriarchs of the peculiar institution.

Margaret Garner's testimony concluded with statements that all three
children were hers and, of course, born after the visit. Jolliffe then
wrapped it up with a crucial question:

[Mr. Jolliffe] Do you know who claims to own you?
[Margaret Garner] As far as I understand, old Mrs. Gaines owns
me. I live with her and have often heard her say, when Mr. [Ar-
chibald] Gaines was by, that I was her servant. I never heard him
deny it.

Jolliffe then turned to Colonel Chambers with an invitation to "take the
witness," but Chambers smugly rebuffed him: "I've nothing to say to
her."

With that snotty remark, testimony concluded.[46] Pendery scheduled
closing arguments for Tuesday morning, beginning at nine. Outside on
Monday afternoon the snow flurries had turned to a light misting rain.
Streets and sidewalks were heavily coated with slush and as temperatures
fell with the darkness that slush turned to a thick plate of ice.

Tuesday, 12 February. Samuel T. Wall presented the closing statement on behalf of Archibald K. Gaines, casting the drama as a sectional
fight dividing South and North even while promising to avoid sectional
rhetoric and stick to the matter at hand: "I shall not pander to the
passions of the people of the South," he said. "I shall not discuss the
chivalry of the Southern people, nor the magnanimity and benevolence
of the people of the North." Still, Wall immediately pushed his rhetoric
into a field of familiar, divisive clichés:

[Mr. Wall] What was the condition of these people in Kentucky?
They were well cared for, as is evidenced by their appearance in
Court. They were enjoying the comforts of a family in which themselves and their ancestors have long been held as slaves and from
whom they always received great kindness. The slavery of Kentucky
is in so mild a form that I infinitely prefer it to the poverty of the
North. The condition of slaves in the South is much better, I assure
your honor, than the half-starved free-colored people of the North.
The desire of these people to go into the seething cauldron of

Northern fanaticism is not attended with any beneficial results, either to themselves or their brethren in the South. It only serves to fasten the chains of slavery more firmly around them. It only serves to bind the fetters closer.

Wall was ignoring the obvious "evidence" of Margaret's scars and ticking off the favorite Southron clichés. Northern free labor was inferior to slavery at the South, with its patriarchal benevolence; and Kentucky slavery was the best of all worlds—if only those abolitionist fanatics would leave it alone.[47]

Fracturing common sense, Wall blamed "fanatical" abolitionists for prolonging Kentucky slavery; indeed, forcing masters to "abolish" slavery in the state by selling their trusted and beloved chattels to the Cotton South's Simon Legrees. He continued for some time in this groove. His own father, Wall claimed, used to discuss how to "gradually emancipate" his many slaves and "get rid of the evil," but abolitionism, "a weed of recent growth," had disrupted Nature's course. Now, he said, "in Kentucky thief and abolitionist are synonymous terms." In this or any of the recent fugitive cases Kentucky was "not the aggressor. The debt which Ohio owes to Kentucky, and which she in turn owes to the mother of States, Virginia, ought to be better repaid than by stealing slaves from these States." We can well imagine Archibald Gaines, son of a Virginia immigrant, approving that statement of filial allegiance. His friend and neighbor Benjamin Franklin Bedinger regularly penned such arguments in guest editorials for the *Covington Journal*.

Wall reminded the court of the city's upcoming Washington's Birthday celebration. Using it to call up images of the founding fathers and their worries over disunion, he charged that Jolliffe and his cohort were deliberately fomenting sectional division and civil war, imaged as "an ocean of blood" loosed by Ohio fanatics. He began to conclude:

Abolitionists have united together, for what purpose? Why, sir, to steal Kentucky negroes. To steal that property which is sacred to us, and which is protected by our National Constitution. What effect will your decision have on the interests of the people of the South? It will only restore what is rightful. I need not examine the testimony. We have proved the property to be A. K. Gaines's, and that we are entitled to the possession of that property. We have been disposed to give no offense. Instead of taking these slaves back to Kentucky, as we might have done by aid of the friendly bridge of ice, by force from the house of Elijah Kite, we have appealed to the courts of the country.

The claimant, Wall stated, was a man of good will and obedience to the law; and the abolitionist, by contrast, a man-stealer who incited the innocent slave to bloody deeds.[48]

Wall summarized their case without once referring to legal precedent. On the overriding constitutional issue of comity he remained silent, and the defense motion asking Pendery to continue the case until after Ohio tried the murder indictment Wall characterized as a "very singular device," cynically calculated "to avoid the responsibilities of the Fugitive Slave Law." As for defense arguments that Margaret (and therefore her children) were emancipated as a consequence of her trip to Cincinnati with John Gaines in 1840, Wall sidestepped legal precedent on the question and attacked Margaret herself:

This, sir, is the testimony of this woman who has barbarously murdered one of her children, whose hands have been imbued in the blood of her offspring. Of what benefit can her testimony be? Not being competent as to herself, how can it avail her children?

Wall was insisting on having it both ways. First the slave mother's infanticide should not be tried in a Northern court because, in effect, it did not matter; killing little Mary Garner was only a "singular device" calculated to avoid being returned to that kinder, gentler slavery of Kentucky. In short, it was a rational, sane act. But on the other hand her infanticide mattered enormously to the Southerner's argument for return of his property, because her deed proved the slave mother's insanity and thus her complete untrustworthiness as a witness.

By its end, Wall's summation was a hive of contradictions. Having earlier argued the moral goodness of Kentucky slavery, compared to freedom at the North, he concluded by saying, "It is not my province to argue the moral right or wrong of slavery." And he had spoken but little on the facts and even less about legal precedent, but wound up his speech saying, "I have only given to the Court my humble views upon the facts in this case." With that Wall was content to leave "the

matter with the Court" and sit down. It was ten-thirty. During the first
trial, James Marshall's attorneys made their summations into lengthy
orations running two to three hours each. This time, increasingly confident of Pendery's decision, they wanted a swift conclusion of the
drama.

Pendery called on Jolliffe, who, in a surprise move, yielded to Samuel
S. Fisher, a Cincinnati attorney and sometime abolitionist, who took up
the question of comity. Jolliffe, it was plain to all, did not feel well this
morning and had therefore divided the summation into three parts.
Fisher took the first shift. Speaking until the noon recess, he detailed
case law on the subject of comity and attacked as "almost unthinkable"
the claimants' petition to override those precedents with the 1850 fugitive law. Pendery, he argued, could not grant their plea because in
denying Ohio the right to prosecute crimes against its citizens, the Commissioner would deny its sovereignty, destroy the rules of comity, and
thus nullify the Union.

After the recess Jolliffe's assistant James Gitchell took the second shift,
speaking as in the first trial by reviewing case law on slaves emancipated
when their masters sojourned with them on free soil. Then Gitchell
argued that because Pendery would not grant a continuance to get testimony from John Pollard Gaines the Court had no choice but to accept
as fact Margaret's 1840 visit to Cincinnati. This being the case, he argued that Margaret's sojourn, however brief, automatically freed her and
therefore all three surviving Garner children.

Around three in the afternoon Jolliffe rose. We know very little about
his final remarks in defense of Margaret Garner. The *Gazette* simply
remarked that he "closed on the part of the fugitives"; the *Enquirer*, that
he spoke "in his usual pathetic and forcible manner." The *Commercial*,
our best source, still supplies only a brief summary of his speech. Apparently Jolliffe briefly reiterated his argument from the first trial, concentrating again on the fugitive laws of 1793 and 1850, acts that (he
said) required Christians to do evil and that fatally conflicted with First
Amendment guarantees. As before, Jolliffe addressed Pendery from behind the defendants' table and often rested his hand on Margaret or on
one of her children. As before, he was roundly applauded, or hissed.
Jolliffe concluded at four in the afternoon and Pendery scheduled Colonel Chambers's rebuttal for ten the next morning.

Thus far Margaret's trial had moved considerably faster than the first.

Also unlike the first, it hadn't been punctuated with bizarre outbursts: no drunks raging from the audience, no assaults on Levi Coffin's hat, no shillelagh-wielding deputy marshals, and only a bit of the notorious Jacob Flinn. Either Pendery had taken command of courtroom decorum or, what is more likely, the first trial's protracted length had tempered everyone. In any event, the drama's penultimate act had been staged with deliberate speed.

Act V: "He promised me he would make her free!"

Late Tuesday afternoon, a remarkable confrontation occurred before deputies escorted Margaret and her children from the courthouse. Abolitionist speaker Lucy Stone first met briefly with Deputy Marshal Brown, probably asking him to delay returning Margaret to her cell. Then she strode up to Archibald K. Gaines, introduced herself, shook hands with him, and pulled up a chair. For fifteen minutes Lucy Stone and Archibald Gaines had what the *Enquirer* described as a "considerable conversation, the nature of which we did not ascertain." Neither did anyone else know what they spoke about, Gaines's attorneys having exited the courtroom. After meeting with Gaines, Stone crossed the room and "conversed with Margaret for some time. We have heard it said her object is, in case the slave-mother should be sent back into slavery, to purchase her freedom, if found out on what terms her emancipation can be secured."[49] Later reports indicate that Gaines promised to submit a fair price for Margaret and the children; in turn Stone promised to start a charitable subscription and meet his price. John Jolliffe listened intently as the famous feminist and abolitionist described this plan to Margaret, whose hopes must have soared at the possibility even though nothing was said about plans to purchase Simon, Mary, and Robert Garner from James Marshall.

Wednesday, 13 February. "Col. Chambers commenced his argument a little after 10 o'clock . . . and closed at ten minutes before 2 P.M."[50] With Pendery recessing for just fifteen minutes at noon, Chambers orated for three and a half hours, fewer than his effort in the first trial yet still a prodigious job. From the little that newspaper accounts tell us of his closing rebuttal, it is clear Chambers walked Pendery over the same ground as before: acres of statutes and precedent-setting decisions that he endlessly quoted. Once more he fantasized a bloodbath if the Commissioner failed to uphold the 1850 fugitive law. Once more he dismissed the murder indictment as a cynical attempt to deny Southern gentlemen their "property." Once more he attacked Ohio abolitionists for "inciting" Margaret Garner to child-murder.

Then he unleashed a surprise attack. Chambers charged that when marshals were leading Margaret from the courtroom on Tuesday afternoon, Lucy Stone had approached and "asked of the Deputy Marshal, Mr. Brown, the privilege of giving [Margaret] a knife, that she might destroy herself in case she was remanded back to slavery." Chambers also alleged that Jolliffe, already sympathetic to the fugitives' claim they would go "singing to the gallows" rather than be remanded to slavery, now had masterminded this "nefarious" conspiracy to deny Kentuckians their property and to defy the court. Jolliffe's training in Quaker non-violence worked overtime to control his rage.

When Chambers finished his rebuttal argument Jolliffe immediately rose to deny the charge. He regretted "that Mrs. [Stone] was not present to answer the attack the gentleman had made upon her." Colonel Chambers rose to say he regretted it too; he would like to interrogate Stone about the plot. Providentially, the *Enquirer* tells us, just at that moment "Mrs. [Stone] entered, and, on application by Mr. Jolliffe, opposed by counsel on the other side, the Court gave her permission to reply to Col. Chambers. She, however, preferred not to speak at the bar, but, as it was near the time of closing, requested the audience to remain a few moments after the adjournment." This was deftly managed. A practiced antislavery activist, Lucy Stone resisted answering a court whose legitimacy the movement questioned. She would take her case before the tribunal of American public opinion.

With that, the hearing on Archibald Gaines's claim to "the labor and service" of Margaret, Tom, Sam, and Cilla Garner concluded. Pendery was very brief:

> [Commissioner Pendery] As many new points have arisen in this case which have never been fairly adjudicated, the Court should, in justice to all parties and itself, take ample time for investigation. This it should do conscientiously, endeavoring to know nothing but the law and the facts in this case. Therefore the Court fixes

Wednesday, the 12th of March, four weeks from today, to give its decision.

[Col. Chambers] Your honor, I object, because in fixing so distant a day, the Court only increases the expense to my clients.

[Jacob Flinn] Your honor, I think it would be better not to announce the day, so as to avoid collision between the Sheriff and the United States.

Flinn's thought was that if Pendery gave no advance notice of his decision, marshals could speed the Garners over the river and avoid jurisdictional conflict. Chambers was thinking of money. Jolliffe said not a word, doubtless delighted with a four-week delay. Here Pendery was giving attorneys more time to work up both public opinion and a habeas corpus appeal, and giving the Garners at least four weeks more on free soil. Jolliffe was pleased when Pendery dismissed Flinn's and Chambers's objections.

Deputy Marshal Brown escorted Margaret and her children to the waiting omnibus, Pendery retired to his chambers, and the court "then resolved itself into a meeting." Archibald Gaines remained seated with his attorneys; Jolliffe and Gitchell likewise kept their seats at the defendants' table. By acclamation, a Mr. Pullen "was appointed chairman" and invited Lucy Stone to speak. "She was dressed in a black silk gown, had a brown merino mantle over her shoulders, a bonnet of the same material on her head, and a green veil." Thus mimicking Pendery's judicial robes, Stone added to the effect by mounting the bench, where she "took the Judge's desk." She addressed the packed courtroom "in an easy, assured manner, without excitement or violence, never so much as raising her voice beyond the low, penetrating tones peculiar to her."[51]

[Lucy Stone] I have been informed that Mr. Chambers has spoken of my having offered to the poor woman now under examination a knife. I wish to explain in the right place, where the matter has been spoken of, what I said, and the motives that led me to say what I did.

I did not ask of Deputy Marshal Brown the privilege of giving a knife. If Mr. Brown were here, he would acknowledge as much. I have been out of town ever since the commencement of this examination until the day before yesterday, or I should have been here every day, doing what I could to show my sympathy for my afflicted sister. When I came here and saw that poor fugitive, took her toil-hardened hand, and read in her face deep suffering and an ardent longing for freedom. Her eye beamed with the dull light of despair, the tear of anguish trickled down her cheek, her lip quivered in silent agony as I took her hand and expressed my sympathy. I told her that a thousand hearts were aching for her, and they were glad that one child of hers was safe with the angels. Her only reply was a look of deep despair—of anguish such as no word can speak.

I thought, as I looked upon her unexpressed grief, that if ever there was a time when it was a good deed to give a weapon to those who fought the battle of liberty on Bunker's Hill—if those patriots had the right to use the arms supplied to them—she who had said, "Let us go to God rather than go back to slavery," had the same right.

So that was it: Lucy Stone had wanted weapons for these people to fight for their liberty like heroic Patrick Henry, and perhaps to die in the effort rather than fail and be returned to slavery. She had been talking revolution, not suicide. Or had she?

I turned to Mr. Brown and expressed my wish that she could have a knife to deliver herself, dreading as she did slavery to such an extent that she had taken the life of her dear child rather than return it.

Thus it was both: the slave's suicide destroyed Massa's property and was therefore a revolutionary act. But Stone's rhetoric reached still further, to encompass sentimental nineteenth-century discourses of mother love and Christian sacrifice:

Who that knows the depths of a mother's love does not estimate the sacrifice she had made? If she had a right to deliver her child, she had a right to deliver herself, so help me Heaven! I would rather tear open my own veins, and let the earth drink my blood, rather than wear the chains of slavery. How then could I blame her for wishing her child to find freedom with God and the angels, where there are no chains?

Then Stone made a still more extraordinary reference. Conjuring the image of those Garner children just taken from the courtroom, she asked the audience to read their faces:

The faded faces of the negro children tell too plainly to what degradation the female slaves submit. Rather than give her little daughter to that life, she killed it. If in her deep maternal love she felt the impulse to send her child back to God, to save it from coming woe, who shall say she had no right to do so? That desire had its root in the deepest and holiest feelings of our nature—implanted in black and white alike by our common Father.

There it was: the whole previously unspoken subtext of Margaret's sexual bondage to Archibald Gaines and the paternity of her children. Spectators gasped, then the courtroom erupted in cheers and counterpointing hisses.

It was an amazing moment. If the Garner case could not find justice before the federal bar it might find recompense at the bar of public opinion. For abolitionists this was one purpose for the drama since its opening scenes two weeks earlier and now, though Margaret and her children were absent, Lucy Stone had grabbed the chance to indict Archibald K. Gaines to his face—shaming him, all but naming him an adulterer and miscegenator. This done, she defended herself against Chambers's charge:

I asked no privilege of the Marshal—I beg my rights of none. I had a right to put a dagger in the woman's hand—the same right that those who had seized their weapons to fight about a paltry tax on tea! I hoped to see her liberty rendered her—I hope it still. I do not know the Commissioner of this Court, but I doubt not he is accessible to the cry of the oppressed. He should act true to his conscience, true to right, true to Heaven, and deliver this victim from the hands of oppression.

I know not whether he has little children, else I would appeal to him to know how he would like to have them torn from him;

Cincinnati-based abolitionist and feminist
Lucy Stone, ca. 1860
FROM ALICE STONE BLACKWELL, *LUCY STONE:*
PIONEER OF WOMEN'S RIGHTS (1930)

but I feel that he will not disregard the Book which says: "Thou shalt not deliver unto his master the servant which is escaped from his master unto thee; he shall dwell with thee, even among you, in that place which he shall choose in one of thy gates, where it liketh him best."

I make no apology to this Court, or to anyone, for wishing to give this woman a dagger. I apologize to nobody; I exercised the same right as those who distributed weapons to the combatants on Bunker's Hill. God gave this woman a love of liberty, and she has a soul worthy of the gift. If she prefers liberty with God to oppression with man—if she desires for her children the guardianship of angels rather than the scorn and lash of slavery—let her have them, and find in immortality a refuge from wrong and insult.

Next Stone turned directly to the man whose honor she had most extraordinarily blackened:

I told him who claims her—I do not say her owner, for God has made no man owner of another—I told him that this was a historic period; that the deeds now doing would employ the pen of genius, and be handed down to future generations; that his name would be connected with the events now occurring, with execration if he continued to enslave one capable of such deeds as this woman, but with honor if he gave her the freedom that was her right. As I looked into his kindly face, his mildly beaming eye, I thought he had a generous heart, and so it proved. He kindly said, when he had her back in Kentucky under his own care, he would render her liberty. He said, "If I get her back to Kentucky, I mean to make her free." I hope he will fulfill his promise.

I give all notice here, and say it in the hearing of my sisters who are present, that whenever and wherever I have an opportunity of offering opposition to the Fugitive Slave Law, and thwarting its operation, whatever may be the consequence, *I will do it!*

For some minutes, reporters tell us, "there was considerable applause, mingled with hisses, the applause predominating."[52]

Lucy Stone took a seat beside John Jolliffe, then Colonel Chambers rose and, after the spectators were quieted, "begged to offer a statement" before them:

[Col. Chambers] I desire to say, on behalf of my client Mr. Gaines, that he made no such promise as had been spoken of. He had agreed to consider what the lady said, when he returned to Kentucky.
[Lucy Stone] He promised me he would make her free!
[Col. Chambers] I do not care how it is. I speak to a point of law to prevent a claim.

With its obvious insinuations of sexual infidelity, miscegenation, and clandestine paternity Lucy Stone's carefully staged oration had outraged Archibald Gaines's honor before his entire community. She had broken through the Southron's code of silence about such matters. But in thus placing on view issues that social and legal decorum left unspoken, had she also changed Gaines's mind? At that moment did he decide to renege on his promise to sell Margaret and her children? The slaves' fate was his great trump card. To many, it looked as though Lucy Stone forced him to play it. Then the impromptu meeting adjourned.

Near Florence, in Boone County, Kentucky, six slaves belonging to planter Robert Wilburne took advantage of the weather and the ice bridge to make their break for liberty. The party included three men, one of whom brought his mother, wife, and two children. Rumor had it that the party crossed over into Cincinnati during the early morning hours, made it to Levi Coffin's store at Sixth and Broadway, and were "put on the northbound cars of the U.G.R.R." Asked by their pursuing master to hunt down the slaves, Deputy U.S. Marshal George Bennet told Wilburne he declined to "have anything more to do with runaway niggers."[53] Weeks later there was still no word on the fugitives, who probably made it safely to Canada.

4

SLAVE

❦

"A question of property"

Warm southern breezes pushed into the Ohio Valley on Wednesday, 13 February. For the first day in over two months temperatures rose above freezing and stayed there, and the next day, Thursday, highs in the fifties began melting packed snow from Cincinnati streets and once more raising steamboatmen's hopes. By Friday, with the thaw still holding, crews packed gunpowder into gallon-size crockery jugs and attacked the river. All that morning blasts echoed up city streets and off the hills, but by day's end the bombs had merely punctuated the ice with another set of meaningless black asterisks. Mayor Farran rejected a call to bring in Army artillery. How could troops get a correct angle to fire on the ice? Or control cannonballs ricocheting off of it? There was no choice but to wait out the thaw.[1]

Pendery had adjourned court nearly into the spring, although nobody involved with the case thought he would really wait until 12 March before remanding the Garners to Kentucky slavery—the decision everyone anticipated. Cincinnati newspapers surmised that Pendery set aside four weeks because he knew attorneys would file a spate of habeas corpus writs in various courts and he meant to give judges ample time to rule on them, the last legal barriers keeping James Marshall and Archibald Gaines from the Garners. Pendery certainly wanted all court dockets cleared of Garner case business before issuing his own ruling; that way deputies could immediately escort Margaret and her family over to Kentucky and perhaps avoid the civil chaos worrying U.S. Marshal Hiram Robinson.

Action in the case was about to shift from Pendery's courtroom to other courts, city offices, and Cincinnati streets. Everyone connected with the case expected the Commissioner to rule in favor of the slave masters and thought it was only a matter of when he would do it and how he would manage the fugitives' return to Kentucky. Would sheriffs sworn to uphold Ohio laws resist when federal marshals tried to take people indicted for murder outside the state? If so, what course would Pendery take? Could the dispute flare into physical rather than merely oratorical confrontation? How would John Pendery—just a Commissioner—react to threats of Kansas-like violence?

These were legitimate questions, following the previous weeks' zealous courtroom rhetoric. But first came the legal issues, and Pendery's cooling-off period gave antislavery attorneys time to test the wills of local and federal judges, sheriffs, and marshals. Their means of attack, all knew, would be with habeas corpus writs, highly problematic in such cases because of the fugitive law's "peculiar," hybridized status.

Following the United States' first (1793) Fugitive Slave Law, federal authorities treated fugitive hearings as civil suits rather than criminal trials. Runaways were neither charged with nor punishable for crimes, and habeas corpus writs—typically used to force arresting officials to either charge or release suspects—therefore should have been wholly out of place during fugitive processes. Yet deputies routinely kept runaways in state and federal jails; treated them, in short, *as criminals*, and abolitionist lawyers soon learned to block fugitive processes by using habeas corpus—a tactic that the 1850 Fugitive Slave Law was designed to block. The new law prohibited the use of habeas corpus writs in fugitive cases and allowed federal marshals to house alleged runaways, in addition to anyone suspected of aiding or abetting them, in federal cells. It also granted marshals authority to compel help from bystanding citizens during a fugitive's arrest and detention—the sweeping police power that John Jolliffe attacked as a violation of his First Amendment rights to religious liberty. Despite the new law, 1850s court battles still concentrated on the fundamental legal questions: Was the fugitive a criminal or civil defendant? Depending on the answer to that question, what rights did she have? The standard proslavery reply held that she was neither a criminal defendant nor a party in a civil suit but a "species of property." Therefore, even while (technically) a person before the bar of justice she had none of a citizen's ordinary civil liberties—for example, the right of habeas corpus. In 1850 John Crittenden, a former Kentucky governor, who had become Millard Fillmore's Attorney General, wrote in an opinion that fugitives had no access to habeas corpus rights.[2] But in 1856 few believed a federal Attorney General's opinion had legal force over the state judges, who typically issued such writs. Indeed, the U.S. Supreme Court wouldn't give Crittenden's opinion the full force of law until 1857, in *Dred Scott v. Sandford*. Thus for both sides in the Garner case, the whole matter was still debatable. This is why, in his summation for client James Marshall, Colonel Francis Chambers spoke a half hour to back his claim that "they [the Garners] have no rights, except such as their master gives them."

Fugitive cases turned on questions of rights and jurisdictions. In 1856, Ohio statutes treated Margaret Garner and her family as persons having claim to (almost) all civil rights. (The exceptions: Ohio blacks couldn't vote or sit on juries.) Although, like other Northern states, Ohio accepted Kentuckians' rights to hold slaves and deny their civil rights, still Ohio said: once those blacks walked on Ohio soil their natural rights were restored. On the other hand, Kentuckians claimed that slaves had no civil liberties, wherever they might go; moreover, Kentuckians thought that *Strader v. Graham* (a highly problematic case) upheld their claim and therefore that Northerners used habeas corpus writs in defiance of federal law. Northerners replied that defiance was exactly their point.

These habeas corpus battles repeatedly demonstrated how U.S. fugitive slave law was wrought from a brittle alloy. Seizing it in the name of states' rights and, eager for the irony, applying to it the massive torque of Calhoun's classically Southron argument against federal intervention in local institutions, the abolitionists' aim was to break the Slave Power down. Over and over, in state after state, their method was powerful but simple: petition a sympathetic state judge for a habeas corpus writ, use it to remove the fugitive from federal authority, and then, on grounds that Ohio (or Pennsylvania or New York or Massachusetts) statutes do not recognize slavery, ask the judge to order her immediate release and thereafter count on her stealthy disappearance or an abolitionist "rescue." Sometimes it worked. Sometimes federal marshals simply rearrested the fugitive outside the state courthouse and the cycle began anew. Exactly the circus Commissioner Pendery wanted to avoid.

So familiar were these strategies that, within a day after Margaret's infanticide, proslavery papers like the *Cincinnati Enquirer* and the *Covington Journal* angrily predicted a habeas corpus battle, while antislavery papers like the *Cincinnati Gazette* and the *Cincinnati Commercial* eagerly anticipated it. And rightly so. Federal courts never had decided a case where the fugitive committed a capital crime on free soil. Never had the jurisdictional dispute been more perfectly defined than in Margaret's case, and never was there a more crucial habeas corpus battle. Now Pendery expected it to commence in earnest.

Instead nothing happened. For a week after Pendery's adjournment interested attorneys refused to let Pendery call their hand. Determined to wait him out, they held off petitioning state courts for help. Hamilton County sheriff Gazoway Brashears similarly did nothing to execute his outstanding *capias*, the writ commanding officers to formally take custody of the adult Garners under indictment for Mary Garner's murder. It looked like a stalemate. Meantime the Garners themselves were reported as resting comfortably but anxiously in their adjacent cells. The *Gazette*'s court news indicates that John Jolliffe and James Gitchell appeared in Probate Court on Monday, 18 February, to represent a contested will.[3] U.S. Marshal Robinson still kept over four hundred deputies on his roster, though antislavery crowds no longer thronged city streets. Cincinnatians turned their attention to the ongoing thaw and prepared to celebrate Washington's Birthday, planned as a massive (and new) patriotic festival. Archibald Gaines had returned to Maplewood, his pregnant wife, and a workforce of slaves almost halved during the last month.

Finally, on Wednesday, 20 February, Brashears and then Pendery made their moves. At nine in the morning an impatient Judge Carter, of the Ohio Court of Common Pleas, commanded the sheriff to carry out Ohio's *capias* for murder, now outstanding for twelve days. Brashears replied that he found "the defendants . . . confined in the Jail of Hamilton County" but formally "in custody of the U.S. Marshal," whose deputy, George Bennet, refused to part with them. The prosecuting attorney, Joseph Cox, immediately protested. Housing the Garners in the county jail, he argued, meant that marshals already *had* "parted with the custody of them," for Ohio statutes gave sheriffs "entire charge" of prisoners lodged there. Then Cox began to lay grounds for a habeas corpus hearing: "The only use for which a jail in this State can be applied," he said, "is for the confinement of those who have violated the laws of this State," or for prisoners who committed offenses against federal statutes. Yet the Garners weren't charged with a federal crime. Quoting from the 1850 compromise, Cox reminded Judge Carter that "the Fugitive Law does not declare [the fugitive] a criminal—does not subject him to any punishment for escaping from his master." On the other hand, Cox said in conclusion, the four Garner adults *had already been indicted* under state murder statutes. Federal marshals should therefore give up custody, under the *capias*, or answer to a habeas corpus writ. Judge Carter agreed: "The responsibility is on the Sheriff to perform his duties according to law"; in short, carry out the *capias* and take sole custody of the prisoners.[4]

As during the Garner trial, attorney George Mills represented Brashears's office. He didn't know what could be done to head off a jurisdictional war over the Garners and noted that "present appearances" pointed to "a grand scramble for the prisoners." He pleaded with Judge Carter: "if the city could be saved from riot or bloodshed by the action or advice of the court, it should be given." But Carter once more affirmed Cox's claim: the *capias* had to be carried out. Standing all this time before the bench, a frustrated Brashears angrily turned over the writ and scribbled on it words to the effect that he "had the parties in his custody," which was practically the case (they were in his building) but not legally correct (federal marshals still detained them there on John Pendery's 28 January fugitive slave warrant).[5] Accepting his claim, Judge Carter let federal marshals off the hook—now they needn't formally *surrender* custody—but then he set the hook deeply into Brashears. What would the sheriff do the next time marshals tried to move the Garners?

Pendery had gotten details about events in Judge Carter's court and meant to test Gazoway Brashears's will. His court recorder, J. Bell Pollock, announced early Wednesday afternoon that Pendery would "give the decision in the Fugitive Slave cases at ten o'clock Thursday morning," the day before Washington's Birthday. Wednesday night Jolliffe visited the Garners and advised them to prepare for the worst; reporters implied that Margaret once again reaffirmed a desire to die rather than return to Kentucky slavery.[6]

Thursday morning brought a brilliant sun, blue skies, and a continuing thaw. In the streets "a very large crowd assembled in the neighborhood"—overflow from a jammed courtroom that Pendery entered promptly at ten. By quarter after, neither the Garners nor Jolliffe had arrived and Pendery sent the marshal over to the county jail "for intelligence." There Robinson found Brashears and his deputies armed with pistols and repeating rifles. The sheriff had ejected federal deputies from the building and absolutely refused to give up custody of his prisoners. Here, then, was Brashears's answer to Judge Carter's tacit question, and to Pendery's test of his will. At the jailhouse door, Robinson argued that Judge Carter's *capias* named only the Garner adults and that Tom, Sam, and Cilla Garner were therefore his prisoners, under the federal fugitive warrant. Still Brashears resisted. This confrontation lasted about thirty minutes, within eye- or earshot of the Garners, who must have been altogether frightened at the guns and commotion, confused about its meaning, yet perhaps satisfied to be its cause. Back at the U.S. Courthouse, Robinson urged Pendery to order his marshals to seize the children using any force required. He was clearly itching for a fight, but a more reluctant Pendery "decided not to bring [the children] down at that time." Technically this meant the Garners were now Ohio prisoners. Brashears had won the first round, and a vanquished Commissioner adjourned (again) until the following Tuesday morning, 26 February.[7]

With the habeas corpus battle finally underway, Jolliffe made his first move early Thursday afternoon. He asked Jesse Beckley, a member of the Life Guards and brother of William Beckley (whom Jolliffe had previously asked Pendery to use in subpoenaing defense witnesses), to petition Probate Court Judge John Burgoyne, "alleging that [the Garners] were unlawfully detained in custody by the marshal of said district."[8] Burgoyne immediately issued a habeas corpus writ (his third in the case). This one meant that nobody, not even Brashears, could dispose of the Garners without Burgoyne's consent—an important condition in coming days.

The Beckleys and John Jolliffe were well acquainted. (In May 1857 Jolliffe would sue three Cincinnati Ward Judges for denying Jesse Beck-

ley an election ballot "on grounds he was colored."⁹) Jolliffe knew the
Beckley brothers because he often argued cases on behalf of black abolitionist groups such as the Life Guards; on this day Jesse Beckley
accompanied John Jolliffe as sheriff's deputies served the habeas corpus
writ on Hiram Robinson at the U.S. Courthouse. While there Jolliffe
extracted from the marshal a pledge, "on his word as a gentleman, that
they [the Garner children] should be brought before Judge Burgoyne
before being returned to the master." This in the words of reporter
Edmond Babb, who also witnessed the confrontation for *Gazette* readers
and added that Robinson's wording hinted yet again "that the decision
of the Commissioner will be against the fugitives."[10] Coming days would
spotlight the marshal's promise too.

Then came Robinson's turn. He secured from U.S. District Court
Judge Humphrey H. Leavitt two habeas corpus writs, one for the Garner
children and another for the adults, both to be returned by Saturday,
when Leavitt promised to hear arguments from attorneys on either side.
Finally, late Thursday afternoon Pendery made a surprising move when
his office issued without comment a warrant for the arrest of nineteen-
year-old Thomas Marshall on a charge that he committed perjury in
testifying that masters had never allowed Robert Garner to sojourn in
Cincinnati, a claim Jolliffe's witnesses had demolished.

Friday, 22 February. For weeks Hiram Robinson's newspaper had
been advertising for sale at the *Cincinnati Enquirer* offices various flags,
staffs, and buntings for Queen City residents preparing "to celebrate the
anniversary of the birthday of the FATHER OF HIS COUNTRY."
Overnight, residents had draped Robinson's wares "everywhere from
buildings" in town. At sunrise, a cannon salute opened the festivities
and church bells pealed for a half hour. By nine, a "thick" crowd
blocked city streets in a half-mile-square area. A parade commenced at
ten and the procession was so long that during its looping course
through town the U.S. Army band marching at its head was forced to
pause for the procession's rear to pass through an intersection. Leading
the parade were Mayor Farran, Sheriff Brashears, and Governor Chase,
followed by members of the Ohio Senate and General Assembly, a regiment of U.S. Cavalry, the city's Sarsefield and Shield Guards, Masons,
Odd Fellows, and the American Protestant Association. The first of
many "decorated cars" featured "America and Her Institutions," a tableau formed by a bevy of white-gowned young ladies. A second group

of young women modeled "The Union." A third car, "filled with boys, displayed the words *Our Hope is Young America!*"[11]

What hope indeed for those Young Americans? Many would soon enough demonstrate how, as historian William Freehling so concisely puts it, "the world's most advanced republic could end slavery only by one of the bloodiest fratricides in human history." Of course, those boys hadn't the benefit of our hindsight, but on 22 February 1856 they did have Margaret Garner, a symbol of slavery for Americans, detained just off the parade route. They had read news reports and some of their fathers and mothers had even sat in John Pendery's courtroom and heard attorneys on both sides drawing out elaborate metaphors of the blood-stained, grapeshot-blazed fields of fratricidal war. Were those images mere hyperbole? Perhaps so, for it is true that visions of civil violence had cropped up in American political rhetoric ever since the Constitutional Convention, and had become so commonplace during the last antebellum decade that many dismissed them as unreal. John Jolliffe's or John Finnell's metaphors should be seen in this broader context. Yet images of Margaret's unthinkable infanticide, of heavily armed county sheriffs and federal marshals facing each other down after her arrest, and of Hiram Robinson's four hundred special deputies suppressing abolitionists, all gave a special reality to attorneys' metaphors. Moreover, the regiment of gaily festooned Sarsefield Guards, each bearing one of those surreptitiously obtained Sharps rifles, had to have galled thousands in the crowd who understood the militia's proslavery role during recent weeks of struggle over the Garners.[12]

Yet here people from throughout this strife-torn border zone, Ohioans and Kentuckians, were celebrating "The Union." Following the Army regiments, local militias, Protestant societies, and Masonic lodges rolled "decorated cars" from the Queen City's ethnic subcultures. The German community had fitted up a "Lager Bier Wagon" featuring "a portly Bohemian" holding an enormous stein. After it, bystanders cheered wagons representing several "Roman Catholic Societies," the "Ancient Order of Druids" (an Irish fraternity), and "Sons of the Covenant" (from a neighboring synagogue). Among them came the "Improved Order of Red Men" (an all-white fraternal organization) escorting a huge canoe with "a group of savages surrounding a young lady representing the Goddess of Liberty."

Just days before, newspapers had been ringing alarms for a looming civil war. Now they touted this display as a grand celebration of the United States' motto, *e pluribus unum*—"out of many, one." The *Cincinnati Gazette* proclaimed it "an index of our population and of our country. All classes, the Protestant and the Catholic, the native and the foreigner, German and Irish, Jew and Gentile, all united to do honor to the Father of our Country." But again: just twenty-four hours earlier, right outside the Garners' cells, gun-toting sheriffs and marshals had faced off.

What kind of schizophrenia was this? Answering such a question means realizing how Cincinnatians were employing Washington's Birthday to construct *white* social identity. For each group parading behind Governor Chase and Mayor Farran, the point was to filiate (in the legal sense of signifying paternity) with the nation's body, symbolized in Washington. Each paraded a sign of national or ethnic *difference*— German lager beer, druidic costumes, the Torah, Native American regalia—in a ritual celebration indexing their *similarity*, as "Americans" descended from a common "Father." Yet this patriotic rite combined and thus erased marks of national origin or ethnic difference for another socially vital reason: to confirm a rigid social hierarchy. From beginning to end, the Washington's Birthday parade displayed stereotypes every Cincinnatian would have recognized: "hardworking" Germans marched before "lazier" Irish Catholics, who took precedence over more "oriental" and therefore degraded Jews, as well as the "Improved" version of "Red Men" who demonstrated that improvement principally by being whites *masquerading* as Indians. An American panorama unscrolling before streetside spectators, this parade descended the social ladder into a carnival of beer and blarney and mock Indians.[13]

Missing from that parade and virtually detached from the entire celebration were Ohio's free blacks. For what kind of "decorated car" might Cincinnati's Life Guards have mounted? A tableau of fugitives in flight? An overseer tying a Kentucky slave to the whipping post? A few of Massa's own "nearly white" children waving to bystanders? After Lucy Stone's courtroom insinuations that Archibald Gaines fathered the child that Margaret Garner nearly decapitated, *that* would have been a tableau of filiation suitable to the times. Yet such scenes had to be excluded not only because they would be unsavory or subversive but because African-American lives counted as the zero against which other "ethnic" minorities could gauge and claim their identity on the status hierarchy.

Blacks were the sine qua non of that hierarchy, but how could their essentiality be represented? Only, perhaps, in American pop culture when whites mimed "the colored" by "blacking up" for the minstrel stage or, as the instance of those "Improved" Native Americans illustrates, putting on red faces. In sum, the drama of inclusion, named *e pluribus unum*, worked according to a logic of *exclusion*. Recognizing how that exclusionary process operated can help us to understand Margaret Garner's disappearance in and from American cultural and social history, her eventual eclipse behind an array of sermons, poems, and fictions, thus her transformations into legend and myth.

Near the Fifth Street marketplace on Friday afternoon Mayor Farran and Governor Chase orated for hours on patriotic themes—"The Union" and "The Constitution." Chase was in Cincinnati for the first time since assuming the governorship, and it was the first occasion for this ardent abolitionist to speak out on the era's most dramatic fugitive case. Yet newspaper summaries and transcriptions record neither a single mention of nor even the most oblique reference to the Garner case, even though proslavery partisans hooted their dislike of Chase throughout his speech.[14] Instead of addressing slavery and its "impending crisis," speakers simply shoved the whole topic off their podium, a temporary amnesia or interdiction consistent with the festival's inner logic. And more: for it would soon develop that Chase's silence on the topic was consistent with his general distaste for strong action on the Garners' behalf, and it would turn out that Chase's reluctance was crucial. For if state authorities planned to dispute federal marshals for custody of the fugitives, they had to count on the governor. This day, his silence symbolized much.

Sometime during the day's festivities Chase did manage to meet privately with Sheriff Brashears and prosecuting attorney Joseph Cox. Three weeks later Chase would recall that he encouraged them to stand firm for Ohio sovereignty and "told them plainly . . . that he [Brashears] should be assisted with all the force needed." This could only have meant that Chase indicated his willingness to call out Ohio militia, the only "force" capable of matching Robinson's battalion of special deputies.[15]

As for the Garners, after the morning began with cannon fire and pealing church bells, they at least heard and perhaps were allowed to peer out windows and view the parade that passed near the county jail.

They knew from John Jolliffe that four days later Pendery would render his decision, that it would surely go against them, and that they should expect Gaines and Marshall to attempt their immediate return to Richwood Station. The day's celebration of liberty and union outside their cells must therefore have been especially bitter. At dusk jailers probably let the Garners once again peer from jailhouse windows at "the grand illumination" commencing outside. Residents and owners had placed candles in every window of city buildings, which shone for hours in the night "like light houses." It had turned cold once again but reporters tell us that city streets, "notwithstanding their wet and icy condition, were filled with people."[16]

Saturday, 23 February. This morning's *Covington Journal* printed a notice for "A Mass Meeting" scheduled to begin at midday "in Florence, Boone County, . . . to take into consideration what is proper to be done in the present crisis of our affairs, touching our rights as slave-holders and union-lovers." Benjamin Franklin Bedinger of Forrest Home addressed the meeting and briefly introduced before a crowd of about a hundred planters their neighbor Archibald K. Gaines, then on his way to Cincinnati. Dr. Elijah Clarkson also spoke "in a brief and eloquent style" about "the crisis in our affairs as slave-holders." He complained about Northern "foot-dragging" in terms he might well have grabbed from that day's newspaper. For, in an editorial that ran several columns away from the notice for that day's meeting, *Covington Journal* editors renewed their refrain that the 1850 law prohibited habeas corpus writs, and that indulgent state and local judges who granted such writs blocked justice, leaving all parties with "no decision" and therefore an ongoing crisis. Looking over the Garner dispute, the *Journal* thought "a conflict between State and National authority would seem to be inevitable. At present the Fugitive Slave Law is very near a nullity. The sooner the South knows what it has to depend on, the better."[17]

Boone County residents attending the afternoon meeting unanimously approved several resolutions. They complained: "for the love of our glorious Union we have borne this species of [abolitionist] plunder," and all pledged to fight for their "rights" to property in slaves. They resolved to send Clarkson and another representative to meet with Governor Morehead and the legislature at Frankfort. There they hoped to secure a bill providing for funds to reimburse James Marshall and Archibald Gaines "the costs and charges they have been compelled to incur in this shamefully protracted case." They also resolved that the Kentucky legislature should start a permanent fund to make such reimbursements in future cases.[18]

This was also the day that U.S. District Court Judge Leavitt had scheduled to hear arguments on Robinson's application for a habeas corpus writ, but he postponed them until Tuesday morning, just before Pendery would issue his decision. So the wait continued through Sunday and Monday, as did warm weather. By Monday morning the Ohio River ice pack showed signs of breaking up and constables began prohibiting any more foot traffic on the ice. Late that day a channel suddenly opened and, even though large floes still kept ferries at their docks, after six long weeks the ice bridge was finally severed. With it, at least until ferries could navigate the waters, went any link between Covington and Cincinnati. James Marshall and Archibald Gaines must therefore have crossed into Cincinnati just in time, probably Saturday evening or Sunday, as both were in Cincinnati for Tuesday's decision.

Tuesday, 26 February. This morning angry crowds once again thronged streets and traded insults with each other. Outside the courthouse abolitionists harangued Hiram Robinson's four hundred deputy marshals. Inside, Lucy Stone and her sister-in-law Antoinette Blackwell found seats near James Gitchell and Levi Coffin. The other spectators were also (apparently) all white, Robinson having once more ordered deputies to exclude "persons of color."

First came the habeas corpus hearing before Judge Leavitt, and these arguments produced one intriguing twist. Cincinnati attorney James Headington represented Marshal Robinson, who had applied for the writ. Headington's position was that on Wednesday Sheriff Brashears had illegally taken sole custody of the Garners. He claimed that "the only legal way for him [Brashears] to have reached them was" not by the *capias* outstanding for Mary Garner's murder but "by a writ of habeas corpus." Then, say reports, Headington claimed the Garners "were *not property, but persons,* and as such were properly [the marshal's] 'prisoners' and came under the resolution of Congress" and the Fugitive Slave Law.[19] Of course this is exactly what Headington *had* to claim, because habeas corpus writs apply only to *persons*; if he argued otherwise Brashears's attorneys would have shredded his application before Judge Leavitt. Still, Headington's admission contradicted the proslavery logic behind the very fugitive slave process that his own client, Robinson, was zealous to fulfill. Certainly Headington's move surprised Brashears's attorney, former Cincinnati Criminal Court judge George Hoadley. He was "glad to agree" that slaves were "sensible human beings" whom authorities could only detain as prisoners, not property. As *persons* (Hoadley continued) their crime of murder necessarily overrode any other transgression. Therefore Ohio detained them legitimately and Leavitt should deny the marshal's habeas corpus plea. At noon Leavitt adjourned, promising a decision the next morning. Most spectators thought Hoadley had won this round and eagerly kept their seats for the next.

Pendery "opened his Court" at one-thirty.[20] Archibald Gaines and James Marshall sat with attorneys Wall, Finnell, and Chambers. John Jolliffe and James Gitchell sat alone at the defense table because Pendery, no doubt recalling the Louis rescue, had decided not to risk bringing the Garners through jammed city streets when nothing in the fugitive slave statute required their presence for a Commissioner's ruling. (It also meant the Commissioner would not have to face the subjects of his decision.) Pendery moved swiftly. He summarily overruled Jolliffe's motion, pending for three weeks, that the court "discharge Margaret Garner, Simon Garner senior, Simon Garner junior, and Mary Garner, from custody of the U.S. Marshal, and deliver them into the possession of the Sheriff" on a charge of murder. He recited facts listed on the fugitive warrant and then turned immediately to Marshall's claim, framing it around two questions: First, should prior sojourns on Ohio's free soil drop the Garners' chains? Second, what did the Fugitive Slave Law require him to do?

That first question consumed the greatest part of Pendery's argument, and it suggests how crucial was John Finnell's decision to concentrate on *Strader v. Graham*:

[Commissioner Pendery] The only question which we propose to discuss in this case is, "does the fact of the temporary visit to Ohio of Simon Garner, junior, and Mary Garner, with consent of their master, prior to their escape, affect the rights of the claimant?" Or, in other words, James Marshall having permitted these persons to come into Ohio, and they having voluntarily returned into his service, is their relation as master and slave changed?

Pendery answered with an elaborate summary of facts in *Strader* and recited from Taney's obiter dicta on its key issues. This and similar cases, the Commissioner decided, posed no particular challenge to Ohio's constitutional prohibition. When Ohio said, "There shall be no slavery or involuntary servitude," the intent was "to prevent slavery as an institution within her limits, rather than to execute the act of manumission upon foreign slaves temporarily upon our soil with the master's consent."

Pendery then stipulated as facts defense claims that Robert (whom he called "Simon junior," using his slave name) and Mary had both sojourned on free soil, which had the practical effect of calling their masters liars. Still those sojourns did not matter, Pendery ruled, because to win their liberty slaves in transit on free soil had to assert their right to freedom, but in returning with their master these slaves waived that right. "In coming to Ohio the master voluntarily abandoned his legal power over his slave, and in returning voluntarily the slave has equally abandoned his claim to freedom," Pendery said. He concluded that when they escaped on Sunday night, 27 January 1856, the Garners were legally the slaves of their Boone County masters. This was a very limited application of Chief Justice Taney's remarks in *Strader*, one that pulled up much shorter than proslavery thinkers like Finnell went with the same material. Perhaps it was a bow to Jolliffe.

The Commissioner then turned to the crucial second question: What did the fugitive law require? Here he cast aside Jolliffe's whole summation:

[Commissioner Pendery] The question is not one of humanity that I am called upon to decide. The laws of Kentucky and of the United States make it *a question of property*. It is not a question of feeling, to be decided by the chance currents of my sympathies. There are to be adjudicated the rights of an institution so agreed to in the formation of our Government as to make it both municipal and federal in its character. It is the essence of the institution that the slave does not possess equal rights with the free-man. The abstract rights to *life, liberty, and property* are in his case replaced by statutes providing expressly for his condition. It has been our duty, as a Court, to listen with attention, and, we trust, with courtesy to all those arguments which have urged the decision of this question upon moral rather than legal grounds. We conceive that our highest moral obligation in this case is to administer impartially the plain provisions of the law.

However painful the result may be to the defendants in this case, it is my duty to deliver them, Simon Garner senior, Simon Garner junior, and Mary Garner, fugitives from service, into the custody of their claimant, James Marshall.[21]

The courtroom erupted in cheers on one side and hisses on the other. Marshall, Gaines, and their attorneys celebrated with gentlemanly handshakes.[22] The record does not tell us how Jolliffe responded but even though expecting this result he must have been utterly downcast.

When the commotion subsided Pendery moved just as swiftly to his decision on Archibald Gaines's claim to Margaret and the children. Again he summarized facts inscribed on the fugitive slave warrant of 28 January; then, again using the slave names listed on that document, he announced:

These facts present for our consideration the same question which was raised in the case of *Marshall v. Simon Garner et al.*, and the decision which we have just announced applies equally in this case.

We shall therefore make the order that the parties named, to wit: Peggy, Tom, Sam, and Cilla, be delivered into the custody and possession of the claimant, Archibald K. Gaines.

Press reporters say that at this point many women in the courtroom began openly weeping.[23] Word of Pendery's decision shot through city streets.

With stunning brevity it was over. Apparently Jolliffe departed straightaway for the Garners at the county jail; by two, deputies were clearing the courthouse. Observers had foreseen this result, but during the minutes afterward they must have been stunned to ponder the total victory Pendery had just handed proslavery forces. Contradicting Hoadley's appeal that morning before Judge Leavitt, this U.S. Commissioner wholly rejected the slaves-as-persons argument. As would any respectable Southron, he understood slaves as a "peculiar" form of "property." In fact, Pendery's remarks on the "rights to life, liberty and *property*" accomplished a startling resurrection of Thomas Jefferson's original phrasing for the Declaration of Independence, phrasing edited away so as to avoid conflicts *over slavery* when the colonies launched their rebellion against England eighty years earlier. Pendery thus handed Southron interests a deeply rooted as well as overarching defeat of abolitionist arguments. His decision anticipated by almost exactly a year the Supreme Court's ruling, in *Dred Scott*, that slaves had no rights as persons.

Four weeks and a day after it began, the longest-running and most expensive fugitive slave trial in American history came to a close.[24]

Remanded to Slavery

Tuesday afternoon Jolliffe told Margaret Garner of Pendery's decision. Wednesday's *Gazette* reported that afterward she was "suffering great agony, not knowing what moment her babe [Cilla] will be taken from her arms."[25] From this it appears someone (probably Jolliffe) led Margaret to believe that Gaines might soon take her three children back to Richwood Station but that she and the three other adults would remain in Cincinnati on the murder charge. Events would play out differently, though it was true that nothing now stood between the children and Archibald Gaines's desire for their return to Maplewood. The *Gazette* thought weather was the only thing still blocking Gaines from taking the Garner children: "in the present state of the river (the ice running) it would be impossible to get them over to Kentucky." A hard freeze might extend their stay; otherwise the children's situation was precarious. The news writer (probably Babb) closed with an appeal: "Will not the mothers of Cincinnati buy for this poor woman her child?" Apparently he thought Cilla's whiteness and infancy made her a special case.

While Jolliffe met with the Garners, Archibald Gaines and his attorneys adjourned to Pendery's chambers to make "an affidavit that he [Gaines] was apprehensive said fugitives would be rescued by force." He therefore asked that Pendery order marshals "to deliver his slaves to him in the state of Kentucky . . . pursuant to provisions of the act of congress."[26] Citing "Section 9" of the 1850 fugitive law, Pendery agreed and wrote the order to Marshal Robinson, after which a satisfied Gaines retired to his lodging at the Galt House hotel.[27] There he waited out the continuing thaw and U.S. District Court Judge Humphrey Leavitt's decision on the habeas corpus writ.

Wednesday, 27 February. At nine in the morning, John Jolliffe appeared before Probate Court Judge John Burgoyne and made his last appeal for a habeas corpus writ to keep the Garner children in Cincinnati.[28] After bringing developments in the case up to date, he resumed his attack on Commissioner Pendery's authority:

> [Mr. Jolliffe] The Constitution says that all judicial power shall be exercised by certain judges. But here is an individual pretending to such power, holding his court with officers swarming about him like the lictors of a Roman tribunal. And whence did he derive his authority? Under the statute of 1850, which was unconstitutional and void, because it proposed to confer judicial authority on a man who had not been appointed by the President, who does not receive a salary, but a fee of $5 if he decides the case for the defendant, and $10 if in favor of the plaintiff, and he holds his office according to the pleasure of Judge McLean.
>
> [Judge Burgoyne] I shall require some time to render a decision, but I estimate, however, that a majority of the Supreme Court having passed on the constitutionality of the Fugitive Slave law, is no reason why I should not take up the Constitution and read it for myself, being sworn to support both the Constitution of the United States and of the State of Ohio.
>
> [Mr. Jolliffe] Your honor, I ask the Court to make a special order that the children shall not be removed until the final decision.

Burgoyne made the order and, promising Jolliffe a decision by Saturday, 1 March (1856 being a leap year), adjourned just after ten. That afternoon Judge Leavitt's office announced that the next morning at nine-thirty he would render a decision on the habeas corpus Marshal Robinson requested. Things were moving fast and timing would be everything.

Even at this critical moment, however, observers close to the case legitimately believed Marshal Robinson would have to obey Judge Burgoyne's order and keep the Garners in Cincinnati for a decision on John Jolliffe and Jesse Beckley's application for a habeas corpus writ. Most also thought Sheriff Brashears was determined to resist any attempts to take the adult Garners from his custody; at least that's what his armed standoff, the previous Thursday, had suggested. Most therefore believed the Garners had at least a few more days on free soil, as attorneys urged their rights before local courts.

On all counts they were dead wrong.

Thursday, 28 February. The weather was still moderate, although heavy clouds had blown into the Ohio River valley. Early in the morning a heavy rain melted still more of the snow and ice pack; that morning for the first time in six weeks ferries resumed service between Covington and Cincinnati. Now the only thing standing between the Richwood Station masters and their runaway slaves was Burgoyne's order, a barrier that an opposing habeas corpus ruling from Judge Leavitt might remove because his was a federal and superseding court.

Sometime between eight and nine that morning John Jolliffe had his last interview with the Garners. No details of this meeting have come down to us, but Jolliffe probably still thought that even if Leavitt granted Robinson's petition for habeas corpus, only the children could be taken South on this day, and taken despite Marshal Robinson's pledge "as a gentleman" that he wouldn't do so without first taking them before Judge Burgoyne. Perhaps Jolliffe knew more, and feared the worst. From the man's character we know Jolliffe would have assured the Garners that no matter what happened he and other abolitionists would press the Ohio courts and officials to return Margaret, Robert, Simon, and Mary for trial on the murder charges—in their view, still a better option than lifelong slavery. Yet he may well have sensed that this was goodbye.

By nine in the morning outside the U.S. Courthouse a dense crowd had gathered and its "anticipation was keen, to know the slaves' fate," said the *Gazette*'s Edmond Babb. Leavitt had set nine-thirty for his announcement, but that time passed by without news. Spectators waited through the noon hour, and several heavy rain showers; still there was no word. A deputy named Pic Russel kept the door barred against anyone without official business at the building.[29]

At two forty-five, Russel admitted spectators to the courtroom. At three, Leavitt began reading from a prepared document. He quickly reviewed the main facts, recited statutes governing the issuance of federal habeas corpus writs, and rejected Hoadley's argument that a state process for murder necessarily took precedence over a federal fugitive slave warrant. He said the 1850 statute was, for now, "a valid and constitutional law, and as such must be respected. . . . Any other principle must lead to anarchy in its worst form, and result inevitably in the speedy overthrow of our institutions."[30] That said, he granted Robinson's petition for habeas corpus. It was three-fifteen.

At four, Marshal Hiram H. Robinson left the courthouse "with a large number of assistants." As they marched through city streets the crowd of spectators followed in solemn procession. At the county jail, Sheriff Brashears brought all seven of the Garners into a foyer or "reception room." Robinson handed over the habeas corpus writ, and Brashears handed over custody of the state's prisoners.

Here we must pause in the story and consider Gazoway Brashears's predicament. Judge Burgoyne had not yet decided Jesse Beckley's habeas corpus application. In fact, so far the judge had only issued an "order" stipulating that Robinson should leave the Garners in state custody. But a federal judge *had* issued a habeas corpus commanding sheriffs to produce the Garners. Leavitt's writ not only had the greater priority, compared to Burgoyne's bench order, it also (arguably) had the superseding authority of federal law. Yet this was only half of the matter.

When he was in Cincinnati on Washington's Birthday the governor had promised to assist Brashears "with all the force needed." Now where was Chase's assistance? Brashears must have felt betrayed, for this Thursday afternoon federal deputies completely overwhelmed his office and the small force of sheriff's deputies representing Ohio sovereignty. Within the city Marshal Robinson commanded a battalion-strength posse armed with repeating rifles and pistols. About three hundred of these men now stood outside the county jail, eager to enforce Pendery's order. Another one hundred or so were at the ferry dock. Waiting in the wings were perhaps an equal number of local militia from the Sarsefield Guards and Shield Guards, also armed with repeating rifles. Opposing them, according to our best accounts, Brashears commanded several dozen men. Pondering Governor Chase's silence since his visit six days ago, and his failure to send needed militia, Brashears must have sensed a waning interest in the Garner case at Columbus. He had good reason to feel betrayed.

Looking at white antislavery activists like John Jolliffe, Levi Coffin, the Reverend Bassett, and Lucy Stone—good religious people who had for years operated in a mode of nonviolent resistance to slavery and the fugitive law—Brashears had to have become still more pessimistic about his chances for a successful resistance to Robinson's overwhelming force. And as for black activists like the Beckleys, men perhaps willing

Steamboats at the Cincinnati levee, ca. 1860
COURTESY THE CINCINNATI HISTORICAL SOCIETY

to defend the Garners by force, Brashears well knew that local racists would use any strong resistance from that quarter as provocation for another race riot, whose consequences for free blacks in nearby Bucktown would be absolutely disastrous.

Did it matter, as some later claimed, that Sheriff Brashears was never a committed abolitionist? Recalling these events in 1864, George Hoadley would remark the fact but hasten to add that through it all Brashears strove "to do his whole duty and did not shrink from responsibility." Chase, of all people, was harsh on Brashears; he thought a sheriff with stronger antislavery principles would have "held on to his custody" at any cost. But Chase, who had promised the sheriff all necessary assistance and then failed to deliver it, wasn't at the jail when Marshal Hiram Robinson arrived with Leavitt's habeas corpus writ and three hundred armed men to enforce it. It's fair to say Brashears did his utmost, short of making himself and his deputies into antislavery martyrs.[31]

As Robinson emerged triumphantly under cloudy skies, Deputy U.S. Marshal Pic Russel followed him carrying Cilla. Behind Russel came Deputy Brown, who "offered his arm to Margaret"; next came court reporter J. Bell Pollock walking "arm in arm with Simon," then Mary Garner, who apparently declined to take any but the arm of her son Robert. Deputies walked before and behind them. The seven Garners passed through a double gauntlet of special deputies and boarded an omnibus, accompanied by their escorts. Robinson mounted an open buggy, Bennet took the reins, and the special deputies formed a solid phalanx around the vehicles. After twenty or thirty yards "Robinson motioned the driver to stop. Some of Margaret's clothes (given to her since in jail) had been left."[32] Brashears brought them out and the procession resumed its progress.

Down Sycamore to Ninth Street, over to Walnut, then straight down to the ferry landing. All along, says the *Gazette* "a large crowd which had gathered around the jail followed, but with the silence and order of a funeral procession." At the dock waited another one hundred or so of Robinson's special deputies arrayed like a wall. It yawned open for the buggy and omnibus, then closed its maw behind them. From the Cincinnati side several thousand silent spectators watched as both vehicles drove straight on board the ferryboat *Kentucky*. Reports indicate the omnibus was no sooner aboard the ferry than "she was cut loose." James Marshall stood "on the bow deck, surrounded by crowds of his friends." They exchanged "warm congratulations."

"Oh," said one, "ain't this worth a thousand dollars?"

"Yes," replied another, "we've got that damned abolition State under foot now, and by God we'll keep it there."

"Oh, it's too good!" said a third.

The *Gazette*'s man Edmond Babb observed all of this from inside the passengers' cabin, where he rode near Archibald K. Gaines. That "thousand dollar" figure was Gaines's rough estimate of costs in reclaiming his escaped slaves. And he wasn't done paying yet.

Looking out from her seat in the omnibus, Margaret Garner passed her first ferryboat ride since 1840, deputy marshals surrounding them the whole way. When they docked at Covington a "large, cheering crowd" greeted the *Kentucky* and even as deckhands tied her off at the piers Robinson's buggy led the omnibus down a ramp. The posse marched three short blocks to Second and Greenup streets, where Hiram Robinson handed over custody to his northern Kentucky counterpart, U.S. Marshal Clinton Butts, who hadn't seen the Garners since the day of their capture. As they passed through lower Covington, says the *Gazette*, "women with children in their arms came to the door steps and in the street, and beautiful, dark-haired girls, gleaming with jewels, filled the open windows—all to see the procession pass."

After they "deposited" the Garners at the Kenton County jail, Hiram Robinson, George Bennet, James Marshall, and Archibald Gaines "adjourned" to the Magnolia House, where John Finnell and Samuel Wall met them. John Jolliffe's old nemesis Jacob Flinn was there. Joining them were Richwood Station neighbors and northern Kentucky friends: Dr. Clarkson, Major Murphy, William Timberlake, Peter Nolan, and others who had stood in gentlemanly solidarity around Archibald Gaines during the trial. They made a crowd of perhaps eighty to a hundred packed inside the Magnolia House. "The bar was opened, and for some time liquor flowed freely," noted Edmond Babb.

Outside milled an excited crowd of hundreds more. They demanded speeches, and so Hiram Robinson, "being loudly called for," eventually appeared on the Magnolia House balcony to sustained cheers. Reporters at the scene tell us he toasted their success in maintaining Ohio's sovereignty "by vindicating the sovereignty of the state of Kentucky." In a brief speech he "denounced in good round terms" Ohio's abolitionists and "spoke of his own personal courage," while also claiming that he had "not done anything more than his duty." The crowd called for John Finnell, who commended Robinson (to more sustained applause) and then proclaimed his own "love of the Union," now "far dearer to him than it was two hours ago." "I tell you," Finnell concluded, "the salvation of Kentucky and of the South, and the continuance of our domestic institution, depend upon the integrity and continuance of our Federal Union (tremendous applause)."

The crowd called for Jacob Flinn, and Finnell disappeared inside for a few minutes before producing him. The burly Irishman launched into what the *Gazette* termed a "Glorious Union Speech" that continued through several rounds of applause before Flinn "stopped short, said he was dry, and must go down to get a drink." Good old Jacob Flinn.

They called for Archibald Gaines, but Robinson joked that he was not available, "stating that he [Gaines] had been appointed a committee of one to go over the river and invite Mr. Jolliffe to come over and get a drink"—a foreshadowing of Gaines's 1857 attack on Jolliffe. For some minutes "the multitude persisted in calling 'Gaines, Gaines, Gaines,'" and when he finally came forward it was clear that Archibald was not like his loquacious brother John. When the crowd quieted he turned to Finnell, Robinson, and Flinn and said, "I am ten thousand times obliged to you gentlemen, for your diligence in preserving the laws and carrying them out. But I am no speech maker. Mr. Flinn will speak for me." A re-lubricated Flinn spoke for several minutes, assuring the crowd "that no pecuniary motive actuated Mr. Gaines in pursuing these slaves. It was purely a matter of principle with him, for they had cost him more money than would boulder that whole street with wooly heads." On that racist note the crowd began dispersing into the dark. It was just after seven o'clock. Margaret and her family had been back on "ground consecrated to slavery" for nearly three hours.

Standing in the crowd to record these events, Edmond Babb recognized some of the cheering partisans as Hiram Robinson's special deputies, several "of whom he had seen in the Court Room" during the Garner trials. Soon they also recognized him: "See that damned abolition reporter," Babb overheard one of them say, "what business does he have over here from Ohio?" Walking back to the ferry dock from the Magnolia House, Babb realized a crowd had surrounded him. Before he could react one of the "rowdies" brought his fist down on the back of Babb's head. Others pitched in, Babb fell, the encircling mob began to kick him, and onlookers shouted encouragement. One wanted to tar and feather the "damned abolitionist," another suggested they duck him in the frigid Ohio River, while still another wanted to "put him on a cake of ice and let him go to the devil!"[33]

Determined to do just that, they prodded a bleeding and semiconscious Babb to his feet and began hustling him toward the dock. His upper jaw was fractured from just below the right eye socket down to his mouth and he could barely walk. The *Cincinnati Commercial* reporter thought that if it weren't for Robert Lee, a former deputy U.S. marshal from Cincinnati, the mob would probably have tossed the *Gazette*'s reporter off the wharf and watched him drown. Recognizing Babb, Lee recruited several acquaintances, who "drew their shooters," ordered the mob back, and surrounded him until a ferry arrived. When the boat chugged off, "the Kentuckians crowded on the wharf shouted their curses and threatenings, swearing that if they ever again caught the damned abolitionist reporter on that side of the river they would kill him."

From their cells just three blocks away from the Magnolia House, the Garners must have heard the tumult and suspected what it was about. Earlier in the evening, when he watched Marshal Robinson's procession toward the Kenton County jail, Babb "was reminded of the recent jubilee" on Washington's Birthday. Probably the Garners had similar thoughts, but with a deeper sense of the ironies.

Within a week, Covington sheriffs had charged five men for assaulting Babb. One of them was John Butts, brother of U.S. Marshal Clinton Butts. All were working-class men in their twenties, one was over from Cincinnati, another was from nearby Mason County; and while willing to fight for the South's "peculiar institution" none of them, interestingly, owned a slave.[34] Deputies never did find a sixth man named Johnson, though it "was said he took the most active part in striking, kicking, and menacing" Edmond Babb. At trial the defense argued that the men's assault, though illegal, was "the natural method of dealing out justice" to those who "ridicule our people and institutions." Apparently the jury rather agreed. They returned guilty verdicts but imposed only light fines of ten to forty dollars.[35]

At the same time "rowdies" were attacking Edmond Babb in Covington, a small "committee" of Cincinnati abolitionists took John Jolliffe to supper and afterward presented him "a well filled purse" intended to offset his lost income during the Garners' long trial. This group's letter of commendation, published in the *Gazette*, reassured a still downcast Jolliffe and assailed the Fugitive Slave Law as unconstitutional and Southern slavery as "most odious and cruel":

We have seen a child perishing by the hands of its mother! That tragedy gives to us an illustration of the ruin wrought by that system, upon the tenderest sensibilities of our nature. . . . Such laws pour contempt upon the dictates of justice and humanity, and are calculated to harden the heart, and benumb the conscience of every man who assists in their execution.

The great conflict between freedom and slavery must sooner or later come to a crisis. All neutral ground upon this subject will be unknown. These two principles so opposite in their nature can never be made to harmonize.

There it was again—the shadow of fratricidal strife. Margaret Garner's child-murder continued to serve as touchstone for other signs of an imperiled Union. During the early months of 1856 American newspapers broadcast further news of disunion: an eight-week battle in the House of Representatives over appointment of a new Speaker, itself symptomatic of a fractured political party system; and civil strife in "Bleeding Kansas" leading up to charges of "high treason" against the territory's antislavery government.[36] The slave mother's infanticide aptly symbolized these images of a national family murdering itself from the inside out.

Jolliffe thanked his supporters in a letter written the next morning, stressing once again the Fugitive Slave Law's threat to religious liberty and underscoring the committee's sense of wartime urgency:

> You say that sooner or later the crisis between freedom and slavery must come. Gentlemen, it has come. It is upon us *now* and *here*. We must meet it as men, or shrink from it and bear the responsibility of desertion from our posts of duty. Religious liberty, without which man is deprived of the highest dignity of his nature, lies today in dishonored dust in Ohio by the decision of Pendery; and the right of the State—a right which every wandering horde of savages possesses—to inquire into an accusation of homicide within its limits—is made subordinate to the will or judgment of officers from another State. All this is without law, and against law, and it remains only to be seen whether the people of Ohio will arise as one man and assert their rights, or tamely submit to outrages upon them that would drive any other people to the very verge of madness.[37]

Writing these words on Friday, Jolliffe well knew the drubbing Kentucky "rowdies" administered to Edmond Babb on Thursday night. Though still a Quaker at heart, he was thinking revenge.

On Friday, the day after she was remanded to Kentucky slavery, Margaret Garner's story was far from over. Her own future remained highly complex and uncertain. Would Kentucky governor Morehead compel

Archibald Gaines to honor a requisition if Ohio governor Chase asked
for Margaret's return, along with her husband and in-laws, to stand trial
for murder? In any case, what could Gaines *do* with such a slave, now
that he'd spent a thousand dollars or more to win his legal right to
reclaim her? Obviously her continued presence at Maplewood would
be much too disruptive and risky and he'd have to hire out or sell the
woman. But this was only the half of it. For the Garner case had also
left behind a welter of legal problems for Cincinnatians to sort out. What
about Judge Burgoyne's "special order" issued to keep the Garner children in Ohio? In removing them, Marshal Robinson had not only dis-
honored his gentleman's pledge made to Jolliffe but also opened himself
up to possible arrest for contempt of Burgoyne's court. Additionally,
Robinson was technically in contempt of Ohio's Judge Samuel Carter,
who still claimed legal custody of the Garner adults on that murder
indictment. Would Carter, or perhaps Burgoyne, force a showdown with
Leavitt's court?

From here, Margaret Garner's story runs along three parallel paths.
One involves the fate of Margaret and her family, a path difficult to
trace but increasingly dramatic. A second plot line involves the social,
political, and legal consequences for a great range of people affected by
her deeds. A third traces Margaret's story through texts written to memorialize her, texts that failed in that purpose, and failed for vexing
reasons we must try to understand.

A few examples. Since early February, newspapers in Kentucky and
throughout the North had used the image of Margaret's child-murder
to argue for or against slavery. Typical was a *Chicago Tribune* editorial
of 6 February 1856 that concluded: "When a mother can draw a knife
across the throat of her own child to ensure it freedom and heaven, it
is time the slaveholders should pause and war against a system which
debases every human being connected to it."[38] While thus politicizing
the Garner case, it wasn't long, however, before newspapers were adding
layers of mythic references to the Garner infanticide, as Hiram Robinson's paper had already done by imagining her as "Virginia," the tragic
heroine of Thomas Babington Macaulay's famous poem. A long editorial on 8 February in Horace Greeley's *New York Tribune* compared
Margaret Garner to Greek hero Mithridates, who sacrificed his wife and
sister rather than give them up to a life of concubinage. Then the writer
recalled Virginius and asked how his tragedy differed "from that of the

poor slave-mother on the banks of the Ohio?" The only difference the *Tribune* could see was that the ancient legend "becomes classic; history celebrates it; artists spread it upon their canvas; [and] poets embalm the memory of it in undying lines."[39]

Some years would pass before an American painter would "spread" Margaret's image on canvas, but one day after Greeley's editorial the *Tribune* published our first known literary text seeking to "embalm" her child-murder within "undying lines." The author—an Auburn, New York, versifier named Mary A. Livermore—datelined her poem Sunday, 3 February 1856. She opens with "the Sabbath sun" shining "through the clear and frosty air"; church bells are ringing and believers arriving "to renew to God their pledges," but the poem's speaker cannot join their worship:

> *For my soul is sick and saddened with that fearful tale of woe,*
> *Which has blanched the cheeks of mothers to the whiteness of the*
> *snow;*
> *And my thoughts are wandering ever where the prison walls surround*
> *The parents of their children, in hopeless bondage bound.*

Her next stanza invokes Margaret's image, gleaned (evidently) from newspaper accounts:

> *Oh, thou mother, maddened, frenzied, when the hunter's toils*
> *ensnared*
> *Thee and thy brood of nestlings, till thy anguished spirit dared*
> *Send to God, uncalled, one darling life that round thine own did*
> *twine—*
> *Worthy of a Spartan mother was that fearful deed of thine!*

Note that even while Mary Livermore imagines her infanticidal slave mother as a noble "Spartan," she cannot accept the deed itself as anything other than that of an irrational ("maddened, frenzied") person. This reading of Margaret was becoming typical—for example, during attorney Samuel Wall's summation at Margaret's trial, although she herself insisted the deed was coolly and pragmatically done.[40] Jolliffe himself wasn't above such inferences, as his 29 February reply to the Cincinnati committee illustrates.

More significantly, though, in this poem the black mother's infanticide has the paradoxical effect of *whitening* free mothers. Mary Livermore imagines that it "blanched" them to a snowy paleness, a way of saying Margaret's deed made them become *more white* than these free white mothers already were, while acquiescing to slavery. But her lines also imply that heroic infanticide is what the dominant culture expects not of black but of *white mothers*—a rhetorical move that becomes clearer in the poem's very next stanza, which appropriates Margaret Garner's deed to the poet's *own* self-conception:

> *Yet (oh, God of heaven, forgive me!), baby sitting on my knee,*
> *I could close thy blue eyes calmly, smiling now so sweet on me!*
> *Ay, my hand could ope the casket, and thy precious soul set free:*
> *Better for thee Death and Heaven than a life of slavery!*

Trusting to this heroic rationale (she might well have quoted Patrick Henry's famous motto: "Give me liberty, or give me death!"), the speaker imagines making a plea for Margaret "before the Judge Eternal" and wins for her a pardon and—for humanity—God's awful indictment against those "hunters of His children," the slave catchers, slated for trial and execution on judgment day:

> *But the day of vengeance cometh—He will set his people free,*
> *Though he lead them, like his Israel, through a red and bloody sea;*
> *For the tears and gore of bondmen are staining deep the frighted*
> *sod,*
> *And the wailing cry of millions riseth daily up to God!*[41]

Mary Livermore's vision of impending millennial violence undamming a "red and bloody sea" was fully consistent with images of fratricidal war preached in Pendery's courtroom, by attorneys on either side. Her poem illustrates how, as Americans abstracted Margaret's child-murder from its context, they also brought it into the dominant culture. Indeed they *whitened* the story, and thereby increased its mythic resonances for those on either side of the political spectrum. Thus Americans were already learning to forget or, practically the same thing, not to think about *why* she did it.

Central to the Garner infanticide were questions about this slave mother's moral and political capacity to act. For Northerners her bloody deed could be a profoundly moral act of resistance, comparable to those of other heroic slaves like Frederick Douglass or Harriet Jacobs—whose writings used Patrick Henry's famous motto.[42] For Southerners, black slaves were benighted subjects for whom questions involving the "higher morality" were unthinkable. "High and peculiar characters, by elaborate cultivation, *may be taught to prefer death to Slavery*," argued Southron ideologue William Harper, but he thought "it would be folly" to imagine slaves having that capacity.[43] Whole hierarchies of class and race depended on such beliefs.

Consider one more example that Cincinnati-area readers might have encountered during February 1856. Hiram Martin was a forty-five-year-old Covington brickmaker with a house and shop valued at $10,000 in the 1850 census. In 1856 Martin and his wife had four children, ages fifteen to twenty-two, and owned a twenty-five-year-old black female slave whom they probably employed in domestic service.[44] Like Mary Livermore of Auburn, New York, Hiram Martin of Covington, Kentucky, was another from that horde of amateur versifiers then publishing in the nation's penny papers. During the 1850s he averaged a poem per month in the weekly *Covington Journal*. In fact, Hiram Martin was far and away the *Journal's* most published local poetaster. His favorite topics included the seasons, children, duteous wives, and local celebrations.

During the awful winter of 1856 a persistent rumor circulated through Covington about a distressed, homeless mother found dead in a snowdrift. This young woman was rumored to have perished by freezing but had clasped her infant daughter so tightly to her bosom that the baby survived. Some even said that the child, when sheriffs discovered the tragic scene, still suckled at its deceased mother's breast. Two times in January the *Journal* dispelled this rumor. After the Garner case, however, Hiram Martin found poetry in that phantasm. In five galumphing pentameter stanzas, his poem, titled "A Mother Found Dead in a Snow Drift with a Living Infant in her Arms," composes the story as a parable about maternal love. Martin's world-weary mother never abandons her child: "She bared her breast, to nourish and console/ And slept in death, to God resigned her soul." Around this tableau winter weather roars— "a night more dismal yet was never hurled/ Against the face of this benighted world"—and when deputies scrape away the snow from her face the woman seems to serenely "smile in death."[45]

Hiram Martin's poem appeared in the *Covington Journal*'s edition of Saturday, 9 February 1856, just when Margaret Garner's trial had reached its ultimate stage. The poem is very much about that trial despite how, or even *because of how*, its verses have nothing factual to do with Margaret's case. Martin's poem simply inverts the Garner plot: here, mother dies so infant survives. His poem thus composes a tableau of normative, *white* motherhood to stand against and correct the horror that an abominably erring Margaret Garner had spread through his region's domestic institutions. Hiram Martin writes to disinfect Southern culture, as if to say: "Look, even our local legends, apocryphal though they be, know better than to heroize the infanticidal slave mother." By indirection and inversion, his stanzas represent Margaret Garner as an amoral and even nonhuman actor.

These literary texts were cultural means for rewriting and thus diminishing the facts of Margaret Garner's story. In February 1856, when Margaret was still in custody, these processes were already well underway, across a broad range of texts and situations. Now that slave catchers had taken her South, what would become of her story?

Shell Game

After U.S. marshals remanded the Garners to Kentucky the chief question was whether some or even all of them could ever be returned to free soil. Lucy Stone had claimed that Gaines promised to strike a deal with abolitionists for the children. Meanwhile the adults might be extradited, *if* Ohio governor Chase could persuade Kentucky governor Morehead to give them up. Yet this was a crucial *if*: For who could trust Archibald Gaines to relinquish his "property," now that he had paid so dear a price to get it back?

After the expense and, more important, after all the public disrepute this case had brought on him, it was wholly unreasonable to think Gaines would suffer further wounds to his "honor" by caving in to abolitionist demands. What, then, would he do? During Margaret's trial several Richwood Station whites testified that Gaines had brothers residing in New Orleans, the Natchez area, and Arkansas—where Archibald Gaines himself had old ties. An obvious solution would be to ship or sell Margaret and the children south to one of the brothers. As for

James Marshall, his record of frequently hiring out the Garners didn't bode well either. All signs therefore pointed up the need for quick and decisive action, if Ohio officers expected to get the fugitives back.

We know that from this time forward Gaines made the Garners travel in leg irons. Hinged bands clasped around the ankles and linked with heavy chain just long enough for the slave to shuffle but not to stride, much less run, leg irons weighed up to five pounds each. They caused chafing and blistering that often left permanent scars.[46] From the day Robinson and Bennet handed the fugitives over to Covington marshal Clinton Butts, witnesses who saw the adult Garners in transit noticed the irons. Some remarked that Margaret also wore handcuffs. But why use the irons and cuffs? The reason could not simply have been to prevent their escape, because even while Gaines frequently moved the Garners about in coming days he always sent them in the custody of armed deputies who would put them up overnight in local jails. Escape was practically impossible. Gaines's real reason for the restraints therefore had to be punitive. He wanted to break the slaves' wills and humiliate them, especially Margaret, for the disrepute they had cast on his family. As for Margaret's handcuffs, they indicate that Gaines took seriously her threat to take the children's lives before she would see them returned to slavery.

So Gaines meant these punishments to do physical as well as psychological work on his chattels, and on Marshall's as well, because from here on Archibald K. Gaines appears to have had sole authority to dispose of all seven Garners. James Marshall—perhaps suffering again from his gallstones (or "gravel")—simply disappears from the print record.

The Garners were truly back in the South. Shackled and chained, and liable to be traded or sold south in the blink of an eye. Perhaps separated for good. No more sympathetic, kindly white abolitionists like John Jolliffe, the Reverend Bassett, and Lucy Stone to visit them, or gifts of clothing or encouraging words from free blacks. As for food, after a month of the Hamilton County jail's relatively varied and healthful dishes, they were back to the slave's diet, a deficient and boring regimen of cornmeal and the least cuts of pork. They were also back to the slave's most deeply rooted anxieties: What future for them? Would Massa put them "under the whip," as Kentucky statutes entitled him to do? Would he "put them in his pocket," selling the family away and apart?

The Garners knew how Lucy Stone had cornered Archibald Gaines and made him promise to give abolitionists a price for the Garners' freedom. John Jolliffe had also promised that he would get them back to Ohio for trial on the murder warrant. But what good were those promises now? Despite all that Cincinnatians had done on their behalf, right now the Garners were in chains. Anyway, they had little experience trusting white people and many reasons to be deeply apprehensive. They knew the master's power, now that he'd gotten them back on Southern soil. The hot-tempered Gaines wouldn't have told them much (if anything) about his plans. In the darkness of their Kenton County jail cells on Thursday, 28 February, the Garners must have spent a frightened and restless night.

That night Gaines slept at the same place where Margaret stayed during her 1840 sojourn to Cincinnati, the house of his sister's husband, Percival Bush, now advertising his services as a "General Agent" in the Covington real estate trade.[47] Before retiring for the night Gaines telegraphed Richwood neighbors to look for his arrival the next morning. By sunup Friday he and Marshal Clinton Butts were taking the Garners from the jail to Covington Station. A southbound "Express Train" of the Covington & Lexington Railroad departed the city every day (except Sunday) at 7:25, "stopping at all regular stations," including the depot at Richwood, where Gaines disembarked with Margaret and the children.[48] Clinton Butts stayed aboard and escorted Simon, Mary, and Robert on to Lexington and there changed trains for Frankfort. Several days later, the *Cincinnati Gazette* reported that James Marshall's three slaves had "already been hired out" in Kentucky's capital, but this turns out to have been erroneous. From the little we know, it appears Marshal Butts simply lodged them in a local jail and made his own way back to Covington.[49]

Archibald Gaines was deftly manipulating the Garners. During the two weeks after Pendery adjourned court to await his decision, Archibald had contacted his brother at Gaines Landing, Arkansas, and Benjamin agreed to take the slaves, pending or perhaps even in defiance of any requisition that Ohio governor Chase might soon issue. Now on Friday morning Gaines was making his first moves in a plan to ship the Garners south by steamboat out of Louisville, thus to avoid any further commotion in the Covington-Cincinnati area. Putting Marshall's three slaves in a Frankfort jail kept them within easy reach of both Richwood and Louisville. It also put them at the state capital, should Kentucky governor Morehead force Gaines to give the Garners over to Ohio deputies. Meantime, he brought Margaret and her children "home" to Maplewood for the weekend. Why? Because, compared to James and Thomas Marshall, the attachment Gaines felt to these runaway slaves was stronger and probably, as key evidence suggests and many Cincinnatians suspected, much more intimate. Margaret the reclaimed fugitive had claims of her own.

Here again we have to imaginatively reconstruct the scene. A week's worth of southern breezes had melted most of the winter snow.[50] Thermometers were rising rapidly into the fifties under a brilliant sun as Margaret and the children rolled past Richwood Presbyterian Church and the rendezvous where, over a month ago, under cover of darkness and a winter storm, Robert had met her with James Marshall's sleigh. Perhaps some of the neighboring slaves stood in silent observance of Margaret's arrival. Benjamin Franklin Bedinger was just the sort of master who would have wanted his slaves to look upon her—as a bad example. Archibald Gaines probably took Margaret by Mary Garner's still fresh grave, evidently on Maplewood itself.

The Gaines family had their Peggy back, for now. Archibald's wife, Elizabeth, was nearing the end of her pregnancy, his aged mother was as much an invalid as ever, and they had been shorthanded around the place for weeks. Gaines needed to begin the spring plowing. Still it's unlikely that he gave Margaret any actual chores during her several days' stay at Maplewood. Archibald's wife wouldn't have wanted an infanticidal slave anywhere near her little Margaret Ann or William, and Gaines may therefore have confined Margaret to one of the slave cabins, and probably kept her in the handcuffs and leg irons. Meantime she surely both lamented and rejoiced in the absence of familiar faces, her own mother and the resisting Hannah, who had evidently run off with the party of Gaines slaves that successfully fled Maplewood in the days right after Margaret's failed attempt.

In Cincinnati that Friday afternoon, Hamilton County prosecutor Joseph Cox took before Judge Carter a formal complaint against U.S. Marshal Hiram Robinson for reneging on his agreement to produce the four Garner adults named in the Ohio *capias* for murder. Carter agreed: he said the marshal was obliged not only to his promise but to constitutional rules for comity and therefore should have accepted the Garners' arrest for murder "no matter what may have been their position

in reference to any other court in the land." Homicide was a capital
crime that took precedence over any other except perhaps treason, Carter said, and he advised prosecutor Cox "that he had better get a requisition from the Governor." Cox replied that he had "already done
so."[51]

But what in fact *had* the prosecuting attorney already "done"? The
Cincinnati Gazette, our best source on this important detail, thought
Cox meant that he had not only applied for but already *received* a requisition from Governor Chase. Their impression was that on 29 February—presumably in response to a telegram from Cox—Chase had
dispatched "a party" of officers to hand-carry the requisition from Columbus to Cincinnati. Subsequent comments in the *Enquirer* indicate
that Robinson's reporters had the same impression.

This becomes a crucial point because six days would pass before—
on 5 March 1856—Cox and two other attorneys actually departed Cincinnati for Frankfort, Kentucky. There they put the requisition and
Chase's cover letter before Governor Morehead. They also learned that
Archibald Gaines had himself been in Frankfort, and that just hours
ahead of the Ohioans' arrival he had left for Louisville to put the Garners on a steamboat bound for Arkansas. This misadventure had fatal
consequences. Who, then, was to blame? The *Gazette's* story would
point the finger at Cox, for irresponsibly and inexplicably laying over at
Cincinnati.[52]

Letters archived among the Chase papers tell the true story. When
prosecutor Joseph Cox appeared in court on Friday afternoon and Carter
advised him to "get a requisition from the Governor," Cox's reply—that
he "had already done so"—really indicated that he had only just written
the governor, not that he had "already" received the requisition itself.
We know this from Cox's own message to Chase, dated "Feby 29/56."
Enclosing a certified copy of the grand jury's murder indictment, Cox's
letter recounts the latest developments—Pendery's decision, Leavitt's habeas corpus ruling, Brashears's surrender of the Garners to Robinson's
posse—but then actually stops short of formally asking Chase to write a
requisition. "I cannot make any affidavit or even statement that these
parties are fugitives from justice," Cox complains, because "they did not
flee from justice in this State." Just as attorneys Jolliffe and Mills had
predicted, Cox now cautioned that Chase might have no legal basis on

Salmon Portland Chase,
Republican Governor of Ohio, ca. 1855
COURTESY THE CINCINNATI HISTORICAL SOCIETY

which "to issue a requisition upon the Governor of Kentucky for these defendants." His closing left the decision entirely in the governor's hands: "*If* you deem it proper," Cox wrote, deftly leaving Chase a way out, *then* he would volunteer to take the requisition to Frankfort, Kentucky.[53]

The record shows that Chase did not write his final draft of the requisition until five days later, on Tuesday, 4 March 1856. That was the date on his personally inscribed cover letter, a five-page legal brief that took Governor Morehead to school on constitutional issues. In it Chase reviewed international laws respecting the return of fugitives, laws he said were affirmed in the Articles of Confederation between "the original thirteen American states," thus to be written "into the Federal Constitution." He claimed "the framers of our Constitution" never intended to make slavery an exception to time-honored laws, and claimed moreover that "actual flight" was never an absolute condition for requisitioning criminals; rather, any kind of "leaving" qualified a chief magistrate to petition his counterpart in another jurisdiction. After four densely argued pages of this, Chase finally stated his "conclusion that the persons mentioned in the issued indictment are properly subject to extradition and I therefore make the usual requisition."[54]

Chase asked Columbus attorney Edward S. Hamlin to present the requisition at Frankfort. When Hamlin initially declined, Chase appointed another Columbus attorney, Joseph Cooper, but with Chase's blessing Hamlin also went along, not interested in the requisition but determined instead "to secure, if possible by purchase, the freedom of the children and also, in the event of her acquittal or upon the expiration of her sentence, that of the mother." In the event Gaines might agree, Hamlin took an $800 purse that Ohio abolitionists had already raised for the purpose.[55] On Wednesday, 5 March, Cooper and Hamlin arrived in Cincinnati and joined with prosecuting attorney Joseph Cox. Early the next day these three finally departed Ohio, bound for Frankfort via Covington and Lexington.

This explains why six days passed before the "party" of Ohio officers "reached Frankfort on Thursday evening [6 March], and had an interview with Gov. Morehead, and placed in his hands the official papers relating to the case."[56] Interestingly, though, published accounts also suggest that before Ohio deputies handed him the formal requisition, Governor Morehead already knew it was being sent. Perhaps he had received a telegram from Chase, or else from Cox, giving advance notice of their impending arrival in Frankfort. In any case, Morehead *must* have gotten some kind of advance notice. By Wednesday, 5 March, the day before Joseph Cooper said they left Cincinnati, Morehead had already extracted a promise from Archibald Gaines "that he would not send the woman [Margaret] out of the State, and that she should be given up if he [Governor Morehead] should so require."[57] Archibald Gaines later admitted that he had made such a promise but claimed he was forced to wait so long for the formal requisition to arrive from Ohio that he had given up. He said that when Thursday came and no extradition request had arrived he felt "constrained by the accumulation of cost and a desire to get rid of such an encumbrance as the woman necessarily was"; therefore he proceeded "to send her, in company with her husband and children and her husband's parents, to the State of Arkansas."[58] Purely a business decision.

It turns out that we also have good reason to question Gaines's account, particularly after examining his complicated actions and asking what motivated them. Once again the print record gives us a little but perhaps just enough to go on. For example, within days of returning empty-handed from Frankfort, Joseph Cooper wrote a letter explaining to Chase why the party failed to return with Margaret. In the letter he included an important anecdote. Cooper said that when his party changed trains at Lexington he met an acquaintance "who had in charge four slaves." This meeting happened early Thursday afternoon and we know from other sources that the acquaintance was Marshal Clinton Butts. The four slaves in his charge were Robert, Robert's mother, Mary, and "a light-colored mulatto girl with a still lighter-colored infant in her arms"—obviously Margaret and Cilla.[59] Cooper erroneously thought the elder woman was "Margaret's mother" and also made a bad guess at Robert's age ("about thirty," he thought). Still, Cooper remembered this "Negro" as the same tall, well-built man that other observers described from courtroom appearances.[60] When they met, Marshal Butts volunteered information that he was taking the Garners "to Louisville, where Mr. Gaines's other slaves were lying in jail, and that, on his arrival, they would all be shipped down the river." If this is so, then Gaines had obviously been continuing his shell game with the Garners. During the previous days, and for reasons unknown, Gaines must have ordered Robert and Mary back from Frankfort *and then* sent Margaret's boys, Tom and Sam, over to Louisville, where they now lay in jail with their grandfather, Simon. Deception is the likeliest motive for all this complicated and costly shuffling.

Gaines was in Frankfort as early as Tuesday, when he could have given those assurances to Governor Morehead, and he spent Wednesday night there. On Thursday, Gaines departed Frankfort for Louisville "in the morning train of cars" after explaining to marshals in the Kentucky capital that he intended to reunite the Garner children with their mother, then in transit via Lexington. He also reaffirmed his intention to obey any requisition order. But if this is so, why didn't he simply keep the Garners in jail at Frankfort? Moreover, why did Gaines move them all to Louisville just at the moment when Cooper, Cox, and Hamlin were in transit from Covington to Frankfort? His timing was so precise, indeed almost preternatural, that someone must have tipped him off.

Who? That part would have been easy. In the Cincinnati-Covington area Archibald Gaines had well-placed, powerful allies like Marshal

Hiram Robinson, John T. Finnell, and Samuel Wall. On Wednesday evening any of them could have gathered intelligence about how Governor Chase's party had (finally) arrived in Cincinnati and were completing preparations to depart from there on Thursday morning. A telegram from any of these allies addressed to his Frankfort hotel could have tipped Gaines, who just as easily set Marshal Butts in motion from Lexington. Eight years later, Chase would still believe something like this must have happened.[61] As for Cooper's running into Marshal Butts at Lexington, that was just blind luck for his side, for otherwise Gaines played a deft game whose strategy was to keep dividing up the Garners and moving them among Richwood Station, Lexington, Frankfort, and Louisville. The game's object: stay just ahead of Ohio antislavery people, placate Kentucky governor Morehead, and finally ship the Garners south—all the while playing the exasperated yet cooperative gentleman.

Gaines had time enough to play this game because it took Cooper, Cox, and Hamlin six crucial days to reach Frankfort, and they took so long because Chase had been laboring over the requisition. This delay resulted in a tragedy like that following Elijah Kite's belated return to his Mill Creek cabin on the morning of 28 January, when the eight Garners were craving to get on to the next Underground Railroad station. It was another awful foul-up. While less notable than Kite's, over the years it has demanded inquiry and answers.

Was Chase to blame? For months and even years afterward, radical abolitionists accused him of failing to throw state government across the path of federal judges and marshals responsible for remanding the Garners to slavery. In a May 1856 keynote speech for an American Anti-Slavery Society convention at New York, Theodore Parker accused Chase of foot-dragging—he thought because of racism. Had Margaret Garner been white, Parker claimed, the governor would have swiftly bugled Ohio's militia forces to a Cincinnati "rescue," for "the only constitution which slave-hunters respect is writ on the parchment of a drumhead."[62] Salmon Chase had built his reputation on an unyielding sympathy for fugitive slaves and he had long regarded Parker as an abolitionist friend, but after reading Parker's speech in printed form he felt betrayed and misunderstood. In a private letter he told Parker that what really stung him was the "intimation that my constitutional views on the Slavery question are determined by considerations of the color or origin of the Enslaved. God forbid!"[63] In public, however, Chase never answered accusers who said he acted indecisively or slowly and thus gave the Garners up to the Slave Power. So the charges lingered.

After eight more years of public life Chase was serving as Lincoln's Treasury Secretary and pondering a run for the 1864 Republican presidential nomination as a hard-liner on Reconstruction issues. War hadn't wholly shadowed critics' memories of the Garner case and some still grumbled about Chase's foot-dragging. The worst had come in late 1863. In November, old-line abolitionist Wendell Phillips charged in a Boston lecture that Chase "sacrificed Margaret Garner," proving he had neither the "heart" nor the "principle" for the presidency. Phillips followed that attack with a series of letters to Horace Greeley's *New York Tribune* arguing that Chase's delays in the Garner case well indicated his lack of "vigor" for "the cause."[64] This time Chase's Republican Party supporters urged a public response, and the former governor begged testimonials from old Ohio friends such as George Hoadley, William Dennison, and W. H. Brisbane. He rummaged through his papers for copies of 1856 correspondence, then (in early 1864) contacted a former Treasury Department colleague, Edward L. Pierce, about publishing all the documents in a pamphlet. At the same time he began sending the first of twenty-seven letters to Boston journalist John T. Trowbridge, who had proposed writing a campaign biography of Chase. Answering Trowbridge's queries about the Garner case, Chase penned a six-thousand-word reply that began with his recollection of the "tragic circumstances" and erred only in a few minor matters. Overall, Chase portrays himself as a newly inaugurated governor whose mostly practical concerns prevented him from acting on the Garners' behalf. The legal proceedings unfolded just two weeks after he assumed the governorship, Chase complained; and at that key moment he was simultaneously dealing with a just convened Ohio legislature as well as with Pittsburgh-based committees planning for an upcoming Republican Party convention.[65] He praised Jolliffe's "able counsel" and thought every available legal defense had been tried. Still, Chase admitted to feeling "keenly the humiliation" of seeing the 1850 fugitive law override Ohio statutes.

Chase's letter to Trowbridge is an obvious attempt at self-vindication, and so was the projected pamphlet of documents he was compiling with Edward Pierce. But months later, in May 1864, Chase withdrew from the presidential race. Trowbridge's biography would appear in heavily edited form, a volume in a series of popular biographies printed for juveniles. The documents Edward Pierce assembled never saw print.

Perhaps it was well for Chase that his actual letters and documents never saw publication, for a minor but persistent motif running through them is Chase's reluctance to act. Writing to Trowbridge, for example, he noted (in phrasing later edited out) that when Cox asked him for the requisition his first thought was: Ohio had no claim on them as "fugitives from justice" because a legal process had sent them away. "I overcame my reluctance," Chase said, "and issued the requisition." One of his letters to Dennison repeated that theme: "I hesitated about making a demand for them on the Governor of Kentucky. I hesitated the more because I was unwilling to characterize the homicide as murder. I yielded however to my sympathies for the poor mother & to my wishes in some way to vindicate the outraged laws of the State, & sent an agent on to Kentucky with a formal demand for the fugitives."[66] It all boiled down to this: Chase "hesitated" before sending his agent with the requisition, and that "reluctance" to act would prove fatal.

Chase certainly added to his critics' doubts by never speaking publicly about the Garner case, not even at the 1856 Cincinnati Washington's Birthday festivities with the fugitives jailed a few blocks away from the speakers' platform. It's also true—as Theodore Parker charged—that by never deploying Ohio sheriffs or militias against federal marshals Chase weakly avoided what might well have become a decisive states' rights confrontation. Resolutions passed in the Ohio Senate immediately following Margaret Garner's child-murder demonstrate that Chase could have counted on strong legislative support. Tallying all these factors, Chase's most recent biographer concludes that, had he risked it, Ohio antislavery forces might well have turned aside the Garners' rendition to Kentucky. That he didn't risk it is all the more baffling because Chase was maneuvering even then for his first run at a presidential nomination, and one of his likely competitors would be Supreme Court Justice John McLean. Chase must have seen how the Garner fugitive trial gave him a signal opportunity. He could have pointed up the proslavery role of McLean's Commissioner John Pendery and thus seized a chance to characterize Taney's fellow Supreme Court justice as exactly the "old fossil" that many antislavery Republicans were saying he was.[67] More generally, resisting Franklin Pierce and the Slave Power could only have bolstered Chase's standing with those emerging antislavery forces who would take Republicans to the White House in 1860.

Chase therefore had compelling political reasons to take up the Garners' cause. But he had equally compelling personal reasons to stand aside. Among the Chase papers housed at the Library of Congress is a bound notebook containing miscellaneous notes, quotes, meditations, facts, and drafts for speeches from 1841 through the late 1850s—all on the subject of slavery and Chase's antislavery activities. Among the entries in Chase's tiny and at times nearly illegible handwriting is one accounting or list written just before Chase's gubernatorial inauguration, probably in early 1856, and having no explainable connection to the notebook's subject. Chase titled the page "Family Memoranda" and on it he detailed grim genealogical facts. "Catherine Jane Chase, wife of S.P.C., died December 1, 1835 (post-partum)," reads the first item. Below it he wrote the name of his first-born daughter, Catherine Jane, born two weeks before the mother's death. This little girl died at age four (in February 1840, as Chase noted), months after Chase's second marriage (in 1839) to Eliza Ann Smith. A year later Eliza bore Chase another daughter, *another* Catherine Jane, who survived. Another daughter, Lizzie, died at four months (in 1842), as did a second Lizzie at thirteen months (in 1844). Below these Chase listed the death of his second wife, Eliza (in 1846), followed by his marriage to Sarah Ludlow (in 1847), then the births of their first child (who lived) and their second (who did not). Finally he listed Sarah Chase's death ("at Clifton, near Cincinnati, where she was then residing, January 13, 1852").[68] These birth dates and death dates imply a chilling story. They say that by February 1856 this man had buried three wives and four daughters, only one of whom had lived past thirteen months, so that even in that era of high infant mortality rates, of tuberculosis and cholera epidemics and scarlet fever, Salmon Portland Chase must have been one of the most star-crossed husbands and fathers among the Garner tragedy's dramatis personae.

How did his losses affect his view of Margaret Garner? When reporters electrified newspaper readers with accounts of "the slave mother's infanticide," Chase must have felt deeply the horror of her actions. In his religious view, inscrutable Providence had hung a string of tragedies on the Chase family tree. But they were God's doing; Margaret Garner's doings usurped divine authority. After burying four daughters of his own, Margaret's child-murder probably left Chase feeling a deep revulsion. It was true that through the antebellum decades he had lawyered tirelessly and passionately for fugitive slaves. This time, however, he showed little stomach for the work. Not that Chase shirked his duty, exactly. For in the first days of March he did after all write that meticulously argued brief to Governor Morehead. This document was a dry, scholastic exercise in overkill—as it turned out—a legal brief whose research and writing consumed five precious days, time Gaines used to stage his shell game.

Should Chase have thought he had that kind of time to "hesitate" over the legal issues? He shouldn't have. All his prior experiences fighting slave masters had taught him to expect deception and to act swiftly, especially in a case like this one. And yet Chase took too much time. Five years later abolitionist Samuel May would write that Chase's waiting so long to send his agents to Kentucky for the Garners was "an unpardonable delay."[69] It remains a fair judgment.

At least prosecuting attorney Joseph Cox put Chase's delay to some kind of good use: he began to pursue U.S. Marshal Robinson from court to court. On Friday, 29 February, the day he told Judge Carter of having asked the governor for a requisition, Cox was in court to file a complaint against Robinson for hindering the *capias*. The next morning Cox was in Judge Burgoyne's Probate Court to challenge Robinson's motion to quash Burgoyne's still outstanding habeas corpus writ, now mooted (in the marshal's view) by the fugitives' return to Kentucky. Instead, at Cox's urging Burgoyne turned up the heat: if Robinson wanted it quashed, then he belatedly admitted the writ's legitimacy; and if he granted its legitimacy, then why—Burgoyne wanted to know—hadn't the marshal delivered the fugitives as the writ required instead of taking them over the river? Robinson's attorney, James Headington, kept giving evasive answers until late that afternoon, when a frustrated Burgoyne adjourned, scheduling further arguments for Monday morning, 3 March.

On Monday, and again on Tuesday and Wednesday, there was no action on Robinson's case in Burgoyne's court. The likeliest reason for the delay is that prosecutor Cox was waiting, assuming that a departure for Kentucky with Chase's requisition was imminent. He probably asked Burgoyne for an adjournment until after the Frankfort trip was over. Early Thursday morning Cox finally departed for Frankfort with the others and left arguments against Robinson in the able hands of John Jolliffe, who had asked Burgoyne for the habeas corpus in the first place and therefore had perhaps the better reason to pursue Robinson.[70] As we know, on Thursday afternoon in Lexington, Joseph Cooper ran into Marshal Clinton Butts, already en route to Louisville with Margaret, Cilla, Robert, and Mary Garner. In Frankfort, Gaines was ready to move Simon and the two boys on to Louisville as well. Cooper's party was en route to Frankfort. But too late. Archibald Gaines was about to win his shell game.

Thursday evening Cooper, Cox, and Hamlin laid the requisition, murder indictment, and Chase's cover letter before Governor Morehead, whose written reply to Chase (dated the next day) suggests what was the tenor of that meeting. Morehead first of all characterized the Garner trial and subsequent habeas corpus maneuvering as a wholesale "intervention to obstruct the delivery of these persons as fugitive slaves from Kentucky to their owners." As for an extradition order, Morehead explained that he was always "prepared to act immediately" on any requisition and to return the Garners promptly; Chase, however, had used up precious time in researching and writing his lengthy essay on constitutional law. Then Morehead twisted the knife still further: he said that looking over Chase's five dense pages of argument had had an unintended effect; for if the issue had to be so exhaustively argued, Morehead remarked, then that gave rise "to doubts whether they [the Garners] come within the description of the second clause of the second section of the fourth article of the Constitution." In sum, now that Chase had brought it up, Morehead was compelled to study the legal matters himself. That effort took him only an evening instead of Chase's five days and even then, Morehead snidely remarks in his letter, "I saw no reason to change my previous opinion." A polite way of saying Chase had wasted his breath.

Then Morehead chided him further. Perhaps, he speculated, Chase exercised his legal expertise with the design of giving "such doubts under color of which I might refuse" the requisition. If so, then Chase misunderstood Kentucky's willingness "to acknowledge the paramount obligation in letter and spirit of the Federal Constitution, and the supremacy of all laws made in pursuance thereof. *They* would be the last to justify their suasion by any mere quibble or technicality." That last was clearly a gibe at antislavery Ohioans, whose "mere quibble" over a "technicality" or two had only "obstructed" the Garners' necessary return to slavery. Finally, Morehead even rebuked Chase for sending "distinguished counsel to argue this question," an action that (he said) betrayed a distrust of "Kentucky character." And of course, he remarked in closing, should "these slaves be acquitted" in Ohio, then he trusted Chase would return them to Kentucky with "the same promptitude" that Morehead was then demonstrating.[71] In all, Morehead's formal reply was a masterful exercise in sarcastic criticism masking itself as cooperation and comity.

We don't know how much of his irony surfaced Thursday evening when Cooper presented the requisition. That meeting lasted an hour and closed with Morehead promising to "examine [the documents] and give his answer tomorrow [Friday]." In any case, that Cooper found the whole episode exasperating is clear even in his restrained narration of events in a letter to Chase. Cooper also must have felt that Archibald Gaines, perhaps with Morehead's approval, had ultimately succeeded in manipulating everyone. For that evening as Cooper's group left the governor's mansion someone ran up with late news that Gaines had already taken his slaves by train from Frankfort to Louisville.

First thing Friday morning, Morehead formally granted Chase's request. Cox, Cooper, and Hamlin barely made the midmorning train. They reached Louisville that afternoon only to learn that hours earlier Gaines had already put the seven Garners aboard a boat bound down the Ohio and Mississippi rivers for New Orleans. Clinton Butts was transporting them in leg irons and had orders to deliver the slaves to Benjamin Gaines's plantation in southeastern Arkansas.

Sold Down the River

The *Henry Lewis* was a Cincinnati-based Mississippi steamboat in the classic style. While not one of those sumptuously decorated, three-hundred-foot-long "floating palaces" like the *Sultana* or the *Eclipse*, two famous steamboats then making the Cincinnati–New Orleans run in an average of five to six days, the *Lewis* had an identical design. It was somewhat over two hundred feet long, a multidecked side-wheeler painted white and with the ornate, boldly colored green and red filigree in the "steamboat gothic" style, all topped by twin black stacks. Poorer passengers, including any slaves other than body servants, traveled on a steerage ticket and rode with cargo stacked on the lower or main deck. Largely unprotected from weather and noise from the boat's twin boilers and engines, they often sat on or amidst crates or fuel and slept on packed cargo. For a washroom they had the river. Regular passengers sat, strolled, washed, dined, and slept on the second or boiler deck. For better views of passing villages and landscapes they might climb stairs to the roof or hurricane deck and stroll past the texas, or crew's quarters, atop which stood the pilothouse.[72]

The *Louisville Journal*'s "Shipping News" column tells us that the *Henry Lewis* arrived from Cincinnati on Wednesday evening; on Thursday the boat laid over to fill its cargo manifest and take on more passengers. Gaines arrived in town on Thursday, reunited the Garners, and, one supposes, informed them it was final: no requisition had arrived from their abolitionist friends, so he was obliged to send them all to his brother. If Gaines hadn't already made the Garners' travel arrangements before arriving in Louisville, he might well have scanned the morning's *Journal* for notices about departing packet boats and read this small advertisement, just following the universally used steamboat logo: "For NEW ORLEANS. The fine steamer *Henry Lewis*, Emerson, master, will leave Friday, the 7th inst., at ten o'clock a.m. For freight and passengers apply on board." Gaines purchased eight tickets: seven in steerage, costing about thirty-five or forty dollars total, and one for a stateroom on the main deck, probably costing another twenty dollars. That night Archibald Gaines slept at the Exchange Hotel, just up from the waterfront. The Garners slept at the Jefferson County jail, lodging for which their master probably paid the usual fee of fifty cents per adult, twenty-five per child. Most likely Clinton Butts also spent the night on a bunk at the jail—his meals, lodging, and service imposing still more expense on an already exasperated Gaines.[73]

Friday, 7 March 1856. Overnight the weather turned cold once again. Morning snow flurries would give way to dark, overcast skies in the afternoon and a high temperature in the upper thirties. When Clinton Butts escorted the Garners from the county jail they confronted a biting cold—memento of recent days in Cincinnati. Evidently they passed through Louisville streets practically unnoticed. No white and black abolitionists kept vigil outside the jail, no disturbances were recorded in the next day's papers, they were just another slave family in transit. At the waterfront, roustabouts—most of them slaves—loaded and secured final items of cargo on board the *Henry Lewis*. Later reports indicate that Captain Emerson had loaded the boat down to its gunnels with seven hundred tons of barreled pork and lard oil, crated candles, and cheeses, all bound for New Orleans markets. Roustabouts had stowed some of this cargo up on forward sections of the hurricane and main decks, stacking crates so high that newspapers would later wonder whether the Lewis's running lights were obscured from view, and if the cargo had made the boat's fore section top-heavy.[74]

Once aboard with the other forty or so passengers, Clinton Butts arranged the Garners and their few belongings in the "nursery," that portion of the lower or main deck at the stern, behind the twin paddle wheels and under cover of the boiler deck. Butts shackled them by twos, like other slaves in transit on the Henry Lewis, and evidently chained them to an iron ring. Margaret carried little Cilla. When Butts had his final instructions for the journey and the Garners were settled in, Gaines must have made what he assumed would be a final farewell to them. Clinton Butts took to his stateroom and the Garners huddled against the cold. At ten Emerson ordered the crew to cast off and pilot James Patterson turned the boat downstream.

They steamed past the falls of the Ohio, easily navigable with the river running so high, then through a sequence of short stops to load or unload passengers, mail, and fuel. Evans Landing and Rome, Indiana, Cloverport, Kentucky—the villages and towns slid by. Along the way Marshal Clinton Butts evidently strutted about the boiler deck heavily armed "with an immense amount of cutlery and firearms." Passengers also noted him making quite a show of keeping close watch over "his niggers," and later he exchanged "some sharp words with a gentleman on the steamer about the Fugitive Slave case." Several times he checked up on the slaves, then retired to his stateroom about ten Friday night.

The boat made good time. Seventeen hours out, at three Saturday morning, the Henry Lewis reached Hawesville, Kentucky, a coaling stop. If they had been asleep the Garners were awakened by, and perhaps Simon and Robert were also required to assist in, the loading of fuel, a common requirement for those traveling in steerage. At four in the morning the boat reached Troy, Indiana, about a hundred and fifty miles below Louisville and twenty-five miles upriver from Owensboro, Kentucky. There pilot James Patterson handed over the wheel to his brother and before retiring to his bunk in the texas spent a while with Adam Patterson, "conversing together in the pilot house." Outside it was a cold but also "a clear, starlit morning." They could see several miles downriver.

Just after four the Pattersons glimpsed a steamboat "coming up, still about two miles distant." It was the *Edward Howard*, steaming to Cincinnati. "She was running the Indiana shore," James Patterson later wrote. Watching her course, the brothers figured that the *Howard*'s pilot would keep hugging that north shore, "as is customary with steamboats when the river is high." Adam Patterson continued steering the *Lewis* down the middle of the Ohio, but as the boats drew nearer he became anxious for a signal whistle that would indicate the side on which the *Howard* wanted to pass, another customary practice among river pilots. No whistle came. Patterson was just about to pull the whistle himself when his counterpart signaled that the *Lewis* should pass on the *Howard*'s left or port side, between the *Howard* and the Indiana shore. But this was an illogical and impossible maneuver, now that the two boats were so close. Adam Patterson immediately whistled back "for the larboard [right side] and stopped our engines and commenced backing as soon as we saw that she was headed across the river."[75]

The *Edward Howard* plowed into the *Henry Lewis* just forward of its starboard-side boiler. The impact turned the *Lewis*'s bow back upstream. Collapsing under the cargo, the entire cabin and then the hull broke into two sections and the smaller fore portion "careered over" until its hurricane deck was mostly submerged. The aft portion, where the Garners rode, began taking water but miraculously remained upright. The starboard side boiler luckily did not burst and released its pressure in a sustained "hissing," but fire spread from the engine room back through the main deck toward the nursery.[76]

News reports indicate that when the collision occurred all regular and steerage passengers were asleep in their stateroom berths or hunkered among the pork barrels stacked in the nursery. The impact threw stateroom passengers from their beds and pinned a few of the slaves in shifting cargo on the main deck. Within minutes everyone was panicked. Survivors told newsmen that the *Lewis* was soon echoing "alarms of 'Fire!' and cries of drowning wretches" that brought most regular passengers, "including a number of ladies and children," onto the boiler deck in their night clothes.[77] Below, on the main deck, they could hear cries from slaves calling for help. Wouldn't someone come down to unshackle them?

The impact also tumbled Marshal Clinton Butts from his berth, and, like other passengers, he ran first onto the boiler deck to survey the *Lewis's* dire condition. Evidently he then hustled back to his stateroom "to get something"—apparently the key to unshackle the Garners. While he was back inside, part of the heavily laden hurricane deck—the stateroom's roof—collapsed, trapping Butts inside. One of the cabin boys heard Butts's calls for help and begged the assistance of several male passengers. They failed in several attempts to pry off cargo and wreckage to get at his door.

Finally one of the cabin boys found an ax and chopped a way through the debris above Clinton Butts's stateroom. One of the passengers reached down to pull up the trapped man and, although the *National Anti-Slavery Standard* discounted this next detail as an apocryphal bit of poetic justice, the man was said to be "the same gentleman" who had earlier argued with the marshal over the Garner trial and Pendery's decision. Looking into the stateroom, he allegedly exclaimed, "Halloo, Butts, is this you? Damn you, if I'd known that, you might have drowned. And you shall anyhow, if you won't give your word to let those niggers go." With the gentleman now "holding the axe of deliverance or death," Butts surrendered the key.

About fifteen minutes had passed since the collision. After impact, the *Edward Howard* had backed off, and the pilot, seeing the *Henry Lewis's* fore section break away and nearly capsize, decided to nudge his boat's damaged prow against the still upright aft section in order to remove frantic passengers. As he approached the *Lewis's* slowly sinking stern on its starboard side, stateroom passengers ran downstairs behind steerage passengers who cried for the *Howard's* mates to throw them ropes. Fire was still spreading from the boiler rooms.

What happened next is unclear. Cradling Cilla in her arms a now unshackled Margaret Garner was standing at the gunnel with a white woman who traveled with them in steerage. Behind her were other slaves and steerage passengers. Then, either the *Edward Howard* gave the *Lewis's* aft section a sudden push, throwing the white woman and Margaret and Cilla into the icy river. Or, seeing that she "had an opportunity," Margaret "threw her child into the river and jumped after it." Or she "tried to jump upon the boat alongside, but fell short." An inadvertent slip? A suicidal leap? Or a desperate jump to save her child? No newspaperman who wrote this part of the story could say exactly which it was, but it is certain that ten-month-old Priscilla Garner drowned and that her body was never recovered. James and Adam Patterson, pilots of the *Henry Lewis*, confirmed these details in a published description of the accident that was followed by a tally of other dead passengers. They had no interest in these fugitives' recent case, therefore no reason to misrepresent events.

Witnesses did describe to newsmen how "a black man, the cook on the *Lewis*, sprang into the river and saved Margaret." They also relayed details that make Margaret's actions somewhat clearer. Apparently, when rescuers brought Margaret aboard the *Edward Howard* she "displayed frantic joy when told that her child was drowned, and said she would never reach alive Gaines's Landing, in Arkansas, the point for which she was shipped, thus intimating a desire to drown herself."[78] Such actions, of course, were consistent with what we know of Margaret Garner. Yet this recognition compels us to ask: How did events unfold in the steamboat's nursery just after the collision? Did Robert and his parents once again sense Margaret's destructive design? Did they share it? If not, could they have done anything to stop her? Did Tom and Sam, witnesses (and near-victims) just five weeks earlier, not only sense the other passengers' terror but also feel, once again, that mortal dread of their own mother? Here again the record falls silent and we can only ask speculative questions.

In the confusion and darkness, rescuers never recovered the bodies of the unnamed white woman and Cilla, lost along with others who were consumed in the fire. The Garners, the surviving passengers, finally even Marshal Butts and his abolitionist savior were all pulled from the *Henry Lewis*. The fore section broke apart and drifted downstream. The aft section sank in fifteen feet of water eighty yards off the Kentucky shore. James Patterson wrote that crew members worked tirelessly to cut three others besides Clinton Butts from their staterooms, then abandoned the scene. Exaggerated reports in Louisville and Cincinnati papers later counted twenty or even twenty-five victims of drowning or injuries because of the impact and fire. Later tallies brought that number down to nine. Known victims included three "gentlemen" crushed to death in their staterooms near the *Howard*'s point of impact, a steward from New Orleans and a cabin boy from Ohio who were evidently burned, and finally the unnamed white woman in steerage and her two children who were drowned along with Priscilla Garner.

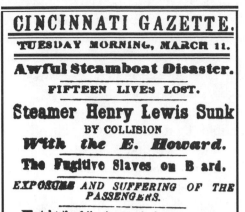

CINCINNATI GAZETTE.

TUESDAY MORNING, MARCH 11.

Awful Steamboat Disaster.

FIFTEEN LIVES LOST.

Steamer Henry Lewis Sunk
BY COLLISION
With the E. Howard.

The Fugitive Slaves on B ard.

*EXPOSURE AND SUFFERING OF THE
PASSENGERS.*

We take the following particulars of the loss of
the Henry Lewis, announced in our river column
yesterday, from the Louisville *Courier :*

The disaster occurred in the Obio river, about
4 o'clock, Saturday, a clear starlight morning. The
Henry Lewis, with a full cargo for New Orleans,
from Cincinnati, and about forty passengers on
board, was descending the river, just belyw Troy,
"hugging the Kentucky shore," at the head of Anderson's bar, when the E. Howard, ascending, came
up, or rather out, from behind the point, and a collision occurred, sinking the Henry Lewis in three
minutes, in about twenty feet of water.

At the moment of the collision the wildest scene
of terror and excitement ensued among the passengers and crew of the ill-fated boat ever conceived of or experienced on the Western waters.
The passengers were all asleep in their berths
but a moment before, and at the next instant were
hurried forth amid the crushing of timbers, the
hissing of steam, the hurrying to and fro, the
alarm of fire and cries of drowning wretches to find
themselves surrounded by death in its most hide-
ous forms. The shock of the collision threw the
boat around with her bow up stream, and the entire cabin broke in two, or was rather crushed in
by the great weight o' freight upon the roof and at
the same time it careered over, a portion of the
roof on one side, being entirely under water. The
passengers including a number of ladies and children, escaped in their night clothes, and took refuge on the hurricane-deck, exposed to all the in-
clemency of the weather. Many of them were
sorely bruised by the boxes of glassware and other
articles that fell in upon them from the roof. The
boat also caught fire, and amid the smoke, falling
ruins, and rushing waters their chances of escape
seemed hopeless indeed. The boat luckily settled
to the bottom of the river, leaving the hurricane-
roof above water, and there the survivors congre-
gated to await assistance.

*More shocking news: headlines and opening
paragraphs from the* Cincinnati Gazette
of 11 March 1856

A *Cincinnati Commercial* story indicates that after gathering all possible survivors the *Edward Howard* turned back downriver for Evansville. There Clinton Butts rebooked their passage aboard another Louisiana-bound steamboat, the *Hungarian,* embarking late Saturday afternoon, and telegraphed Archibald Gaines news that all were safe except the infant Priscilla. "The last that was seen of Peggy," according to the *Commercial,* "she was on the *Hungarian,* crouching like a wild animal near the stove, with a blanket wrapped around her." This reporter thought the tragedy had all but completed its denouement: "Our readers will, we presume, be struck with the dramatic features of the Fugitive Slave Case, and that it progresses like a plot wrought by some master of tragedy."

According to this logic, the "drama" only makes sense through the unfolding of its concluding scene, when readers can work backward from effects to their causes and trace Fate's designs in mortal lives. "Peggy" had finally been "sold South" into the "seething Hell" of slavery, but she had vowed to die rather than go there. So it was time to give a précis of the plot, time to calculate on the necessary conclusion or "catastrophe" that seemed (literally) just around the bend:

First, there was the flight and the crossing of the frozen river in the twilight of the morning, the place of fancied security, the surprise of the officers, the fight with them, the murder of the child, the arrest, the scenes about the Court-room and in the jail, the long suspense, the return to Kentucky, the removal to Frankfort, the separation there, her removal to Louisville, the pursuit of the messengers [from Chase], the boat on which she was to have been taken South leaving two hours ahead of Cooper with the writ from Governor Morehead; then the speedy catastrophe of the steamer, the drowning of the babe of the heroine, and her own rescue, as if yet saved for some more fearful and startling act of the tragedy; and lastly the curtain falls, leaving her wet and dismal, on a boat bound South, perfectly careless as to her own fate, only determined never to set foot on the soil of Arkansas. There is something fearfully tragic about this, which must occur to every mind, and we shall look with much interest for information of the catastrophe which will complete the dramatic unity of the affair.[79]

What "catastrophe" would unify Margaret's drama? This *Commercial* writer anticipated hearing momentarily of her violent death and expected it would occur just beyond Northerners' view—offstage, like the bloody finale of a classic tragedy. Cincinnatians would get word of it as the merest snippet of hearsay forwarded up from the South. For him the curtain had fallen and Margaret's drama was all but concluded; nothing left for it but the chorus's final recitative. Margaret had become the modern Medea, departing the stage leaving two children dead by her own hand and her world in flames and wreckage, just as Euripides scripted it.

Perhaps the point was to *make* Margaret disappear. Euripides has Medea ride off in her sun chariot, tormented yet unpunished, an ending producers have rewritten ever since because culture cannot cope with mothers who murder their children. Since we are all of mothers born, we are all conflicted to the point of wordlessness over maternal infanticide. We say it is against nature, unthinkable, but also demand rational reasons for it; we wish it away but want it answered. Thus in his 1813 opera *Medea in Corinth*, Giovanni Mayr scripted a Medea goaded to child-murder by a vengeful Aegeus; she then exits the drama on an inrush of self-destructive guilt. In 1856 Ernest Legouvé portrayed a Medea driven to infanticide by altruistic mother love. His Medea takes up the knife to spare her boys from a torturous death at the hands of Corinthian mobs, and the exit figures her as a tragically doomed heroine.

Antebellum Americans knew the Mayr and Legouvé scripts because touring companies had brought the operas Stateside. The Euripides version they knew through Richard Porson's translation and through American poet Harriet Fanning Read's popular 1848 adaptation of the story. Read's dramatic script is particularly telling because she depicts a Medea motivated solely by the desire for vengeance against a Jason who jilted her for a racially purer wife. In fact, Harriet Read's Medea could well have been played *as* a black woman.[80] By 1856, therefore, it would have been possible to understand Margaret Garner in terms of three different Medeas: a Southron version in which abolitionists goad her to child-murder (Mayr), a bourgeois Northern view of her as murdering from an altruistic mother love (Legouvé), and an abolitionist view of her as a wronged woman of color wreaking vengeance on her white husband for his sexual and racial betrayal of her. These differences were already clear on the day after Margaret's infanticide, when her story first electrified telegraphic wires. Yet both sides now shared a common cultural problem: the ending. How would the *real* Margaret Garner exit her drama?

Many American readers would have expected the last scene to unfold in a popular sentimental mode. Harriet Beecher Stowe's phenomenally successful 1852 novel *Uncle Tom's Cabin* includes a brief anecdote (in the "Eliza's Escape" chapter) narrated by Haley, the slave catcher, who could easily have been played by Clinton Butts. Sharing a jug of corn whiskey with compatriots, Haley complains that "notions" infect women slaves facing the sale of a child; they turn wild, uncontrollable. He tells of transporting a fugitive slave mother and her infant aboard a steamboat and, during the journey, swapping her child for "a keg o' whiskey." Then the slave mother learned of his perfidy: "I hadn't got my gang chained up, so what should she do but ups on a cotton bale, like a cat, ketches a knife from one of the deck hands, and, I tell ye, she made all fly for a minit, till she saw 't wasn't no use; and she jest turns round, and pitches head first, young un and all, into the river,—went down plump, and never ris."[81] Margaret's daring escape over the ice, like Eliza's; her resistance and then her despairing suicide and child-murder, like Haley's slave woman: these had a "familiar" ring and observers saw them as scenes torn from a popular text.

Soon a welter of poems, polemics, and plots representing her as a mostly fictional "Tragic Slave Mother" would practically eclipse Margaret's historical presence. The *Commercial* writer's synopsis demonstrates how details of her life were already susceptible to a pat kind of scripting. As sure as she would disappear into the miasmatic air of Southern slavery, Margaret Garner was evaporating into the thin air of Northern texts written to memorialize her.

In Boston, *The Liberator* of 7 March narrated the Garners' rendition to Kentucky as "the last act of the drama of the fugitive slaves."[82] In Cincinnati the *Gazette* also wondered if the drama had concluded. Would Chase—for that matter *could* Chase—requisition Arkansas for Margaret's return? Probably not, and so they chided Archibald Gaines to return her voluntarily or forever surrender his reputation "as an honorable man."[83] Throughout the coming week, *Gazette* and *Commercial* editorialists kept pressing the issue of Gaines's honor—a canny move, as things turned out. Meanwhile the antislavery *Gazette* and the proslavery *Enquirer* sustained a running argument over the amount of Hiram

Robinson's bill to the Pierce administration for remanding the Garners. Was the *Gazette*'s $22,400 figure an "extravagant" inflation? Robinson's own *Enquirer* had a tough time claiming the number should be half that much because just his own battalion of special deputies, employed at two dollars per day, most of them for four weeks, added up to something very close to the *Gazette*'s number.[84]

Cincinnatians also turned their attention to Hiram Robinson himself. After a spirited two-day debate on the marshal's defiance of an Ohio habeas corpus, argued in his Probate Court and spotlighting John Jolliffe, Judge John Burgoyne adjourned and on Tuesday, 18 March, found, "after full examination and calm deliberation," that the 1850 Fugitive Slave Law's empowering of Commissioners was unconstitutional and therefore that Robinson's "defiance" of an outstanding Ohio habeas corpus writ when he returned the Garners to Kentucky put the U.S. marshal in contempt of court.[85] The next day Burgoyne ordered Robinson to appear before his bench and show cause why he should not be cited. In due course he would order the marshal himself jailed and Robinson's lawyers would be asking federal judge Humphrey Leavitt for a habeas corpus writ *to free Robinson from jail*. Here again was the grand narrative of states' rights battles, itself a primary theme in the great drama of disunion or "impending crisis."

But Margaret's drama was still playing. By Monday, 10 March 1856, the six surviving Garners had reached Gaines Landing, situated on that C-shaped arc of the Mississippi where fifty-two-year-old Benjamin Gaines ran the three-hundred-acre plantation he had purchased from Archibald K. Gaines six years earlier, after a pregnant Margaret Gaines tumbled down a stairs and died three days later of internal hemorrhaging. In 1856 Gaines Landing was still little more than a village fronting the river and surrounded by cypress swamps that the slaves had cleared for cotton. The place was isolated. In 1852 the Arkansas legislature had granted charters to the Oachita & Red River Railroad Company to connect a railhead from the Landing to a trunk line fifty miles away, but by 1854 crews had laid only twenty miles of track from Gaines Landing to the west. The rails were never used for anything other than handcar travel.[86]

In 1850 the census taker recorded ninety-nine slaves on Benjamin Gaines's plantation. As at nearby Sunnyside, a plantation for which historians have a rather full archive, Gaines's slaves were primarily engaged in raising cotton for New Orleans markets. Gaines Landing was largely self-sufficient and its slaves raised corn, sweet potatoes, vegetables, and fruits; they maintained herds of about thirty milk cows and eighty head of cattle, several hundred pigs, several dozen mules, oxen, and the master's horses. During fall and winter the male slaves cut, split, hauled, and stacked wood for sale to steamboats. Spring and summer his entire slave force worked the cotton.[87]

The six surviving Garners had never known that kind of regimented, backbreaking work, but they arrived at the beginning of the cotton season and undoubtedly Benjamin Gaines sent them to his overseer for work in the fields, for the slaves' recent resistance ruled out any household service. Thus the Garners resumed their lives of toil and uncertainty.

5

LEGEND

✧

"Just in time to be too late"

The Garners arrived at Gaines
Landing at cotton-sowing time. A horn summoned them to dawn roll
call with Gaines's eighty or ninety other slaves, then the overseer drove
them off to the fields. Men broke clods of freshly plowed ground with
picks and hoes and shaped soil into rows. Women stooped over the rows,
pulling weeds and tossing them into baskets. Other women and children
like Tom and Sam followed, sprinkling the seed and pressing it into the
soil with their toes. Mornings, field slaves worked in cold fogs rising off
the river; afternoons, temperatures pushed into the seventies, a mere
foretaste of summer's suffocating heat and humidity. The tedious rou-
tines of King Cotton.[1]

Then one day Clinton Butts rematerialized. Two weeks after the Garners' arrival at Arkansas he rode up in a carriage (one supposes) and
stepped down with the latest: Archibald Gaines wanted Margaret back,
and Margaret alone. He had instructed Butts to bring her upriver to
Covington on the first available steamboat and lodge her in the county
jail. As for the other Garner adults and children, for now they should
stay at Gaines Landing. Archibald had no intention of sending all four

adults back to Ohio on a governor's warrant he regarded as a pretense for "negro-stealing."[2]

He had nonetheless relented under intense pressure. Newspapers throughout the North had been lashing him for dishonoring his pledge to hold the adult Garners in northern Kentucky until Governor Chase's agents arrived with a requisition. "Is this the boasted honor of a chivalrous Kentuckian?" wondered the *Gazette*, in what became a typical criticism. A widely reprinted *New York Tribune* editorial bluntly called Gaines a liar. No one should have been surprised at Gaines's shell game, said Horace Greeley's paper, because this man had already broken his promise to Lucy Stone (to sell abolitionists the children), and now his dealing the Garners to a Deep South cotton lord who would "administer the patriarchal system after the Simon Legree fashion" only completed the stereotype. Just like Squire Shelby in Harriet Beecher Stowe's *Uncle Tom's Cabin*, this Squire Gaines was also a rank hypocrite, "a member of the Presbyterian church" who "hesitates at no lie" to deal in human "property."[3]

Everything we know about Archibald Gaines tells us that even if these jabs drew blood, at first they only stiffened the man's resistance. Finally, though, he was forced to redeem his honor. As he later told it:

> Soon after she was sent from Kentucky it suited the purposes of the Abolition newspapers of Cincinnati to clamor most vociferously against me for having, as they charged, been guilty of running off and concealing a fugitive from justice from the State of Ohio. After much hesitation and consultation with friends of intelligence and integrity, I concluded that, in order to satisfy even the clamors of fanaticism, I would have her brought back to Kentucky. This I accordingly did, and at heavy expenses had the woman repurchased in New Orleans and brought back to Kentucky, by a special messenger and there held a reasonable length of time, subject again to the demand of Governor Chase.[4]

This from a letter dated 14 April that Gaines published in area newspapers, important evidence of the man's deceit. We know, for example, that he returned Margaret from Arkansas, not New Orleans—probably a deliberate bit of misinformation—for other accounts have Clinton

Butts bringing Margaret upriver from Gaines Landing, and they had no reason to lie.[5]

Moreover, Gaines finally relented not only to redeem his honor but, more important, to obey Governor Morehead. Within days after the *Henry Lewis* disaster, Morehead telegraphed Chase "his extreme regret and indignation at the course taken by Mr. Gaines." In the published version of this message he also promised "that measures have already been taken to cause [Margaret's] return from Arkansas."[6] But Morehead set aside Chase's request for Simon, Mary, and Robert Garner as accessories, which tells us that his resistance had also stiffened.

Clinton Butts arrived at Gaines Landing in the last week of March and soon arranged passage north aboard the *Queen City*. Once again the marshal secured Margaret in leg irons and left her in the boat's nursery among barrels of sugar, molasses, codfish, turpentine, and tar. The journey upriver would have taken five or six days and sometime during the night of 31 March or early the next morning Margaret passed the spot where the *Henry Lewis* crashed and Cilla drowned.

Wednesday, 2 April 1856. At ten in the morning, in a steady rain, Kentucky-bound passengers disembarked at Covington. By afternoon the weather had turned "mild and clear," and Margaret was back in the same jail where Butts had lodged her and her family after Marshal Robinson returned them all to slavery.[7] Nothing in the record indicates that Gaines was present to receive Margaret at Covington, and it's possible that spring plowing and planting kept him at Maplewood throughout this period. In late March his wife, Elizabeth, had given birth to their third child, Jane, another reason for Archibald to stay at home.

Aside from Gaines and Butts, who else knew Margaret was jailed in northern Kentucky? In his public letter to the *Enquirer*, Gaines wrote that his sending for Margaret "was printed in several of the papers of Cincinnati some time before the arrival of the woman." Probably he meant the *Gazette*'s 14 March quote from Morehead's telegram to Chase, the only such reference (itself quite oblique) that a thorough search of surviving newspapers has discovered. But then Gaines also claimed that after her arrival the fact of his lodging Margaret in the Covington jail "was generally announced in the daily papers of Cincinnati." If so, this awaits proof. The *Enquirer* and the *Gazette* were Cincinnati's principal dailies and the only two for which we have nearly complete volumes. Neither of them "announced" the fact, and if any other papers (such as the *Commercial*) had "generally" remarked this crucial news, then the *Gazette*, at least, would certainly have commented. Hardly a day passed when "The Late Fugitive Case" didn't still command space on its pages—the *Enquirer's* too, for that matter.

By early April the newspapers' attention focused on two disputes. One was Marshal Robinson's $24,000 bill for payment of his special deputies. The *Gazette*, in a story printed the day after Margaret's return to Covington, had charged that Robinson sent agents into local taverns—including "a doggery within four doors of the Court"—with cash to buy deputies' pay certificates at a 50 percent discount. These he planned to redeem at full value in Washington, a lucrative scam, if the papers got it right.[8]

Throughout late March and early April the *Gazette* was also reporting new skirmishes in the habeas corpus battle. On Tuesday, 18 March, evidently after reading the United States Constitution for himself (as promised), Probate Court Judge John Burgoyne announced that he considered the marshals' taking of the Garners from Sheriff Brashears "a bold attempt to usurp the powers of this Court and a wanton disobedience of its process." He gave Robinson two days to "show cause why he should not be attached for contempt." On Thursday, Burgoyne found the marshal's reply "insufficient, and adjudged him guilty." He leveled a stiff $300 fine and ordered Robinson directly to the county jail. That evening Robinson's attorney (Headington, again) applied to federal Circuit Court Judge Humphrey Leavitt for a habeas corpus writ directing Sheriff Brashears to release the U.S. marshal.[9] Several days later Leavitt ordered Robinson released and slated a hearing for mid-April. Until then the marshal wouldn't be hand-carrying those deputies' certificates to Attorney General Caleb Cushing in Washington.

But again, who *knew* Margaret was in Covington? Probably very few people, at least among those who mattered. On Wednesday, 9 April 1856, Chase wrote to Hamilton County prosecuting attorney Joseph Cox. In language clearly indicating it was fresh news to him, Chase told Cox that on Tuesday (8 April) an aide had passed him a telegram ("a despatch") conveying information "that Margaret Garner was awaiting my requisition at Covington, and would remain there until tomorrow [10th April]." If Chase did not know until Tuesday, the 8th, then no one else who mattered (such as Joseph Cox or John Jolliffe) can have known either, and we therefore have to ask about Gaines's game. Again, from his mid-April letter:

> Now, while I have no special interest in the administration of the criminal laws of Ohio, and no special motive for forwardness in bringing the murderess to justice, yet a desire to preserve my reputation as a law-abiding man, and to prevent and forever stop even the clamor of the Underground Railroad Abolitionists, induced me, after the woman had been in Covington for several days, to send a telegraphic dispatch, in my own name, to Governor Chase at Columbus, announcing the fact that she was there, and subject to his requisition. Day after day, however, elapsed, and yet no requisition came.

Obviously, for six days Gaines had been smugly twiddling his thumbs while Margaret languished in a Covington jail cell and Ohio officers (who could not know Margaret was back in Kentucky) *did not* come to requisition her, all part of a ruse to justify Gaines in sending "the woman" back to Arkansas. The shell game, all over again.[10]

The likeliest explanation for this latest foul-up is that Archibald Gaines obeyed the letter of Governor Morehead's order: he returned Margaret Garner to Covington, but did nothing more. In this scenario Gaines never bothered to notify (or ordered Clinton Butts to notify) Brashears or Cox. Perhaps Gaines even had Governor Morehead's tacit approval for this passive resistance. When Gaines finally sent his "telegraphic dispatch" with its impossible demand on Chase's agents to arrest Margaret just forty-eight hours later, on Thursday, and to do it (as he'd be sure to have Butts insist) by a legal process, he already knew that he'd beaten Ohio again.

Through Morehead or Butts, Gaines probably knew something about Chase and Cox's predicament. As Chase relates it in his 9 April letter to Cox, the awful fact was that before Deputy Clinton Butts could surrender custody of Margaret, Ohio officers were technically required to present the marshal an arrest warrant and extradition order from Kentucky's governor. But a month earlier Cox, Cooper, and Hamlin had left these documents, issued in response to Chase's belated requisition of March, in the hands of Louisville deputies, who presumably still had them.

As in early March, it was all coming down to timing and technicalities. On Wednesday, 9 April, Chase telegraphed Cox his opinion that "it is competent for any officer to go over into Kentucky and receive Margaret. She sustains in Kentucky the double relation of a slave and a fugitive from justice. In the former relation Gaines has the control of her, and may surrender her to whom he will. In the latter, the officer may receive her and restore her to the custody from which she was taken."[11] Perhaps this stated the common sense of matters in concise phrases; but it also scanted what the law obliged Cox to do when extraditing a fugitive. He needed those documents; otherwise Gaines might well scoff at their request.

Just as he did in March, once again Chase consumed crucial hours thinking things through. The more he ruminated on Gaines's moves in the context of events of February and March, the more riled he became over the Kentuckian's latest gambit. His message to Cox clearly stated his exasperation:

Under the circumstances I feel but little inclination to take any further steps in the matter. . . . I felt keenly the humiliation of being obliged by a federal proceeding in the form of a habeas corpus, to resort to the process of requisition for the purpose of restoring criminals to the precise custody from which they were taken by the writ. . . . Now Margaret alone of the four, is brought back. And I am telegraphed that she will await my requisition forty-eight hours! You will readily imagine with what sentiments I regard this course of action. And yet you as prosecuting attorney have a duty to perform in the process, and I am forced to aid you, so far as my position enables me to do so, in recovering the custody of all fugitives from justice. I therefore inclose to you the [Ohio] warrant [for murder] heretofore issued, and leave it to your discretion to make such use of it as you may see fit.

When Cox received this message and the Hamilton County murder warrant he understood two bitter facts: first, that Ohio's chief executive no longer stood behind their fight to save the Garners; second, that

Chase's hesitation had wasted at least twenty-four of the forty-eight hours Gaines had stipulated.[12]

Meantime the object in this battle of wits and honor between the governors of Ohio and Kentucky lay in a Covington jail cell, now four or five months into her fifth pregnancy, very much alone and bewildered. When Joseph Cox or John Jolliffe had previously spoken to Margaret about returning to Ohio for trial on the murder warrant, it had certainly sounded better to her than slavery. The lawyers' thinking was that after considering her circumstances leading up to the infanticide, no jury in Ohio would return a verdict against Margaret for capital murder. Especially if Jolliffe brought before jurors testimony about Gaines's cruelties to her and evidence about her "nearly white" daughter's true paternity, the worst Margaret might expect would be a conviction and sentencing on some lesser homicide charge. She might spend a few years in the penitentiary, after which, if Gaines tried to remand Margaret back to Kentucky, Ohio abolitionists would purchase her freedom. Jolliffe and others had explained this strategy to her. They had also told the Garners that Simon, Mary, and Robert, if tried as accessories, should expect even shorter sentences and soon rejoin her children, whom abolitionists were planning to purchase in any event. For that, Edward Hamlin had already raised $800 by early March.[13] Despite all their talk, however, by Wednesday, 9 April, Margaret had languished in a Kenton County jail cell for a week and heard nothing except perhaps an earful of Clinton Butts's taunts, to the effect that this only showed how the "damned abolitionists" cared more about spreading disunion than saving slaves like her.

To Margaret's way of seeing, none of this had worked out the way they promised. The Gaines brothers had sent her north alone. Now the likelihood was that Margaret would never again see her husband and children. Massa Archibald and Massa Benjamin might do anything at all with the family: split them up, auction some off, work her boys to death in the mosquito-infested muck of an Arkansas plantation. These doubts and fears kept Margaret company in her Covington jail cell for eight days, a stretch of waiting and unknowing that has to have been one of the more agonizing periods in her extraordinary ordeal.

Wednesday, 9 April 1856. In the afternoon, Chase's letter with its enclosed warrant arrived in Cincinnati by express train and Joseph Cox decided that despite the governor's withdrawal he at least would try to extradite Margaret. That evening Sheriff Brashears supplied him two deputies. Cox instructed the men to do their best; if Clinton Butts refused to release Margaret without Morehead's warrant, then one of them should shadow Margaret while the other returned to Cincinnati for further instructions. Taking Gaines at his word, Cox thought he had until Thursday to claim Margaret and he therefore ordered the officers to get a night's sleep and take a morning ferry over to Covington.[14]

At practically the same moment a man showed up at the Kenton County jail "with a written order" from Archibald Gaines, who wanted Margaret immediately released to this agent's custody. Had one of his friends or sympathizers warned Gaines that Ohio deputies would soon arrive? A fair question, for Gaines had promised to hold Margaret in Covington until Thursday. Now his agent appeared under cover of darkness and acted with a haste that typified events of the next thirty-six hours. Within minutes, Clinton Butts's deputy had Margaret back in leg irons and in the custody of Gaines's man (whose identity passed unrecorded). His carriage took Margaret south on the Turnpike, in "mild and breezy" weather.[15] In what would otherwise have been a beautiful spring night for a drive—starry skies and air scented with forsythia and cherry blossoms—Margaret Garner rode south in an exact reverse of her family's January sleigh ride to free soil.

Thursday, 10 April 1856. Probably she was back at Maplewood before midnight and if sleep came at all, Margaret was awakened early. The first train for Lexington passed through Richwood Station around eight-fifteen and Gaines wanted Margaret aboard it with his man. It had dawned "bright and mild." The neighborhood's oaks and sycamores wouldn't have leafed out yet, but we can otherwise imagine the rolling landscape ablaze in color and redolent with the scents of spring blossoms and grasses. Massa Gaines's two dozen sheep and his three dozen cattle would already be at his pond or grazing his fields; the two male slaves left behind after the winter's calamitous escapes might well have been plowing.

As Gaines drove his man and Peggy through the Maplewood gate and down the gentle slope toward Richwood Presbyterian Church, she took in for the last time in her life Mud Lick Creek and Forrest Home; Richwood Church Road, where the Garners made their rendezvous in the snow seven weeks ago, then James Marshall's plantation, where Robert and her in-laws had passed most of their days in slavery. White folks claiming ownership to it might give their plantations nostalgic names recalling the former wilderness. But Margaret's people had made the land into landscape. In clearing and plowing these fields, running fences and building barns, *slaves* were the ones who *plotted* it.

Her neighborhood passed out of view as Massa Gaines drove them around the bend just behind and east of the church, near the entrance to Marshall's farm. The last Margaret ever saw of Archibald K. Gaines was at Richwood Station. By early afternoon she was in Lexington, and at two-thirty she departed on the westbound train to Frankfort and Louisville. By early evening Gaines's agent had lodged her once again in the Jefferson County jail at Louisville.[16]

Thursday morning the two Cincinnati sheriff's deputies arrived at the Covington jail and (according to the *Gazette*) learned from the jailor that "he had given her [Margaret] up on Wednesday night, to a man who came there with a written order from her master Gaines, but could not tell them where she had been taken." One of the Ohio deputies reportedly inscribed the words "not found" on the warrant's back side and returned it to Joseph Cox.[17]

Friday, 11 April 1856. Events soon told Cox that Gaines had sent Margaret south. Around midday, Sheriff Brashears "received information which induced him to believe that [Margaret] had been sent on the railroad to Lexington, thence via Frankfort to Louisville, there to be shipped off to the New Orleans slave market." With Cox's approval, remarked the *Gazette*, Brashears "telegraphed the Sheriff at Louisville (who holds the original warrant from Governor Morehead, granted to Governor Chase) to arrest her there, and had a deputy in readiness to go down for her."[18]

Incredibly, all of this unfolded an hour, or no more than two hours, too late. Gaines's agent had booked passage for himself and Margaret aboard the *Eclipse*, perhaps the grandest and swiftest of the "floating palaces" then plying the Cincinnati–New Orleans route. Shackled once more in a steamboat's nursery, Margaret settled in with other white and black steerage passengers amidst a cargo of barreled pork, kegged whiskey, and baled hemp. At five o'clock Friday afternoon the *Eclipse's* master, a Mr. Sturgeon, ordered his crew to cast off and his pilot to steer her downriver. By "early evening" Cox's agents arrived and learned from deputies in Louisville that Gaines had already shipped Margaret south. By noon the next day she had once more journeyed past the spot where little Cilla had drowned. Several days later the *Eclipse* was steaming between Tennessee and Missouri shores and Margaret Garner had forever bid goodbye to *her* old Kentucky home.[19]

At the same time Margaret was steaming south on the Mississippi River, her former master's letter explaining these latest moves appeared in the *Cincinnati Enquirer*. Gaines claimed that when Ohio's "Abolition avengers" never showed up to extradite Margaret, they left him with no option but to "send her back with her husband and children." As for Cox's too late arrival at Covington and Louisville, Gaines again laid blame for that failure with abolitionists and especially with Governor Chase:

> How singular it is that after the lapse of eight days before the woman was first sent to the South, and not until then, Governor Chase sent his requisition to Governor Morehead, and that it should arrive just in time to be too late. And how passing strange it is that, after a lapse of nine days, during which the woman was in Covington, subject to the requisition, no step was taken to enforce it until it was ascertained that she had been taken to her home and family in the South!
>
> I am morally sure that the Abolitionists care nothing for Peggy, either through regard for the offended majesty of the laws of Ohio or for any sympathy with her as an oppressed, down-trodden, persecuted, heart-broken, desperate woman; and I am equally sure that the atrocious scoundrels have a wider and meaner object in view—that they care nothing for negroes or their owners, and only wish to use both as material for the promotion of political ends, for the furtherance of objects of treason to the Constitution and the laws of the Union.
>
> It may turn out that the publication of a letter from Governor Chase to Governor Morehead, which accompanied the requisition, will explain why the Abolitionists have managed to be *just in time to be too late* to get Peggy.[20]

The letter was yet another attempt to blame everything on abolitionist "scoundrels."

Chase never did publish the letter to which Gaines referred (that of 4 March 1856). Even if he had released a copy to the papers it would have demonstrated nothing more than this: Ohio's old-line abolitionist governor was guilty of excessive prudence and of naiveté in believing a slave master's promises. More recently, Chase had also been guilty of an understandable impatience; and then, for reasons harder to understand, guilty of losing focus on the real "objects." These were, at a minimum, achieving for the Garners a life on free soil (even if that meant years in the penitentiary) and battling to limit or even to nullify federal power over free states through its exercise of the 1850 Fugitive Slave Act. Archived letters tell us that some Ohioans like Cox and George Hoadley agreed on these objectives. The letters also say that others failed to see through the Kentuckians' deceit.

Gaines's charges were absurd on their face because he produced nothing, except a vaguely imagined abolitionist conspiracy, as a motive for Chase, Cooper, Cox, Hamlin, and the various deputies to arrive in Kentucky just exactly one or two hours too late, two times. Instead it was Gaines who had powerful reasons to be cunning, and those reasons involved more than simple economics. For Gaines had indeed spent large sums, but neighbors had introduced a bill in the Kentucky legislature whose sole purpose was to reimburse him for monetary losses, and before little Cilla died abolitionist Edward Hamlin had already raised $800 to buy all three children, a figure at or above prevailing market value. Even then Gaines could still have applied to federal courts for relief under the 1850 fugitive law.[21]

Honor, not money, explains the man's actions. Archibald Gaines understood that if Ohio put Margaret Garner on trial for infanticide, defense testimony would scarcely touch on her crime. Mary Garner had already testified to the main facts before Coroner Menzies's jury, and Margaret had admitted her deeds before newsmen and others. Gaines could be certain that John Jolliffe would grant those facts and bore in on the extenuating circumstances behind Margaret's child-murder, and this meant putting her master himself on trial. To Gaines that was unthinkable. Cincinnati's antislavery newspapers had already spotlighted Margaret's remarks about her facial scars—the palpable marks, she said, of maltreatment by a "white man," whom most presumed to be Gaines. At trial Jolliffe would surely reprise those themes, with worse to follow. Both Jolliffe and Lucy Stone had all but named Gaines as the father of Margaret's "almost white" children, thus painting him in people's minds as a miscegenator as well as a rapist, for Margaret's deeds signified that she would never have willingly submitted to that man's lust. Unlike fugitive slave processes that barred slaves from the witness stand, this murder trial would turn absolutely on Margaret's testimony. Jolliffe could subpoena Robert Garner, Gaines's neighbors, finally even Gaines himself. Thus a murder trial threatened to open up untold horrors, which the penny papers would blazon across their pages. Gaines therefore had to ship Margaret south, as far away from Chase's requisitions as possible. The short-term damage he might face, for obstructing justice, was minuscule compared with the shame of a trial.

A cardinal rule of Southern Honor required a "gentleman" who indulged himself with a slave woman to do so with utmost discretion and by all means to avoid scandal arising directly or indirectly out of his liaison, scandal that could threaten the entire fabric of genteel relations that was a planter's life. Neighboring planters would generally share the man's permissive attitudes about such miscegenetic relations, and some Southerners (like essayist William Harper) even hinted at practical benefits to their "casual" intercourse. But that code demanded discreet silence, or else ostracism. Gaines knew that his whole claim to power and prestige, to property and even his children's patrimony, hung in the balance.[22]

Archibald Gaines therefore had the most powerful motive for evading Chase's requisition. He also had the most obvious means to *make* Chase's agents arrive too late. For it was not Chase or Cox or even Governor Morehead who had custody of Margaret, and held her on Southern soil, with friends and sympathizers everywhere about. After obeying Morehead's order in only the most literal sense, by holding Margaret at Covington but doing nothing more until he could ensure that Ohio deputies would arrive "just in time to be too late," Gaines got Margaret out of Louisville barely ahead of them. Several days later, on the theory that the best defense is a slashing offense, he wrote his letter to the *Enquirer*, laying off blame on abolitionists and Chase.

Thursday, 17 April 1856. Margaret Garner would have disembarked from the *Eclipse* by this day and rejoined her family. She soon learned that Benjamin Gaines had decided (in brother Archibald's phrasing) not to permanently "take so dangerous an inmate as [Margaret] was into his family of slaves."[23] Following Archibald's directions, Benjamin made plans to have his younger brother Abner transport the Garners to New Orleans. Abner LeGrand Gaines was a former New Orleans cotton broker with a residence over the river and further south at Natchez. Through his wife, Sally Watson Gaines, he also owned a cotton plantation on the river in Issaquena County, Mississippi, some thirty-five miles south of Gaines Landing.[24] Until Abner arrived, probably about five days later, the Garners sat tight at Gaines Landing.

On Saturday, 26 April 1856, Abner L. Gaines checked into the St. Charles Hotel in New Orleans and by month's end he had temporarily resettled the Garners.[25] Fourteen years later Robert Garner would recall that in New Orleans "the brother of one of their old masters, LeGrand Gaines" (as Abner sometimes signed himself), hired them out. In 1870 Robert also recalled that there in the Crescent City his family survived through "hard work and destitution" in several homes, a familiar curse for Robert (who had now known four different masters in six years), but not to Margaret or the children, or his parents, Simon and Mary. Who hired the Garners' time in New Orleans, and how long did their indenture last? Robert didn't supply dates and no other records appear to have survived, though such terms typically concluded in late December.

From Archibald Gaines's vantage point, this temporary arrangement made excellent sense. New Orleans put Margaret well beyond the reach of requisitions and subpoenas, should Cox decide to serve papers for the slaves. Also, should word of Cox's departure from Cincinnati once more reach Boone County, as it apparently did in March and April, Archibald could easily telegraph Abner or Richard (another New Orleans–based brother) and direct either one to hide the Garners. He could do it long before the officers completed their seven- or eight-day steamboat trip. In New Orleans, then, the Garners were quite secure. Hamilton County prosecutor Joseph Cox soon conceded Gaines's victory. On 15 May 1856, Cox wrote Governor Chase one more time and asked "that a requisition be made by you upon the Governor of Louisiana if you deem it proper under all the circumstances." Chase was then swept up in the whirl of Republican Party politics leading toward summer campaigns, and either did not reply or simply declined. No requisition was ever issued, and seven years later Cox lamented the Garners' sale to Louisiana: "What was their fate after this I know not."[26] They had disappeared into "the seething Hell" of Deep South slavery.

History's archive yields up only a few more traces of Margaret and her family. When the Garners' indenture concluded, Abner Gaines sold them all to his Issaquena County neighbor Judge DeWitt Clinton Bonham. At Bonham's Willow Grove plantation, at Tennessee Landing, six miles northwest of the present-day town of Eagle Bend, the Garners made their last home in Southern slavery.

Bonham, born in Pennsylvania, was a thirty-six-year-old Probate Court judge and the county's eleventh-wealthiest planter. He and his wife, Mary, employed a governess for their six-year-old daughter Belle (an only child), and an overseer named R. G. Maxwell had command of the sixty to sixty-five slaves who worked Bonham's more than six hundred acres of cotton.

DeWitt Bonham knew Abner Gaines as a neighbor who managed his plantation after the fashion of other Deep South absentee landlords, spending much of his time in Natchez and New Orleans. Throughout the period 1850–60, however, Bonham periodically saw Abner Gaines in his capacity as Probate Court judge, for he had the duty to decide a hopelessly contested will probated back in August 1846, following the death of Abner Gaines's wife's grandfather, Homer Ledbetter. When he died at age eighty-two Ledbetter left behind a recently witnessed, hand-written will providing that his mulatto mistress, Violet, and her three "infant" children, Daniel Boon [sic], Elizabeth, and Laura, be the sole legal heirs of his estate. Ledbetter's will directed the executor, his grand-daughter's husband, William Deeson, to "take Violet and her three children to some free state," purchase them a home, and arrange for the children's education. Apparently Deeson was sympathetic to the deceased man's purposes. He swiftly transported Violet and her children North and vigorously began to execute Ledbetter's will. By 1850 he had even liquidated some of Ledbetter's movable goods and had the man's "negroes" appraised for sale or hiring-out. From then on the four surviving Ledbetter heirs, including Sally Watson Gaines, tied up the will in Bonham's court. Abner and Sally fought tooth and nail to prevent Deeson from executing the will, persistently demanding $27,252 as their one-eighth share of Ledbetter's real estate. They also demanded a proportionate share of his slaves. In 1859 Bonham finally awarded Abner and Sally Gaines $3,406 in legal expenses, apparently the only settlement ever reached in this case before—and evidently even after—the Civil War erupted.[27] Abner Gaines's dealing the Garners to DeWitt Bonham, no doubt at a bargain price given their reputation, may have been a consideration for the judge's friendship and diligent service in blocking the Ledbetter will.

Willow Grove plantation sat on a rise not far from the river. Groves of scrub pine, willows, a few live oaks and cypress trees studded the mostly flat landscape. Slaves worked his cotton on the rich, sienna-colored soil and, on Saturday afternoons, scratched at vegetable patches surrounding their cabins.[28] Here in 1857 the record almost entirely gives out and we are compelled, for a while, to leave them.

"The romance of our history"

The same day that federal marshals returned the Garners to slavery, on 29 February, William Lloyd Garrison's abolitionist paper, *The Liberator*, published two more poems about Margaret. "Carrie" from Barre, Massachusetts, submitted "Plea for the Fallen"; the second, "LINES, Suggested by Reading the Late Slave Tragedy in Cincinnati," appeared over an "Anonymous" byline. Solemn, earnest writers wanting to understand the Garner infanticide and to make its power of horror do antislavery work, both condemned slavery for destroying Margaret's family and causing her child-murder. Yet both also claimed for Margaret's deed a transcending, sacrificial passion with enough symbolic power to transform American society.[29]

Both poets knew that Americans typically recoiled in horror at the Garners' tragedy ("Ye deem them heartless," writes Carrie), but still blamed the masters for keeping their slaves under a morally and spiritually blighting oppression. But not totally blighting: for even slavery cannot turn a mother's love "to gall and wormwood." Mother love outvies the master's depravity and rises to righteous sacrifice, when godlike love saves her child from death on earth. As "Anonymous" phrased it: "The very love she bears her child/ Has nerved her arm to deal the fatal blow"—Americans' commonest way of explaining slave infanticide.

The author of "LINES" called at last "for VENGEANCE" on slaveholders, but Carrie ends her poem with images of Margaret's sacrificial passion as itself only the shadow (lesser *and* darker) of a divine father's love, thus concluding with a call not for vengeance but for mercy. On the very day when marshals took the Garners back to Kentucky, she implored readers to "lead them gently home!/ Sure in our Father's house there is yet room!" While not the Southerner's noblesse oblige, requiring that he assume the patriarch's responsibility to feed, clothe, and protect his extended slave "family," Carrie's was nonetheless a profoundly white patriarchal burden—to reach down and (as she says) "lead a lost one" back to "our Father's house." By April 1856 the Garners had heard enough such talk, which still hadn't rescued them from the shadow of Massa's house.

These poetic pictures of Margaret Garner illustrate how antebellum Americans saw her infanticide as a cultural icon, whose power to figure political and social agendas and tensions did not require being true to specific, complex facts. Instead, like all icons the poems convey simple, coherent meanings within a generalized system of values and beliefs. Such icons of the all-loving parent—a type of female Abraham, knife upraised over her sacrificial child, in "LINES"—were intended to strike the familiar chord of a transcending and even a healing horror. That way Northern readers might lay claim to her tragedy's power—not because the poems imagined Margaret's child-murder as a singular and almost unspeakable deed—but precisely because they would always already *know it*. It was part of their cultural hardwiring.

But the Margaret Garner case was unique in the annals of American slavery. Of the few documented slave mother's infanticides, none even remotely compared to hers; for the others (as we shall see) involved newborns of mothers still held in bondage, and were committed almost literally under cover of darkness—never, as in Margaret's case, in the master's face. But despite her absolute singularity, antebellum Americans persisted in seeing Margaret as a figure they thought they already knew, through the infanticidal slave mothers in *Uncle Tom's Cabin*, or others in tracts and gift books, in antislavery songs and poems. Far more imaginary than she was ever real, until Margaret Garner's case, the infanticidal slave mother had by January 1856 become a potent icon signifying everything unnatural and unholy about "the peculiar institution." It was almost as if the icon had always awaited or demanded a Margaret Garner.

Her child-murder put the name and face of a real black woman to what had mainly been a fantasied image circulated for decades among genteel white abolitionists. Earnest reformers like Carrie thought they could know and memorialize her "Tragedy" in terms of that icon. Instead, for almost a hundred thirty years the Garner case nearly disappeared from American cultural memory, just as the Garners themselves practically disappeared into Deep South slavery. Had the icon eclipsed the reality? Is it possible that these processes were not merely coincidental, but consequential? It is always crucial for us to ask how culture sponsors such results.

This last problem in the Margaret Garner case forces us to ask some new and different questions. In what terms did Margaret's child-murder become the stuff of stories? Who produced them? Why? Answering such questions requires us to leave aside for now the tools of conventional history and to open a brief inquiry into literary history. Except for instances like Stowe's novel and Browning's poem, the texts for study have never been regarded as important art. Here are poems and stories long shelved and largely forgotten in Special Collections libraries, but whose authors thought they had made lasting literature.

They thought so because abolitionists commonly believed, with Thomas Wentworth Higginson, that "the romance of American history" would draw great literary material from "the lives of fugitive slaves." In fact, this idea was a widely circulated cliché by 1856, when poet James Freeman Clarke advised writers:

> Go ye, who seek in Plutarch's page romantic acts
>   and lives sublime,
> Go to these martyr slaves and learn the Romance
>   of our Land and Time.

In 1842, antislavery activist and fiction writer Lydia Maria Child had speculated that slaves' stories would provide the stuff of "tragic romance," and essayist Edmund Quincy thought writers should find models in white reformers as well. In a piece that appeared along with Child's in *The Liberty Bell* (an annual antislavery gift book), he countered English philosopher Edmund Burke's claim that "the age of chivalry is dead." Just read the penny papers, Quincy argued, and see antislavery reformers enacting chivalric heroism every day.[30] In a key document, "The Philosophy of the Abolition Movement," first delivered as an 1853 speech, Wendell Phillips traced this idea back to its probable source: antislavery writer Fredrika Bremer's 1836 comment that "the fate of the negro is the romance of our history." At the Massachusetts Anti-Slavery Society's annual meeting of 1853, Phillips devoted a portion of his keynote address to the role of reform literature:

Again and again, from my earliest knowledge of the cause, have I heard the opinion, that in the debatable land between Freedom and Slavery, in the thrilling incidents of the escape and sufferings of the fugitive, and the perils of his friends, the future Walter Scott of America would find the "border-land" of his romance . . . and that the literature of America would gather its freshest laurels from that field.

When Phillips made this prediction at Boston's Melodeon Hall on the evening of 27 January 1853, three years to the day before the Garners fled the "border-land" village of Richwood Station, American abolitionism was still riding the groundswell of enthusiasm for *Uncle Tom's Cabin*. That night Phillips praised Stowe's novel ("rather an event than a book," he said) and predicted that still more and better novels would soon appear. More did, but the antislavery movement never produced a more significant work of fiction.[31]

Dead children haunt *Uncle Tom's Cabin*. Two years before she wrote the book Stowe's youngest son, Charley, fell victim to a cholera epidemic that swept through Cincinnati during July and August 1849. Stowe biographer Joan Hedrick writes that the infant's death devastated her, but also had the effect of confirming Stowe's commitment to abolitionism. Northern activists had long complained that masters wielded tyrannical power when they sold slave children away from their mothers, and abolitionist texts commonly called up such auction-block tableaux to grab doubters' hearts. In the summer of 1849 Stowe felt for herself those scenes' power: "It was at his dying bed, and at *his* grave," Stowe later recalled of little Charley's dying and the writing of *Uncle Tom's Cabin*, "that I learnt what a poor slave mother may feel when her child is taken away from her."[32]

Her novel begins with Squire Shelby (a northern Kentucky planter) dealing Tom away to a slave trader along with Eliza Harris's son Henry. Eliza soon flees with her boy over ice floes choking the Ohio River (in the novel's most dramatized scene), and even when she reaches free soil Eliza's ill fortune puts her at the house of a Doughface Ohio politician, Senator Byrd. Will the senator's wife remand them to slavery? "Ma'am," Eliza pleads, "have you ever lost a child?" With that she strikes a nerve: "The question," Stowe's narrator explains, "was unexpected, and it was thrust on a new wound; for it was only a month since a darling child of the [Byrd] family had been laid in the grave."[33] Eliza herself lost two infants to untimely deaths, she tells Mrs. Byrd, and that's why she fled rather than let slave traders take little Henry, "a baby that had never been away from his mother in his life!" On the spot Mrs. Byrd takes up the fugitives' cause and soon converts the senator, scenes that miniaturize Stowe's own conversion and that she hoped *Uncle Tom's Cabin* would spur nationwide.

Such early scenes only prepare readers for the novel's moral and spiritual keystone: the sublime death of little Eva St. Clare, daughter of Tom's ill-fated, next-to-last master, and a sickly but preternaturally moral child. Eva's dying pleas for the common humanity of blacks and whites convert her father, Augustine, who then determines to emancipate his slaves—but too late, as it turns out, for St. Clare himself dies. Still more important, Eva models Christ-like dying when, haunted by cries of black children who "lost their mothers" at slave sales, she tells Tom, "I would be glad to die, if my dying could stop all this misery. I *would* die for them, Tom, if I could." Overhearing those earnest exclamations, the St. Clare "mammy" rightly calls Eva a "little, blessed lamb" (401), and in thus symbolizing potentials for Christian sacrifice Eva prefigures Uncle Tom's all-important role as "The Martyr" in Stowe's plot.

Joan Hedrick locates Eva's symbolic power in mid-nineteenth-century idealizations of the "special child," a powerful icon Americans had wrought during an important historical role shift for middle-class children.[34] No longer regarded as junior-sized adults expected to contribute their labor power to a family's economy, children were increasingly understood as unformed individuals whose nurturing to the practical, moral, and spiritual responsibilities of bourgeois domesticity was a vital result for parents—especially mothers—to ensure. One sign of this change was that Americans extended the term "infant" to include children whom we would call "toddlers" and even "primary grade" schoolchildren—any child up to age six or even seven.[35] That new role also required middle-class parents to become more emotionally invested in their "infant" than ever before, even in the face of infant mortality rates that had only just begun their long decline to significantly lower modern numbers. In 1850 the early death of a child remained a universal experience, and middle-class Americans dealt with such a loss, as of the actual Charley Stowe or the fictional Eva St. Clare, by enshrining his or her memory in family tradition. Typically the infant's presumed dearness to God made it a kind of divine intercessor, and in that role the "special child" had great power in American popular culture. A scan through penny papers from any region of antebellum America will turn up quantities of sentimental verses, essays, and homilies on dead children, a fair amount of it reprinted from religious tracts and periodicals, and a surprising portion of it authored by men. During the 1850s, for example, northern Kentucky's poetastering brickmaker, Hiram Martin, contributed to the *Covington Journal* his fair share of verses on the sublime death of children.[36]

But it was a far leap from these bourgeois ideals to the grim facts of slave children's lives. They *were* required to add their labor power to the master's domestic economy, as seven-year-old Margaret's nursing of Major Gaines's children illustrates. Moreover, infant mortality rates among slaves ran almost twice as high as those for whites, a consequence of poor hygiene and diet.[37] Added to those burdens was the ever present danger that a master might suddenly sell off a healthy slave child, as many plantation owners reckoned on a 5 or 6 percent return on their slave "property" deriving from just that potential for the "natural increase" of slave populations.[38] On these terms middle-class white ideals had practically nothing in common with Southern black realities. Nevertheless abolitionists found in themes of child mortality and mothers' losses a way to make that leap. Summoning white middle-class readers to scenes of their own past bereavements as a means of enlisting soldiers against "the peculiar institution" and its devastation of black families, Garrisonian abolitionists made the "special child" into a potent political tool. Stowe knew its effectiveness and in little Eva she beatified that stereotype.[39]

But it was a still further leap from white America's "special child" to black mothers "saving" their babes from slavery by child-murder. Stowe, however, thought it a natural step because abolitionist sources also claimed infanticide was a regular fact of plantation life. Speaking in her novel's "Conclusion" about the slave trade's "heart-break and its horrors" as a motive for child-murder, Stowe claimed: "There are those living who know the mothers whom this accursed traffic has driven to the murder of their children; and themselves seeking in death a shelter from woes more dreaded than death" (623). Though she provides no further detail Stowe thought these secondhand stories warranted her own pictures of infanticidal slave mothers, for example in the anecdote of Haley the slave catcher, who tells how a slave mother he had in transit leapt from a steamboat, "young un and all, into the river,—went down plump, and never ris" (125). In a late chapter titled "The Quadroon's Story," a mulatto woman, Cassy, tells of being held for years as the concubine of one white master; he sold away their two children, then auctioned her to another, who fathered Cassy's third and last infant:

> But I had made up my mind,—yes I had. I would never again let a child live to grow up! I took the little fellow in my arms, when he was two weeks old, and kissed him, and cried over him; and then I gave him laudanum, and held him close to my bosom, while he slept to death. How I mourned and cried over it! and whoever dreamed it was anything but a mistake, that had made me give it the laudanum? but it's one of the few things that I'm glad of now. I am not sorry, to this day; he, at least, is out of pain. What better than death could I give him, poor child! (521)

What were those "woes more dreaded than death," in Northerners' iconic images? For young male slaves, the burdens of gang labor on mosquito-infested sugar plantations. For young female slaves, such as Cassy and others like her in abolitionist literature, the dread was sexual.

Antislavery texts represent child-murder as a slave mother's last, desperate, loving way to end generations of sexual bondage. In *Incidents in the Life of a Slave Girl* (1861), Harriet Jacobs relates Linda's genealogy as a tale of miscegenation. Then at age fifteen she herself fends off the advances of one white man (her owner) by taking up with another (Mr. Sands) and bearing his children, thus to realize her ancestors' awful predicament: in slavery children are not a blessing but a curse. When Linda's son takes ill she feels "what a mockery it is for a slave mother to pray her dying child back to life! Death is better than slavery." But with the birth of her second child, a girl, Linda feels a still deeper burden: "my heart was heavier than it had ever been before. Slavery is terrible for men; but it is more terrible for women."[40] Jacobs's narrative stops short of infanticide, but other antislavery texts push the slave mother's infanticidal logic to its conclusion. "The Slave and Her Babe," a poem published in *The Liberator* (in 1845) and set to music for communal singing at antislavery conventions, opens on a dreary graveyard scene and a weeping slave mother bending over her mattock. Pondering the grave she's just dug and the outstretched body of an infant girl whose life she's obviously just taken, the woman thinks "that its safety in death was far better/ Than the joy she had felt when she breathed on her cheek." Burying the infant girl will finally shield her from that "tyrant" who was evidently also its father. The first edition of Lunsford Lane's *Narrative* (1842) included on its frontispiece another white-authored poem whose verses develop the same infanticidal logic.[41]

It was not in the least unusual for whites to sing that way, in blackface. Elizabeth Barrett Browning would do it, for example, in "The Runaway Slave at Pilgrim's Point" (1848). What's always striking in such instances is the slave mother begging an advance pardon, and begging it of the same child she's about to kill. Such a scenario makes the slave mother's child her sole earthly judge, a still more powerful judgment since the child is bound "home," to God, source of all liberty. Returning to that source, these works give readers a set of absolute equations: Death is Liberty is Divine. They apotheosize Patrick Henry's appeal, offering it as the only ethical formula for judging the infanticidal slave mother. Still, one has to have made an extraordinary leap of faith to accept it, because such a verdict is only handed down from Heaven, a wholly abstract and transcendent place way beyond the traumas and memories of slavery. It is handed down without experience, without precedent and history, and as such it can always only be a judgment without real judging.

Among abolitionism's earliest and most remarkable imaginary scenes of infanticide that I have found is an illustrated dialogue, "A Mother's Anguish," printed in "The Children's Department" of the 1837 *American Anti-Slavery Almanac*. Under a crude lithograph depicting a slave mother raising an ax over her sleeping children, the dialogue opens with a little girl, Caroline, asking, "What is that woman doing, uncle?" The uncle, a Mr. S., matter-of-factly answers, "She has an axe in her hand, with which she is killing her little children." He explains that the woman was a Missouri slave who loved her children "very much" and always thrilled as she returned from the fields to find their hands outstretched "to take hold of hers, as you do when your father comes home." Still his niece can't fathom the picture: "My mother loves me, too," Caroline replies, "but she wouldn't kill me." The uncle explains further:

You ought to thank God your mother is not a slave. One night when that woman came home, she found that her dear boys had been sold to a man who was going to carry them six hundred miles off, to a place where they would have to work under a driver's lash, and where she could never see them again. I cannot tell you how bad she felt. She felt much worse than your mother would, if a stone should fall on you and kill you. The children did not know what was going to be done to them, and they laid down and slept quietly on their bed of straw, clasped in each other's arms.

There, he says, the mother found them and after anguishing over the "stripes and misery her children must endure, she thought she would rather see them both dead and put in the ground." She killed them, he says, and then fearing her master's retribution "killed herself. I cannot tell you how much torment a mother must suffer, before she would kill her own children. You can judge from this what slavery is." Still Caroline asks, is it still not "wicked to kill"? Her uncle can only answer in conclusion, "She did what she thought was best for her children."[42]

One remarkable aspect of this vignette, along with and even because of its intended audience of genteel Northern children, is how it stages a racial difference nervously verging on a similarity. Caroline's father returns home from his bourgeois employment, while the slave boys' mother returns to the quarters from a "hard day's labor" in the fields; yet both parents yearn to clasp their children's hands. Like the slave mother, Caroline's mother loves her child but still wouldn't commit infanticide, would she? Perhaps she would, Mr. S. suggests, if it meant saving Caroline from an overseer's cruel "stripes." By these comparisons the dialogue attempts to erase the color line and transfer to the black children Caroline's transcendent values in her possible role as the "special child"—a role she would fulfill, Mr. S. points out, if she were killed under a falling stone. The whole ensemble—lithograph and dialogue— is organized to stage that transference as an empathic response of privileged whites, Caroline and her uncle, interpreting a provocative artwork. Precisely what the *Almanac*'s youthful Northerners must do in their turn. And precisely the idea behind abolitionist cultural practice in general and Stowe's in particular.

"You can judge from this what slavery is," concludes Mr. S. But from what, exactly, *should* one judge? After all, Caroline's uncle twice con-

A MOTHER'S ANGUISH.

Caroline. What is that woman doing, uncle?

Mr. S. She has an axe in her hand, with which she is killing those little children.

Ca- What made her hate them so? What had they done to her?

Mr. S. She did n't hate them, my dear.

Car. I should think she did. What *did* she kill them for?

Mr. S. I will tell you. She was a slave. She lived in the state of Missouri, a state seven times as large as Massachusetts, and a thousand miles from here. Those are her own little children, and she loved them very much. When she came home at night, from her day's hard labor, she always hastened to meet her children. It made her feel happy and forget her wretched lot, when she saw them run smiling to meet her, and hold out their little hand to take hold of hers, as you do when your father comes home.

Car. My mother loves me, too, but she would n't kill me.

Mr. S. You ought to thank God that your mother is not a slave.

One night when that woman came home, she found that her dear boys had been sold to a man who was going to carry them more than six hundred miles off, to a place where they would have to work under a driver's lash, and where she could never see them again. I cannot tell you how bad she felt. She felt much worse than your mother would, if a stone should fall on you and kill you. The children did not know what was going to be done to them, and they laid down and slept quietly on their bed of straw, clasped in each other's arms.

Car. Didn't their mother sleep with them?

Mr. S. The mother couldn't *sleep* when her children were going to be carried off. The man who bought them, did not think it safe to let her be where she could get at them, to take them away. So they had her *chained* in a shed near the house. As she lay there, and thought of the toil, and stripes and misery her children must endure, she thought she would rather see them both dead and put in the ground. She tried hard to get loose from her chain, and after some time she

Infanticidal slave mother: "A Mother's Anguish," selection from the "Children's Department" of the 1837 Anti-Slavery Almanac

cedes the inadequacy of speech to express *this* "mother's anguish," so he fails to extenuate what Caroline thought a "wicked" deed. "I cannot tell you . . . ," he simply says. Since words fail, one might try to "judge from this" *picture*. Yet excepting its vague Missouri origin, the image that Caroline and her uncle ponder lacks any historical context of names and dates and events. Therefore it really does function in a condition of innocence, "The Children's Department," without real-world depth. So this icon also fails to capture the actualities of a human subject, and the color line marking a seemingly absolute difference now reasserts itself. The slave mother's anguish and her infanticide remain unknowable phenomena. One can only observe how this woman did "what *she* thought was best." Yet that involves a moral relativism that bedrock Christians would ordinarily reject.

In abolitionist literature these texts imagined slave mothers' infanticides as scenes in "the romance of America." Their ethical purpose was to confer on slave children the idealized, iconic power of the bourgeois "special child." Most typically, but especially when a slave mother takes the life of her infant girl amid coded hints of sexual oppression, these texts formulate a set of absolute equivalences: Death = Liberty = Divine. Thus they attempt to spirit ethical judgment away from the contingent, historical realities of enslaved people and into a domain of absolutes. Try as they may, however, these icons are still freighted with contradictions and tend to treat slave mothers' actions and motives as being wholly enigmatic.

The one exceptional instance I have found is Elizabeth Barrett Browning's poem. In 1845 the Boston Anti-Slavery Bazaar commissioned her to write a work on abolitionist themes, but Barrett Browning didn't respond until 1847, when she sent a long narrative poem in thirty-five ballad stanzas. In 1848 "The Runaway Slave at Pilgrim's Point" finally appeared in the Bazaar's annual gift book, *The Liberty Bell*, an important Christmas season fund-raiser for Boston abolitionists. The poem's speaker is a young black woman who tells of falling in love with a field hand at a Southern sugar plantation where they both were slaves. Their tyrannical master kills the young man and rapes her. The child of that violent union she suffocates because he is too white, like his father, and because the grave restores the infant to blackness. After the infanticide she runs North and reaches Plymouth Rock before pursuing slave catchers surround her, and there the young woman falls to her knees and at poem's end she dies—of an exhaustion that literally breaks her heart. Before dying she not only renounces the whites' view of her as a frenzied, brainsick mother; she also forces the surrounding slave catchers to gaze upon her body, seen both as object of their awful oppression and as human subject that their own violence has transformed into a murderer, a mirror of themselves. In the poem's last lines she also puts a new twist on the typical martyr's role, saying of herself and all slaves, "We are too heavy for our cross,/ And fall and crush your seed."[43]

"The Runaway Slave at Pilgrim's Point" provides an alternative, English view that overthrows every significant aspect of the infanticidal slave mother in antebellum American fantasy. In Barrett Browning's understanding, Liberty is not an unquestionable, abstract term equal to others like Death and God. Instead Liberty is a contested value one must fight to claim, in a contingent history that stretches (in the poem) from the rock where *Mayflower* pilgrims kneeled in 1620 to bless their God to the same point where she now kneels ("I bend my knee down on this mark") and curses those pilgrims' seed. Concisely situated in space and time, and laying claim to a very problematic past, Barrett Browning's slave mother rejects any abstract ethics and insists that the good and the wicked may only be known through experience and memory, through history. She demands that the slave catchers acknowledge her relative moral superiority, a claim Barrett Browning's authorial voice never intrudes upon. Still more interesting, this slave mother denounces the "special child" as a repressive bourgeois fantasy. She laughs it away ("Ha, ha!") as a silly cartoon of child-souls "gathered" like "fruit" around the godhead's feet, in some cheap homiletic picture hanging on middle-class parlor walls; in fact, she charges that such images are a calculated "trick of the angels white." Finally, Barrett Browning lets her slave mother speak a motive for infanticide that I have found nowhere else in the literature. Partly the mother says she killed her infant boy to "save it" from the "curse" of slavery, a familiar motif. But then she claims a deeper motive in vengeful resistance: her infant's white face recalls the master's, and looking on him the mother knew that "he [the infant] wanted his master's right" to dominate and violate others. She therefore kills his "right." Certainly that is one of the most bitterly ironic words in a poem that appears to have passed without comment over the American horizon.

Had Americans been more able to take its outlook, Margaret Garner might not have practically disappeared from written history. People would have realized in Margaret's deeds a tangled skein of motives: despairing desires to "save" her children, urges for violent backlash against the master who had probably made her his concubine and who might in turn victimize little Mary, and a destructive spite for her children's whiteness that was in every sense Massa's "property," his "right." People might thus have reckoned with the singularity of Margaret Garner's child-murder instead of transforming it into iconic clichés or imposing on it a bourgeois ideology that required martyred slaves to evaporate in some abstract spirit kingdom. People would have had to deal with her unique and deeply problematic ethical and historical being.

Also they would have had to substantiate their assumptions about infanticidal slave mothers, and from surviving evidence that would have been difficult. It may well be true, as historian Deborah Gray White remarks, that slave masters always "suspected that midwives conspired with female patients to bring about abortions and infanticides."[44] But White provides no further documentation, a tendency notable in much writing on this topic right back to Stowe's remarks on infanticide in her "Conclusion" to *Uncle Tom's Cabin*. In any case, why should masters' suspicions count for much? What one wants, instead, are testimonies: slaves' testimonies if possible, and preferably court records. Where is that kind of support?

What we have for the entire antebellum period are two problematic cases of child-murder. Legal historian Helen Tunnicliff Catterall records the first, an 1831 case that tried a Missouri grand jury indictment brought against a nineteen-year-old household slave who allegedly administered poison to her infant girl and then smothered the baby "in its bedclothes." A jury convicted Jane but she was later released again into slavery after an Appellate Court overturned the verdict because of a defective indictment. Afterward the Circuit Court apparently never retried Jane, so the question of her guilt remains undecided.

From a slave owner's letters we also know of a second case. In November 1859 on the Georgia plantation of Charles Colcock Jones, a slave named Lucy came under suspicion for giving birth to and then smothering her newborn with assistance from a black midwife. For twelve days Lucy denied even bearing a child, until a physician's examination confirmed that she had. Farmhands then recovered the infant's decomposing body, and Lucy and her midwife were brought to a hearing before three local magistrates. Both women insisted the infant was stillborn and hours of interrogation failed to shake their story. Because Lucy admitted the birth and her deceit, the magistrates summarily convicted her of "concealment" and ordered eight days' imprisonment accompanied by "corporeal punishment to the amount of ninety stripes, inflicted at intervals of two and three days, one third at a time"—a brutally severe penalty.[45]

Neither of these cases produced definitive evidence for infanticide. Scholars may yet turn up evidence in a third, recorded in Lydia Maria Child's 1860 volume, *The Patriarchal Institution as Described by Members of Its Own Family*. Child's anthology reprinted stories that originated from penny papers published below the Mason-Dixon line, a canny way of indicting Southerners with their own news. Among the texts she gathered was a story that "went the rounds of Southern papers in 1853," about a slave woman belonging to a George M. Garrison of a "Polk County" who cut her children's throats as all four of them slept, allegedly because she heard the master intended to sell her south.[46] But did this case ever go to trial? Where? Child doesn't tell us the state; my own efforts to verify the story have uncovered nothing.

American historians have only recently conceded the likelihood that slave mothers' infanticides never were a serious problem. They have long tried to puzzle out mortality statistics revealing that slave infants were twenty-eight times more likely than white babies to die from "smothering," as mothers allegedly lay over them by accident while sleeping. Their studies long assumed that reports of overlaying came from masters who were only trying to hide embarrassing facts about slave infanticide on their plantations. By 1985 the historians' new view was that the higher rates of infants dying while asleep coincided with a sharply higher rate of Sudden Infant Death Syndrome (SIDS) that modern medicine would predict as a consequence of slaves' poorer diet and hygiene. This theory mostly releases slave mothers from suspicion. Indeed one scholar who sifted the mortality schedules and local marshals' reports of slave infant deaths concluded that these data never "produced even a hint of infanticide."[47]

Perhaps it is time we put the Infanticidal Slave Mother on the shelf with other myths about the Old South, for slave infanticides probably occurred with the same (or even less) frequency than among whites. Yet

Southern polemicists must have credited abolitionist stories about child-murdering slaves because they were quick, not to test the stories' bases in fact, but to countercharge that things were far worse in free-labor states. Thus in his *Southern Institutes* (1858), billed as an analysis of slavery's legal and institutional history, Louisiana attorney George S. Sawyer made the bizarre claim that *partus sequitur ventrem* (the doctrine according to which a slave mother's children inherited her condition) actually prevented blacks from abandoning or killing their infants, as whites supposedly often did. Sawyer believed abolition would push emancipated slaves to child-murder because in a wage-labor economy —Europe, he offered for example—parents collapsed under the financial burden of child care. In contrast, Sawyer argued, slavery imposed that burden on masters, who never destroy their own "property." Ebenezer Starnes puts several episodes based on Sawyer's argument into his proslavery novel *The Slaveholder Abroad* (1860). Composed as the narrative of a Georgia plantation master's trip to England for the 1852 World's Fair, just as "Mistress Stowe's book is causing such a row," this novel's strategy is to contrast British "wage-slavery" with the American "patriarchal institution." Along the way Starnes lets Master Jones's black servant, Billy Buck, get his fill of free soil. By novel's end no fewer than five infanticidal episodes have opened Billy's eyes to the horrors of life outside the slave South. Among the worst are a gin-soaked working mother who heaves her son to his death from an apartment window and another downtrodden mother who tosses her infant into a pig pen where a bony sow devours it. Reflecting on these scenes, Billy tells "Marster Jones" that if these mothers lived under slavery's protective arm in Georgia they'd have never been driven to child-murder: "in Georgy, Marster, us slaves has got a plenty, an to spar. An then our marsters has to tote all our cares an troubles, an the troubles o' our families."[48]

These representations probably had a certain force among proslavery advocates because, in contrast with the lack of printed evidence about slave infanticides, newspapers in the North headlined the news of white child-murders. In Cincinnati during the years leading up to Margaret Garner's case, the *Gazette* and *Enquirer* covered numerous murders of infants who were suffocated, abandoned in Cincinnati snowdrifts, dropped down hotel privies, killed by all manner of means. Just two days before Margaret cut little Mary Garner's throat, Coroner Menzies held an inquest over the body of an infant found in a culvert off Western

A WOMAN THROWS HER CHILD FROM A THIRD STORY WINDOW

*Infanticidal white mother: In this pro-slavery version, the impoverished, inebriated
English mother throws her child from a tenement window*
FROM STARNES, *THE SLAVEHOLDER ABROAD: OR, BILLY BUCK'S VISIT,
WITH HIS MASTER, TO ENGLAND* (1860)

Row. In another Cincinnati case that unfolded some months earlier it
had turned out that a newborn dropped down a hotel privy was delivered
by an eighteen-year-old Irish servant girl who had hidden her pregnancy.
Then, as now and perhaps always, infanticide happened as a consequence of immaturity, poverty, shame, despair, mental disease, drunkenness, careless neglect . . . a whole host of conditions about which we
cannot generalize.[49]

As for that, even if new evidence were to arise and reveal slave infanticide as a statistically significant problem in the Old South, on what
basis (again) could we generalize about *its* causes? Certainly we should
have to set aside what abolitionist rhetoric always presumed to be a
universal type: the slave mother's divinely inspired sacrifice of her child
to spare it from a life worse than death. Presuming it so made an otherwise unthinkable and seemingly unnatural act into a "natural" love
offering; like God's sacrifice of Christ. Such was the commonplace that
Stowe and numerous other writers accepted, and it shaped Northerners'
popular understanding of Margaret Garner's case. As "Anonymous"

wrote for *The Liberator*: "The very love she bears her child/ Has nerved her arm to deal the fatal blow." But did slave infanticides fit that type, Margaret's in particular?

Perhaps mother love partly explains the Margaret Garner case. Yet this is no reason to think that her child-murder jibed with white middle-class idealizations of the "special child," an icon from which Margaret was profoundly alienated, as Elizabeth Barrett Browning understood. Evidence in Margaret's case forces us to seek other explanations. For example, the fugitives' armed resistance at Kite's cabin, the Garners' resoluteness about going to the gallows even after their capture, and signs that she was motivated by sexual abuse: all these features of her story demand attention to alternative motives.

Recent anthropological research opens a window on a world that might compare with Margaret's. American field-worker Nancy Scheper-Hughes spent two decades (from the late 1960s to the late 1980s) study-ing the shantytown residents of Alto de Cruzeiro in Brazil's Nordeste (Northeast) region, where mothers often practice a mode of "passive infanticide." They withhold food, medicine, as well as nurturing love from infants who in life's early months show little likelihood of surviving the chronic hunger, disease, and poverty otherwise awaiting them. In effect these mothers triage weak children. Many actively wish or even pray for their children's early deaths, much as slave mothers are often represented as doing in American antislavery literature; and Scheper-Hughes interviewed some who willingly discussed instances when moth-ers took steps to speed their infants' deaths. All frankly admitted to Scheper-Hughes that in any case their infants would be better off dead than growing up to work Nordeste sugar plantations, where labor and wages were scarcely changed from the days of chattel slavery, abolished in 1888.

Nordeste mothers forced Scheper-Hughes to confront the inadequacy of theories that argue or only assume that mother love is "natural." She realized how such theories blind us from recognizing that infant neglect and even infanticide are not "unnatural, inhuman, or unwomanly" but are, to mothers caught in desperate oppression and poverty, "reasonable responses to unreasonable constraints and contingencies."[50] In an im-portant discussion Scheper-Hughes also points out a key paradox. It re-mains true that in triaging their own children the dispossessed mother does what the dominant culture must define as unspeakable. Nevertheless, Scheper-Hughes argues, such mothers also act *in complicity* with a dominant economy unwilling to spend its resources on unproductive elements. In effect, the neglectful or infanticidal mother helps make the system more efficient. In thus doing its business, as it were, she acts out the system's political economy *in spite of its apparent moral economy* Exactly why her complicity must never be spoken: the entire subculture of neglect or infanticide must be shunted into the shadows, though that creates potentials for outlaw practices which Margaret Garner's infanticide might be taken to illustrate. For especially when the infanticidal mother acts out the system's violent logic in the master's face, thus displaying anger and revenge against his class, she mirrors his violent politics in profoundly disruptive ways, as Elizabeth Barrett Browning understood. In such moments the dispossessed mother represents unutterable contradictions that the dominant culture must repress or mask. In nineteenth-century American culture, the solution was to represent the mother as a beast, or to beatify her infant.[51] Those polarized terms defined how writers represented Margaret Garner in poems, essays, sermons, and fictions.

Legend

Three days after Margaret's child-murder the *Cincinnati Commercial* exhorted citizens to contribute funds toward a monument honoring "the heroic woman, who spared not her own child, when she supposed it must be returned to bondage." In reply the *Gazette* remarked that people had better first work to ensure the slaves' liberty; "then it will be time enough to talk about the monument."[52]

One hundred and thirty-two years later Toni Morrison remarked that such a monument had yet to be erected:

> There is no place, here, where I can go or where you can go, and think about or not think about, or summon the presences of, or recollect the absences of, slaves. Or, just one. Something that reminds us of the ones that made the journey, and those who did not make it. There is no suitable memorial, or plaque, or wreath, or wall, or park, or skyscraper lobby, there is no three-hundred-foot tower, there is no small bench by the road, there is not even a tree

scored and initialed, that I can visit, or you can visit, in Charleston,
or Savannah, or New York, or Providence, or the Ohio River, or
better still on the banks of the Mississippi.

Because such a place did not exist, Morrison realized, her novel *Beloved*
"had to."[53]

But how should Margaret Garner's infanticide be committed to public memory? In 1856, proslavery writers were quick to respond. In what
became a familiar refrain, Clarkson laid blame at abolitionists' feet.[54]
Writing under the byline of "Justice," Benjamin Franklin Bedinger also
blamed abolitionists, the "disorganizing, law-breaking, meddling abolitionist fanatics" who (he said) tempted Margaret away from Maplewood
intending to make of her a public sacrifice. That claim was bizarre
enough, but then came another as Justice let loose his racism: "Peggy
is a very common, cross-tempered, flat-nosed, thick-lipped negro woman
whose father was a very bad character. She was cruel to her children at
home . . . [and] the murder of the child was the result of vexation and
disappointment, arousing to a pitch of phrenzy a revengeful and devilish
temper, inherited from her father." By his fourth installment, of 5 April
1856 (when Margaret was languishing in a Covington jail cell, unbe-
knownst to Cox and Jolliffe), Justice was calling on his fellow Southron
ideologues to gird themselves for a bloodletting, if they wanted to heal
the Union's diseased body.[55]

It was becoming a commonplace refrain. Asking why "alienation . . .
between North and South had become so *bitter* that civil war is ready
to burst forth," Kentuckian Henry Field James traced "these *immense
evils* to the fanatical spirit of abolitionism." After the Garner case he set
about writing a kind of fiction arguing that thesis. His *Abolitionism Unveiled; or, Its Origin, Progress, and Pernicious Tendency Fully Developed*
appeared in mid-July 1856 and contains perhaps the first fictionalized
version of Margaret Garner's child-murder.[56] Organized as a travelogue,
Henry James's chapters take a Boone County squire and his nephew on
a journey to Canada and back. In Sandusky and Detroit, Squire Gray
and young David interview jailed fugitive slaves lamenting their errors
and pleading for a return to their kind "Marster"; in Canada the two
Kentuckians narrowly escape a mob of unemployed, starving free blacks
who were deluded into running North after listening to abolitionist "fan-
cies"; at Oberlin College the Squire trounces an abolitionist professor

in a debate over "the peculiar institution"; and while returning to Squire Gray's Boone County plantation via Cincinnati they patiently withstand the verbal harangue of a "Higher Law fanatic" who very much resembles John Jolliffe.

Tedious polemic veiled as fiction, *Abolitionism Unveiled* concludes with a version of Margaret's child-murder. The scene opens at the tranquil slave cabin of "Peggy" and "Sam" (Margaret and Robert, whom witnesses variously called "young Simon" or "young Sammy" during the fugitive trial). The novel imagines for young Sam "a warm, comfortable room, good bedding, a wife, and four pretty children," and therefore hardly a care—until an evil white abolitionist (oddly named "Jim Crow") sneaks onto Gray's plantation. Crow persuades Sam to run for his freedom and gives the young slave a revolver. In turn, Sam commences to work on a doubting Peggy, who ominously confesses (in James's awful imitations of black dialect): "I'm so easily frightened, an' den I don't know what I might do. To be sent to de Souf, de berry notion nearly kills me. All dese t'ings, dear husband, if we should be taken, will rush upon me at once; I shall become de'perate, and what I may be tem'ted to do, God only knows." Finally she agrees to run, young Sam steals "the master's horses and sleigh," and that night the family crosses over the frozen Ohio River to Cincinnati. There, Squire Gray recalls, "they arrived at old Joe Kite's about the dawn of day, too late, as luck would have it, for underground railroad operations." The marshal's posse soon surrounds Kite's cabin and as the men batter their way inside Sam fires wildly while Peggy, "in a fit of desperation" that she had foretold, is seen to have "cut the throat of one of her children, and wounded two others." All of this only sketched key facts in the Garner case that any newspaper reader recognized. But it also required a view of slaves (especially Margaret) as simpleminded children lacking even the free agency to plot escape, much less conceptualize freedom. Squire Gray brushes guilt away from slaves and slaveholders alike and demonizes the abolitionist, "the serpent that crept into the garden of Eden and by his subtlety tempted Adam and Eve to depart from their holy estate."[57]

Ugly as it is, Henry Field James's racism never attains the virulence of *Negroes and Negro Slavery* (1861).[58] The author, Dr. J. H. Van Evrie, was a New York physician who flirted with polygenesis, a theory of mankind's multiple origins that challenged the Judeo-Christian narrative of humanity's common descent from Adam. He could easily have been the model for Toni Morrison's character, Schoolteacher, in *Beloved*. In that novel Schoolteacher orders his northern Kentucky pupils to count and gauge the "characteristics" of whites and blacks, then list them under "human" and "animal" headings in a two-column format. Van Evrie similarly categorizes "the Caucasian" and "the Negro" according to differences such as "Color," "Figure," "Hair," and facial "Features." Later chapters extend this analysis from physiological into psychological characteristics, and in a discussion of "The Domestic Affections" Van Evrie portrays black mothers as more animalistic and instinctual, solely concerned with securing "the mere bodily preservation" of their off-spring. In contrast he depicts white mothers as more given to sentimental affections because of "the elevated intellectualism of the race." Like other thinkers associated with polygenesis, such as Louisiana professor Josiah Nott, Van Evrie understood whites and blacks not as alternate varieties of man but as wholly different *species*. Hence Van Evrie's worst nightmare—miscegenation. He believed any crossbreeding of whites and blacks would produce "mongrel" hybrids prone to mental disease and finally, as with mules, sterility. On his view, prohibiting relations between whites and blacks was simply a matter of rational, benevolent "science"; a matter, as Van Evrie phrased it in the book's "Preface," of confining slaves to their side of the color line and so preventing them from committing "treason to themselves, to their posterity, to the country, and to American civilization."[59]

In the Garner infanticide Van Evrie thought he saw an important test case for his theory. Revising his book for 1861 rerelease, he erred in recalling a few factual details (he has Margaret killing her daughter while *returning* to Kentucky) but clearly recollected newspapers' depictions of Margaret's child-murder as an act of "Roman sternness and French exaltation." Here was the old challenge to proslavery thought: Could a slave mother enact Patrick Henry's heroic passions? Had she the "higher sensibility" to elect death over slavery? For Van Evrie this was an especially telling question because his theory claimed that only whites exercised that superior intellectual faculty. Moreover, his theory claimed for black mothers an absolute, instinctual protectiveness over their children. If so, what explains Margaret Garner's infanticide? Van Evrie thought he found the answer right in front of American readers, in the penny papers' accounts. Witnesses had described this woman, he recalled, as "a mulatto or mongrel." To him that explained all: Margaret's "unnatural crime was quite possible, as indeed any unnatural vice or crime is always possible in the mixed element, [but] it is scarcely possible to the [pure] negress, whose imperative maternal instinct, as has been observed, shields her from such atrocity."[60] Case closed.

Wholesale exercises in denial, proslavery versions of the Garner infanticide pardoned the slave master and his "peculiar institution," indicted and demonized "fanatical" abolitionists, and rested the matter on principles of divinely authored "Nature." Few such texts appeared, however, and excepting Van Evrie's (New York) treatise all cropped up in the Cincinnati area, as Southrons seemed content to let Margaret fade from public memory. In contrast, the literary response of Northern abolitionists was broadly broadcast and sustained, as the Garner case remained a vital cause célèbre.

In early April 1856 a Cleveland minister named Henry Bushnell preached a widely reprinted sermon on a scripture from Judges 19, the story of a sojourning old Levite taken in at a stranger's house.[61] In the Old Testament narrative, a band of rioting Benjaminites surrounds them in the night and demands that the host give up his guest to satisfy their lust. Instead the Levite sends out his concubine, the Benjaminites rape the woman until she dies, and the outraged Levite divides her body into twelve portions and sends them throughout Israel's tribes as an exhortation for them to "take counsel" over the horror. They do: Judges 20 narrates the outbreak of civil war as Israel's other eleven tribes rise up and nearly exterminate the Benjaminites. Aligning the Garner story with this Old Testament allegory of righteous civil war required several revisions of historical fact. For instance, Bushnell ignores Margaret's relation to the Kites and pictures the Garners as wandering Cincinnati's snowbound streets, unwelcome and unhoused until "a poor laboring man," quite a stranger, "gave them the shelter of his humble cabin." Then, nodding to the subtext of miscegenetic rape that has always haunted the Garner case, he makes Margaret the "concubine" demanded to slake Southern lusts and Margaret's daughter Mary the innocent lamb sacrificed on freedom's altar—a motif that recurs in the literature, though Bushnell wasn't the first to use it.

Probably the first writer to develop that motif at any length was Harvard professor and poet William Wallace Hebbard. On the evening of Tuesday, 18 March 1856, he recited 798 lines of verse (heroic couplets, mostly) in a "rotund and musical" voice before a disappointingly thin but apparently enthusiastic audience gathered for an abolitionist fundraiser at Boston's Tremont Temple. Hebbard titled his opus *The Night of Freedom: An Appeal in Verse, against the Great Crime of our Country, Human Bondage!* and after slight revision published it as a chapbook in 1857. Hebbard's invective style scored its best hits against prominent figures like President Pierce, Doughface Northern senators like Daniel Webster, and those marshals and judges who remanded fugitive slaves Anthony Burns and Thomas Sims to slavery.[62]

By all accounts, though, Hebbard's audience was most deeply moved when he narrated Margaret Garner's escape to Cincinnati ("the Rome of the West") and her search in vain for sanctuary there. At last the "Powers of Darkness" surround her and, no hero coming to her aid, a cornered Margaret raises up a knife as the slave catchers stop in horror:

> *All hope of Liberty on earth has fled—*
> *"But shall they not be free in heaven?" she plead;*
> *And from that heart by man's oppression riven,*
> *Up went the dread appeal of woe to Heaven:—*
> *"Forgive, O righteous God, if sin it be,*
> *I give these treasures back, unstained, to Thee!"*
> *The blade flashed in the light!—one babe was free!*

Margaret's sacrificing her babe on "Freedom's Altar" ushers in the poem's uttermost darkness and a world turned on its head: Tyranny has made "Infanticide a virtue in our land." By Hebbard's closing stanzas, descendants of the Pilgrims and the heroes of 1776 can no longer await God's judgment, "in awful ire,/ And vialed wrath, outpouring from above." Charging "forth to the field, as Freedom's living men," they're armed for "Civil War."

Meantime abolitionist critics and editors sustained a running critique of peripheral issues. In mid-February, Archibald Gaines had evidently professed (to Lucy Stone, during the impromptu meeting in Pendery's court) his staunch membership in "the Old School Presbyterian Church" of the Richwood neighborhood, and Northern clergymen and journalists were quick to capture the irony. The *National Anti-Slavery Standard* hooted that it was certainly comforting to understand how the same squire who hounded "his chattels" over the brink to child-murder was also "a strictly 'evangelical' man and a firm supporter of the gospel!" In April, Judge Leavitt came in for similar treatment after local newspapers broadcast his election to Cincinnati's Presbyterian synod. From Boston, *The Liberator* editorialized that Leavitt had turned the bar of justice into "the altar of the great American Moloch," at which he then assisted Gaines at Margaret's child-murder.[63]

More followed in this vein. "Dear Garrison," wrote Cleveland's Henry C. Wright in a public letter to *The Liberator*'s famous editor on 28 March 1856. "The end of the Cincinnati tragedy is not yet. Margaret Garner is a name that will long be preserved and consecrated in the hearts of the people of Ohio. That heroic mother, in the deep, holy love of her maternal heart, cut the throat of one child and tried to kill her three others to save them from the lash and the lust of a leading member of the Presbyterian Church of Kentucky." Summarizing Margaret's shipment to the South and little Cilla's drowning, Wright pointed (again) to the underlying theme of sexual violence, remarking that she "saved two of her babes from the pollutions and horrors" of Master Gaines. Next Wright turned his ire against Governor Chase, who "saw the tragedy proceeding . . . and opened not his mouth till the deed was finished, and the victim beyond his reach." When Wright sent this letter he had no way of knowing that Clinton Butts was steaming upriver with Margaret Garner for a second round of Gaines's deceitful game.[64]

In early May, Boston abolitionist Theodore Parker seconded Henry Wright's indictment during his keynote speech at the American Anti-Slavery Society meetings in New York. Parker argued that in standing by while federal marshals returned the Garners to Kentucky, Chase had virtually caved in to the Slave Power. Why? Answering, Parker went even further than Wright. The Ohio governor failed to rescue the Garners not only for reasons of political expediency, Parker thought, but also for reasons of *race*. If she had been a white woman and not "a black African," Parker believed, then Chase would have called on his "four hundred thousand able-bodied men" and their "half a million firelocks" to protect the Garners, for if he had not done so the governor's "head would not have been on his shoulders" the next day. These remarks were generally reported in Northern papers and wounded Chase, who wrote Parker for the full text of his speech. A week after receiving a newly bound volume of it Chase responded, in a letter marked "Private," complaining that whether inside or outside federally recognized slave states he hated "the peculiar institution": "There is no spot on earth in which I would sanction slavery." As to Parker's "intimation" that his actions were guided by an unacknowledged racism, Chase replied: "God forbid!"[65]

Though she herself was in New Orleans, Margaret Garner haunted the City Assembly Rooms on Broadway, during the New York antislavery meeting of 7 May 1856. Before Parker took the podium that Wednesday evening Lucy Stone addressed the membership for over an hour and had even more to say about "the recent Cincinnati Tragedy." Her main point: that abolitionism had entered a new stage. She claimed that by spring 1856 the objective of containment—summarized in abolitionism's early rallying cry, "No slavery outside the slave states!"—lacked any further credibility. And why? Because the Garner case demolished the motto's meaning: "What, to that mother, that father at her side, and those children clustered around them, are those words?" Squire Gaines's slaves had "the love of liberty which God had implanted in their souls," and so "they started to make their way to Canada" over the "bridge of ice." In vivid detail Stone sketched how slave catchers surrounded Kite's cabin, how Margaret drew "a dagger she had concealed" and, "knowing too well from her own experience the life that awaited," took the life of little Mary, "a child of surprising beauty." The audience heard again the story they already knew from Northern newspapers, of the trial, the failed habeas corpus battle, the Garners' shipment to the South, little Cilla Garner's drowning (Margaret's second infanticide, according to Stone), then Margaret's last return to Covington and Archibald Gaines's final victory. Gaines's agents had stretched forth the hated arm of federal authority outside the slave states and into Ohio, Stone argued, and so obliterated any difference between free and slave states.

Quoting from John Jolliffe's summation as well as from Mary Livermore's *New York Tribune* poem, Lucy Stone understood the Garner case as a popularly circulated story, already told in familiar texts. In short, she understood it as *a legend*. Stone thought it spoke especially to women, "disenfranchised" but willing to "make a common cause," as mothers, to "root out the system of slavery."[66] Her speech was a powerful appeal for solidarity and action that brought a standing ovation and loud hurrahs. When he followed her to the podium, Theodore Parker said Stone's speech had been "more eloquent than the philosophy of noblest men."

Margaret Garner was fast becoming a story and a byword. Remembered in the speeches of Frederick Douglass and Charles Remond, summoned before Republicans at their nominating convention, the image of her child-murder symbolized for some that the time for words had passed. Douglass was telling audiences: "Every thing connected with the struggle portends the rapid coming of the final crisis. And I for one welcome it. Almost any thing is better than a suspense."[67] Time to gird oneself for civil war, Douglass thought.

Summer 1856 also brought publication of a work that is, if not the first fictional treatment of the Garner infanticide (with Henry Field James's despicable book), at least the first full-length novel based upon it—a rare book titled *Liberty or Death!; or, Heaven's Infraction of the Fugitive Slave Law*. Of its author, Hattia M'Keehan, we know little beyond representations in her 1859 autobiography, *The Life and Trials of a Hoosier Girl*. She was raised in Madison, Indiana, and married a "heartless" New Orleans slave owner. Months later the man was mortally wounded in a duel and left his new wife an estate mortgaged to the hilt. In 1854, at age twenty-five, she moved to Cincinnati and made her living as a "colporteur," an itinerant peddler of Bibles, concordances, and religious tracts.[68] To her wares she also added antislavery novels.

When the Garner case broke, winter weather was confining M'Keehan to Cincinnati, where she must have followed the case intensely, for *Liberty or Death!* novelizes practically every significant detail of the Garner case that was available from newspaper accounts. M'Keehan simplifies some things: her Robert Garner character, for example, has already been sold South as the novel opens. M'Keehan also changes characters' names: Archibald and Elizabeth Gaines become "Mr. and Mrs. Nero," Clinton Butts a "marshal Bullethead," and Pendery a "Commissioner Leadhead." Even Hiram H. Robinson makes an appearance, as "a certain proslavery, prowhiskey editor of Cincinnati." But the most significant change comes with the Margaret character, the bizarrely named Gazella: "In form fragile, but stately; her complexion almost fair—for in her veins ran but a tincture of African blood." This revision, a whitening of Margaret's mulatto identity, becomes crucial because *Liberty or Death!* plays out themes of rape and miscegenation that few, excepting Lucy Stone, had been willing to name. In fact, M'Keehan's novel not only identifies Gazella as her mas-

ter's half sister (through Squire Nero's father); it also remarks that Gazella's child Rosetta—fated to die, in little Mary Garner's role—is in
turn Mr. Nero's daughter, thus adding incest to this book's indictment.[69]

Approaching "the late tragedy at Cincinnati" as "a romance of the
most exciting character," M'Keehan also plots *Liberty or Death!* as a
ghost story. After Gazella's infanticide, staged exactly as newspapers reported Margaret's, little Rosetta's specter twice haunts the Kentuckians.
She first appears to Bullethead and Nero at the "Broadhorn" (Magnolia
House) hotel, where they have stopped for whiskey before riding on to
Nero's with the child's body. "Vile assassins!" the spirit warns them,
"accuse not my mother; ye are the murderers." At Nero's Boone County
plantation she appears again, begins stalking the halls and in Mrs. Nero's
outraged presence calling to Nero as her "Father!" before damning them
all to Hell.[70]

With its allusion to Patrick Henry's famous declaration, *Liberty or
Death!* suggests much about popular perceptions of the Garner case.
M'Keehan's desire to indict Southern slaveholders as well as Northern
Doughfaces (including Governor Chase, for his "tardiness"), her treatment of sexual themes, analogies to heroic infanticidal mothers in classical legend, and obvious fascination with the Garners as romantic
spectacle: all are consistent with themes and tendencies evident in
newspaper coverage since day one. Certainly M'Keehan felt she'd struck
a nerve. Traveling the upper Ohio Valley with trunks full of copies, as
well as the plates needed to print off more on demand, she claimed a
$500 profit in the first several months—even after paying for initial type-
setting costs at a Cincinnati print shop. By 1863 the book had gone
through at least seven printings from the original plates, including one
1862 printing under a new title page: *Liberty or Death!: or, The Mother's
Sacrifice*, by Mrs. J. P. Hardwick. (Apparently the Hoosier girl had re-
married.)[71]

Hattia M'Keehan wasn't the only novelist before Toni Morrison to
write the Garner infanticide as a ghost story. In 1858 John Jolliffe published his second novel, *Chattanooga*, a rambling, uneven narrative that
also uses the murdered child's ghost to indict her slave master. But
where M'Keehan works close to actual events, Jolliffe treats them with
far greater license. Significantly, he sets his story twenty years in the past
and frames it with the narrative of a Connecticut Yankee, Hezekiah
Strong, who has traveled to Tennessee in search of witnesses to the

"strange tragedy" he recalls from New England penny papers. In Chattanooga, Strong begins unraveling that story, now become a local legend ("an old time story") that treats a fugitive slave mother, her child, and a haunted cave "that you wouldn't dare to go into."[72]

An awkward device whenever the novel reverts back to it, this frame story becomes so disruptive that one finally wonders why Jolliffe kept it. I think the answer is that he needed some way of expressing his dismayed realization that events had swept past Margaret Garner. By 1858 she was fading from memory, except as a curious episode in the region's legendary battles over slavery, and this not twenty but just two years after her "tragedy." Jolliffe knew how the memory of Margaret had become a popular icon. But the efforts of Jolliffe's well-meaning researcher Hezekiah Strong illustrate the near-impossibility not only of finding reliable documents but also of piercing through witnesses' petty bigotries and monstrous hatreds to get at anything resembling historical "truth" behind the icon.

The story Strong recovers, despite its too numerous and complex digressions, tells of a slave master's purchase in Charleston of a beautiful sixteen-year-old slave girl named Huldah, a quick-witted, literate, and "nearly white" girl torn from her crying mother's arms. Her new master, Norton, transports Huldah to his Chattanooga plantation, intending to "breed the wench" with another slave, a rather crude and illiterate black man. Before Norton can impose marriage, however, Huldah meets a local Cherokee chieftain, Grey Eagle. He's literate, eloquent, "born to command." The two elope and Huldah lives for a while at the Cherokee Nation, but just when she gives birth to a son, Norton learns of her hideout. He mounts a posse to recapture his fugitive slave and her infant, but Huldah eludes the slave catchers by taking refuge in a cave known only to local Cherokees, and eventually Grey Eagle takes her North, then to Europe. When the family returns to Chattanooga after a four-year absence Norton mounts another slave hunt, assisted by local Presbyterian preacher Jabez Clitters. They trail the fugitives to the secret cave, a cathedral-like room with "Corinthian" stalactites forming arches and buttresses, and, at its center, an altar-like stone. From there Huldah and Grey Eagle hold them off at gunpoint and send out word to nearby tribespeople "that at midday she would offer a sacrifice in the great hall." There, with Indians and slave catchers looking on, Huldah embraces her son Willie, proclaims, "No child of mine shall ever be a slave!" and plunges a dagger into his heart: "He fell upon the altar, and Huldah threw upon his bleeding wound the flag of her country." Months after the infanticide Willie's ghost begins haunting the Reverend Clitters, who insists "I—I—I did not kill that child. Oh no—I did not kill that child. Its own mother murdered it."[73]

Jolliffe's gothic adventure story tells us much about how he understood the Garner case. Huldah's cool deliberateness in planning the child-murder and her staging the scene as both sublime sacrifice (the altar) and political resistance (in draping Willie with the flag) suggest how Jolliffe rejected any view of Margaret as an ignorant woman driven by "phrenzy," and that he fully accepted her deed's symbolic power for abolitionism. Imagining the Garner case as a ghost story, Jolliffe tacitly accepts and puts to use the popular perceptions of Margaret as a figure out of tragic romance, perceptions that surfaced within days of little Mary Garner's death. But he also realizes how those cultural processes eclipse facts behind the stuff of legends, and this explains why Jolliffe had to intrude the otherwise awkward frame story, with its central figure of Hezekiah Strong questing for the true story behind those hazy myths—one way of characterizing my own commitment to understanding the Margaret Garner case.

Finally, it is interesting that, like other writers, Jolliffe not only imagines a much more "whitened" tragic slave mother than Margaret ever was; he also writes Robert Garner out of the story. M'Keehan's novel simply deleted his character; Jolliffe's move is still more troubling. Having imagined with horror this "nearly white" woman's forced mating to a rather ordinary black plantation slave, on the very next page Jolliffe solves his problem by bringing in the noble, literate, and all but white Cherokee chief, a man welcomed among monarchs when he takes Huldah to Europe. Thus *Chattanooga* keeps the color line solidly fixed. For John Jolliffe, the man who among all others in Cincinnati best knew and sympathized with the Garners' hopes and designs, still does not (or cannot) represent them as fleeing slavery in order to preserve the integrity of their *black family*.

At the end of *Chattanooga*, he quickly sends his Huldah/Margaret character off alone to a Louisiana plantation, where after several "sad and cheerless years" of grieving to herself and avoiding other slaves, she dies under the overseer's lash. When the novel was published in midsummer 1858, no one had heard anything of Margaret for over two years. It probably seemed a likely fate.

"Live in hope of freedom!"

Late summer–early autumn 1858. It would have begun as a drowsiness she could not shake. Nights, she craved sleep but tossed and turned in a cold sweat. Days, Margaret had no appetite, and even when she gave in to family telling her she must eat, nausea soon followed. Despite her low-grade fever Margaret probably continued to answer work calls, at least for the first week or so. Then her illness would have been severe enough for Mr. Maxwell, the overseer, to order Margaret quarantined with any other slaves showing similar symptoms of typhoid—for it soon enough became clear that this was Margaret's latest trouble. Whether or not she beat the disease would depend on a range of factors, but women in her age group were for some reason particularly liable to die from typhoid.

Initially, typhoid fever presents a range of symptoms that nineteenth-century doctors and laymen often misdiagnosed—as yellow fever, cholera, or a cold. An infectious bacterial disease usually caused when typhus bacilli seep from infected cesspools into the water supply, it spreads in epidemic fashion even while it remains localized among users of particular springs or cisterns. July through September were always the months of greatest incidence. By late summer 1858 yellow fever began working its way up the Mississippi River from New Orleans, and with it came outbreaks of typhoid. By September *The Mississippian* reported "yellow jack" and typhoid as far north as Memphis. Taken altogether, it was a bad season. The usually fatal black tongue disease was devastating herds of Mississippi cattle; "rust" and boll weevils were wrecking the cotton crop. It was a season of omens: in late September a comet cut a swath across the night skies.[74]

The Garners had been laboring a year and a half at Willow Grove plantation and had come to know cotton's seasonal rhythms. This was their second crop for Master Bonham and by now Tom and Sam, ages eight and six, would be in the fields with their parents. As for Margaret's baby, the one she was carrying in 1856, Robert omitted any mention of it in his interview published years later, in 1870. A stillbirth, perhaps? Or did Robert avoid speaking of it to the Cincinnati reporter because the child was not his? Maybe the reporter's questions simply didn't lead Robert to speak of the child (though he does mention Tom and Sam). In June 1860, however, Deputy Marshal Thomas A. Sellers recorded in the census rolls the presence at Willow Grove of a single four-year-old slave—the age of Margaret's child if it survived. This child was listed as a mulatto female, one of only two mulatto children at Willow Grove, the other a boy whose age in 1860 corresponds to that for Samuel Garner. The same census data also indicate that the Garners now lived in a neighborhood where blacks outnumbered whites by a ratio of 12.4 to 1, an extraordinary change for Margaret and her family.[75]

In 1858 the Garners had acclimated themselves to a slave culture with more autonomy, solidarity, and continuity than they had known in Richwood Station. Bonham's plantation fit a Deep South pattern in which a predominantly black population included seven times fewer mulatto slaves than in the Border South, indicating that miscegenation and concubinage and rape were relatively less significant factors in slaves' lives. The census also indicates that Issaquena masters did not usually hire out their bondsmen, bringing more stability to the slave community than anything the Garners had known at Maplewood.[76]

By 1858 the Garners had found their place in Willow Grove's slave quarter. They had learned to negotiate their way in a more complex internal hierarchy with more rigidly assigned roles. At Maplewood, for example, a nursemaid and house servant like Margaret would have been trained to a range of tasks such as spinning and sewing, and during seasons of peak demand for agricultural labor she was probably sent to labor in the fields alongside her master's other slaves, at times even with white family members and Master Gaines himself. At Willow Grove she was initiated into a slave culture in which those holding superior positions—as domestics, artisans, and drivers—might be keenly protective of precisely defined responsibilities and privileges.[77] At the same time, old hands probably schooled the Garners in new ways (at the same time learning old Kentucky tricks) to outwit Bonham and overseer Maxwell. These modes of covert resistance were vital items of knowledge for slaves laboring on Deep South plantations. In *Roll, Jordan, Roll*, Eugene Genovese describes the seasonal rhythms of plantation labor, during which masters and overseers accepted slaves' minor resistances during off-peak periods, but in exchange demanded extraordinary exertion from them during seasons when they planted corn and cotton (in late March and April) and harvested it (in late summer and autumn). How and to what extent slaves might exploit and resist these concessions and demands, all the while avoiding the overseer's lash, were matters the Garners had to learn during their first year at Willow Grove.[78]

At the same time they would have encountered a more variable and rich culture. In Boone County, Margaret Garner had been raised among slaves who, like their masters, had all either immigrated or descended from those who immigrated out of Virginia. Now at Willow Grove she and her family had come to know a more heterogeneous slave population. Like other Mississippi slaves, residents in Bonham's slave quarters might trace their origins to southern Virginia and North Carolina tobacco farms, to the rice fields of South Carolina and Georgia, and to southern Louisiana's sugar plantations. These people sustained a richly creolized, polyglot culture of folktales, slave songs, proverbs, jokes, and aphorisms, as well as medicinal and spiritual practices. Less assimilated to the dominant white culture than their Border State counterparts, they preserved many cultural practices and beliefs surviving from the African diaspora. Their Christianity blended African rites and myths and involved a more covert, resisting outlook than anything Margaret had known from Richwood Presbyterian Church and neighborhood "hush harbors."[79]

This was Margaret's world in 1858; for all she knew it was her future. In some ways it was worse than Maplewood, in other ways it was better. If Margaret was freer from the kinds of white sexual oppression that once drove her to despair about her daughters' futures, nevertheless she still despaired over her sons' prospects in Bonham's cotton fields. At all events the Garners were still together, their lives had taken on regular rhythms in a large community, and at times these things seemed like real blessings. Then came her fevers and night sweats.

After the disease's merely uncomfortable one- or two-week incubation period, Margaret's gastric disorders and night sweats gave way to full-blown typhoid. Her fever began a steady, stepwise march up to the 105–106-degree range, especially at night; and if her case followed the general pattern she was also wracked by chills and body ache, intense stomach cramps, headaches, and a roaring in her ears. If DeWitt Bonham or his overseer, Maxwell, brought in a physician to treat Margaret,

it would have been during this stage, although a doctor's remedies—
from doses of castor oil and "Glauber salts" (sodium sulfate) to bleedings
and blisterings (usually of the chest)—cannot have provided any relief
and probably only tortured Margaret all the more. Perhaps a physician's
use of steam inhalation relieved her dry throat and mucous membranes,
but the help was only temporary.[80]

About three weeks into the disease Margaret's condition turned critical. Soaring fevers brought on delirium and dried her lips and tongue
so terribly that they began to split and hemorrhage. She suffered from
a dry cough. Roseolate spots that appeared on her chest and abdomen
during the onset of fever turned to open pustules. At the end, as delirium
brought on tremors and paralysis, Margaret could no longer speak and
probably became comatose. Before she lapsed into silence, her last
words to Robert "were, never to marry again in slavery, but to live in
hope of freedom, which she believed would come in some way."[81]

Liberty thus came to Margaret Garner in the way it came to her
daughters, Mary and Cilla, whom she had claimed were better dead
than slaves. But her dying was prolonged and excruciatingly painful.
Certainly it must have seemed to her family that, after all she endured
at the hands of masters, slave catchers, all degrees of racists, even some
well-meaning abolitionists who could not or would not make good on
their promises, inscrutable Providence should have devised a kinder ending to Margaret Garner's story. They buried her at Willow Grove. We
may imagine them singing about crossing "over Jordan."

Margaret Garner's last words to Robert, among the few bits of her
reported speech that we have, spoke volumes about her view of black
women's lives in the Old South. For Margaret did not enjoin Robert
from remarrying; she enjoined him from taking another wife *in slavery*,
a promise consistent with all her twenty-five years under the patriarchal
institution. For it was slavery that made marriage some kind of hell to
her parents, enough that when she was first coming into womanhood
at thirteen, Margaret's master, John Gaines—by all accounts a relatively
gentle slave owner—became so persuaded Cilla would bolt North with
Peggy that he used threats of selling the girl away as a means to coerce
the family's obedience. Some time afterward, Duke, the slave who may
or may not have been Margaret's actual father, either ran away from
Maplewood or was sold or died. Despite this legacy she married Robert
and by him bore Thomas. For the next five years James Marshall hired

her husband away to masters all over northern Kentucky. She saw Robert only on Sundays if he could get a pass and if old Eliza Gaines or Master Archibald's new wife, Elizabeth, with her nursing children would allow Peggy to join him. Then came the worst: Archibald Gaines made Margaret Garner's life into some kind of hell that neither she nor Robert ever cared to talk about with white people. Her children's faces told part of that story.

When the Garners finally bolted for Cincinnati on 27 January 1856 they did it as a family. After reaching free soil their fatal mistake was to seek shelter with family. At the house of her cousin Elijah Kite, Margaret Garner picked up a butcher knife because—as she later explained to abolitionists—she had to put as many of her children as possible in a place where slave catchers could never reach them. That Robert's parents did not block Margaret's strokes of the knife says that they, too, understood and tacitly accepted her motive for infanticide. Later, Robert told John Jolliffe that as a family they would all "go singing to the gallows" rather than return to slavery.

The day after her arrest, a *Cincinnati Gazette* headline put Margaret Garner's story in spare words that expressed the dreadful logic at its heart: "A Slave Mother Murders her Child Rather than See it Returned to Slavery." This phrasing said it straight out, but time swiftly translated Margaret Garner's infanticide into different terms. A case study in the conflict of laws, a drama of disunion, a prelude to fratricidal war, thus a chapter in the tragic romance of this republic—for nineteenth-century Americans the Garner case lit up all of these complex themes. And more: her story was used in support of the most poisonous racist theory, or it was a tableau of the most divine mother love. Then it was all but forgotten.

"Never marry again in slavery!" Margaret Garner's final testament claimed for her life story an essential understanding about black families and the awful wreckage that slavery spread through them. The damage involved domestic, intimate matters that were always "unspeakable things unspoken," in Toni Morrison's phrasing. For historians these "things" tend to resist anything beyond suppositions and inferences—a good enough reason (if we need it) to have historical novels like *Beloved*.

Margaret Garner's child-murder electrified a range of other themes it was always also about. Working back through them, however, we come at last to recognize how core facts in her life form a pattern that reveals a meaning. For her, slavery made child rearing an awful counterpart of child-murder, yet this oppression never froze her soul in despair. With her family she sought freedom, fought for it, and determined when all was lost that they should find freedom in death, and claim it in plain sight of Massa Gaines himself. Then, indomitable and inscrutable, she endured jail, her trial, Gaines's shell game, and her family's sale to the Cotton South. The story of Margaret Garner is all about slavery and child-murder, family and freedom.

On her deathbed Margaret implored Robert, "Never marry again in slavery!" But then Margaret Garner added, "Live in hope of freedom!"

EPILOGUE

❧

During Sunday services on 1 June 1856 the Richwood Presbyterian Church publicly lamented the parishioners' "many sins with which we as a people and a church have provoked the withdrawal of Divine favor and influence from our midst." The deacons appointed "Friday the 13th day of June as a day of solemn fasting and humiliation before God on account of our sins and departures" and enjoined the congregation "to practice bodily abstinence on that day as shall be suitable to abasing themselves in the dust before the great God whom we have offended." Squire Gaines was not listed among the penitents.[1]

In April 1857 he had a close scrape with death. "Mr. Gaines," reported the *Covington Journal*, "while plowing Monday last, had a very fine team of horses killed by lightning." Two months later, in early June 1857, he publicly reclaimed his "honor" by terrifying John Jolliffe outside Timberlake's store. Two weeks after that, his neighbors elected Gaines president of Boone County's chapter of the proslavery American Party, the Know-Nothings. At northern Kentucky agricultural fairs his sheep, mares, calves, and hogs annually won top awards throughout the remaining antebellum years, and in 1859 his wife, Elizabeth, gave birth to a healthy boy, Archie.[2]

When civil war broke out, however, northern Kentucky politics seemed to take a U-turn. Like the northern Kentucky squires who stood by him during the Garner trial, Gaines had always played the staunch Southron, but in 1860 he joined John Finnell, Clinton Butts, William Timberlake, and John Menzies in signing resolutions *opposed* to secession. Finnell took an appointment as Kentucky Adjutant General, in charge of enlisting Union volunteers, and in 1861 Menzies won John Gaines's old Tenth District congressional seat for the Democratic Party's antisecession or "Union" wing. They all seem to have put on the blue uniform. Even young Thomas Marshall enrolled in a Boone County unit of the Home Guards, a militia pledged to protect central Kentucky railroad and telegraph lines against rebel depredations.[3]

Archibald Gaines's family rode out the civil war at Richwood Station, and the record tells us nothing more of him until 1871. The afternoon of 11 November, a day of cold, drizzling rain, found Gaines

> in the barn yard, looking at a colt that had been lamed. The colt made a movement as if to kick, and Mr. Gaines moving back suddenly, stepped on a nail sticking up in a plank. The nail penetrated his foot, and lock jaw ensued.

A *Covington Journal* writer completed his obituary:

> The best medical skill and the most devoted attention on the part of his family and immediate friends could not avert the dread result. Mr. Gaines was one of the oldest citizens of Boone county, and universally respected for those traits of character which mark the kind husband and father—the good citizen—the upright man.

His will left Maplewood to Elizabeth and the six children.[4]

During the war, former Kentucky governor Charles S. Morehead was arrested at Louisville and charged with treason for supporting Confederate rebels. Receiving the news, former Ohio governor Salmon Portland Chase—then serving in Washington as Lincoln's Treasury Secretary—rubbed his hands in satisfaction.[5] Another time John Jolliffe visited the white-pillared Treasury Building and found his way to the reception area outside Secretary Chase's spacious office, there for an appointment with an undersecretary. Chase stepped out to greet him, but Jolliffe, Chase would later recall, turned aside all pleasantries with an obvious and deep-rooted "hate, for he carried matters [that is, old resentments] to that point."[6]

Jolliffe had moved to Washington, D.C., in 1862 because twenty years of antislavery lawyering had left him all but bankrupt, and the war had brought extraordinary opportunities to the nation's capital. As Union forces swept through the South, they were confiscating property, at times the lands and goods of planters still loyal to Washington. These Unionist planters, many of them former slaveholders, brought suits before the U.S. Court of Claims, later before the newly formed Southern Claims Commission. Jolliffe represented them and saw the first large fees of his career—a $31,000 attorney's bill in one case.[7] His caseload picked up during Reconstruction, and, after decades of boardinghouse life, he and Synthelia moved into a home five blocks from the White House.

On 23 March 1868 a blaze spread through Jolliffe's law offices, at 15th and F streets. Fire companies contained the blaze, and Jolliffe darted inside to salvage his papers—a complete loss, as it turned out. Overcome by smoke, he was carried semiconscious from the building and five days later died of pneumonia. In Washington, the eulogist remembered John Jolliffe as a "quiet and unostentatious" Quaker who early in his career fixed on the goal of achieving liberty and equality for slaves: "He devoted, nay he concentrated to that idea his time, his talents, his learning, his labors, and his life. His destiny has been accomplished." The *Cincinnati Gazette* ran the obituary article on its front page, next to a report on "Ku-Klux Outrages" in Alabama.[8]

We know precious little about the surviving Garners. In 1870 Robert Garner told a Cincinnati newspaper interviewer that the war's outbreak found them still at Willow Grove plantation. Their master, Judge Bonham, was an ardent Southron who had presided over Issaquena County's Democratic Party caucus that sponsored resolutions for secession. With Lincoln's election in December 1860, Bonham ushered in the county's near-unanimous vote to secede. By October 1861, he was a Confederate Army colonel commanding "928 rank & file volunteers" of the 22nd Mississippi Infantry Regiment, which he himself had raised. Among the troops was his farm overseer, twenty-eight-year-old R. G. Maxwell.[9]

After minor skirmishing in northwestern Tennessee during the early autumn of 1861, Bonham led his troops into Kentucky, south of Paducah, where they "built log cabins for Winter quarters." Dysentery and pneumonia swept through the 22nd Regiment's makeshift camp during the late autumn, and Bonham died shortly before Christmas.[10]

Willow Grove therefore must have fallen into the hands of Mary Bonham and perhaps—if they followed a pattern typical of the wartime South—a specially trusted slave. Unstable conditions, at best. Still worse were rumors of slave insurrections that shot up and down the riverside counties (Adams, Washington, and Issaquena) during the war's first year. The situation at Tennessee Landing must have been particularly threatening to whites because that area of Issaquena County was sparsely populated, with poor roads and no railheads. The best access was via the river, but by early 1862 and especially after the Confederate losses at Shiloh, in early April of that year, Union gunboats patrolled the river practically at will. Runaways were everywhere in the forests and swamps lining the river.[11]

Robert soon joined them. In his 1870 interview Robert says that he served on Union gunboats and fought at the siege of Vicksburg in 1863. Thus far no record of those activities has surfaced, and it's quite possible that Robert was one of many informal (and unrecorded) former slaves who gathered around Union camps and volunteered their labor in exchange for food and supplies. In fact, the first Colored Infantry regiments in western Mississippi weren't formed for months after the surrender of Vicksburg (on 4 July 1863), exactly when the archives yield up a tantalizing reference. A month after General Benjamin Butler commissioned the 71st Regiment of the United States Colored Infantry at Natchez, on 3 March 1864, the paymaster noted among his personnel in Company A one "Robert Gardner," a misspelling that had cropped up in some 1856 news stories about the Garners. For six months this volunteer complained that though he had "cooked for the Company since April 11 64" he had "received no pay for any part of the time," perhaps because (as it says in the last of the "Remarks" on his record), the man was never formally enlisted on the regiment's muster rolls.[12]

If this man is our Robert, as seems likely, then we can well imagine his frustration. The Army's failure to pay his wages was just one more link in a chain of white men's lies and sellouts. Finally, when he had made good his run for freedom, and even fought against Judge Bonham's old regiment at Vicksburg, they wouldn't pay his wage. Well, he didn't need "Massa Linkum's Army."

By November 1864 Robert had evidently just walked away. After the war he resettled the teenaged Tom and Sam on a small farm outside Vicksburg. What happened to Simon and Mary Garner is unknown. None of the Garners appear in the 1870 Mississippi census, suggesting they had either died or migrated. But where? By 1870 Robert Garner was living with his new wife at Cincinnati and listed in the city directory as a laborer.[13] Then he vanished in the great African-American diaspora.

Thomas Satterwhite Noble, "The Modern Medea," photographed by Mathew Brady and lithographed for reproduction in Harper's Weekly Magazine, 18 May 1867. *During spring 1867, copies of the photolithograph also appeared in the* St. Louis Guardian, *the* New York Daily Standard, *and the* American Art Journal

Margaret became "The Modern Medea." In Thomas Satterwhite Noble's painting of spring 1867, the slave catchers confront her over the outstretched bodies of two boys, a departure from historical fact that the myth demanded. A youth pointing at the children, palm down, may have been intended to represent young Thomas Marshall. The bearded figure of Archibald Gaines fixes an angry stare on Margaret, while the other two men (one holding the fugitive slave warrant) avert their eyes in horror and disbelief. Without a hint of "phrenzy," Margaret glares back at Gaines in clear-eyed defiance. Noble, who had been a Lexington, Kentucky, teenager when the Garner case was front-page news,

completed "The Modern Medea" on commission for a New York col-
lector. Evidently he intended it as one in a series of canvases on slavery
themes, among them a long-lost painting, "Fugitives in Flight," that
resurfaced in 1993. "Fugitives" depicts a slave family crossing the placid
Ohio River on a moonlit summer's night, in a configuration that refers
ironically to Emanuel Leutze's famous painting, "Washington Crossing
the Delaware."[14]

These paintings indicate that in 1867 Noble, like antebellum abolitionists, still saw fugitive slaves as heroes and heroines in "the romance
of our history," and Mathew Brady's widely circulated photolithograph
of "The Modern Medea" certainly recalled the famous case to popular
memory. But the recollection was fleeting. Frances E. W. Harper's 1874
poem, "The Slave Mother: A Tale of the Ohio," retold the story of
Margaret's child-murder as an offering of profoundest mother love, the
commonplace approach to the Garner case and slave infanticides in
general. In Harper's 1892 novel, *Iola Leroy; or, Shadows Uplifted,* set
during Reconstruction, a character speaks of the Garner case in vague
terms ("that slave mother who . . . killed one of [her] children").[15] After
that, the almost century-long silence was profound.

Margaret Garner's story had vanished too.

NOTES

༺ৡৢৢৣৡ༻

Prologue

1. Details on the Beckley suit are from the *Cincinnati Gazette* and the *Cincinnati Enquirer* of Thursday, 14 May, and Friday, 15 May 1857.

2. The following reconstruction of Archibald Gaines's 30 May 1857 assault on John Jolliffe draws principally from accounts in the *Gazette* and the *Enquirer*, who covered the story in their editions of Monday and Tuesday, 1 and 2 June 1857. Further details were drawn from their coverages of Gaines's trial, in editions of Thursday, 4 June 1857. The *Covington Journal* of Saturday, 6 June 1857 provides "a southside view" of the case.

3. On Timberlake's loss of slaves and his hiring of slaves from Archibald Gaines's Richwood Station neighborhood, see below in Chapter 1, "Fugitive."

4. The phrase is Paul Finkelman's, in his study *An Imperfect Union: Slavery, Federalism, and Comity* (Chapel Hill: University of North Carolina Press, 1981), 8.

5. Emerson's 21 January 1855 "Lecture on Slavery," delivered at Boston's Tremont Temple, denounced the federal government's role in the Burns case of May 1854; see *Emerson's Antislavery Writings*, ed. Len Gougeon and Joel Myerson (New Haven: Yale University Press, 1995), 91–106. Published initially in the 1855 edition of *Leaves of Grass*, Whitman's poem "A Boston Ballad" imagines the fracas over Anthony Burns summoning from their graves disgusted Revolutionary War "phantoms"; see *Leaves of Grass: A Textual Variorum of the Printed Poems*, Vol. 1, ed. Sculley Bradley et al. (New York: New York University Press, 1980), 146–48. Douglass related his outrage at the Burns case in *My Bondage and My Freedom* (1855) and in several speeches during the months after Burns was remanded to the South. One such address, delivered at Rochester on 22 May 1856, names Margaret Garner and Burns in a long list of martyrs and resisters; see *The Frederick Douglass Papers,*

Series One, Vol. 3; *Speeches, Debates, and Interviews*, ed. John W. Blasingame (New Haven: Yale University Press, 1985), 114–33. For modern-day treatments of the Burns case, see note 6, below.

6. On the Anthony Burns case, see, for example, *The Boston Slave Riot and Trial of Anthony Burns* (Boston: Fetridge and Co., 1854); Charles Emery Stevens, *Anthony Burns: A History* (Williamstown, MA: Corner House, 1973); Jane H. Pease, *The Fugitive Slave Law and Anthony Burns: A Problem in Law Enforcement* (Philadelphia: J. B. Lippincott, 1975); as well as a book written for juveniles by Virginia Hamilton, *Anthony Burns: The Defeat and Triumph of a Fugitive Slave* (New York: Alfred A. Knopf, 1988). On the Dred Scott case, see, for example, Vincent C. Hopkins, *Dred Scott's Case* (New York: Russell and Russell, 1967); Stanley Kutler, ed., *The Dred Scott Decision: Law or Politics* (Boston: Houghton Mifflin, 1967); Donald E. Fehrenbacher, *The Dred Scott Case: Its Significance in American Law and Politics* (New York: Oxford University Press, 1978); Walter Ehrlich, *They Have No Rights: Dred Scott's Struggle for Freedom* (Westport, CT: Greenwood Press, 1979). The literature on Scott even includes a biography of his attorney, Roswell M. Field; see Kenneth C. Kaufman, *Dred Scott's Advocate* (Columbia: University of Missouri Press, 1996). Still the matchless study of these and other fugitive cases is Stanley W. Campbell's *The Slave Catchers: Enforcement of the Fugitive Slave Law, 1850–1860* (Chapel Hill: University of North Carolina Press, 1970).

7. From an interview reported in "Toni Morrison's *Beloved* inspired by a slave who chose to kill her child," *New York Times*, 26 August 1987, III, 17. Evidently Morrison first learned of the Garner case in the early seventies, when she was editing two projects for Random House publishers. Gerda Lerner's anthology *Black Women in White America: A Documentary History* (New York: Random House, 1972) contains Brady's photolithographed image of Noble's "The Modern Medea" along with an article about the case reprinted from an 1856 Baptist magazine. M. A. Harris's *The Black Book* (New York: Random House, 1974) reuses these two texts.

8. See Toni Morrison, *Beloved* (New York: Alfred A. Knopf, 1987). A voluminous and rapidly burgeoning scholarship has grown up around Morrison's novel, and among the most useful on *Beloved*'s historical claims on readers are the following: Bernard Bell, "*Beloved*: A Womanist Neo-Slave Narrative; or, Multivocal Remembrances of Things Past," *African American Review* 26.1 (1992): 7–15; Elizabeth B. House, "Toni Morrison's Ghost: The Beloved Who Is Not Beloved," *Studies in American Fiction* 18.1 (1990): 17–26; Linda Krumholz, "The Ghosts of Slavery: Historical Recovery in Toni Morrison's *Beloved*," *African American Review* 26.3 (1992): 395–408; Andrew Levy, "Telling *Beloved*," *Texas Studies in Literature and Language* 33.1 (1991): 114–23; Caroline Rody, "Toni Morrison's *Beloved*: History, 'Rememory,' and the 'Clamor for a Kiss,'" *American Literary History* 7.1 (1995): 92–119; Charles Scruggs, "The Beloved Community in Toni Morrison's *Beloved*," in *Sweet Home: Invisible Cities in the Afro-American Novel* (Baltimore: Johns Hopkins University Press, 1993), 167–204. An extensive treatment of the Garner case, based on Levi Coffin's memoir, Julius Yanuck's historical essay, and 1850s newspaper accounts also appears in Chapter 4 of Avery Gordon's *Ghostly Matters: Haunting and the Sociological Imagination* (Minneapolis: University of Minnesota Press, 1997), 137–192.

9. Morrison, *Beloved*, 6.

1. Fugitive

1. Details about Margaret Garner's sojourn to Cincinnati are from her testimony of 11 February 1856, as transcribed by the *Cincinnati Enquirer*, 12 February 1856; as well as from her deposition before the U.S. Commissioner, quoted verbatim in the *Enquirer* of Thursday, 31 January 1856.

2. Mary Lipscom, testifying during the Garner fugitive slave hearing on Monday, 11 February 1856, as quoted in the *Cincinnati Gazette*, 12 February 1856. The employment of young slave girls as "nurses" was commonplace, and Jacqueline Jones concludes that "mistresses entrusted to the care of those who were little more than babies themselves the bathing, diapering, dressing, grooming, and entertaining of white infants"; see her *Labor of Love, Labor of Sorrow: Black Women, Work, and the Family from Slavery to the Present* (New York: Basic Books, 1985), 24. Jones also quotes testimony from a slave named Hannah who was "only eight" when she began "minding her master's children" (13). Similarly, in her 1861 slave narrative Louisa Picquet relates that from age five on she nursed her master's children: "I was a nurse. I always had plenty to do. Fast as one child would be walkin', then I would have another one to nurse." See "Louisa Picquet, the Octoroon; or, Inside Views of Southern Domestic Life," in *Collected Black Women's Narratives*, ed. Anthony G. Barthelemy (New York: Oxford University Press, 1988), 15.

3. Two excellent sources on Cincinnati in 1840 are William Cheek and Aimee Lee Cheek, "John Mercer Langston and the Cincinnati Riot of 1841," and Henry Louis Taylor, Jr., and Vicki Dula, "The Black Residential Experience and Community Formation in Antebellum Cincinnati," in *Race and the City: Work, Community, and Protest in Cincinnati, 1820–1970*, ed. Henry Louis Taylor, Jr. (Urbana: University of Illinois Press, 1993), 29–69 and 96–125, respectively. Also useful: Daniel Aaron, *Cincinnati, Queen City of the West: 1819–1838* (Columbus: Ohio State University Press, 1992); Carter G. Woodson, "The Negroes in Cincinnati Prior to the Civil War," *Journal of Negro History* 1.1 (1916): 1–22; and David L. Calkins, "Black Education in a 19th Century City: An Institutional Analysis of Cincinnati's Colored Schools, 1830–1887," *Cincinnati Historical Society Bulletin* 13.3 (1975): 161–71.

4. Working with maps and 1850 census records (easily the most thorough accounting) it is possible to tally the numbers of whites and slaves residing on property immediately bordering on that of Gaines, Bedinger, and Marshall—an area of about one-half a square mile. In 1850, 63 whites lived alongside 61 slaves, who made up 49.2 percent of the neighborhood population. These numbers appear to have been fairly constant throughout the antebellum decades. But in Kentucky as a whole, slaves, in 1830, comprised 24 percent of the state population. By 1860 a long decline had reduced their percentage to 19.5. See J. Winston Coleman, *Slavery Times in Old Kentucky* (Chapel Hill: University of North Carolina Press, 1940); and Marion B. Lucas, *A History of Blacks in Kentucky*, Vol. 1: *From Slavery to Segregation, 1760–1891* (Frankfort: Kentucky Historical Society, 1992), 2–3.

5. Lucas, *A History of Blacks in Kentucky*, 30–32.

6. Reprinted in the (Covington, KY) *Licking Valley Register*, 26 February 1848.

7. Quoted in W. C. Woodward, "The Rise and Early History of Political Parties in Oregon," *Quarterly of the Oregon Historical Society* 12.1 (1911): 37.

8. See Merrill S. Caldwell, "A Brief History of Slavery in Boone County, Kentucky"

(1957), unpublished paper in University of Kentucky Special Collections; as well as Paul Tanner, "Slavery in Boone County, Kentucky (and Its Aftermath)" (October 1986), unpublished paper at Boone County Library, Florence, Kentucky.

9. *Third Census of the United States, 1810: Kentucky. Bell and Boone Counties*, 59. Because this tally did not even record the sex or ages of slaves, we can say nothing certain about Gaines's slave property, but Margaret Garner's comments indicate her grandmother was among them.

10. For studies of the diets of Kentucky slaves, using recent archaeological evidence, see Kim A. and W. Stephen McBride, "From Colonization to the 20th Century," in *Kentucky Archaeology*, ed. R. Barry Lewis (Lexington: University Press of Kentucky, 1996), 196–97; and Matthew M. Walters, "Faunal Remains at Waveland," *Proceedings of the Symposium on Ohio Valley Urban and Historic Archaeology* 3 (1985): 145–50.

11. Lucas, *A History of Blacks in Kentucky*, 14–19. Lucas's generalized picture of the role of Kentucky blacks in clearing the wilderness was stated in 1849 by Gaines's neighbor, B. F. Bedinger: "the negroes were wanted to clear the lands, to open the farms and perform the hard labor and drudgery incident to commencing business in a new country." From a letter by Bedinger in the *Licking Valley Register*, 1 June 1849.

12. The Abner Gaines house is described by Collins Gaines, Introductory Letter to "The Diaries of John Pollard Gaines," unpublished manuscript, ed. Martha Woods Gaines, Fort Worth (TX) Public Library, 1–2. On the masters' practice of turning over their log huts to slaves, see Francis Fedric, *Slave Life in Virginia and Kentucky; or, Fifty Years of Slavery in the Southern States of America* (London: Wertheim, Macintosh, and Hunt, 1863), 17–18.

13. Quoted in J. Winston Coleman, *Stage-Coach Days in the Bluegrass: Being an Account of Stage-Coach Travel and Tavern Days in Lexington and Central Kentucky, 1800–1900* (Louisville: Standard Press, 1935), 46–47; see also 268–69.

14. At Malden, Gaines served in the regiment of a Colonel Porter; see the John Pollard Gaines Papers, Box 7, Folder 11. Gaines's trading in land warrants comes up in several surviving letters of the Gaines Papers. See, for example, G. S. Theobald to JPG, 21 February 1843, Box 1, Folder 4; G. S. Theobald to JPG, 27 December 1845, Box 1, Folder 4; A. K. Gaines, Jr., to JPG, 14 February 1848, Box 2, Folder 1; J. W. Menzies to JPG, 24 December 1848, Box 3, Folder 3. Subsequent to the Mexican War he was also notified by the Pension Office, in a letter dated 13 March 1848, that his "claim under the 9th section of the act of February 11, 1847, allowing bounty land or scrip, at the option of the claimant, has been allowed, and the Commissioner of the General Land Office has been duly notified thereof"; Gaines Papers, Box 2, Folder 3. John P. Gaines would use this 1848 grant when he took up residence in Oregon Territory, near Salem, where he proudly displayed his 1814 regimental sword, a "relic" held at the Oregon Historical Society; see the untitled note in the *Quarterly of the Oregon Historical Society* 6.3 (1906): 342.

15. The man supervising construction complained about the high cost of white hirelings in a letter to Gaines: "Labor is worth $3.00 a day and board . . . so you can see I am spending no small amount of money." George Davidson to JPG, undated (but probably 1842–43); Gaines Papers, Box 1, Folder 3. George Davidson was the son of James Davidson of Louisville, who served alongside John P. Gaines during the War of 1812. Gaines employed young Davidson intermittently during the 1840s to

oversee construction projects at Maplewood and to manage the planting of crops in springtime. In 1846, when Gaines formed the regiment of Kentucky Volunteer Cavalry, young Davidson rode off with them to Mexico as a lieutenant.

16. The last record of Gaines's tobacco dealings comes in a receipt from A. S. Soughery, a Louisville tobacco trader, who writes JPG in November 1837: "your tobacco, eighty-one Boxes was shipped on 29th September last, consigned to Messrs. A. L. Gaines & Co., Natchez"; Gaines Papers, Box 1, Folder 3.

17. See, for example, the letter of G. S. Theobald to JPG, dated 21 February, discussing Gaines's work as "receiver" of lands and slaves currently mired in bankruptcy proceedings, and mentioning also Gaines's possible bids for those and other lands. Throughout the 1840s the *Licking Valley Register* printed notices for land sales in which John Gaines served as agent. Typical of these is a November 1845 advertisement that ran for several months in early 1846, offering for sale a 300-acre tract of Richwood Station land in Gaines's "neighborhood."

18. G. S. Theobald to JPG, 21 February 1843; Gaines Papers, Box 1, Folder 4.

19. Details on Elijah Clarkson's 1850 holdings of property and slaves are from the 1850 census, and the 1850 census of slaves.

20. *Congressional Globe.* Proceedings of the 30th Congress, 1st Session (Washington, DC: Blair and Rives, 1848), 105.

21. According to the *Abridgment of the Debates of Congress*, Vol. 16: *1846–1850* (New York: Appleton, 1861), which recorded the yeas and nays of representatives on key votes, Gaines did not record a single vote on the Oregon bills that occupied the 30th Congress during its first session in 1848. His one vote on this and related measures came at the very end of the second session, on March 2, 1849, when Gaines voted with Southern representatives in favor of an amendment that would have allowed "the coastwise slave trade" in the new state of California. The amendment was defeated, by 100 yeas to 114 nays. Given Gaines's interest in a territorial governorship (see below), his seemingly total disinterest in the territorial bills may well define a man more interested in winning spoils than in legislating.

22. Of twelve petitions Gaines presented before the 30th Congress, nine involved bounty lands or veterans' survivors' pensions. He worked hard securing monetary relief for men who served under him in Mexico, especially Cassius Clay. The only two resolutions Gaines presented involved military pensions, as did the only three bills he sponsored. Gaines also seems to have been rather inept at parliamentary procedures. Two months into the session he sponsored a bill to create a select committee to investigate the expediting of extended Revolutionary War benefits, unaware that a standing committee on Revolutionary War pensions already had an extension ready for an upcoming vote. Ibid., 541–42.

23. Florella Gaines to JPG, March 7, 1848, Gaines Papers, Box 2, Folder 3.

24. The *Covington Journal* reported Mrs. Gaines as being "dangerously ill" in its 20 October 1848 edition; news of Gaines's departure for Washington, in company with Senator Benton, appeared in the 1 December 1848 edition. For Harriet's comments to JPG, see her letter from Richwood, 9 December 1848; Gaines Papers, Box 3, Folder 2.

25. G. S. Theobald to JPG, undated (circa 1845); Gaines Papers, Box 1, Folder 4.

26. Archibald K. Gaines, Jr., to JPG, 14 March 1848; Gaines Papers, Box 2, Folder 3.

27. Brenda Stevenson, *Life in Black and White: Family and Community in the Slave South* (New York: Oxford University Press, 1996), 73.

28. George Davidson to JPG, undated (circa 1844), Gaines Papers, Box 1, Folder 3.
29. See the *Covington Journal*, 21 December 1849: "Dr. B. F. Bedinger drove to market, last week, 400 hogs of his own feeding, with corn of his own raising. The aggregate weight was 113,097 pounds; an average weight of 270 pounds. They were sold at $3.05 per hundred—the highest price paid for any lot of hogs." The article further notes that he'd also delivered 21 two-year-old sheep averaging 200 pounds live weight.
30. Bedinger to JPG, 7 November 1846; Gaines Papers, Box 1, Folder 6.
31. Archibald K. Gaines, Jr., to JPG, 8 February 1848; Gaines Papers, Box 2, Folder 1.
32. Archibald K. Gaines, Jr., to JPG, 14 February 1848; Gaines Papers, Box 2, Folder 1.
33. Abner L. Gaines to JPG, 1 October 1846; Gaines Papers, Box 1, Folder 6.
34. "Uncle James's health is not good by any means—he is to settle in Covington very shortly, having already prepared himself with a house": young Archibald Gaines to JPG, 14 March 1848, Gaines Papers, Box 2, Folder 3. James M. Gaines was dead by 24 February 1854, when an obituary for his twenty-three-year-old son, William T. Gaines, appeared in the *Covington Journal* and referred to "the late Col. James M. Gaines, of Boone County."
35. Harriet Jacobs, *Incidents in the Life of a Slave Girl* (1860; New York: Oxford University Press, 1988), 44–45.
36. Frederick Douglass, *My Bondage and My Freedom* (1855; New York and London: Dover, 1969), 263.
37. "To the People of Cincinnati," *Covington Journal*, 22 March 1856. Bedinger's editorial continued for eight more issues of the *Journal*.
38. Historians using statistical methods have focused considerable energy on the onset of menarche and childbirth in the slave population of the South, beginning with Robert W. Fogel and Stanley Engerman, *Time on the Cross: The Economics of American Negro Slavery* (Boston: Little, Brown, 1974). From demographic surveys they claim that slave women did not begin childbearing as early as was commonly believed, an important assertion because it bears on the whole issue of slave masters' intrusions into the sexual behavior of their chattels. Menarche is important too, because it bears on questions of diet—clearly a factor influencing women's maturation. The Fogel and Engerman interpretation was questioned several years later by James Trussell and Richard Steckel, "The Age of Slaves at Menarche and Their First Birth," *Journal of Interdisciplinary History* 8.3 (1978): 477–505. They corrected Fogel and Engerman's calculations by factoring in other data, such as mortality figures; still, they report that the mean age for a first birth among slave women was 20.6 years, whereas the postulate that slave fertility was "manipulated" by masters should have produced a mean around 16.5 to 17 years. For further discussions of the issue, see Richard Steckel, *The Economics of U.S. Slave and Southern White Fertility* (New York: Garland, 1985); as well as Robert William Fogel, *Without Consent or Contract: The Rise and Fall of American Slavery* (New York: W. W. Norton, 1989), especially 147–53.

    On the strategy of using marriage and childbirth to defend against white sexual predators, see Harriet Jacobs's *Incidents in the Life of a Slave Girl*. "Linda" determines on a marriage to Mr. Sands, not out of love, but in order to block the advances of her master, Dr. Flint. In her narrative Louisa Picquet describes taking similar steps.

39. Facts about Robert's hirings-out derive from his deposition of 30 January 1856, transcribed in the next day's *Cincinnati Gazette*; and from trial testimony offered by Thomas Marshall one day later and reported in the *Gazette* of 1 February 1856.

40. William Timberlake to JPG, in "Washington City," 1 December 1848; Gaines Papers, Box 3, Folder 2. Though they misspelled the town's name, the *Licking Valley Register*'s coverage of the "Casiopolis Outrage" began in the issue of Friday, 3 September 1847, and continued for some weeks afterward.

41. Details about Robert Garner's different owners are taken from testimony by Thomas Marshall and other white witnesses, as well as from Robert's affidavit, transcribed in both the Cincinnati *Enquirer* and *Gazette*, for their editions of Friday, 1 February 1856.

42. On Gaines's appointment as Oregon governor and his preparations for departure, see the *Covington Journal* during October–November 1849; Gaines's journal, "Around Cape Horn: A Voyage from New York to Oregon Territory by Sailing in 1850," in "The Diaries of Major John Pollard Gaines"; and the Gaines Papers, especially the receipts and documents in Box 7, Folder 9, detailing his New York purchases and the hiring of Isaac Farr and his wife on a one-year bond of service (terms: passage to Oregon and wages of $20 per week).

43. See the 1850 census for Boone County, 165. A thorough search has turned up no marriage record for Archibald and Elizabeth Gaines; its date, her maiden name, and place of birth therefore remain unknown. Theirs may have been a common-law marriage.

44. The value of Maplewood real estate is from the 1850 census; the value of the slaves is estimated using widely available scales based on age, sex, and possible premiums (such as a slave's special skills) or discounts (such as those for a known runaway or troublesome slave). See, for example, Michael Tadman, *Speculators and Slaves: Masters, Traders, and Slaves in the Old South* (Madison: University of Wisconsin Press, 1989); and Fogel, *Without Consent or Contract*, especially 69–73.

45. See Robert B. Walz, "Arkansas Slaveholdings and Slaveholders in 1850," *Arkansas Historical Quarterly* 12 (1953): 38–60; Desmond Walls Allen and Bobbie Jones McLane, *Arkansas Land Patents: Arkansas, Chicot, and Desha Counties* (Conway, AR: Arkansas Research, 1990), 77–78; Willard B. Gatewood, "Sunnyside: The Evolution of an Arkansas Plantation, 1848–1945," *Arkansas Historical Quarterly* 50 (1991): 1–12. On Gaines Landing, see also Stephen E. Wood, "The Development of Arkansas Railroads," *Arkansas Historical Quarterly* 7 (1948): 103–18.

46. Marriage Book B (Boone County, Kentucky), 70. Subsequent to their marriage on 23 February 1843, on the "3rd sabbath in December [1843]," Mr. John Dudley & his wife Mrs. Jane Dudley & their daughter Mrs. Margaret Ann Gaines, were added to the church on certificate from the session of the church at Georgetown, Kentucky." This from the Session Books of the Richwood Presbyterian Church: Session Book 1.

47. Benjamin F. Bedinger to JPG, 7 November 1846; Gaines Papers, Box 1, Folder 6.

48. Elizabeth M. [Gaines] Hubbell to JPG, 12 March 1848; Gaines Papers, Box 2, Folder 3.

49. The description of Archibald Gaines is from the *Cincinnati Gazette* of 11 February 1856, as the fugitive slave hearing for Margaret Garner was first getting underway.

50. Bedinger to JPG (then in Washington, DC), dated 20 January 1849; Gaines Papers, Box 3, Folder 5.

51. See the *Covington Journal*, 22 June 1856; and the journal of John Pollard Gaines, "Around Cape Horn," 3–5.

52. *Covington Journal*, 30 November 1850; cause of the blaze was unknown.

53. This news was first announced in the *Covington Journal*, 11 October 1851; the following week's issue (18 October) published details of her accident.

54. Abner L. Gaines to JPG, 12 September 1851; Gaines Papers, Box 5, Folder 1.

55. Archibald K. Gaines, Jr., to his father JPG, 14 September 1852: "I hope you have rec'd the papers of settlement with Uncle A. I have a claim of trust of $344 against him which he thinks he ought not to pay—I should like your opinions as to the propriety of the claim. I hope you have sent a deed to Uncle A. with the certificate of the Clerk and the seal of the Notary as this is necessary." Gaines Papers, Box 5, Folder 2.

56. A. K. Gaines, Jr., to JPG, 14 September 1852; Gaines Papers, Box 5, Folder 2.

57. J. W. Menzies to JPG, 8 August 1851; Gaines Papers, Box 4, Folder 5.

58. On Kentucky masters' punishments of slaves, see Lucas, *A History of Blacks in Kentucky*, 47–48.

59. The phrase is Winthrop Jordan's, from *White over Black: American Attitudes toward the Negro, 1550–1812* (Chapel Hill: University of North Carolina Press, 1968), 174. On the unspeakable nature of miscegenation, see also Jacqueline Jones, *Labor of Love, Labor of Sorrow*, 12–17; and Deborah Gray White, *Ar'n't I a Woman?: Female Slaves in the Plantation South* (New York: W. W. Norton, 1985).

60. Gordon-Reed's case is one of history's most difficult: that involving the paternity of children born to Thomas Jefferson's mulatto slave Sally Hemings. Generations of American historians have summarily dismissed the charge that Jefferson fathered Hemings's children, a dismissal for which Gordon-Reed effectively pillories them. See Annette Gordon-Reed, *Thomas Jefferson and Sally Hemings: An American Controversy* (Charlottesville: University Press of Virginia, 1997), 99–100.

61. Gordon-Reed, *Thomas Jefferson and Sally Hemings*, 100–2. On the "gander months," see Bertram Wyatt-Brown, *Honor and Violence in the Old South* (New York: Oxford University Press, 1982), 113. Historian Brenda Stevenson also reports that the period of sexual inaccessibility generally lasted from one to six weeks postpartum; see her *Life in Black and White*, 104–5.

62. See Larry Gara, *The Liberty Line: The Legend of the Underground Railroad* (Lexington: University Press of Kentucky, 1961), 22–24.

63. All details on the weather are from the 15 November 1855 through 30 January 1856 editions of the *Cincinnati Gazette*, which provided daily data on climate and on river conditions. The sixty-year record was claimed in the 11 January 1856 edition; remarks on the icebound ferries, regular foot traffic, and the ice bridge appeared, respectively, in the editions of 16, 17, and 25 January 1856. Stories on iron shipments from Covington, droves of hogs being taken over the ice, and sleighing on the river appeared on 23 and 29 January 1856.

64. Details on city life over the weekend of 26–27 January 1856 appeared in the *Cincinnati Gazette* and the *Cincinnati Enquirer* editions of 26 and 29 January 1856. Advertisements for Warden's minstrel troupe appeared in the *Covington Journal*, 26 January 1856. The Hutchinson Family Singers were Judson, John, Asa, and Abby Hutchinson, from Milford, New Hampshire. Barbara White has discovered that Rebecca Hutchinson Hayward, model for Mrs. Belmont, the "she-devil" of Harriet E. Wilson's fictional autobiography, *Our Nig* (1859), was an aunt of the Hutchinson

singers, whose place in the culture of abolitionism was significant; see her "*Our Nig* and the She-Devil: New Information about Harriet Wilson and the 'Belmont' Family," *American Literature* 65.1 (March 1993): 19–52. Further details on the Hutchinsons and their lyrics are from Carol Brink, *Harps in the Wind: The Story of the Singing Hutchinsons* (New York: Macmillan, 1947), 87–89, 135, 176–80; as well as from Sam Dennison, *Scandalize My Name: Black Imagery in American Popular Music* (New York: Garland, 1982), 165–70.

65. See Taylor and Dula, "The Black Residential Experience and Community Formation in Antebellum Cincinnati"; and Henry Louis Taylor, "Spatial Organization and the Residential Experience: Black Cincinnati in 1850," *Social Science History* 10.1 (1986): 43–69. The quote is from Cheek and Cheek, "John Mercer Langston and the Cincinnati Riot of 1841," 34. See also Charles Theodore Greve, *Centennial History of Cincinnati and Representative Citizens* (Chicago: Biographical Publishing, 1904), 750–51.

66. Weather data for Sunday, 27 January 1856, are from the 28 January edition of the *Gazette*, which also ran a story, "Rowdyism," about the assaults on the Allen Chapel congregation, in addition to the story on Catharine Beecher's address to the city's corps of women teachers. Catharine Beecher's forthcoming books, derived from her recent visits to European women's schools, were *Physiology and Calisthenics for Schools and Families* (1856) and *Letters to the People on Health and Happiness* (1856).

67. Archibald Gaines had twelve slaves listed in the 1850 census. Assuming that none of them died (which seems reasonable, the oldest of them—a male—being fifty years old in 1850), then Margaret's three children born after 1850 would bring his holdings of slaves to fifteen by 1855. See *United States Census Schedules, 1850: Census of Slaves; Boone County, Kentucky* (Washington, DC: National Archives Trust), 193 and 211. Data on his agricultural holdings derive from both the John Pollard Gaines Papers, especially letters from Gaines's eldest son, Archibald (named for his uncle), his neighbor Dr. B. F. Bedinger, and his sometime farm manager, George Davidson, all of whom discuss in extensive detail such matters as crops, harvests, and stock management and sales; as well as from the 1850 *Census of Agriculture*. These are undoubtedly reliable figures for 1855, as Gaines did not add or subtract from his total acreage, or from the percentages of it tilled for crops or used for grazing, between 1850 and his death in March 1872, when the property was inventoried and surveyed for the settlement of his will. See Will of Archibald K. Gaines, 13 March 1872, Boone County, Kentucky, Willbook I, 392–96.

68. On the seasonal rhythms of slave labor in Kentucky, see Lucas, *A History of Blacks in Kentucky*, Chapter 1, "Labor, Living Conditions, and the Family," especially 3–6. Also useful is Coleman, *Slavery Times in Old Kentucky*. On the household and other duties of slave women, see Jones, *Labor of Love, Labor of Sorrow*, 22–35; and Deborah Gray White, "The Lives of Slave Women," in *Black Women in United States History*, Vol. 4, ed. Diane Clark Hine (Brooklyn: Carlson, 1990), 1–14. Of Gaines's slaves other than Margaret and her children we know little beyond brief references in letters archived among the John Pollard Gaines Papers; see in particular letters to JPG from George Davidson, his son A. K. Gaines, Jr., and (in particular) an 8 August 1851 letter to JPG from J. W. Menzies (Box 4, Folder 5). At the Second Annual Exhibition of the Northern Kentucky Agricultural Society, held at Florence, KY, in October 1856, Gaines was awarded prizes for his merino sheep;

as he was the following year, in addition to other awards for best cow, best yoke of oxen, best bull, and best saddle horse (age 1–2 years). See the *Covington Journal*, 16 October 1856; and 17 October 1857.

69. Details about Margaret's household duties are taken from testimony at her fugitive slave hearing, summaries and transcriptions of which were published in both the *Cincinnati Gazette* and the *Enquirer*. For details on the membership and attendance of area residents—including slaves—at Richwood Presbyterian Church, we have the records of the church's Session Books, on microfilm at the University of Kentucky Library, Special Collections. Archibald K. Gaines was married to Margaret Ann Dudley there on 23 February 1843: ten months later the following notation recorded her formal admission to church membership: "3rd Sabbath in December. At this meeting also Mr. John Dudley & his wife Mrs. Jane Dudley & their daughter Mrs. Margaret Ann Gaines were added to the church on certificate from the session of the church at Georgetown, Kentucky" (Session Book 24). Ten months later, in October 1844, Elizabeth M., "daughter of Mrs. Margaret Gaines [was] baptized" (Session Book 27). From this record, Archibald Gaines does not appear to have been at all active in church affairs, though his in-laws were. The Richwood Presbyterian congregation numbered fifty to sixty whites during these years, and six to ten persons "of color"; notations about the slaves always supply only first names— as with one called "Sister Hannah," who was once remonstrated with for "insubordinate conduct as a servant and for the use of bad language unbefitting her profession" (Session Book 53).

70. See Mechal Sobel, *Trabelin' On: The Slave Journey to an Afro-Baptist Faith* (Westport, CT: Greenwood Press, 1979), 333–43. These black churches could be sizable. Georgetown's Colored Branch of the First Baptist Church boasted a congregation of nearly two hundred in 1855; in the same year Lexington's Second African Church numbered over one hundred and fifty, and when the owner of Pastor George Depuy put him up for sale, white residents purchased him—on condition that members repay them at $8.30 per week.

71. Albert J. Raboteau, *Slave Religion* (New York: Oxford University Press, 1978), Chapters 3–5. See also Peter Randolph's "Plantation Churches: Visible and Invisible" and Sister Kelly's narration in *Afro-American Religious History: A Documentary Witness*, ed. Milton C. Sernett (Durham, NC: Duke University Press, 1985), 63–68, 69–75.

72. See Julius Yanuck, "The Garner Fugitive Slave Case," *Mississippi Valley Historical Review* 40 (1953): 50, n. 18; summarizing comments in a *Daily Times* story of 16 February 1856, Yanuck writes: "It is likely that their determination to escape was strengthened by two English ladies who were at that time guests in the home of Archibald K. Gaines. Soon after the slaves fled the ladies were accused of encouraging them by pointing out the possibilities of escape. They hastily terminated their visit because of threats to their lives." Not only do the "two English ladies" appear in no other archival source; they do not appear in the *Covington Journal*, a paper that kept an interested, close watch on and reported the goings and comings of foreign visitors. In the chapter on *Beloved*, Avery Gordon incisively comments that whites needed the "two English ladies" to diminish the Garners' agency; see her *Ghostly Matters: Haunting and the Sociological Imagination* (Minneapolis: University of Minnesota Press, 1997), 222, n. 17.

73. See Hugh Honour, *The Image of the Black in Western Art*, Vol. 4, No. 1: *From the*

American Revolution to World War I: Slaves and Liberators (Cambridge: Harvard University Press, 1989), 207–14.

74. The original *Cincinnati Commercial* story is unavailable but it was reprinted by other newspapers, for example in *The Press* of Philadelphia, 18 March 1870, under the headline "A REMINISCENCE OF SLAVERY: The Slave Mother, Margaret Garner—Her Tragic Sacrifice of a Child—Interview with Her Husband—Subsequent History of the Family." On Robert's affidavit submitted at the fugitive slave hearing, see the *Cincinnati Gazette*, 31 January 1856; the Kites' testimony during the fugitive slave hearing was transcribed in detail and appeared in the *Gazette* of 2 February 1856. The 1850 Fugitive Slave Law imposed fines on anyone assisting slaves in their escape, a provision clarified by Justice McLean. Ruling in a Pennsylvania case, McLean found that a Mr. Kaufman was guilty of harboring thirteen fugitives and therefore liable for damages. In rejecting the pleas of Kaufman's defense, McLean excluded acts of kindness or charity toward fugitives, holding that under the 1850 law the acts in question must be intended "to encourage the fugitive in his desertion of his master, to further his escape and impede and frustrate his reclamation. This act must evince an intention to elude the vigilance of the master" (*United States v. Kaufman*, 2 McLean, 608 [1852]). Intent was everything, McLean ruled; and by this standard the Kites might well have been charged.

75. These figures are based on a survey of the two major Cincinnati papers, the *Enquirer* and the *Gazette*, as well as the *Covington Journal*, from September 1850 to January 1856, for all reported instances of slave escapes from the northern Kentucky counties of Boone and Kenton. Stories of escapes from other areas, such as Louisville, KY, from whence slaves often fled over the Ohio River into the woods of southern Indiana, were not counted in this survey because we want to assess local practices, the knowledge of slaves such as the Garners about previous attempts, and how past patterns may have affected the vigilance of local whites in January 1856. Incidentally, the numbers and details in this survey compare favorably with those gathered by Stanley W. Campbell, in *The Slave Catchers: Enforcement of the Fugitive Slave Law, 1850–1860* (Chapel Hill: University of North Carolina Press, 1970). See especially the tables of his "Appendix," 199–205. The term "negro stampede," used with reference to groups of fugitives (typically families) on the run, was common in Southern newspapers; see Gara, *The Liberty Line*, 22.

76. Willard Rouse Jillson, *Pioneer Kentucky* (Frankfort: State Journal Company, 1934), 43–45; and Coleman, *Stage-Coach Days in the Bluegrass*.

77. *Cincinnati Enquirer*, 29 January 1856.

78. The *Maysville* (KY) *Eagle*, 11 February 1856; reprinted in the *National Anti-Slavery Standard*, 23 February 1856.

79. *Cincinnati Commercial*, 29 January 1856; reprinted in the *National Anti-Slavery Standard*, 9 February 1856.

80. *The Revised Statutes of Kentucky* (1852), Chapter XCIII, Article III, paragraphs 9, 11, and 12; and Article VII, paragraph 10.

2. Captive

1. Unless specifically indicated all the narrative details that follow were culled from news reports published in the Cincinnati daily papers, the *Gazette* and the *Enquirer* (the two most accessible), as well as the *Columbian* and *Commercial*; in addition I

have used the *Covington Journal*, a weekly paper invaluable for its "south-side view" on events.

2. See Levi Coffin, *Reminiscences of Levi Coffin, the Reputed President of the Underground Railroad* (Cincinnati: Western Tract Society, 1876), 558–59. A 4 January 1853 *Cincinnati Gazette* article about Stowe's novel commented on John Van Zandt: "The first station north of Cincinnati was a few miles up Mill Creek, at the house of the pious and lion-hearted John Van Zandt, who figures in chapter nine of *Uncle Tom's Cabin* as John Van Tromp. . . . He now sleeps in the obscure grave of a martyr."

3. Beginning with an erroneous report in the *Cincinnati Commercial* on Tuesday, 29 January 1856, a story perpetuated in Coffin's *Reminiscences* (558), one version of the Garner escape has it that the eight Garners and nine other slaves, seventeen persons in all, piled atop Marshall's sleigh for the eighteen-mile sprint to Covington. Nothing of the sort occurred, as we learn from details related in subsequent editions of the *Cincinnati Gazette*, the *Cincinnati Enquirer*, and the *Covington Journal*, and synthesized here. Probably it was Marshal Clinton Butts who told the *Cincinnati Gazette* reporter about the other slaves' escapes, and left that man with the false impression that all seventeen Kentucky slaves escaped in a well-orchestrated "stampede."

4. *Covington Journal*, 2 February 1856.

5. *Cincinnati Gazette*, Tuesday, 29 January 1856; *Covington Journal*, 2 February 1856.

6. The *Cincinnati Commercial* implies, probably erroneously, that it was Deputy Marshal John Ellis who got the warrant from Commissioner Pendery; the *Enquirer*, *Gazette*, and the *Covington Journal* all state that it was Bennet who secured the warrant and enlisted the other deputies. Details narrated in the subsequent paragraphs are culled from these accounts, with differences noted as pertinent.

7. Julius Yanuck, taking his cue from Levi Coffin's erroneous claim that the Garners were out on Cincinnati streets searching for Kite's Mill Creek house in "broad daylight" and amidst pedestrians, speculates that their betrayers were unknown persons "of whom the Garners asked directions." But this would have been unnecessary because Robert *already knew* the location of Margaret's cousin's house, having found it during a Christmas 1855 sojourn in Cincinnati. See Coffin (559), as well as Yanuck, "The Garner Fugitive Slave Case," *Mississippi Valley Historical Review* 40 (1953): 51.

8. *Cincinnati Enquirer*, 2 February 1856.

9. *Covington Journal*, 22 March 1856.

10. On the *Harper v. Kite* lawsuit, see the *Cincinnati Gazette*, 10 November 1853; on the reactions of Boone County residents to the court's judgment in this case, see the *Covington Journal*, 14 and 21 November 1853. The *Gazette's* story notes that when Elijah Kite escaped from William Harper in 1849, it was with his "wife, Amanda," and a son named Robert. Apparently Elijah lived out of the city for several years; but when back in Cincinnati during the autumn and winter of 1855–56 his "wife," according to court testimony by the Kites, is "Mary."

The case is, by any yardstick, a curious one. Why Harper didn't seek a fugitive slave warrant for the return of Elijah Kite remains unclear from newspaper accounts, though one probable reason is that throughout the 1840s he had willingly let the young slave drive his hogs to Cincinnati markets and thereby endangered his status under the 1793 Fugitive Slave Law. It is also apparent that Harper had signed papers in which he agreed to manumit Kite, and that the contract for Joe Kite's purchase of his son was drawn up in Ohio.

11. The *Enquirer* report of these details—like the *Gazette*'s published in the Tuesday, 29 January 1856, editions—differs only in stating that Deputy Bennet "received information of the hiding place of the fugitives." On Robert's suspicion of his wife's cousin, see his 1870 testimony quoted in "A REMINISCENCE."

12. *Covington Journal*, 22 March 1856. Justice's letter continued through three subsequent issues and prompted several lengthy replies, discussed in a subsequent chapter. The evidence that Justice was Benjamin F. Bedinger rests upon his claim of being a "near neighbor" of Archibald Gaines, and on stylistic comparisons of the Justice letters with other texts subscribed by Bedinger, including correspondence by him addressed to J. P. Gaines, in the John Pollard Gaines Papers, as well as other letters he published in the *Licking Valley Register* and *Covington Journal*; see in particular his lengthy endorsement of Major J. P. Gaines for reelection to the U.S. Congress, in the *Licking Valley Register*, 1 June 1849.

13. See, for example, James Oliver Horton and Stacy Flaherty, "Black Leadership in Antebellum Cincinnati," in *Race and the City: Work, Community, and Protest in Cincinnati, 1820–1970*, ed. Henry Louis Taylor, Jr., (Urbana: University of Illinois Press, 1993), 70–95; and Carter G. Woodson, "The Negroes of Cincinnati Prior to the Civil War," *Journal of Negro History* 1 (January 1916): 1–22.

14. Lucy Stone quoted in the *National Anti-Slavery Standard*, 12 April 1856: 3.

15. Quoted from the *Enquirer*, which reported (from witnesses) that Robert fired one shot through the window, striking Patterson immediately, whereas the *Gazette* and the *Commercial* both reported that this first shot was errant and it was one of the three fired inside the house that struck Patterson.

16. The *Enquirer* here gets the boys' ages wrong—Thomas was six and Samuel four— but all other details in this description are consistent with other news reports, themselves taken from statements of the posse members, and more importantly with testimony offered during the coroner's inquest held Monday afternoon and Tuesday, 28–29 January 1856, as reported in all the city papers.

17. The following paragraphs narrate details and events culled from all available 29–30 January 1856 newspaper summaries of testimony before the coroner's jury: the *Enquirer*, most detailed of the lot; the *Gazette*, a rather tightened version of the former; the *Commercial*, briefest of them all; and the 2 February 1856 edition of the *Covington Journal*, whose summary gets a number of details wrong, such as the sex of the deceased Garner child.

18. *Cincinnati Commercial*, 29 January 1856; reprinted in the *National Anti-Slavery Standard*, 9 February 1856.

19. Both, however, did speak after their trials. See Douglas R. Egerton, *Gabriel's Rebellion: The Virginia Slave Conspiracies of 1800 and 1802* (Chapel Hill: University of North Carolina Press, 1983); Henry I. Tragle, *The Southampton Slave Revolt of 1831: A Compilation of Source Material* (Amherst: University of Massachusetts Press, 1971); and Albert E. Stone, *The Return of Nat Turner: History, Literature, & Cultural Politics in Sixties America* (Athens: University of Georgia Press, 1992).

20. Eric Sundquist, *To Wake the Nations: Race in the Making of American Literature* (Cambridge, MA: Harvard University Press, 1993), 176.

21. George Fitzhugh, *Cannibals All!*, ed. C. Vann Woodward (1857; Cambridge, MA: Harvard University Press, 1960), 204–5.

22. Summarizing the views of Southern intellectuals like Albert Taylor Bledsoe, Thomas Roderick Dew, and James Henley Thornwell, Eugene Genovese concludes: "In southern doctrine the family meant the extended household, defined to include 'servants'—dependent laborers. Their familiar expression, 'my family, white and black,' far from being a propagandistic ploy, expressed the essence of a worldview. For good reason Abraham loomed as the principal Old Testament figure among the slaveholders, much as Moses was among the slaves. Abraham was, in their oft-expressed view, simultaneously a great slaveholder and God's favored patriarch of a household that included his many slaves." See Genovese, *The Slaveholders' Dilemma: Freedom and Progress in Southern Conservative Thought, 1820–1860* (Columbia: University of South Carolina Press, 1992), 38. In Bledsoe's defense of slavery, in a chapter of *An Essay on Liberty and Slavery* (1856), the idea of family looms paramount and its key logic is that of reciprocity. "No fact is plainer than that the blacks have been elevated and improved by their servitude in this country. We cannot possibly conceive, indeed, how Divine Providence could have placed them in a better school of correction. If the abolitionists can conceive a better method for their enlightenment and religious improvement, we should rejoice to see them carry their plan into execution" (Philadelphia: J. B. Lippincott, 1856), 299.

23. Lydia Maria Child uses the term "brothel" in the antislavery pamphlet she compiled, aptly titled *The Patriarchal Institution as Described by Members of its Own Family* (New York: American Anti-Slavery Society, 1860). Harriet Jacobs, in her *Incidents in the Life of a Slave Girl* (1861; New York: Oxford University Press, 1988), spoke rather more in code; using the commonplace trope of a brothel as a "bird cage," Jacobs calls the typical Southern household a "cage of obscene birds" that "makes the white fathers cruel and sensual; the sons violent and licentious; it contaminates the daughters, and makes the wives wretched" (see Chapter 9, "Sketches of Neighboring Slaveholders"). During the 1850s the idea of the South as "brothel" was an especially prominent figure used by Garrisonian abolitionists; see Kristin Hoganson, "Garrisonian Abolitionists and the Rhetoric of Gender, 1850–1860," *American Quarterly* 45.4 (December 1993), especially 570–71.

24. These details are from a Cincinnati "Correspondent" writing for the *National Anti-Slavery Standard*, 23 February 1856. There may well have been grounds for the nepotism charge. The relation of Pendery's wife to McLean is confirmed in Francis Phelps Weisenburger, *The Life of John McLean: A Politician on the United States Supreme Court* (Columbus: Ohio State University Press, 1937), 219–20. Moreover, McLean's correspondence reveals that after Commissioner Samuel Carpenter resigned in protest over the Fugitive Slave Law, in 1855, Ohio lawyers led by Flamen Ball strongly recommended replacing him with William Wallace Warden, a man with strong antislavery views. McLean appointed Pendery instead, further angering Ohioans displeased at McLean's sending the fugitive named Rosetta back to slavery that spring. See Flamen Ball to John McLean, 5 June 1855; in the McLean Papers, Box 18.

25. *Cincinnati Commercial*, 29 January 1856.

26. On Burgoyne's abolitionism, see Coffin, *Reminiscences of Levi Coffin*, 377.

27. Testimony of Friday, 1 February, transcribed in the *Cincinnati Gazette*, 2 February 1856.

28. The phrasing is the *Gazette*'s, from its main story of Tuesday, 29 January 1856.

29. *Cincinnati Enquirer*, Tuesday, 29 January 1856.
30. The study was done by historian David Carl Schilling, and is summarized in Stanley W. Campbell, *The Slave Catchers: Enforcement of the Fugitive Slave Law* (Chapel Hill: University of North Carolina Press, 1920), 57.
31. See Stephen W. Middleton, "The Fugitive Slave Crisis in Cincinnati, 1850–1860: Resistance, Reinforcement, and Black Refugees," *Journal of Negro History* 72.1–2 (1987), especially 27.
32. Ibid.
33. This lyric has been variously documented in the literature on American slave songs. In the pathbreaking collection by William Francis Allen, Charles Pickard Ware, and Lucy McKim Garrison, *Slave Songs of the United States* (1867; New York: Peter Smith, 1929), a variant of the song appears as "I Wish I Been Dere" (see 28–29). For other versions, see Miles M. Fisher, *Negro Slave Songs in the United States* (New York: Russell and Russell, 1953), 56–57; and Sam Dennison, *Scandalize My Name: Black Imagery in American Popular Music* (New York: Garland, 1982), 171.
34. *Cincinnati Enquirer*, Tuesday, 29 January 1856.
35. James Sheridan Knowles, *Virginius: A Tragedy in 5 Acts* (Philadelphia: Turner and Fisher, 1826); available more recently in Knowles, *Dramatic Works* (London and New York: Routledge, Warnes, and Routledge, 1959), 59–111. The Virginius child-murder was also related in Livy, a source (along with Cicero) that Knowles acknowledged. The *New York Tribune* reported that when it was staged in New York the drama stirred "the inmost depths of emotion in large audiences, in whose shuddering sympathy for the child was always mingled a lurking admiration for the stern heroism of the parent." This comparison surfaced in a *Tribune* story on the Garner case in its edition of 8 February 1856—a comparison doubtless triggered by that in the *Enquirer*.
36. Thomas Babington Macaulay, "Virginia," in *The Lays of Ancient Rome* (London: Longman, Brown, Green, and Longman, 1842). Eleven years later the first American edition appeared (Philadelphia: E. H. Butler, 1853), and went through a number of printings.
37. In Macaulay's version, after the trial verdict Virginius takes his daughter aside and remarks that Claudius " 'little deems that in this hand I clutch what still can save/ Thy gentle youth from taunts and blows, the portion of the slave;/ Yea, and nameless evil, that passeth taunt and blow—/ Foul outrage which thou knowest not, which thou shalt never know./ Then clasp me round the neck once more, and give me one more kiss;/ And now, mine own dear little girl, there is no way but this.'/ With that he lifted high the steel, and smote her in the side,/ And in her blood, she sank to earth, and with one sob she died." In that "nameless evil" Macaulay has Virginius emphasize precisely the sexual degradation that Americans in speaking about the plight of slave women also stressed, but only in code. See Macaulay, *The Lays of Ancient Rome*, 166–67.
38. These details on the coroner's inquest are from the *Cincinnati Enquirer*, Wednesday, 30 January 1856.
39. From the report on the inquest published in the *Cincinnati Gazette*, Wednesday, 30 January 1856.
40. Jolliffe's professional address can be found in *Williams's Cincinnati Directory, City Guide, and Business Mirror*. The Cincinnati Historical Society maintains copies ranging from the early 1840s. Descriptions of Jolliffe are drawn from various sources,

including his obituary, published in the *Cincinnati Gazette*, 10 April 1868; various newspaper reports of the Garner fugitive slave hearing, including especially the "Letters from Our Cincinnati Correspondents" printed in the *National Anti-Slavery Standard*, 16 February 1856; and Elizabeth A. Jolliffe, "John Jolliffe," in *Historical, Genealogical, and Biographical Account of the Jolliffe Family of Virginia, 1652–1893* (Philadelphia: J. B. Lippincott, 1893), 223–32.

41. Details on the Jolliffes' philanthropic and antislavery works, and especially John Jolliffe's legal practice, are drawn from surveys of the *Cincinnati Gazette* and the *Cincinnati Enquirer* from 1850 to 1860.

42. Of course, it was not always such plain sailing as this. In July 1855 the steamer *Mediator* docked at Cincinnati from New Orleans; aboard were a Mississippi master named John Wilson and his mulatto slave mistress, Celeste, whom he intended to emancipate and for whose voyage he had secured an expensive stateroom. On arriving in the city Wilson left Celeste in a stateroom, went looking for a lawyer, was directed to Jolliffe, and explained his intention to emancipate the woman. Then Wilson apparently commenced a binge of drinking and card playing, and mysteriously disappeared. Celeste remained aboard ship, twenty dollars of her passage still unpaid and the *Mediator*'s captain demanding either payment of the sum or the rights to Wilson's slave. Jolliffe filed a writ of habeas corpus before Judge Burgoyne, and on his own pulled together the money to satisfy the ship captain. Celeste was freed, but Jolliffe went unpaid. See the *Cincinnati Gazette*, 8–10 July, 1856.

43. Flamen Ball was the law partner and lifetime affiliate of Salmon Portland Chase, during his career as senator, governor, and Chief Justice of the U.S. Supreme Court; see John Niven, *Salmon Portland Chase: A Biography* (New York: Oxford University Press, 1995).

44. On the "Gaines and Jolliffe Affair," see my "Prologue," above.

45. See *The Jolliffe Family*, 66–72.

46. On William Jolliffe, see *The Jolliffe Family*, 108–12. On Quaker abolitionism during the Revolutionary period, see Robert William Fogel, *Without Consent or Contract: The Rise and Fall of American Slavery* (New York: W. W. Norton, 1989), 241–52; and Peter Kolchin, *American Slavery: 1619–1877* (New York: Hill and Wang, 1993), 75–78.

47. For the Tucker genealogy and general history, see Beverly Randolph Tucker, *Tales of the Tuckers* (Richmond, VA: Dietz, 1942). On St. George Tucker's antislavery views, see D. S. Bryman, "St. George Tucker and the Complexities of Antislavery Advocacy in Jeffersonian Virginia," Master's thesis, College of William and Mary, 1972; and Charles T. Cullen, *St. George Tucker and Law in Virginia, 1772–1804* (New York: Garland, 1987), 149–53. A useful general introduction to Tucker's life and thought also appears as the introduction to *The Poems of St. George Tucker of Williamsburg, Virginia, 1752–1827* (New York: Vantage, 1977).

48. About this move the family genealogist offers only vague cliché: "The great West had become the El Dorado of youthful aspirants for fame and fortune . . . [and] towards Ohio, especially, the steps of Virginia's young men were turned." See "John Jolliffe" in *The Jolliffe Family*, 224. Probably the facts were much more prosaic. Jolliffe's professing the law would have embarrassed his devout Quaker mother; also, Tucker's law school had probably produced something of a lawyer glut in Winchester.

49. *The Jolliffe Family*, 224–25.

50. Letters quoted in "John Jolliffe," in *The Jolliffe Family*, 225–26. Jolliffe's sister wrote him the family's concerns about his moving South, perhaps even to New Orleans, in search of remunerative work: "Should you go to the South we might forever relinquish all hope of ever seeing you again, a hope which cheers mother in her hours of deepest sadness."

51. *Belle Scott; or, Liberty Overthrown! A Tale for the Crisis* (Columbus and Cincinnati: Anderson and Blanchard, 1856); and *Chattanooga* (Cincinnati: Anderson, Gates, and Wright, 1858). Neither of these titles was published over Jolliffe's name during the 1850s, though early reviews of both books in the Cincinnati and Columbus papers readily identified him as their author. (A title-page note penned into the copy of *Chattanooga* in the Special Collections at the University of Kentucky's King Library reveals that someone wrongly attributed the book to "Wm. Gilmore Simms.") Publisher's notices for *Belle Scott* indicate that it was published in mid-July 1856; and the first review (in the *Cincinnati Gazette*) appeared on 2 August 1856. Three thousand copies were in print when Heath (of Boston) published a fourth edition of the novel in late 1856 for wider distribution in New England. It was also reprinted in 1971 (Freeport, NY: Books for Libraries Press). *Chattanooga* was a much lesser book for Jolliffe: no antebellum reprintings (indeed scarcely any notices), though the novel has been reissued on microfiche (Louisville, KY: Lost Cause Press, 1969).

   When did Jolliffe complete *Belle Scott*? The question is important because one wonders if, and how, the Garner case might have influenced its writing. For a novel published in mid-July, one suspects that Jolliffe would have been reading galleys by March; the 426-page novel must have been substantially completed, therefore, when the Garner case broke in late January. The influence of that most recent case — Jolliffe's most famous — would therefore have been minor.

52. As a 3 February 1840 letter from Gamaliel Bailey to James G. Birney makes clear. From Cincinnati, Bailey writes Birney at the New York offices of the American Anti-Slavery Society that the supporters in Clermont County have raised one hundred dollars under Jolliffe's guidance, and wish to use it for employment of a lecturer, a Mr. Kedzie. "He [Jolliffe] wished me to write on to you, to know whether the Parent Committee [of the AAS] would be willing that the money should be expended by the friends in Clermont in this way." See *The Letters of James Gillespie Birney, 1831–1857*, Vol. 1, ed. Dwight L. Dumond (New York: Appleton-Century, 1938), 523–24.

53. Again, from the genealogical account written by his niece: "Finding that the prejudice engendered by his antislavery course had infected even the judges of the Courts of Clermont and Brown counties to the prejudice of his clients, Mr. Jolliffe, about the year 1841, removed to Cincinnati." See "John Jolliffe," in *The Jolliffe Family*, 226.

54. See *The Cincinnati Directory for 1842* (Cincinnati: R. P. Brooks, 1842).

55. *Cincinnati Gazette*, 21 April 1851.

56. News of the Free Democracy Party's nominations and resolution appeared in the newspapers throughout the late summer and autumn months of 1852. For final election tallies, see the *Cincinnati Gazette*, 11 October 1852.

57. See, for example, Eric Foner, *Free Soil, Free Labor, Free Men: The Ideology of the Republican Party before the Civil War* (New York: Oxford University Press, 1970).

Foner's view forms the basis of the narrative constructed by Fogel, in *Without Consent or Contract*, 254–386.

58. Quoted in the *Cincinnati Gazette*, 22 June 1852.

59. See Jolliffe's obituary, published in the *Cincinnati Gazette*, 10 April 1868.

60. This narrative of Flinn's assault on Jolliffe is a composite drawn from the *Cincinnati Gazette*, the *Cincinnati Enquirer*, and the *Cincinnati Commercial* for the period 27 August through 9 September 1853.

61. Again, this account of the *Tropic* slaves is a composite drawing from the *Gazette*, *Enquirer*, and *Commercial* for the period 23–26 August 1853; an additional source is Middleton, "The Fugitive Slave Crisis in Cincinnati," 26–27.

62. Moderately stiff by comparison to other fines for assault cases reported in the *Gazette* and *Enquirer*. The typical range: five to forty dollars and court costs.

63. From the list published in the court reports of the *Cincinnati Gazette*, 7 September 1853.

64. The consensus of historians is that Chase won by forging a coalition of former Conscience Whigs, Free-Soilers, and Know-Nothings within the newly fledged Republican Party, and also because he tirelessly stumped the state while the incumbent, William Medill, stayed too much in Columbus. Another (though secondary) consideration was that in the spring of 1855 disruptions in the streets of Cincinnati pitting Irish and German immigrants against each other had raised fears of civil disorder. In that light, Governor Medill's apparent arming of the Irish militias looked very damaging. See Foner, *Free Soil, Free Labor, Free Men*, 244–45; and Niven, *Salmon P. Chase*, 172–75.

65. Wendell Phillips, "Public Opinion" [speech delivered 28 January 1852], *Speeches, Lectures, and Letters* (Boston: Lee and Shepard, 1892), 39, 47, 40, and 36.

66. The "scoundrels" quote is Phillips again (48), but his interpretation of changing strategy was widely held. Indeed, outside the movement per se Ralph Waldo Emerson would argue along the same line. "The Fugitive Slave Law," Emerson's March 1854 address, opens with similar comments on "the silent revolution which the newspaper has wrought," and argues further that the penny papers are—in place of Europe's universities—the "core of rebellion" against oppression in America. Notably, too, Emerson's essay reworks the familiar formula: after the "heart" is educated by the press so that "heads" are changed, action becomes the third and final imperative: "Liberty is aggressive," he remarks in closing. See *Emerson's Antislavery Writings*, ed. Len Gougeon and Joel Myerson (New Haven: Yale University Press, 1995), 73–90. On the influence of steam-driven presses and penny papers in the slavery debate, see also William Lee Miller, *Arguing about Slavery: The Great Battle in the United States Congress* (New York: Alfred A. Knopf, 1996), 93–105.

67. *Cincinnati Gazette* and *Cincinnati Enquirer*, Friday, 9 September 1853.

68. See Campbell, "Appendix" to *The Slave Catchers*, especially Table 12, 199–207. For the story of Celeste, the mulatto woman abandoned in Cincinnati, see n. 42, above.

69. Jolliffe, *Belle Scott*, 237. Entitled "Mr. Ives' Speech," the chapter is number 23, a centerpiece of the novel and its longest chapter by far (others average seven or eight pages each). Comparisons of this chapter with newspaper summaries of Jolliffe's speech, as reported in the *Enquirer* and *Gazette*, for both the McQuerry and Garner cases, show that the chapter is probably a virtual transcript (somewhat digested) of the argument Jolliffe typically made in fugitive cases.

70. *Belle Scott*, 258.

71. *Belle Scott*, 401, 86–87.

72. Cushing in a 29 September 1853 letter to the *Boston Post*, quoted in Campbell, *The Slave Catchers*, 104.

73. "A Fugitive Case in Cincinnati: First Trial before a Supreme Judge of the United States," *Cincinnati Gazette*, Wednesday, 17 August 1853. Unless otherwise indicated, details of the following account are taken from this story in the *Gazette*; from Charles Theodore Greve, *Centennial History of Cincinnati and Representative Citizens* (Chicago: Biographical Publishing, 1904), 759–60; and from Campbell, *The Slave Catchers*, 115–18.

74. For the text of McLean's ruling, see *Miller v. McQuerry*, 5 McLean 469 (1853).

75. On the Louis escape, see Middleton, "The Fugitive Slave Crisis in Cincinnati," 26; Greve, *Centennial History*, 760–61; and Coffin, *Reminiscences*, 548–54.

76. *Belle Scott*, 358.

77. In the novel Belle Scott proclaims, "Oh! I can from my heart of hearts say, with Patrick Henry, 'Give me liberty or give me death!' " (276); for the second quote, see *Belle Scott*, 181.

78. *Belle Scott*, pp. 267–68. His description of a jail in the fictional Ohio town of "Guyandotte" looks notably close to descriptions given of the jail facilities by Cincinnati journalists in the *Enquirer* and *Gazette*.

79. See the *Licking Valley Register* of 11 June 1848.

3. Defendant

1. From "The Weather," a detailed summary of the prior week's storms and climatological conditions in the *Cincinnati Enquirer*, 5 February 1856.

2. Here and in the paragraphs following, my narrative is composed from stories published in the city's newspapers. Unless otherwise indicated, observations or quotations attributed to particular newspapers are from the *next day*'s edition (i.e., the *Gazette*'s observations about events of Wednesday, 30 January, appeared in the edition of Thursday, the 31st).

3. The only comparable case was the Christiana riot of September 1851 in Lancaster County, Pennsylvania. When slave catchers urged by Maryland owner Edward Gorsuch surrounded the farmhouse where a large party of fugitives had holed up, the slaves fired on the whites and then fought their way out. Gorsuch was killed and several others wounded. The fugitives succeeded in making their way to Canada and were therefore never formally charged with murder. Hence the legal clash between states at the heart of the Garner case never unfolded at Christiana. See Thomas R. Slaughter, *Bloody Dawn: The Christiana Riot and Racial Violence in the Antebellum North* (New York: Oxford University Press, 1991).

4. On Pollock's American or Know-Nothing Party affiliations, see the story on their activities in the *Cincinnati Enquirer* of 5 April 1856.

5. Joseph Cox, letter to the editors, *Cincinnati Commercial*, 21 November 1863. A copy of the news story, clipped and sent to Salmon Portland Chase, can be found in *The Salmon Portland Chase Papers* (microfilm edition), ed. John Niven (Frederick, MD: University Publications, 1987), Reel 30, 0073.

6. Common enough that Harriet Beecher Stowe, for example, includes several mentions of the practice in *Uncle Tom's Cabin*. In Chapter 1 she introduces readers to

Tom's great honesty by having the kindly slave's master, Shelby, proclaim to the slave trader Haley, "Why, last fall, I let him go to Cincinnati alone, to do business for me, and bring home five hundred dollars. 'Tom,' says I to him, 'I trust you, because I think you're a Christian—I know you wouldn't cheat.' Tom comes back, sure enough; I knew he would. Some low fellows, they say, said to him—'Tom, why don't you make tracks for Canada?' 'Ah, master trusted me, and I couldn't.' " Similarly, in Chapter 11 a certain tall ("long legged") Kentuckian who prides himself on earning the loyalty of his slaves by treating them well proclaims, "Why, my boys have been to Cincinnati, with five hundred dollars worth of colts, and brought me back the money, all straight, time and again." See *Uncle Tom's Cabin; or, Life Among the Lowly* (1852; New York: Penguin, 1981), 43, 179.

7. From the *Cincinnati Enquirer* of Sunday, 3 February 1856, in its main story on the Garner case.

8. He says as much in a letter published in the next day's *Cincinnati Gazette* of Friday, 1 February 1856; other details about Elliott's life appeared elsewhere in the same issue in an article with news from the state capitol in Columbus, which partly details the progress of Elliott's nomination to the Canal Commissioner's post.

9. See the *Covington Journal*, Saturday, 2 February 1856; as well as the *Cincinnati Commercial* for Monday, 4 February 1856. The 1860 census of slaves tells us that the slaves formerly matching the descriptions of Hannah, Cilla, and Duke were not resident on Gaines's Maplewood plantation four years later.

10. Twenty years later Coffin retold the anecdote of his hat in his autobiography: "The story of my adventure with the marshal, respecting my hat, soon became extensively known. The accounts given of it in the Cincinnati papers were copied by other papers in various parts of the country . . . [and for] several days I could not walk the streets without being accosted by some one who would assert that I had whipped the marshal. My general reply was: 'I didn't hurt a hair of his head.' " See Levi Coffin, *Reminiscences of Levi Coffin, the Reputed Head of the Underground Railroad* (Cincinnati: Western Tract Society, 1876), 574. In her meditation on this episode Avery Gordon writes that it can "only be read as Coffin's assertion of the right to claim one's property [the hat] against the state or the law," an assertion contradicting the very point of the Garner case for antislavery activists: that it was morally and spiritually illegitimate to claim property in people. This is striking but also, I think, something of a stretch. Certainly Coffin *intends* the story to illustrate Quaker principles of passive resistance. Moreover, the full narrative in *Reminiscences* stresses Coffin's disinterest in the hat, and his Quaker commitment not to "make obeisance to men" (*Reminiscences*, 571). Gordon rightly detects Coffin's note of "pride" in offering up the seven anecdotal pages on the hat, but the pride is in his successful resistance and not the pride of ownership successfully asserted. See Avery Gordon, *Ghostly Matters: Haunting and the Sociological Imagination* (Minneapolis: University of Minnesota Press, 1997), 159–61.

11. "General Correspondence, Feb. 1–Feb. 9 [1856]," File 4, Container 76, Cushing Papers, Manuscript Division, Library of Congress, Washington, DC.

12. In 1923 his biographer wrote of him that Cushing was "not a figure whom . . . abolitionists and their descendants could regard or remember with affection." A lapsed antislavery Whig, then a Democrat and staunch Southern ally or Doughface, Cushing well knew how deeply Republicans distrusted him. Known in the Pierce administration as "a Northern man with Southern principles," Cushing vigorously

enforced the Fugitive Slave Law but never publicly discussed his actions, preferring instead to stay above the fray. Cushing was at that time preoccupied with writing Pierce's Kansas proclamation of 11 February. See Claude M. Feuss, *The Life of Caleb Cushing*, Vol. 1 (New York: Harcourt, Brace, 1923), 3–4; as well as Vol. 2, 133–34, 144.

13. A 27 May 1854 directive from Cushing charged federal judges to enforce the Fugitive Slave Law by any means. He authorized judges, Commissioners, and marshals to "call upon any and all organized force, whether militia of the state, or officers, sailors, soldiers, and marines of the United States." If these forces weren't available he authorized them to "summon the entire able-bodied force of [their] precinct, as a *posse comitatus*." Later in 1854 he also directed that alleged fugitives *never* be discharged from federal authority on writs of habeas corpus. As an officer of the court Robinson knew all of this. See Feuss, *Life of Caleb Cushing*, 144–46.

14. Typical was the story in the *Chicago Tribune* of Tuesday, 29 January 1856. Composed from telegraphic accounts, their published story was packed with errors: "A stampede of slaves from the border country of Kentucky took place last night. The whereabouts of several having been discovered here, officers at noon to-day proceeded to make arrests. Upon approaching the house where the slaves were secreted, the latter fired, wounding two or three spectators but not seriously; one slave woman escaped, cut the throats of her children, killing one instantly, and dangerously wounding others. Six of the fugitives were apprehended, but eight are said to have escaped." By Thursday the *Tribune* had received copies of the *Cincinnati Commercial* and thereafter published more accurate news of the "Dreadful Tragedy."

15. The *New York Tribune*, Horace Greeley's paper, was typical of those along the northeastern seaboard. It first ran a story (taken from the 29 January *Cincinnati Gazette*) in the edition of Friday, 1 February, and thereafter followed the case intently. Greeley often editorialized on issues raised by the case, especially the states' rights issue. On 4 February, he wrote that while the 1850 fugitive law had so far been allowed to trample "every civil right [granted] under the State laws," the question of whether it could "override the criminal jurisdiction" of states had not yet been decided, and he urged newly elected Governor Chase to maintain Ohio's jurisdiction.

16. For the principal antislavery newspapers, published weekly, this meant that news of the Garner case wouldn't appear until the following week. The *National Era* of Washington, DC, John Greenleaf Whittier's newspaper, commenced its coverage of the Garner case with the issue of Thursday, 7 February, and thereafter reprinted extensive copy from the *Gazette*. The *Liberator* (out of Boston) began its coverage the next day, Friday, 8 February, with stories that synthesized information from all the principal papers. The New York–based *National Anti-Slavery Standard* commenced its coverage with the Saturday, 9 February, issue.

17. A case in point: throughout this winter the *Charleston* (SC) *Daily Courier* published news from Cincinnati, especially weather-related stories taken from the *Enquirer*. A still more obvious instance of blackout-style selectivity occurred later in the Garner trial. From the *Enquirer* of 11 February, the *Daily Courier* extracted for publication (on 16 February) a relatively minor piece about a lawsuit being tried in the Cincinnati Court of Common Pleas, against Charles Rowecraft, a British consul there. In doing so the *Daily Courier* editors ignored both the *Enquirer*'s lead stories about the case and letters from Gaines's supporters in Boone County.

18. *Cincinnati Gazette*, Friday, 1 February 1856.
19. *Cincinnati Gazette*, Saturday, 2 February 1856.
20. Babb, the *Gazette*'s reporter, transcribed Rice's German accent in the forms quoted here; see the edition of Monday, 4 February 1856.
21. The September 1850 census of slaves for Boone County lists Bowen's slaves as including a thirty-six-year-old black female, a twenty-six-year-old female mulatto, a twenty-one-year-old black male, a sixteen-year-old black female, three male children ages twelve, four, and four months, and a one-year-old female. Of course, by January 1856 some of the children may have been sold away and the slave couple may have given birth to still more.
22. See the *Gazette*, 4 February 1856. These six fugitives are also *not* tallied among those who were ever captured, much less brought to trial, during the antebellum years: see Stanley Campbell, *The Slave Catchers: Enforcement of the Fugitive Slave Law, 1850–1860* (Chapel Hill: University of North Carolina Press, 1970), 203–7.
23. On Brisbane, see John Niven, *Salmon Portland Chase: A Biography* (New York: Oxford University Press, 1995), 68, 213–14. Brisbane was also the author of a 51-page antislavery novella, *Amanda: A Tale for the Times* (Philadelphia: Merrihew and Thompson, 1848).
24. In a complicated finding, the Chancery Court dismissed Graham's suits for damages in the loss of two slaves, Henry and Reuben, who were specifically mentioned by name in Graham's letter to Williams. The question of liability for George was put before a jury, which awarded Graham a thousand dollars. For a summary of these facts, see the Kentucky Appellate Court's decision in *Graham v. Strader*, 5B Monroe 173 (Kentucky 1844); as well as Paul Finkelman, *An Imperfect Union: Slavery, Federalism, Comity* (Chapel Hill: University of North Carolina Press, 1981), 197.
25. For Taney's opinion, see 10 *Strader v. Graham*, 10 Howard's Supreme Court Reports 83 (1851). The best analysis of the Court's complex ruling in this case is in Donald Fehrenbacher, *Slavery, Law, and Politics: The Dred Scott Case in Historical Perspective* (New York: Oxford University Press, 1981), 135–39. In addition see William M. Wiecek, "Slavery and Abolition before the United States Supreme Court, 1820–1860," *Journal of American History* 65 (1978): 53–54; Finkelman, *An Imperfect Union*, 196–200; and Arthur Bestor, "State Sovereignty and Slavery: A Reinterpretation of Proslavery Constitutional Doctrine, 1846–1860," *Journal of the Illinois State Historical Society* 55 (1961): 160–66.
26. Reported in the *Gazette*, Thursday, 7 February 1856; in fact, this large force of special marshals had begun to stir considerable controversy. The *Gazette* wondered if "they are not legally employed," a question echoed (eventually) by others, from Mayor James Farran to Governor Salmon Chase.
27. How do we know this? Evidence for Jolliffe's position, movements, and address to different individuals during the summation comes from the *Gazette* and the *Enquirer*. Both papers, and the *Gazette* in particular, report such things (often parenthetically). For example, the *Gazette* tells us that during one long stretch of the summation, when Jolliffe was summarizing testimony about their master-sponsored errands to Cincinnati, he stood behind each one and touched them, "(putting his hand on the old man's head)" in Simon's case, as in the others (quoted from the *Gazette* for Thursday, 7 February 1856; but see also that day's *Enquirer*).
28. The only other instance of such an argument that I know about is that of Albert Barnes, in his *Inquiry into the Scriptural Views of Slavery* (Philadelphia: Perkins and

Purves, 1846). Barnes claims that enforcing antislavery laws "interferes with the natural right which every human being has, to worship God according to his own views of what is true" (30). But Jolliffe took Barnes's argument a crucial step further by claiming that enforcing the law interfered with Americans' *constitutional* right to religious liberty—that is, in avoiding what they view as "sin."

29. *Macbeth*, I, vii, 54–55.

30. Joseph Cox to Salmon Portland Chase, 29 February 1856, *Salmon Portland Chase Papers*, Reel 11, 0094.

31. In a larger sense Chambers was right, for Southerners really *did* fear slave uprisings and treasured laws empowering them to combat such threats. Robert W. Fogel concludes that slave revolts were so infrequent because "revolution grows out of the barrel of a gun" and slaves had none; see his *Without Consent or Contract: The Rise and Fall of American Slavery* (New York: W. W. Norton, 1989), 196–98. Nevertheless, white paranoia about slave rebellions ran high throughout the antebellum decades. See, for example, William F. Freehling, *The Road to Disunion: Secessionists at Bay: 1776–1854* (New York: Oxford University Press, 1990), 108–18; Lawrence Shore, "Making Mississippi Safe for Slavery: The Insurrectionary Panic of 1835," in *Class, Conflict, and Consensus: Antebellum Southern Community Studies*, eds. Orville V. Burton and Robert McGrath (Westport, CT: Greenwood Press, 1982), 96–127; and Herbert Aptheker, *American Negro Slave Revolts* (New York: International Publishers, 1952). Interestingly this generally Southern fear of slave rebellion could even infect some putatively antislavery texts of the North. A notable case in point, and one contemporaneous with the Garner case, appeared under the heading "About Niggers," an essay that might have been sitting in folks' parlors as Colonel Chambers spoke. This essayist meant to use the San Domingo revolution as evidence of slaves' refusal of the "nigger" role; but he also fed the paranoia about insurrection by focusing on the "terrible capacity for revenge" demonstrated by those events. See "About Niggers," *Putnam's Monthly* 6 (December 1855): 608–12.

32. "A Little More Weather," *Cincinnati Enquirer*, Saturday, 9 February 1856.

33. Details taken from the *Cincinnati Commercial* and the *Cincinnati Gazette*, from their issues of Saturday, 9 February 1856.

34. George Mills was a partner in the prominent Cincinnati firm of Mills & Hoadley and one might well ask why he would argue the constitutional issue rather than Jolliffe. The answer is probably that his firm worked on retainer for the Hamilton County sheriff, for example in defending a deputy sued for breaking the arm of one Asahel Lister while arresting him for public drunkenness (reported in the *Cincinnati Gazette*, Friday, 13 July 1855). Mills & Hoadley represented other commercial and manufacturing clients in lawsuits, defended a few clients in criminal trials, but never argued any of the Queen City's fugitive slave cases.

35. This estimate appeared in the first of two letters "From our Cincinnati Correspondent"—identified only as "P."—published in the *National Anti-Slavery Standard*, Saturday, 16 February 1856. Letter 1 was dated 7 February; Letter 2, the next day. The writer's identity is unknown, though his (or her) estimate was fairly close to the mark.

36. *Cincinnati Enquirer*, Saturday, 9 February 1856. Traditionally, states grant comity more out of respectful deference than legal obligation. One state's remanding to another a fugitive from justice is still a commonplace instance of comity; others

include provisions for interstate commerce and relations of all kinds. The Constitution's Article IV included not only the "Fugitives from Labor or Service" clause underwriting the 1793 and 1850 Fugitive Slave Laws but also the "Full Faith and Credit" and "Privileges and Immunities" clauses. But all of these existed in sharp conflict during the antebellum decades, and while players in the Garner drama affected supreme confidence about what were their practical effects and requirements, things were never really settled.

Taken together the three comity clauses said: (1) that "fugitives from labor and service" shall be remanded to their masters, (2) that "Full Faith and Credit shall be given in each State to the public Acts, Records, and judicial Proceedings of every other State," and (3) that "Citizens of each State shall be entitled to all Privileges and Immunities of Citizens in the several States." But did those clauses require Virginia to extend full citizenship rights to a free black from Massachusetts sojourning in the South? Did they entitle a slave owner sojourning in the North with his chattels to have his property rights in them fully respected? These were highly conflicted issues and the best study to date of their snarled interrelations and of their complex interpretations by state and federal courts can be found in Finkelman, *An Imperfect Union*; the "acid test" observation is his (8). In addition see Robert Cover's *Justice Accused: Antislavery and the Judicial Process* (New Haven: Yale University Press, 1975).

37. Mills quoted from *The Revised Statutes of Kentucky* (Frankfort, KY: 1852), Chapter XCIII, Article 7, whose twenty-five paragraphs detailed a range of punishments— from "stripes" to the death penalty—for felonies. Of specific interest in this case was paragraph 4: "If any free Negro or slave be guilty of murder, rape committed upon a white woman of any age, or the attempt to commit such rape, or be accessory before the fact to either of the aforesaid crimes, upon conviction he shall suffer death" (639).

38. See Stone's letter of 3 February 1856, in *Loving Warriors: Selected Letters of Lucy Stone Blackwell to Henry B. Blackwell, 1853–1893*, ed. Leslie Wheeler (New York: Dial, 1981), 154–55. About Lucy Stone's name, and the question of "Stone" or "Blackwell": when she married Henry Blackwell on 1 May 1855, she insisted on maintaining her name (a decision that later inspired other American women to do the same, for which they were called "Lucy Stoners"). In deference to Stone's wishes, I use that name throughout even though Stone's contemporaries—newsmen especially—called her "Lucy Blackwell." For the story behind Stone's decision, see Alice Stone Blackwell, *Lucy Stone: Pioneer of Women's Rights* (Boston: Beacon, 1930).

39. "Third Day of the Trial of the Mother and Her Children," the *Cincinnati Gazette* of Wednesday, 13 February 1856.

40. Again from Lucy Stone's letter of 3 February 1856, in *Loving Warriors*, 154–55.

41. *Cincinnati Gazette*, Monday, 11 February 1856.

42. See especially the *Cincinnati Enquirer*, Monday, 11 February 1856.

43. *The Liberator*, 14 March 1856, 43.

44. See Fehrenbacher, *Slavery, Law, and Politics*, 93–95.

45. The *Gazette* indicates that Finnell specifically offered "from page 627 to 648," which is indeed the entire section of *The Revised Statutes of Kentucky* (1852) dealing with slaves.

46. Jolliffe had intended to call George Guilford, the *Cincinnati Commercial* reporter

who (on Monday afternoon, 28 January) had heard the Garners talking about being over the river. When Guilford couldn't be found—it turned out he was ill—Pendery agreed to admit the man's testimony from the first trial. One further note: in what turned out to be an inconsequential move Chambers recalled James Marshall and three other white male witnesses, who all rebutted testimony about slave girls working as nurses.

47. A classic instance of this Southron ideology, again, is William Harper's 1837 "Memoir on Slavery," reprinted in 1852 as *The Pro-Slavery Argument* and again in 1860 as *Cotton is King and Pro-Slavery Arguments*. Like other Southern intellectuals such as Albert Taylor Bledsoe and Thomas Dew, Harper saw Northern capitalism providing the least relief for its laboring classes whenever the economy suffered a downturn: "In periods of commercial revulsion and distress, like the present [1837 inflation], the distress, in countries of free labor, falls principally on the laborers. In those of Slave labor, it falls almost exclusively on the employer." But this gentle, patriarchal benevolence is wholly upset, Harper continued, when antislavery forces turn slaves against masters. In fact, he argues, their interference has the still worse effect of making masters destructively suspicious of slaves: "Is it not cruelty to make men restless and dissatisfied with their condition, when no effort of theirs can alter it? The greatest injury is done to their characters, as well as to their happiness. Even if no such feelings or designs should be entertained or conceived by the slave, they will be attributed to him by the master, and all his conduct scanned with a severe and jealous scrutiny. Thus distrust and aversion are established, where, but for mischievous interference, there would be confidence and good will, and a sterner control is exercised over the slave who thus becomes the victim of his cruel advocates." As should be clear from Harper's words, it was commonplace to assume that slaves left to themselves cannot conceive dissatisfaction with their state. Instead they are "made" so; it is an "injury" that is "done to their characters" by abolitionists. See Harper, "Memoir on Slavery," in *The Ideology of Slavery: Proslavery Thought in the Antebellum South, 1830–1860*, ed. Drew Gilpin Faust (Baton Rouge: Louisiana State University Press, 1981), 95, 132.

Albert Taylor Bledsoe was another representative Southron who argued the ennobling effects of "the peculiar institution": see his *Essay on Liberty and Slavery* (Philadelphia: J. B. Lippincott, 1856), 299.

48. How widely Samuel T. Wall's claim was accepted may be gauged from a chapter treating the Garner case in a proslavery propaganda novel published during the summer of 1856. The book is Henry Field James's *Abolitionism Unveiled; or, The Origin, Progress, and Pernicious Tendency Fully Developed* (Cincinnati: E. Morgan & Sons, 1856). Field, who billed himself as "A Kentuckian," represents the Garner escape and infanticide as entirely motivated by Ohio's "damned abolitionists." To such a person he writes: "As the serpent crept into the garden of Eden, and by his subtlety tempted Adam and Eve to depart from their holy estate, so hast thou sought to entwine thyself around the part of the poor, ignorant, confiding Slave, and lead him through the labyrinth of ruin. Happy and contented at his home, thou didst find him and poured thy poisonous breath into his ear, and brought upon him irretrievable ruin. The blood of infants, like Moloch of old, has stained thy hands, because thou didst induce the mother to escape, who, if not tempted by thee, would have remained at her home" (244–45).

49. "The Fugitive Case," *Cincinnati Enquirer*, Wednesday, 13 February 1856.

50. "Conclusion of the Argument," *Cincinnati Gazette*, Thursday, 14 February 1856. Thursday's *Enquirer* added but little more to our sense of Colonel Chambers's closing rebuttal.
51. "The Cincinnati Fugitive Case," in the *National Anti-Slavery Standard*, 23 February 1856. Their story was drawn primarily from the *Gazette* and the *Commercial*. What follows is a composite of Lucy Stone's speech drawing from all available accounts. The *Commercial* gave the most thorough transcription of her speech but chose not to print her remarks about the Garner children's "faded faces" signifying Margaret Garner's sexual degradation; the *Gazette* did print them; it also printed Lucy Stone's quote from Archibald Gaines, to the effect that on returning with his slaves to Kentucky he intended to "make her [Margaret] free."
52. "The Cincinnati Fugitive Case," *National Anti-Slavery Standard*, 23 February 1856.
53. "Escape of Slaves," *Cincinnati Gazette*, Thursday, 14 February 1856. In the following day's paper Bennet denied having uttered that dismissal.

4. Slave

1. See the *Cincinnati Enquirer* and the *Cincinnati Gazette* of Thursday, 14 February 1856.
2. See Lowell Harrison and James C. Klotter, *A New History of Kentucky* (Lexington: University Press of Kentucky, 1997), 114–15; Gary Collison, *Shadrack Minkins: From Fugitive Slave to Citizen* (Cambridge, MA: Harvard University Press, 1997), 89; and Stanley W. Campbell, *The Slave Catchers: Enforcement of the Fugitive Slave Law, 1850–1860* (Chapel Hill: University of North Carolina Press, 1970), 49–55.
3. See the court news reported in the *Cincinnati Gazette* of Tuesday, 19 February 1856.
4. See the *Cincinnati Gazette* and the *Cincinnati Enquirer* of Thursday, 21 February 1856.
5. *Cincinnati Gazette* of Thursday, 21 February 1856.
6. *Cincinnati Enquirer* of Thursday, 21 February 1856.
7. *Cincinnati Enquirer* of Friday, 22 February 1856.
8. Quoted from Judge Leavitt's summary of facts in his April 1856 decision, *Ex parte Robinson*, 20 Federal Cases 965 (1856). Further details are from the *Cincinnati Enquirer*, 22 February 1856.
9. For specifics on Jesse Beckley's suit, see my "Prologue"; other facts about the Beckley family are available in the *Cincinnati Gazette*, 14 May 1857, which covered the case in detail.
10. Here and following, details about the day's court activities are drawn from the *Cincinnati Gazette* of Friday, 22 February 1856.
11. The advertisements ran in all *Cincinnati Enquirer* editions of late January and February, with the newspaper's masthead on page 3. Details on the Washington's Birthday festivities are drawn from the *Cincinnati Enquirer* and the *Cincinnati Gazette* of Saturday, 23 February 1856.
12. William Freehling, "The Divided South, Democracy's Limitations, and the Causes of the Peculiarly North American Civil War," in *Why the Civil War Came*, ed. Gabor S. Boritt (New York: Oxford University Press, 1996), 129. On fratricidal rhetoric in American political discourse of the antebellum period, see Robert V. Bruce, "The Shadow of a Coming War," in *Lincoln, the War President: The Get-*

tysburg Lectures (New York: Oxford University Press, 1992), 1–28; and David Potter, *The Impending Crisis, 1848–1861* (New York: Harper & Row, 1976).

13. In recent years scholars have done considerable work on the historical and social construction of whiteness in America, and especially on the functions of race and ethnicity in that process. In the wake of this research we can no longer assume that race and ethnicity are structurally different categories. Formerly, the argument was that racial minorities were treated differently than immigrants who could be identified as "white ethnics." In *Hierarchical Structures and Social Value: The Creation of Black and Irish Identities in the United States* (New York: Cambridge University Press, 1990), historian Richard Williams persuasively argues that ethnic categories were made possible by those of race; that ethnically defined social status was assigned to immigrants who, even though consigned to lower-paying jobs, were still exempted from racialized discrimination or slavery. In America, enslaved blacks were thus the sine qua non for the social hierarchy. On this point see also David Roedigger, *The Wages of Whiteness: Race and the Making of the American Working Class* (New York: Verso, 1991).

14. In its 3 March 1856 edition the *Cincinnati Gazette* reported that a committee of abolitionists had gathered to "formally pass on the city's regret" at that rough treatment, and to invite Chase to dinner. Among those appointed to this group were a number of the city's prominent abolitionists, including John Jolliffe, James Gitchell, James Birney, and John Burgoyne. Eight years later the fact of Chase's appearance in Cincinnati had faded from his memory as the former governor, serving in Lincoln's cabinet as Treasury Secretary, was contemplating a run for the Republican presidential nomination. In a November speech in Boston, abolitionist Wendell Phillips chastised Chase for dodging the Garner issue. Chase claimed that he was never in the city during the Garner case, a fact overlooked by old Cincinnati contacts who sprang to his defense. Joseph Cox and George Hoadley, for example, both wrote Chase letters intended for publication and stated that when the Garner case first broke the former governor was in Columbus, preoccupied with legislative business. They evidently chose not to contradict him by discussing Chase's Washington's Birthday visit. See, for example, Joseph Cox to Salmon P. Chase, 28 November 1863, *The Salmon Portland Chase Papers* (microfilm edition), ed. John Niven (Frederick, MD: University Publications, 1987), Reel 30, 0070–0071; and George Hoadley to Salmon P. Chase, 6 January 1864, *Salmon Portland Chase Papers*, Reel 31, 0799–0802.

15. Chase to Timothy Day, 13 March 1856, *Salmon Portland Chase Papers*, Reel 11, 0130.

16. *Cincinnati Gazette* of Saturday, 23 February 1856.

17. See the *Covington Journal* of 23 February 1856 and, for a report on the meeting, their issue of 1 March 1856.

18. "Public Sentiment," a formal statement approved by the Florence meeting, was published in the *Covington Journal* of Saturday, 1 March 1856. All quotes are from that text.

19. *Cincinnati Gazette* of Wednesday, 27 February 1856; my emphasis.

20. This account of Commissioner Pendery's decision is a composite of reports published in the *Cincinnati Enquirer* and the *Cincinnati Gazette* of Wednesday, 27 February 1856, as well as the *Covington Journal* of 1 March 1856. In what follows, all quotations are from the *Gazette* unless otherwise indicated.

21. From the *Cincinnati Gazette* of Wednesday, 27 February 1856; the emphases, however, are mine.

22. *Cincinnati Enquirer*, 27 February 1856.

23. *Cincinnati Commercial*, 27 February 1856.

24. In *Shadrack Minkins*, Gary Collison remarks that in a great number of fugitive cases decided after September 1850 the slaves "were lucky if their hearings lasted five minutes" (117), and that the longest-running fugitive trial he could find, of fugitive Henry Long, who was returned from New York City to Virginia, had lasted "more than two weeks" (108). Testimony in the Garner case had taken two weeks and a day to complete. The overall case, from its opening to Pendery's judgment, consumed twenty-nine days. Expenses in the case were a matter of dispute for months afterward; sorting through conflicting accounts, historian Julius Yanuck concluded that by the time the Garners were delivered to Covington on 28 February there were "about 400 marshals holding certificates for 28 days' employment at $2.00 per diem; the total cost was $21,456." See his essay "The Garner Fugitive Slave Case," *Mississippi Valley Historical Review* 40 (1953): 63.

25. See the *Cincinnati Gazette*, Wednesday, 27 February 1856.

26. See Judge Humphrey Leavitt's summary of these events in *Ex parte Robinson*, 20 Federal Cases 965 (1856).

27. "Sec. 9. *And be it enacted*, That, upon affidavit made by the claimant of such fugitive, his agent or attorney, after such certificate has been issued [i.e., for the fugitive's return to slavery], that he has reason to apprehend that such fugitive will be rescued by force from his or their possession before he can be taken beyond the limits of the State in which the arrest is made, it shall be the duty of the officer making the arrest to retain such fugitive in his custody, and to remove him to the State whence he fled, and there to deliver him to said claimant, his agent, or attorney. And to this end, the officer aforesaid is hereby authorized and required to employ as many persons as he may deem necessary to overcome such force, and to retain them in his service for so long as circumstances may require." The Fugitive Slave Law of 1850, in *United States Statutes at Large*, IX, 465. Pendery and Robinson also cited this section of the law as justification for the four hundred-plus special deputies paid at the rate of $2/day (a rate fixed in Section 10).

28. See the Thursday, 28 February 1856, editions of the *Cincinnati Enquirer* and the *Cincinnati Gazette*, from which the following quotations have been taken and adapted.

29. This and the following narration of the Garners' return to Kentucky is a composite, taken from the *Cincinnati Enquirer*, *Cincinnati Gazette*, and *Cincinnati Commercial* of Friday, 29 February 1856, as well as the *Covington Journal* of Saturday, 1 March 1856.

30. *Ex parte Robinson*, 20 Federal Cases 969 (1856).

31. Chase to Timothy C. Day, 13 March 1856, in *Salmon Portland Chase Papers*, Reel 11, 0130; for similar complaints, see also Chase to Hoadley, 16 March 1856, Reel 11, 0133, a letter whose remarks indicated that Hoadley shared Chase's anger. For Hoadley's recollection, see his letter to Chase, 6 January 1864, Reel 30, 0801.

32. *Cincinnati Gazette* of Friday, 29 February 1856.

33. Details of the assault on Edmond Babb are drawn from the *Cincinnati Gazette* and the *Cincinnati Commercial* of 29 February 1856. Though hospitalized from his

injuries, on the same night Babb evidently dictated his story for publication in the next day's paper.

34. Census records are useful additions to newspaper comments. In September 1850, John Butts was a twenty-four-year-old Kentucky-born tobacco worker residing in Covington's Fifth Ward, a neighborhood of ostlers, ropemakers, barkeepers, and slaughterers. Arrested with him was Joseph Hall, not listed as a Kentucky resident in 1850 but described in news accounts as a twenty-six-year-old slaughterer from Covington. Another of those arrested, Henry Wilson, was in 1856 a twenty-six-year-old Virginia-born farm laborer living in Boone County's northern 2nd district, just outside Covington. Adam Fisher was the Mason County visitor; in 1856 this Kentucky-born wagon maker was twenty-three years old. John Hardin was over the river from Cincinnati, whose census taker listed him in 1850 as a twenty-three-year-old plasterer. See the *Seventh Census of the United States, 1850: Kentucky Population Schedules* for Boone, Kenton, and Mason counties; in addition to the *Ohio Population Schedules* for Hamilton County.

35. See the *Covington Journal* of Saturday, 8 March 1856; as well as the *Cincinnati Commercial* and *Cincinnati Gazette* of Wednesday, 5 March 1856.

36. A useful summary of the violent and at times "hysterical" events that "traumatized the nation" in early 1856 can be found in Robert William Fogel, *Without Consent or Contract: The Rise and Fall of American Slavery* (New York: W. W. Norton, 1898), 376–80. On battles in the House and Senate over the speakership and the rise of the Republican Party from the old system's ruins, see especially William E. Gienapp, *The Origins of the Republican Party, 1852–1856* (New York: Oxford University Press, 1987); and Eric Foner, *Free Soil, Free Labor, Free Men: The Ideology of the Republican Party before the Civil War* (New York: Oxford University Press, 1970).

37. The committee's commendation of Jolliffe was dated 28 February 1856; Jolliffe's reply was dated 29 February. He handed them both to the *Cincinnati Gazette* for publication in its edition of Saturday, 1 March 1856.

38. Compare similar instances of this infanticidal image, used to argue pro- or antislavery positions, in the *Lexington Atlas*, 8 February 1856, and in the *Cleveland Herald*, 4 February 1856.

39. *New York Tribune*, 8 February 1856.

40. For example, when Cincinnati Baptist minister P. S. Bassett visited the Garners in jail on Sunday, 10 February 1856, he specifically inquired of Margaret: Was she "not excited almost to madness when she committed" the child-murder? According to Bassett, "she replied, I was *as cool as I now am*; and would much rather kill them at once, and thus end their sufferings, than have them taken back to slavery, and be murdered by piece-meal." In so saying, Margaret denied the claims of, for example, attorney Samuel T. Wall, who argued before Pendery, on Tuesday, 12 February, that Margaret's were the bloody deeds of a "frenzied" woman. Bassett's memoir, published under the headline "A Visit to the Slave Mother who Killed her Child," was first published in the *American Baptist* newspaper; *The Liberator*, one of several newspapers to pick it up, reprinted the piece in its issue of 14 March 1856, 43.

41. Mary A. Livermore, "Slave Tragedy at Cincinnati," *New York Tribune*, 9 February 1856.

42. Thus Douglass: "Patrick Henry, to a listening Senate, thrilled by his magic elo-

quence, and ready to stand by him in his boldest flights, could say, 'Give me liberty, or give me death,' and this saying was a sublime one, even for a freeman; but, incomparably more sublime, is the same sentiment, when *practically asserted* by men accustomed to the lash and chain." See *My Bondage and My Freedom* (1855; New York: Dover, 1969), 284. And thus Jacobs: "I had resolved that, come what would, there should be no turning back. 'Give me liberty, or give me death,' was my motto." See *Incidents in the Life of a Slave Girl* (1860; New York: Oxford University Press, 1988), 151. The quotation was also widely circulated in texts of white abolitionist writers. For example, see John Greenleaf Whittier's well-known poem "Massachusetts to Virginia." Or there is John Jolliffe's use of the phrase in his first novel when he has the title character, Belle, exclaim: "Oh! I can from my heart of hearts say, with Patrick Henry, 'Give me liberty or give me death!' " See *Belle Scott; or, Liberty Overthrown! A Tale for the Crisis* (Columbus and Cincinnati: Anderson and Blanchard, 1856), 276.

43. Harper, "Memoir on Slavery," in Drew Gilpin Faust, ed., *The Ideology of Slavery: Proslavery Thought in the Antebellum South, 1830–1860* (Baton Rouge: Louisiana State University Press, 1981), 131.

44. *Seventh Census of the United States, 1850: Kentucky. Kenton County*, 179. Information on his slave is from ibid., *Slave Schedules*, 164.

45. Hiram Martin, "A Mother Found Dead in a Snow Drift with a Living Infant in her Arms," *Covington Journal* of Saturday, 9 February 1856. Denials of the rumor about such a case actually happening in Covington appeared in the *Journal's* editions of 5 January and 12 January 1856.

46. On leg irons and other disciplinary measures that Kentucky masters commonly used, see Marion B. Lucas, *A History of Blacks in Kentucky*, Vol. 1: *From Slavery to Segregation, 1760–1891* (Frankfort: Kentucky Historical Society, 1992), 45–48; and J. Winston Coleman, *Slavery Times in Old Kentucky* (Chapel Hill: University of North Carolina Press, 1940), 46–52.

47. Throughout this period, P. S. Bush ran advertisements in the *Covington Journal* for "handsomely situated" lots on Covington's outskirts; he was now a "General Agent" in real estate sales, with an office "at Madison & Robbins streets" in the city.

48. Completed in 1853, the Covington & Lexington rail line passed within a half mile of Maplewood. Schedules and fares were printed daily in the *Covington Journal* during these years.

49. Details about the Garners' departure from Covington, their trip south, division at Richwood Station, and Gaines's plans are available in the following sources: the *Cincinnati Enquirer* of Saturday, 1 March, and Monday, 3 March 1856; the *Cincinnati Gazette*, Monday, 3 March 1856; the *Louisville Journal* of Monday and Tuesday, 3 and 4 March 1856; and in a letter Archibald Gaines published in the *Cincinnati Enquirer* of 15 April 1856, reprinted also in the *Covington Journal* of 26 April 1856.

50. Weather data are available in the *Cincinnati Enquirer* of Saturday, 1 March 1856, and the *Cincinnati Gazette* of Monday, 3 March 1856.

51. See the *Cincinnati Gazette* of Saturday, 1 March 1856.

52. This chronology is reconstructed from an extensive account published in the *Cincinnati Gazette* of Tuesday, 11 March 1856, and from related stories in the *Cincinnati Enquirer* of Friday, 7 March 1856, and Monday, 10 March 1856.

53. Joseph Cox to Salmon Portland Chase, 29 February 1856, *Salmon Portland Chase Papers*, Reel 11, 0094.

54. Chase to Governor Charles S. Morehead, 4 March 1856, *Salmon Portland Chase Papers*, Reel 11, 0108–0111.

55. Edward S. Hamlin to Salmon Portland Chase, 11 March 1856, *Salmon Portland Chase Papers*, Reel 11, 0127–0128. Apparently this fund-raising had begun early in February, for the *New York Tribune* would comment in a story written "Special to the Tribune" that within a few days after the Garner infanticide a prominent Cincinnati merchant had stepped up to Jolliffe and promised that "to buy the children" abolitionists should "draw on him for $100" while other "business men of the city would make up the purse"; see the *Tribune* of Monday, 3 March 1856.

56. *Cincinnati Gazette* of Tuesday, 11 March 1856.

57. Ibid.; supporting this chronology are remarks from Gaines, published in his letter to the *Cincinnati Enquirer*, dated 14 April and printed in the following day's edition. Gaines said he held Margaret over in Kentucky "for the space of eight days"—that is, from 29 February through the early morning of Friday, 7 March—before shipping her south via steamboat. Other key statements supporting this chronology appear in Joseph Cooper's 11 March 1856 letter to Governor Salmon Portland Chase, reprinted in the *National Anti-Slavery Standard*, 29 March 1856.

58. See Gaines's letter to the *Enquirer*, 15 April 1856.

59. We know it was Clinton Butts from (first) Archibald Gaines's letter published in the *Enquirer*, in which Gaines indicates that the same unnamed person ("my man") escorted the Garners around Kentucky and down the Ohio and Mississippi rivers; and we know it (second) from both the *Covington Journal* and the *Cincinnati Gazette*, which in various stories mentioned Butts as the Garners' official escort. See, for example, the *Gazette* of Tuesday, 11 March 1856.

60. Joseph Cooper to Salmon Portland Chase, 11 March 1856, *Salmon Portland Chase Papers*, Reel 11, 0123–0126; Cox also sent the letter on to the *National Anti-Slavery Standard* for reprinting (in its edition of 29 March 1856). Clinton Butts may also have deliberately misled Joseph Cooper about the identities of the four slaves he had in transit, for Cooper (who had been in Columbus throughout the previous month's trial) evidently had no idea what the Garners looked like.

61. See Salmon Portland Chase to William T. Dennison, 31 December 1863: "Probably somebody telegraphed the claimants, for though the Governor [of Kentucky] issued his warrant, Margaret & the rest had been shipped south from Louisville before the agent arrived there with it." *Salmon Portland Chase Papers*, Reel 30, 0713–0714.

62. Theodore Parker, *The Great Battle between Slavery and Freedom; Considered in Two Speeches, Delivered before the American Anti-Slavery Society at New York, May 7, 1856* (Boston: Benjamin H. Greene, 1856), 7.

63. Chase to Parker, 17 July 1856, in *The Theodore Parker Papers, 1826–1862* (Ann Arbor: University Microfilms, 1979), Reel 3, Vol. 9; original housed in Manuscripts Collection of the Massachusetts Historical Society.

64. See the *New York Tribune*, 23, 24, and 25 December 1863.

65. Salmon Portland Chase to John T. Trowbridge, 13 March 1864, *Salmon Portland Chase Papers*, Reel 31, 0342–0349. Among several minor errors of fact in this letter, Chase said that Margaret Garner's victim was "a little girl of ten years of age," whereas Mary (whose name he did get right) was just short of three; he also said

nothing further was heard of the Garner family after they were remanded to Kentucky, but this—as it turned out—was also untrue; Cincinnati papers followed the Garners' course for several more weeks. In a 28 March 1864 letter, Edward L. Pierce wrote Chase that the anthology of documents on the Garner case "is essentially prepared" and only awaiting further material from former judge George Hoadley, but thereafter nothing further was said of it and the project appears to have died on the vine; see ibid., Reel 31, 0700. Trowbridge's book may have been planned as a campaign biography, but after Chase's candidacy ended in late spring 1864, he issued it as one in a series of books on famous Americans, designed for juveniles and titled *The Ferry-Boy and the Financier* (Boston: Walker, Wise and Co., 1864).

66. Once again, see Chase to Trowbridge, 13 March 1864; and Chase to Dennison, *Salmon Portland Chase Papers*, Reel 30, 0714.

67. See John Niven, *Salmon Portland Chase: A Biography* (New York: Oxford University Press, 1995), 183–87, for a discussion of Chase's handling of the Garner case in the context of the upcoming Republican convention. For some Republicans' characterizations of McLean as an "old fossil," see 187.

68. Salmon Portland Chase Papers, Library of Congress, Container 36, Miscellany, Notes on Anti-Slavery (File 1). Chase's notebook is not included in Niven's superb microfilm edition of the Chase Papers, and I am grateful to Joan Higbee and Rosemary Plakas of the Library of Congress for steering me to the Manuscripts Collection, where I found it.

69. Samuel J. May, *The Fugitive Slave Law and Its Victims* (New York: American Anti-Slavery Society, 1861), 58.

70. Jolliffe and Gitchell argued that Burgoyne should cite Robinson for contempt and imprison him; again Headington appeared for the marshal. They were still debating the case at six o'clock Thursday evening (6 March); arguments continued during the next morning. Burgoyne ruled against Robinson and required him to "show cause why he should not be attached [i.e., fined and imprisoned]." See the *Cincinnati Gazette* of Saturday, 8 March 1856.

71. Charles S. Morehead to Salmon Portland Chase, *Salmon Portland Chase Papers*, Reel 11, 0112–0116.

72. Information on the steamboat *Henry Lewis* derives from Frederick Way, *Directory of Western Rivers Packets* (Sewickley, PA: n.p., 1950), a volume in the Special Collections at the University of Kentucky Library. On Mississippi and Ohio River steam or "packet" boats in general, see Louis C. Hunter, *Steamboats on the Western Rivers: An Economic and Technological History* (Cambridge, MA: Harvard University Press, 1949); and G. L. Eskew, *The Pageant of the Packets: A Book of American Steamboating* (New York: Henry Holt, 1929).

73. The *Henry Lewis*'s arrival was recorded in the 7 March 1856 issue of the *Louisville Daily Journal*, in its "Shipping News" section; in the same issue's "Arrivals at the Hotels" column the paper also recorded the arrival of "A. K. Gaines—Boone" at the Exchange Hotel. Advertisements for southbound passage on the *Henry Lewis* had run for several days before the 7th; the same edition announced its departure at ten in the morning.

74. See, for example, the *Cincinnati Gazette*'s main story, "Awful Steamboat Disaster," in its issue of Tuesday, 11 March 1856.

75. Quoted from a letter James and Adam Patterson submitted for publication in the *Louisville Journal*, 10 March 1856.

76. Unless specifically noted, what follows is a composite narrative of the *Henry Lewis* disaster drawn from three accounts that come down to us: one in the *Louisville Journal*, 10 March 1856; another from the *Cincinnati Gazette*, 11 March 1856; and a third from the *Cincinnati Commercial*, also 11 March 1856, and reprinted in the *National Anti-Slavery Standard*, 29 March 1856.
77. Quoted from the *Cincinnati Gazette*, 11 March 1856.
78. Quoted from the *Cincinnati Commercial*, 11 March 1856.
79. Ibid. Note that the *Commercial* writer has stretched some of the details. After the Garners were taken to Evansville it was some hours before they were put aboard the *Hungarian*, bound for New Orleans. By this time Margaret would have dried off and changed clothes, after her ordeal, but for pity's sake the writer wants her wet and cold before the shipboard stove.
80. Harriet Fanning Read, "Medea," *Dramatic Poems* (Boston: Wm. Crosby and H. P. Nichols, 1848). In Act V, Medea proclaims to Jason over their dead sons' bodies: "By thee they perished! Thy foul wrongs to me,/ Thy vows profaned, thy household gods deserted/ Thy wife, thy sons, abandoned, to indulge/ Thy roving fancy and thy black ambition,/ Called on the thunder's voice on Heaven for vengeance!/ And it is granted!" (95).
81. Harriet Beecher Stowe, *Uncle Tom's Cabin; or, Life Among the Lowly* (1852; New York: Penguin, 1981), 124–25.
82. *The Liberator*, 7 March 1856, 38.
83. *Cincinnati Gazette*, Tuesday, 11 March 1856.
84. In an editorial entitled "The Price of Returning a Slave" the *Gazette* opened this argument in its issue of Wednesday, 5 March 1856. The next day's *Enquirer* charged that their figure of $22,400 was inflated by a factor of two; the ensuing debate lasted for two more weeks.
85. *Cincinnati Gazette*, Wednesday, 19 March 1856.
86. On Gaines Landing and Chicot County agriculture, there is useful information in Margaret Ross Smith's paper "Sandford C. Faulkner," *Arkansas Historical Quarterly* 14 (1955): 301–14; further information on the area, its isolation, and frustrated attempts to run a rail line to it is available in Stephen E. Wood, "The Development of Arkansas Railroads," *Arkansas Historical Quarterly* 7 (1948): 103–18.
87. Data of the 1850 census, including the census of slaves and census of agriculture, are available in useful summaries compiled by Robert B. Walz, "Arkansas Slaveholdings and Slaveholders in 1850," *Arkansas Historical Quarterly* 12 (1953): 39–63. This survey revealed Benjamin Pollard Gaines as the state's twenty-fifth-largest slaveholder. Sunnyside plantation, which survived well into this century, left behind a rich archive and was the subject of a special issue of the *Arkansas Historical Quarterly* 50 (1991). Especially useful are Willard B. Gatewood, "Sunnyside: The Evolution of an Arkansas Plantation," 1–12; and Bertram Wyatt-Brown, "Leroy Percy and Sunnyside: Planter Mentality and Italian Peonage in the Mississippi Delta," 60–84.

5. Legend

1. Patterns of Arkansas, Louisiana, and Mississippi agricultural practice are available from a number of sources; for example, Willard B. Gatewood, "Sunnyside: The Evolution of an Arkansas Plantation," *Arkansas Historical Quarterly* 50.1 (1991): 1–

12; and Chapter 3, "Of Water, Land, and Work," in Winthrop D. Jordan, *Tumult and Silence at Second Creek: An Inquiry into a Civil War Slave Conspiracy* (Baton Rouge: Louisiana State University Press, 1993), 29–45; J. Carlyle Sitterson, "The William J. Minor Plantations: A Study in Ante-Bellum Absentee Ownership," *Journal of Southern History* 9 (1943): 59–74. I have also consulted William J. Minor's diary for 1856, containing a wealth of information about climate, agriculture, and slave life at his northern Louisiana plantation; see the microfilm edition of the William J. Minor Family Papers, available at the Louisiana State University library.

2. This was Gaines's characterization in his 14 April 1856 public letter to the *Cincinnati Enquirer*, printed in the next day's edition (and reprinted in the *Covington Journal*, 19 April 1856).

3. See the *Cincinnati Gazette*, 12 March 1856; and the *New York Tribune*, 24 March 1856.

4. Gaines's letter to the *Enquirer*, 14 April 1856.

5. Other sources include: Kentucky governor Charles Morehead's telegram to Chase, quoted below (see note 6); a story in the *Cincinnati Gazette* for Tuesday, 11 March 1856 (titled "The Fugitives—The Requisition," it concludes by wondering whether Chase will "demand her [Margaret's] return from Arkansas"); and a story in the *Covington Journal* for Saturday, 15 March 1856, whose informant was Clinton Butts (he telegraphed Covington after the *Henry Lewis* accident).

6. As reported in the *Cincinnati Gazette*, 14 March 1856.

7. The *Covington Journal* of 19 April and Gaines's 14 April letter both state that Margaret arrived in Covington on Wednesday, 2 April. We know from the *Cincinnati Enquirer*'s "Steamboat Register" that the *Queen City* was the only steamboat arriving that day from southern Mississippi River ports (having departed New Orleans on 25 March); details on the boat's cargo and the day's weather are drawn (respectively) from the "Imports by River" column in the *Enquirer* and the "River Intelligence" section of the *Cincinnati Gazette*.

8. See stories in the *Cincinnati Enquirer* of 23 March 1856 and 1 April 1856; and the 3 April 1856 story in the *Cincinnati Gazette* titled "More About the Fugitive Slave Case—The Special Marshals and the Secret Service Fund."

9. An excellent summary of these events is available in Leavitt's decision on the habeas corpus: *Ex parte Robinson*, 20 Federal Cases (1856), especially 965–66.

10. Gaines's remarks are once again from his 14 April 1856 letter. For Chase's remarks see Salmon Portland Chase to Joseph Cox, 9 April 1856, in *The Salmon Portland Chase Papers* (microfilm edition), ed. John Niven (Frederick, MD: University Publications, 1987), Reel 11, 0166–0167.

11. This is Chase, reiterating the contents of his "despatch" in his 9 April 1856 letter to Cox.

12. After he, Cox, and Hamlin failed to arrest the Garners before Gaines shipped them south from Louisville, Joseph Cooper reported on the group's actions in a letter to Chase dated 11 March 1856. In it he indicated that Ohio's warrant charging the Garners with murder had been returned to Columbus. This is the document Chase then enclosed with his 9 April 1856 letter to Cox. A month later, after failing yet again to take custody of Margaret, Cox once more returned it to Columbus with a 15 May 1856 letter to Chase. See *Salmon Portland Chase Papers*, Reel 11, 0231. Evidently the warrant has not survived.

13. This was the strategy that Edward Hamlin described to Chase in 1856, and that

George Hoadley and Governor Chase both recollected eight years later. See Hamlin to Chase, 11 March 1856; Hoadley to Chase, 6 January 1864; as well as Chase to Edward Pierce, 14 January 1864; in *Salmon Portland Chase Papers*, Reel 11, 0127–0128; Reel 31, 0799–0803; and Reel 31, 1008–1011, respectively.

14. See the *Cincinnati Gazette*, Friday, 11 April 1856.

15. Ibid.; weather information is drawn once again from the *Gazette*'s daily "River Intelligence" column.

16. See the *Cincinnati Gazette* for Monday, 14 April 1856; as well as Archibald Gaines's 14 April letter printed in the *Cincinnati Enquirer* of 15 April 1856.

17. *Cincinnati Gazette*, 14 April 1856.

18. Ibid.; for similar reports, see also the *Cincinnati Enquirer* of 14 April 1856.

19. According to the *Louisville Courier*, 11 April 1856, the *Eclipse* was the only New Orleans-bound steamboat departing on that day. Information on the boat's "master" and her cargo are drawn from the *Courier*'s advertisements and shipping news sections.

20. Gaines to the *Cincinnati Enquirer*, in its edition of 15 April 1856.

21. On 1850s slave prices, see Michael Tadman, *Speculators and Slaves: Masters, Traders, and Slaves in the Old South* (Madison: University of Wisconsin Press, 1989), passim. Section 7 of the 1850 Fugitive Slave Law entitled masters to file claims for money damages against anyone allegedly aiding or abetting a fugitive or fugitives in flight, and, after a favorable judgment, to receive compensation ranging up to $1,000 per slave. For a transcript of the 1850 Fugitive Slave Law, see Marion Gleason McDougall, *Fugitive Slaves (1619–1865)*, Fay House Monograph No. 3 (Boston, Ginn, 1891), Appendix B, especially 113–14.

22. See Bertram Wyatt-Brown, *Honor and Violence in the Old South* (New York: Oxford University Press, 1986); and on rules governing sexual permissiveness, particularly between masters and their slave women, see 94–113. In his "Memoir on Slavery," William Harper admits that "licentious intercourse" occurred between masters and slave women but argues for its benefits as a kind of safety valve on sexual passions, especially for younger members of the planter class. Harper thinks that as young gentlemen inevitably turn from their more "degraded" passions with "enslaved females" to white women with their "greater allurements," they do so without the baggage—such as bastard children—"with which worthless women sometimes entangle their victims." As for the mulatto children of their relations, he says that under slavery "such offspring" are never destined to burden either the mother or the society. See William Harper, "Memoir on Slavery," in *The Ideology of Slavery: Proslavery Thought in the Antebellum South, 1830–1860*, ed. Drew Gilpin Faust (Baton Rouge: Louisiana State University Press, 1981), 106–9.

23. See A. K. Gaines's letter printed in the *Cincinnati Enquirer*, 15 March 1856.

24. Details on Abner Gaines and his wife Sally's Issaquena County holdings are available in summaries of a legal dispute over the will of Sally's maternal grandfather, Homer V. Ledbetter, in Katherine Branton and Alice Wade, *Early Records of Mississippi: Issaquena County/Washington County, 1827–1900*, Vol. 2 (Leland, MS: Bound xerographic copy of original MS, 1985), 24.

25. His name was listed in the "Arrivals at the Principal Hotels" column of the *New Orleans Times-Picayune* on Monday, 28 April 1856.

26. See Joseph Cox to Salmon Portland Chase, *Salmon Portland Chase Papers*, Reel 11, 0231; and Cox to Chase, 28 November 1863, ibid., Reel 30, 0073.

27. William Deeson, an attorney, was married to another of Ledbetter's grandchildren, a cousin of Abner Gaines's wife, Sally, and the long battle over Ledbetter's estate appears to have become a grand family squabble. Evidently, aside from the moral satisfaction of freeing Violet Ledbetter and her three children, the Deesons never realized a cent from Ledbetter's will. See Branton and Wade, *Early Records of Mississippi*, Vol. 1, 1–2; and Vol. 2, 24–25; having examined court records, these compilers conclude: "No part of the will of Homer V. Ledbetter was ever executed."

28. Robert Garner, as reported by the *Cincinnati Chronicle* of March 1870; reprinted in *The Press* (Philadelphia), 18 March 1870.

29. *The Liberator*, 29 February 1856, 36.

30. These remarks are all from volumes of *The Liberty Bell*, edited and published in Boston by the Anti-Slavery Bazaar. For Thomas Wentworth Higginson's remark, see his essay on the fugitives William and Ellen Craft, "The Romance of History," in Vol. 15 (1858), 119; James Freeman Clarke's comment is from the last stanza of his poem "The Ballad of Edward Davis," in Vol. 15 (1856), 32; Lydia Maria Child's comment is from her short story "The Quadroons," in Vol. 3 (1842), 141; and Edmund Quincy's remark can be found in his essay "American Chivalry," also published in Vol. 3 (1842), 73–95.

31. Wendell Phillips, "The Philosophy of the Abolition Movement," *Speeches, Lectures, and Letters* (Boston: Lee and Shepard, 1892). For his comment on Bremer and "the romance of our history," see 132; for his discussion of Stowe, see 131.

32. A December 1852 letter from Harriet Beecher Stowe to Eliza Lee Cabot Follen, quoted in Joan Hedrick, *Harriet Beecher Stowe: A Life* (New York: Oxford University Press, 1994), 193.

33. Harriet Beecher Stowe, *Uncle Tom's Cabin; or, Life Among the Lowly* (1852; New York: Penguin, 1981), 149.

34. Hedrick, *Harriet Beecher Stowe*, 191–92.

35. Some examples from the Cincinnati press: a 4 August 1854 story in the *Cincinnati Gazette* provided a tally of the dead from a recent cholera epidemic; the category "infant" included all children through age five. In popular usage that range could go higher, however. On 22 November 1852 the *Gazette* announced an upcoming appearance by "The Prodigy of Our Age!," an "Infant Violinist" described as "only 7 years old!"

36. Typical of Hiram Martin's output on this theme: a poem entitled "Lines Suggestive of the Thoughts of the Rev. W. McD. Abbott and Wife, on the Death of their Little Daughter, Lizzie Reed," published in the *Covington Journal* of 21 March 1857. Martin's last stanza:

> *Farewell, sweetest angel, but O!, not forever;*
> *The gray in our locks says, time cannot long sever*
> *Thy angelic spirit, from kindred so dear;*
> *Resigned we will wait for a call to thy sphere.*

Poems, homilies, and essays on the "special child" were commonplaces of the age, as any scan through newspapers will demonstrate. Cincinnati and Covington were no exceptions to this rule. The 19 February 1853 issue of the *Covington Journal* published a homily entitled "The Death of Infants," wherein the "capaciousness of an infant's tomb" is extensive enough to heal all, including mourners who send their prayers within it.

37. See Jacqueline Jones, *Labor of Love, Labor of Sorrow: Black Women, Work, and the Family from Slavery to the Present* (New York: Basic Books, 1985). Jones notes that from 1850 to 1860, "fewer than two out of three black children survived to the age of ten" (35). See also Kenneth Stampp, *The Peculiar Institution: Slavery in the Antebellum South* (New York: Alfred A. Knopf, 1956), 319–20; and Robert William Fogel, *Without Consent or Contract: The Rise and Fall of American Slavery* (New York: W. W. Norton, 1989), 142–47.

38. See Deborah Gray White, *Ar'n't I a Woman?: Female Slaves in the Plantation South* (New York: W. W. Norton, 1985), 98; and Tadman, *Speculators and Slaves*, 112.

39. For an incisive example, see Charlotte H. L. Coues, "An Appeal to Mothers," in *The Liberty Bell*, Vol. 6 (1845), 3–8. This short story is set in Kingston, Jamaica, and tells the story of a slave owner who sells all the children of one of his female slaves; the woman then goes mad with grief, and at story's end the narrator steps in for the "Appeal": "Christian mother! has a child ever been removed from you by death? Have you, with the strong sight of faith, watched the sweet spirit ascending, after her departure from the body, led by shining angels, cheered by heavenly music—her new-formed wings tiring not until she reached the footstool of the eternal, where, bathed in bliss, she was to enjoy his presence evermore; where her infant powers were to expand; where she was to go on from glory to glory?" If so, says the narrator, then the slave mother's mad grief will be understandable.

40. See Jacobs, *Incidents in the Life of a Slave Girl* (1861), ed. Henry Louis Gates (New York: Mentor, 1987), 392 and 404, respectively.

41. See *The Liberator*, 15 August 1845, 132. The poem is also included in Vicki L. Eaklor, *American Antislavery Songs: A Collection and Analysis* (Westport, CT: Greenwood Press, 1988), 331–32; in a note Eaklor comments that it was written by the Rev. J. Blanchard, who set his lyric to the tune of "Araby's Daughter." For "The Slave Mother's Address to her Infant Child," an "Original" poem for the edition, see Lunsford Lane, *The Narrative of Lunsford Lane, formerly of Raleigh, N.C., Published by Himself* (Boston: J. G. Torrey, 1842). In its most salient moment the poem's slave mother exclaims: "And gladly would I lay thee down/ To sleep beneath the sod,/ And give thy gentle spirit back,/ Unmarr'd with grief, to God:/ The tears I shed upon that turf/ Should whisper peace to me,/ And tell me in the spirit land/ My lovely babe was free." In helping me think through these ideological equations of Liberty and Death, I am especially indebted to Russ Castronovo for sharing with me the longer draft of his paper "Disembodying the Body Politic," delivered at the International Conference on Narrative at the University of Florida, April 1997.

42. *The American Anti-Slavery Almanac*, Vol. 1, No. 2 (1837), 43–44.

43. Elizabeth Barrett Browning, "The Runaway Slave at Pilgrim's Point," in *The Liberty Bell*, Vol. 9 (1848), 29–44. On Barrett Browning's poem, see Dorothy Mermin, *Elizabeth Barrett Browning: The Origins of a New Poetry* (Chicago: University of Chicago Press, 1989), 156–59; Angela Leighton, *Victorian Women Poets: Writing Against the Heart* (Charlottesville: University Press of Virginia, 1992), 97–102; Ann Parry, "Sexual Exploitation and Freedom: Religion, Race, and Gender in Elizabeth Barrett Browning's 'The Runaway Slave at Pilgrim's Point,'" *Studies in Browning and His Circle* 16 (1988), 114–27; and Ralph Thompson, "*The Liberty Bell* and Other Antislavery Gift Books," *New England Quarterly* 7 (1934), 154–68. Thomp-

son notes that Barrett Browning's poem was "the only original contribution of a notable foreign writer" to any of the antislavery gift books. Thanks to Joseph Gardner for showing me Barrett Browning's poem.

44. Deborah Gray White, "The Lives of Slave Women," in *Black Women in United States History*, ed. Diane Clark Hine (Brooklyn: Carlson, 1990), 4.

45. On the Missouri instance, see Helen Tunicliff Catterall, *Judicial Cases Concerning American Slavery and the Negro* (Washington, DC: Carnegie Institution, 1937), Vol. 5, 139; also *State v. Jane (a mulatto woman, slave)* in 3 Missouri Cases 61, April 1831. On the Georgia instance see Robert Anson Myers, ed., *The Children of Pride: A True Story of Georgia and the Civil War* (New Haven: Yale University Press, 1972), 527–47.

46. Lydia Maria Child, *The Patriarchal Institution as Described by Members of its Own Family* (New York: American Anti-Slavery Society, 1860), 20. Many thanks to Karen Sanchez-Eppler for calling my attention to this instance.

47. See White, *Ar'n't I a Woman?* 87–88. The idea that slave mothers were smothering their infants and blaming the deaths on accidental overlaying was developed from mortality schedules that puzzled even antebellum Southrons like J. D. B. DeBow. The recent historical research on slave infant mortality rates is fairly extensive, but see especially Kenneth F. Kiple and Virginia H. Kiple, "Slave Child Mortality: Some Nutritional Answers to a Perennial Puzzle," *Journal of Social History* 10 (1977), 284–309; Todd L. Savitt, *Medicine and Slavery: The Diseases and Health Care of Blacks in Antebellum Virginia* (Urbana: University of Illinois Press, 1978), 124–27; and Michael P. Johnson, "Smothered Slave Infants: Were Slave Mothers at Fault?" *Journal of Southern History* 47 (1981), 494–520. The quote is from Johnson (495).

48. See George S. Sawyer, *Southern Institutes: or, An Inquiry into the Origin and Early Prevalence of Slavery and the Slave-Trade* (Philadelphia: J. B. Lippincott, 1858), 330–31; and Ebenezer Starnes, *The Slaveholder Abroad; or, Billy Buck's Visit, with his Master, to England* (Philadelphia: J. B. Lippincott, 1860), 334.

49. On the child abandoned in a culvert, see the *Cincinnati Gazette* of Saturday, 26 January 1856; the story of the Irish servant girl who dropped her newborn down a privy appeared in the *Cincinnati Enquirer* of 5 September 1855.

50. See Nancy Scheper-Hughes, *Death without Weeping: The Violence of Everyday Life in Brazil* (Berkeley: University of California Press, 1992), 400. A moving and extraordinary book, I have drawn especially from its eighth chapter, "(M)Other Love: Culture, Scarcity, and Maternal Thinking."

51. See Scheper-Hughes, *Death without Weeping*, 274–76. This process involves what anthropologist Pierre Bourdieu defines as *méconnaissance* or "misrecognition": the generally unconscious or unrationalized recognition or practice of what is otherwise unspeakable, especially when that recognition or practice involves social relations (for example, in relations of dominance and submission) that must be dissimulated or concealed (rendered misrecognizable again) in order to ensure people's complicity with the system. A kind of collective bad faith, it is one (crucial) way that cultures maintain inequality. See Bourdieu, *Outline of a Theory of Practice*, trans. Richard Nice (New York: Cambridge University Press, 1977), 172–83.

52. See the *Cincinnati Commercial* of Thursday, 31 January 1856; and the *Cincinnati Gazette* of Friday, 1 February 1856.

53. Morrison made these remarks during her 12 October 1988 acceptance speech for

the Frederick G. Melcher Book Award, Unitarian Universalist Association (Cambridge, MA: The Cambridge Forum), WVTF, Roanoke, VA, 5 April 1991.

54. Dr. Elijah Smith Clarkson, "Messrs. Editors," *Cincinnati Enquirer*, 14 February 1856.

55. The editorials Justice submitted first appeared in the *Covington Journal* on 15 March 1856 and ran steadily in issues of the following five weeks. Each editorial runs well over 2,000 words—an extraordinary output. By his fifth installment, on 12 April, Justice was countered by Truth, who identified himself as a former Whig and supporter of Cassius Clay's schemes for recolonizing slaves in Africa. Truth submitted three more installments (19 April, 26 April, and 17 May). The ninth and last installment from Justice appeared in the *Journal's* issue of Saturday, 7 June 1856. How may we surmise that Justice was really Benjamin Franklin Bedinger? In his first installment Justice relates details about the Gaines slaves at Maplewood— for example, about Margaret's putative father, Duke—that only a near-neighbor could have known. Moreover, Bedinger was a former co-editor (in 1849–51) and in 1856 still a co-owner of the *Covington Journal*, therefore able to command the great deal of space set aside for his nine epistles—probably the surest evidence for identifying him as the face behind the nom de plume.

56. Henry Field James, "Preface," *Abolitionism Unveiled; or, Its Origin, Progress, and Pernicious Tendency Fully Developed* (Cincinnati: E. Morgan & Sons, 1856), iii. From newspaper advertisements in the *Cincinnati Enquirer* and the *Covington Journal* it appears the novel was released in mid-July but nothing further is known of its author, who appears in neither the 1850 nor the 1860 census records, nor any of the directories for Cincinnati-Covington. From descriptive detail in the novel it is apparent that he knew Boone County's land and people fairly well; Squire Gray's plantation, for example, very much resembles those of Gaines and Bedinger in Richwood Station. Indeed it is quite possible that "Henry Field James" was the pseudonym of a northern Kentuckian like Bedinger, a man used to employing noms de plume for his editorials.

57. See James, *Abolitionism Unveiled*, 240–45.

58. Dr. J. H. Van Evrie, *Negroes and Negro Slavery: The First an Inferior Race; the Latter its Normal Condition* (New York: Van Evrie, Horton, 1861). This edition, containing near its close Van Evrie's thoughts on the Garner infanticide, is a revised version of his first, 1853 edition (Baltimore: J. D. Toy). From 1861 to 1863 the revised book went through three editions. Then in 1868 Van Evrie revised it yet again under a Reconstruction-era title that perhaps best expressed the book's true racist spirit: *White Supremacy and Negro Subordination; or, Negroes a Subordinate Race, and (So-Called) Slavery its Normal Condition* (New York: Van Evrie, Horton). Between 1868 and 1870 this edition also went through three editions.

59. For Toni Morrison's representation of Schoolteacher's categorizing exercise, see *Beloved* (New York: Alfred A. Knopf, 1987), 193. For Van Evrie's comments on mothers and "The Domestic Affections" see Chapter 18 of *Negroes and Negro Slavery* (1860), especially 224–25. For his comments on saving America from the "treason" of race mixing, see his "Preface," vi. Samuel George Morton (1799–1851) of Pennsylvania and Josiah Clark Nott (1804–73) were the professors whose arguments for polygenesis probably had the strongest influence over Van Evrie. Nott's 1846 volume, *Types of Mankind; or, Ethnological Researches, Based upon the Ancient Monuments, Paintings, Sculptures and Crania of Races, and upon their Natural,*

Geographical, Philological and Biblical History (Philadelphia: J. B. Lippincott), was in its eighth edition by 1860. Nott's work built on that of Morton, whose two best-known works were *Crania Americana* (1839) and *Crania Aegyptica* (1844), works that argued from evidence of cranial capacity that the "Ancient Caucasian" and the "Ancient Negroid" were originators of different "races." See also Nott's *Two Lectures on the Connection between the Biblical and Physical History of Man* (1848; New York: Negro Universities Press, 1969). Supporters of polygenesis always had to soft-pedal their theory because it so clearly contradicted the biblical creation story, and Nott's *Two Lectures* well represents both the problem and their attempted solution. For further discussion, see William R. Stanton, *The Leopard's Spots: Scientific Attitudes toward Race in America* (Chicago: University of Chicago Press, 1960), and Dana D. Nelson, " 'Our Castle Still Remains Unshaken,' " Chapter 3 of her forthcoming book *National Manhood* (Durham: Duke University Press).

60. Van Evrie, *Negroes and Negro Slavery* (1861), 225–26.

61. For the full text of Bushnell's sermon, see *The Liberator*, 16 May 1856, itself a reprint from the (Yellow Springs, Ohio) *Free Presbyterian* of mid-April. Partial versions of the sermon had also appeared in the *Cincinnati Gazette* as well as the *New York Tribune*.

62. Reports of Hebbard's recitation appeared in the *Boston Transcript* of 19 March 1856 and *The Liberator* of 21 March 1856. For the poem's full text, see William Wallace Hebbard, *The Night of Freedom: An Appeal, in Verse, against the Great Crime of our Country, Human Bondage!* (Boston: Samuel Chism, 1857; repr. Atlanta: Fisk University Library Negro Collection, 1971).

63. See the *National Anti-Slavery Standard* of Saturday, 23 February 1856. Interestingly, the Richwood Presbyterian Church Session Books, kept continuously after the church's founding in 1833, mention Archibald K. Gaines but once; that was on the occasion of his marriage to Margaret Ann Dudley in 1843. Until 1849, when she died, Margaret Dudley Gaines and her parents were enrolled as Richwood Presbyterian members. Archibald never was, and his affiliation with the church must have been casual, at best. For the newspapers' invective editorials on Judge Harold Leavitt's membership in the Presbyterian synod, see *The Liberator* of 23 May 1856, 81.

64. "Letter from Henry C. Wright," *The Liberator*, 11 April 1856, 59.

65. Parker's speech to the American Anti-Slavery Society was reported, for example, in *The Liberator*, 16 May 1856; the *National Anti-Slavery Standard*, 16 May 1856; and the *Cincinnati Gazette*, 19 May 1856. For the full text see Theodore Parker, *The Great Battle between Slavery and Freedom; Considered in Two Speeches, Delivered before the American Anti-Slavery Society at New York, May 7, 1856* (Boston: Benjamin H. Greene, 1856). For Chase's response, see Chase to Parker, 17 July 1856, Reel 3, Vol. 9 of *The Theodore Parker Papers, 1826–1862* (Ann Arbor: University Microfilms, 1979), filmed from the original in the possession of the Massachusetts Historical Society. There is, incidentally, a remarkable hypocrisy in Parker's charge that Chase mishandled the Garner case because of racism. Leading into his remarks on the Garner case, Parker himself displayed a mean streak of racism when he commented that if blacks had the mettle "of Anglo-Saxons" they would have already thrown off the slaveholder's yoke. Northern whites had heard the call to fight slavery and responded because "the slaves themselves were Africans—men not very good with the sword. If the case had been otherwise—if it had been three and a half

millions of Anglo-Saxons—the chief antislavery appeal would not have been to the oppressor to leave off oppressing"; instead, he implied, it would have been necessary to appeal for mercy, lest warlike white slaves rise up and exterminate their masters. See *The Great Battle* (7).

66. From the full text of Lucy Stone's speech quoted in the *National Anti-Slavery Standard*, 16 May 1856.

67. From an address Douglass gave in Rochester on 22 May 1856 (the day Preston Brooks attacked Charles Sumner), an address he apparently adapted and used into the summer. See *The Frederick Douglass Papers*, Series One: *Speeches, Debates, and Interviews*, Vol. 3, ed. John W. Blassingame (New Haven: Yale University Press, 1985), 127–28. For a representative instance of Charles L. Remond's remarks during this period, see his Mozart Hall (New York) speech of 13 May 1858, in *The Black Abolitionist Papers*, Vol. 4, ed. C. Peter Ripley (Chapel Hill: University of North Carolina Press, 1992), 387.

68. The term derives from the French *colporteur:* a peddler or newsmonger. Nineteenth-century colporteurs working on contract for Baptist, Methodist, and Presbyterian publishers combed the Ohio Valley, as elsewhere in the United States. Early on, abolitionist societies adapted colportage as a principal means to distribute antislavery tracts, gift books, and fictions. See Ronald G. Walters, *The Antislavery Appeal: American Abolitionism After 1830* (Baltimore: Johns Hopkins University Press, 1976), 22–23; as well as Richard D. Sears, *The Day of Small Things: Abolitionism in the Midst of Slavery—Berea, Kentucky, 1854–1864* (Lanham, MD: University Press of America, 1986), 38–41. Hattia M'Keehan's autobiographical narrative, *The Life and Trials of a Hoosier Girl* (New York: Printed for the Author, 1860), is our main source of information about her: for example, that she published two other fictions, *The Lover's Revenge* and *The Philosophy of Love*, between 1856 and 1860. About these two books nothing more is known. It remains unclear which work of fiction appeared first, M'Keehan's or Henry Field James's *Abolitionism Unveiled*. Advertisements for both books began appearing in Cincinnati-area newspapers, the *Cincinnati Gazette* and the *Covington Journal*, respectively, during the third week in July.

69. *Liberty or Death!; or, Heaven's Infraction of the Fugitive Slave Law* (Cincinnati: By the Author, 1856), 7, 37, 41.

70. See M'Keehan's "Preface" to *Liberty or Death!*, iii; and for appearances of the ghost, 59–60, 73–74.

71. Details about the book's printing history are available in *The Life and Trials of a Hoosier Girl*. A number of special collections libraries have copies of the book, all printed on cheap paper and bound in rough cardboard. I am grateful to Joan Higbee at the Library of Congress Rare Book Room for helping me to find another copy: Mrs. J. P. Hardwick, *Liberty or Death!; or, The Mother's Sacrifice* (Harrisburg: For the Authoress, 1862), identical with all others except for its title page.

72. *Chattanooga* (Cincinnati: Anderson, Gates, and Wright, 1858), 8–9. The copy housed in Special Collections at the Margaret I. King Library, University of Kentucky, contains someone's penciled inscription of "Wm. Gilmore Simms" as a supposed author, for none was ever indicated on the book's title page. We know Jolliffe as the author because of summer 1858 notices in the *Cincinnati Gazette* referring to him; moreover, his sister Elizabeth acknowledged his authorship in a biographical essay about him. See "John Jolliffe," in *Historical, Genealogical, and Biographical*

Account of the Jolliffe Family of Virginia, 1652 to 1893 (Philadelphia: J. B. Lippincott, 1893), 229.

73. The quotes are from *Chattanooga*, 356–61, 387.

74. My representation of typhoid's progress in Margaret's case is adapted from H. Curschmann, *Typhoid Fever and Typhus Fever*, trans. Alfred Stengel (Philadelphia: W. B. Saunders, 1905), 79–85. For information on yellow fever and typhus epidemics in western Mississippi, see the Jackson, Mississippi, *Semi-Weekly Mississippian*, in particular the issues of 31 August, 10 September, and 14 September 1858. Stories on black tongue disease and boll weevil devastation appear in the issue of Tuesday, 14 September 1858; the comet made its first appearance in the issue of Friday, 24 September 1858.

75. For data on the DeWitt Clinton Bonham family, see *Eighth Census of the United States, 1860: Mississippi. Issaquena County*, 863 (entry 2525). Other data are from the marshal's own summations, noted on the ledger book's final pages. In 1860, Bonham listed none of his slaves as hired out.

76. On these differences between Deep South and Border South plantations and the effects on mating and families, based on analyses of census schedules, see Richard Steckel, "Miscegenation and the American Slave Schedules," *Journal of Interdisciplinary History* 11 (1980): 251–63. For a summary of other studies indicating that miscegenation was far more likely on small (and typically Border South) rather than large (Deep South) plantations, see Fogel, *Without Consent or Contract*, 181–82.

77. See Stampp, *The Peculiar Institution*; and John W. Blassingame, *The Slave Community: Plantation Life in the Antebellum South* (New York: Oxford University Press, 1972).

78. Eugene D. Genovese, *Roll, Jordan, Roll: The World the Slaves Made* (New York: Pantheon, 1974), 292–95.

79. See Lawrence W. Levine, *Black Culture and Black Consciousness: Afro-American Folk Thought from Slavery to Freedom* (New York: Oxford University Press, 1978); and Thomas L. Webber, *Deep Like the Rivers* (New York: W. W. Norton, 1978).

80. See K. David Patterson, "Disease Environments of the Antebellum South," in Ronald L. Numbers and Todd Savitt, eds. *Science and Medicine in the Old South* (Baton Rouge: Louisiana State University Press, 1983), 152–65; and Isaac Wright, *Wright's Family Medicine; or, System of Domestic Practice* (Madisonville, TN: Henderson, Johnston, 1833), 158–59; according to Patterson, *Wright's* was widely used in the Old South, and medicating steam was Wright's best prescription for typhoid's symptoms.

81. Interview with Robert Garner; *The Press* (Philadelphia), 18 March 1870.

Epilogue

1. Entry for 1 June 1856, Book 2, Richwood Presbyterian Church Session Books, 1838–79.

2. The story of Gaines's lightning-struck team of horses appeared in the *Covington Journal*, 11 April 1857. News of his appointment to a two-year term as president of Boone County's chapter of the American Party appears in the *Covington Journal* of 20 June 1857, two weeks after his trial for assaulting John Jolliffe. Reports of award winners in competitions at the Northern Kentucky Agricultural Fair were published

annually in the *Covington Journal*, typically in late September. In 1860, for example, Gaines won top prizes in the categories of "Harness Mare 4 yrs and Older," "Harness Mare 2yr–3yr," and "Bullock 4 yr & Over"; see the *Covington Journal* 22 September 1860. Data on 1860 residents at Maplewood is available in *Eighth Census of the United States, 1860: Kentucky. Boone County*.

3. On the "opposition" resolutions, see the *Covington Journal* of 5 February 1859 and 8 September 1860. Menzies's run for Kentucky's Tenth District congressional seat was widely reported in the *Journal* during the summer of 1861. The enrollment of "Thos. Marshall of Boone" in the northern Kentucky Home Guards is reported in the *Journal* of 21 September 1861.

4. Weather data are from the *Cincinnati Enquirer*, 11 November 1871. See also "Archibald K. Gaines" (obituary), *Covington Journal*, 18 November 1871; and Gaines's will, filed 22 March 1872, available in Boone County (KY) Willbook I, 395.

5. Chase to Edward L. Pierce, 14 January 1863, in *The Salmon Portland Chase Papers* (microfilm edition), ed. John Niven (Frederick, MD: University Publications, 1987), Reel 30, 01011.

6. Chase to Edward L. Pierce, undated (probably late March or April 1864), in *Salmon Portland Chase Papers*, Reel 30, 00739.

7. See Elizabeth A. Jolliffe, "John Jolliffe," in *Historical, Genealogical, and Biographical Account of the Jolliffe Family of Virginia, 1652 to 1893* (Philadelphia: J. B. Lippincott, 1893), 223–31. The Jolliffes' addresses (including that for John's law office) are available in *Boyd's Washington and Georgetown Directory* (Washington, DC: Hutchinson and Brothers), for the years 1863 through 1868.

8. "The Late John Jolliffe," *Cincinnati Gazette*, 10 April 1868.

9. See the "Democratic Meeting in Issaquena," *Semi-Weekly Mississippian*, 23 May 1860, and stories of Issaquena politics in the *Semi-Weekly Mississippian* of 17 October and 24 October 1860. A story on Confederate military movements in the *Semi-Weekly Mississippian* of 20 November 1861 provides some detail on movements of the 22nd Infantry, with a comment by one of his officers that "Colonel Bonham is not only a military man by education, but naturally so"—that in response to some early doubts that had arisen about his abilities. On the 22nd Infantry, see also Steward Sifakis, *Compendium of the Confederate Armies: Mississippi* (New York: Facts on File, 1995), 109–11; and Charles E. Hooker, "Mississippi," in *Confederate Military History*, Vol. 7: *Alabama and Mississippi* (Atlanta: Confederate Publishing Company, 1899).

10. These details are available from Isaac E. Hirsh, "The Life Story of Isaac E. Hirsh: Co. G, 22nd Regiment, Mississippi Infantry, C.S.A.," unpublished ms. (1911), Tennessee State Library, 35–36.

11. On the 1861–62 slave insurrections that originated at Second Creek, west of Natchez, see Winthrop Jordan, *Tumult and Silence at Second Creek: An Inquiry into a Civil War Slave Conspiracy* (Baton Rouge: Louisiana State University Press, 1993); on actions of Bonham's 22nd Mississippi Regiment, see Hooker, "Mississippi," in *Confederate Military History*, Vol. 7, especially Chapter 4.

12. Robert's interview with the *Cincinnati Chronicle* reporter, published as "A Reminiscence of Slavery," is available in *The Press* (Philadelphia), 18 March 1870, 2. The records for Robert Gardner, Company A, 71st Colored Infantry Regiment, are available at the National Archives; his payroll record is page 274, card numbers 7069303, 7069338, and 7069373. There was no other Robert (or Simon, or Simeon,

or Sam) Garner (or Gardner, or Guarner) who served among the U.S. Colored Troops.

13. From Robert Garner's *Cincinnati Chronicle* interview: "[Robert] was in the siege of Vicksburg, and was in active service until the close of the war, when he received an honorable discharge. He subsequently married, and is now living in this city [Cincinnati]. His two boys Thomas and Samuel are living on a farm opposite Vicksburg, in Mississippi." The 1870 census of Mississippi was conducted six months after these words were published; Thomas and Samuel Garner, by then ages twenty and eighteen, do not appear in it.

14. Scholars may yet find other instances, but for now the known lithographic reproductions of Noble's "The Modern Medea" include: the *St. Louis Guardian*, 27 April 1867; the *New York Daily Standard*, 9 May 1867; *American Art Journal*, May 1867; *The Round Table*, 18 May 1867; and *Harper's Weekly Magazine*, 18 May 1867. Two years later the *Boston Herald* of 3 January 1869 also ran the picture and an accompanying story. See James D. Birchfield, Albert Boime, and William J. Hennessey, *Thomas Satterwhite Noble: 1835–1907* (Lexington: University of Kentucky Art Museum, 1987), 68. "Fugitives in Flight" was discovered in a Lexington, KY, attic, then restored and auctioned at Sotheby's in 1993. The painting is currently on permanent display at the Greenville County Museum of Art in Greenville, South Carolina. I am grateful to curator Martha Severens for sharing information about the painting.

15. "The Slave Mother: A Tale of the Ohio," in *Complete Poems of Frances E. W. Harper*, ed. Maryemma Graham (New York: Oxford University Press, 1988), 28–30. The dating of the poem is Suzanne Dietzel's, in a bibliographic survey appended to the volume (221). See also Harper's 1892 novel, *Iola Leroy; or, Shadows Uplifted* (New York: Oxford University Press, 1988), 98.

BIBLIOGRAPHY

⚜

Manuscript Collections

James Birney Papers, Cincinnati Historical Society
Willbooks, Boone County Library, Florence, KY
Salmon Portland Chase Papers, Cincinnati Historical Society
Salmon Portland Chase Papers, Library of Congress
Salmon Portland Chase Papers, Ohio State Historical Society
Caleb Cushing Papers, Library of Congress
John Pollard Gaines Papers, New York State Library, Albany, NY
John McLean Papers, Library of Congress
William J. Minor Papers, Louisiana State University Library
Franklin Pierce Papers, Library of Congress
United States Colored Infantry Records, National Archive

Newspapers

Charleston (SC) Daily Courier
Chicago Tribune
Cincinnati Chronicle
Cincinnati Commercial
Cincinnati Enquirer
Cincinnati Gazette
Clermont (OH) Courier
Cleveland Herald
Covington (KY) Journal
Lexington (KY) Atlas

The Liberator
Licking Valley (KY) *Register*
Louisville Daily Courier
Louisville Daily Journal
Maysville (KY) *Eagle*
National Anti-Slavery Standard
National Era
National Intelligencer
New Orleans Times-Picayune
New York Times
New York Tribune
The Press (Philadelphia)
Semi-Weekly Mississippian (Jackson, MS)

Public Documents

The Revised Statutes of Kentucky (1852)
Third Census of the United States, 1810: Kentucky. Bell and Boone Counties
Fourth Census of the United States, 1820: Kentucky. Bell and Boone Counties
Seventh Census of the United States, 1850: Boone and Kenton Counties, KY
United States Census Schedules, 1850: Census of Slaves, Boone County, KY
United States Census Schedules, 1850: Census of Agriculture, Boone County, KY
Seventh Census of the United States, 1850: Hamilton County, OH
Eighth Census of the United States, 1860: Boone County, KY
United States Census Schedules, 1860: Census of Slaves, Boone County, KY
Eighth Census of the United States, 1860: Issaquena County, MS

Primary Sources

Abridgment of the Debates of Congress, Vol. 16: *1846–1850*. New York: Appleton, 1861.
The American Anti-Slavery Almanac, Vol. 1, No. 2 (1837).
Barnes, Albert. *Inquiry into the Scriptural Views of Slavery*. Philadelphia: Perkins and Purves, 1846.
Bledsoe, Albert Taylor. *An Essay on Liberty and Slavery*. Philadelphia: J. B. Lippincott, 1856.
The Boston Slave Riot and Trial of Anthony Burns. Boston: Fetridge and Co., 1854.
Brisbane, W. H. *Amanda: A Tale for the Times*. Philadelphia: Merrihew and Thompson, 1848.
Browning, Elizabeth Barrett. "The Runaway Slave at Pilgrim's Point." *The Liberty Bell* 9 (1848): 29–44.
Coffin, Levi. *Reminiscences of Levi Coffin, the Reputed President of the Underground Railroad*. Cincinnati: Western Tract Society, 1876.
Congressional Globe. Proceedings of the 30th Congress, 1st and 2nd Sessions. Washington: Blair and Rives, 1848 and 1849.
Douglass, Frederick. *My Bondage and My Freedom*. 1855. New York: Dover, 1969.
———. *The Frederick Douglass Papers*. Series One, Vol. 3: *Speeches, Debates, and Interviews*. Ed. John Blassingame. New Haven: Yale University Press, 1985.

Emerson, Ralph Waldo. *Emerson's Antislavery Writings*. Ed. Len Gougeon and Joel Myerson. New Haven: Yale University Press, 1995.

Ex parte Robinson, 20 Federal Cases 965 (1856).

Fedric, Francis. *Slave Life in Virginia and Kentucky; or, Fifty Years of Slavery in the Southern States of America*. London: Wertheim, Macintosh, and Hunt, 1863.

Fitzhugh, George. *Cannibals All!* 1857. Ed. C. Vann Woodward. Cambridge, MA: Harvard University Press, 1960.

Gaines, John Pollard. The Diaries of John Pollard Gaines. 1850. Typescript prepared by Collins Gaines and Martha Woods Gaines. Fort Worth (TX) Public Library.

Garrison, Lucy McKim. *Slave Songs of the United States*. 1867. New York: Peter Smith, 1929. *Graham v. Strader*, 5B Monroe 173 (Kentucky 1844).

Harper, Frances E. W. "The Slave Mother: A Tale of the Ohio." In *Complete Poems of Frances E. W. Harper*. Ed. Maryemma Graham. New York: Oxford University Press, 1988.

————. *Iola Leroy; or, Shadows Uplifted*. 1892. New York: Oxford University Press, 1988.

Hebbard, William Wallace. *The Night of Freedom: An Appeal, in Verse, against the Great Crime of our Country, Human Bondage!* Boston: Samuel Chism, 1857.

Hirsh, Isaac E. "The Life Story of Isaac E. Hirsh: Co. G, 22nd Regiment, Mississippi Infantry, C.S.A." 1911. Tennessee State Library. Typescript.

Historical, Genealogical, and Biographical Account of the Jolliffe Family of Virginia, 1652–1893. Philadelphia: J. B. Lippincott, 1893.

Jacobs, Harriet. *Incidents in the Life of a Slave Girl*. 1860. New York: Oxford University Press, 1988.

James, Henry Field. *Abolitionism Unveiled; or, The Origin, Progress, and Pernicious Tendency Fully Developed*. Cincinnati: E. Morgan & Sons, 1856.

Jolliffe, John. *Belle Scott; or, Liberty Overthrown! A Tale for the Crisis*. Columbus and Cincinnati: Anderson and Blanchard, 1856.

————. *Chattanooga*. Cincinnati: Anderson, Gates, and Wright, 1858.

Kenny, Daniel J. *Illustrated Cincinnati: A Pictorial Hand-Book of the Queen City*. Cincinnati: R. Clarke, 1875.

Knowles, James Sheridan. *Virginius: A Tragedy in 5 Acts*. Philadelphia: Turner and Fisher, 1826.

Lane, Lunsford. *The Narrative of Lunsford Lane, formerly of Raleigh, N.C., Published by Himself*. Boston: J. G. Torrey, 1842.

The Liberty Bell, Vols. 1–15 (1840–58). Boston: Anti-Slavery Bazaar.

Macaulay, Thomas Babington. "Virginius." *The Lays of Ancient Rome*. London: Longman, Brown, Green, and Longman, 1842.

May, Samuel J. *The Fugitive Slave Law and Its Victims*. New York: American Anti-Slavery Society, 1861.

Miller v. McQuerry, 5 McLean 469 (1853).

M'Keehan, Hattia. *Liberty or Death!; or, Heaven's Infraction of the Fugitive Slave Law*. Cincinnati: By the Author, 1856.

————. *The Life and Trials of a Hoosier Girl*. New York: Printed for the Author, 1860.

Nott, Josiah. *Types of Mankind; or, Ethnological Researches, Based upon the Ancient Monuments, Paintings, Sculptures and Crania of Races, and upon their Natural, Geographical, Philological and Biblical History*. Philadelphia: J. B. Lippincott, 1846.

Parker, Theodore. *The Theodore Parker Papers, 1826–1862*. Ann Arbor: University Microfilms, 1979.

————. *The Great Battle between Slavery and Freedom; Considered in Two Speeches, Delivered before the American Anti-Slavery Society at New York, May 7, 1856*. Boston: Benjamin H. Greene, 1856.

Phillips, Wendell. *Speeches, Lectures, and Letters*. Boston: Lee and Shepard, 1892.

Picquet, Louisa. "Louisa Picquet, the Octoroon: Or, Inside Views of Southern Domestic Life." 1861. In *Collected Black Women's Narratives*. Ed. Anthony G. Barthelemy. New York: Oxford University Press, 1988.

Reed, Harriet Fanning. "Medea." *Dramatic Poems*. Boston: Wm. Crosby and H. P. Nichols, 1848.

Salmon Portland Chase Papers (microfilm edition). Ed. John Niven. Frederick, MD: University Publications, 1987.

Sawyer, George S. *Southern Institutes; or, An Inquiry into the Origin and Early Prevalence of Slavery and the Slave-Trade*. Philadelphia: J. B. Lippincott, 1858.

Second Fugitive Slave Act (signed September 18, 1850). *United States Statutes at Large* 9, 462–65.

Session Books, Richwood Presbyterian Church. Special Collections, University of Kentucky Library.

Starnes, Ebenezer. *The Slaveholder Abroad; or, Billy Buck's Visit, with his Master, to England*. Philadelphia: J. B. Lippincott, 1860.

State v. Jane (a mulatto woman, slave), 3 Missouri Cases 61 (April 1831).

Stowe, Harriet Beecher. *Uncle Tom's Cabin; or, Life Among the Lowly*. 1852. New York: Penguin, 1981.

Strader v. Graham, 10 Howard's Supreme Court Reports 83 (1851).

Trowbridge, J. T. *The Ferry-Boy and the Financier*. Boston: Walker, Wise and Co., 1864.

Van Evrie, Dr. J. H. *Negroes and Negro Slavery: The First an Inferior Race; the Latter its Normal Condition*. New York: Van Evrie, Horton, 1861.

Williams's Cincinnati Directory, City Guide, and Business Mirror. Annual. Cincinnati, 1840–60.

Secondary Sources

Aaron, Daniel. *Cincinnati, Queen City of the West: 1819–1838*. Columbus: Ohio State University Press, 1992.

Abraham, Roger D. *Singing the Master: The Emergence of African American Culture in the Plantation South*. New York: Pantheon, 1992.

Allen, Desmond Walls, and Bobbie Jones McLane. *Arkansas Land Patents: Arkansas, Chicot, and Desha Counties*. Conway, AR: Arkansas Research, 1990.

Aptheker, Herbert. *American Negro Slave Revolts*. New York: International Publishers, 1952.

Bell, Bernard. "*Beloved*: A Womanist Neo-Slave Narrative; or, Multivocal Remembrances of Things Past." *African American Review* 26.1 (1992): 7–15.

Bestor, Arthur. "State Sovereignty and Slavery: A Reinterpretation of Proslavery Constitutional Doctrine, 1846–1860." *Journal of the Illinois State Historical Society* 54 (1961): 159–74.

Birchfield, James D., Albert Boime and William J. Hennessey. *Thomas Satterwhite Noble: 1835–1907*. Lexington: University of Kentucky Art Museum, 1987.

Blackwell, Alice Stone. *Lucy Stone: Pioneer of Women's Rights*. Boston: Beacon, 1930.

Blassingame, John W. *The Slave Community: Plantation Life in the Antebellum South.* New York: Oxford University Press, 1972.

Branton, Katherine, and Alice Wade. *Early Records of Mississippi: Issaquena County/ Washington County, 1827–1900.* 2 vols. Leland, MS: n.p. 1985.

Brink, Carol. *Harps in the Wind: The Story of the Singing Hutchinsons.* New York: Macmillan, 1947.

Bruce, Robert V. "The Shadow of a Coming War." In *Lincoln, The War President: The Gettysburg Lectures.* Ed. Gabor S. Boritt. New York: Oxford University Press, 1992.

Bryman, D. S. "St. George Tucker and the Complexities of Antislavery Advocacy in Jeffersonian Virginia." Master's thesis, College of William and Mary, 1972.

Burton, Orville V., and Robert McGrath. *Class, Conflict, and Consensus: Antebellum Southern Community Studies.* Westport, CT: Greenwood Press, 1982.

Caldwell, Merrill S. "A Brief History of Slavery in Boone County, Kentucky." University of Kentucky Special Collections, 1957. Typescript.

Calkins, David L. "Black Education in a 19th Century City: An Institutional Analysis of Cincinnati's Colored Schools, 1830–1837." *Cincinnati Historical Society Bulletin* 13.3 (1975): 161–71.

Campbell, Stanley W. *The Slave Catchers: Enforcement of the Fugitive Slave Law, 1850–1860.* Chapel Hill: University of North Carolina Press, 1970.

Catterall, Helen Tunicliff. *Judicial Cases Concerning American Slavery and the Negro.* Vol. 5. Washington, DC: Carnegie Institution, 1937.

Cheek, William, and Aimee Lee Cheek. "John Mercer Langston and the Cincinnati Riot of 1841." In Taylor, *Race and the City,* 26–69.

Child, Lydia Maria. *The Patriarchal Institution as Described by Members of its Own Family.* New York: American Anti-Slavery Society, 1860.

Clinton, Catherine. *The Plantation Mistress: Women's World in the Old South.* New York: Pantheon, 1982.

Coleman, J. Winston. *Slavery Times in Old Kentucky.* Chapel Hill: University of North Carolina Press, 1940.

———. *Stage-Coach Days in the Bluegrass: Being an Account of Stage-Coach Travel and Tavern Days in Lexington and Central Kentucky, 1800–1900.* Louisville: Standard Press, 1935.

Collison, Gary. *Shadrack Minkins: From Fugitive Slave to Citizen.* Cambridge, MA: Harvard University Press, 1997.

Cover, Robert. *Justice Accused: Antislavery and the Judicial Process.* New Haven: Yale University Press, 1975.

Cullen, Charles T. *St. George Tucker and Law in Virginia, 1772–1804.* New York: Garland, 1987.

Curschmann, H. *Typhoid Fever and Typhus Fever.* Trans. Alfred Stengel. Philadelphia: W. B. Saunders, 1905.

Dennison, Sam. *Scandalize My Name: Black Imagery in American Popular Music.* New York: Garland, 1982.

Dula, Vicki, and Henry Louis Taylor. "The Black Residential Experience and Community Formation in Antebellum Cincinnati." In Taylor, *Race and the City,* 96–125.

Dumond, Dwight L. *The Letters of James Gillespie Birney, 1831–1857.* Vol. 1. New York: Appleton-Century, 1938.

Eaklor, Vicki L. *American Antislavery Songs: A Collection and Analysis.* Westport, CT: Greenwood Press, 1988.

Egerton, Douglas R. *Gabriel's Rebellion: The Virginia Slave Conspiracies of 1800 and 1802*. Chapel Hill: University of North Carolina Press, 1983.

Ehrlich, Walter. *They Have No Rights: Dred Scott's Struggle for Freedom*. Westport, CT: Greenwood Press, 1979.

Eskew, G. L. *The Pageant of the Packets: A Book of American Steamboating*. New York: Henry Holt, 1929.

Faust, Drew Gilpin, ed. *The Ideology of Slavery: Proslavery Thought in the Antebellum South, 1830–1860*. Baton Rouge: Louisiana State University Press, 1981.

Fehrenbacher, Donald E. *The Dred Scott Case: Its Significance in American Law and Politics*. New York: Oxford University Press, 1978.

Feuss, Claude M. *The Life of Caleb Cushing*. 2 vols. New York: Harcourt, Brace, 1923.

Finkelman, Paul. *An Imperfect Union: Slavery, Federalism, and Comity*. Chapel Hill: University of North Carolina Press, 1981.

Fisher, Miles M. *Negro Slave Songs in the United States*. New York: Russell and Russell, 1953.

Fogel, Robert William. *Without Consent or Contract: The Rise and Fall of American Slavery*. New York: W. W. Norton, 1989.

Fogel, Robert W., and Stanley Engerman. *Time on the Cross: The Economics of American Negro Slavery*. Boston: Little, Brown, 1974.

Foner, Eric. *Free Soil, Free Labor, Free Men: The Ideology of the Republican Party before the Civil War*. New York: Oxford University Press, 1970.

Fox-Genovese, Elizabeth. *Within the Plantation Household: Black and White Women of the Old South*. Chapel Hill: University of North Carolina Press, 1988.

Freehling, William. *The Road to Disunion: Secessionists at Bay, 1776–1854*. New York: Oxford University Press, 1990.

———. "The Divided South, Democracy's Limitations, and the Causes of the Peculiarly North American Civil War." In *Why the Civil War Came*. Ed. Gabor S. Boritt. New York: Oxford University Press, 1996.

Gara, Larry. *The Liberty Line: The Legend of the Underground Railroad*. Lexington: University Press of Kentucky, 1961.

Gatewood, William B. "Sunnyside: The Evolution of an Arkansas Plantation, 1848–1945." *Arkansas Historical Quarterly* 50 (1991): 1–12.

Genovese, Eugene. *Roll, Jordan, Roll: The World the Slaves Made*. New York: Pantheon, 1974.

———. *The Slaveholders' Dilemma: Freedom and Progress in Southern Conservative Thought, 1820–1860*. Columbia: University of South Carolina Press, 1992.

Gienapp, William E. *The Origins of the Republican Party, 1852–1856*. New York: Oxford University Press, 1987.

Gordon, Avery. *Ghostly Matters: Haunting and the Sociological Imagination*. Minneapolis: University of Minnesota Press, 1997.

Gordon-Reed, Annette. *Thomas Jefferson and Sally Hemings: An American Controversy*. Charlottesville: University Press of Virginia, 1997.

Greve, Charles Theodore. *Centennial History of Cincinnati and Representative Citizens*. Chicago: Biographical Publishing, 1904.

Hamilton, Virginia. *Anthony Burns: The Defeat and Triumph of a Fugitive Slave*. New York: Alfred A. Knopf, 1988.

Harris, M. A. *The Black Book*. New York: Random House, 1974.

Harrison, Lowell, and James C. Klotter. *A New History of Kentucky*. Lexington: University Press of Kentucky, 1997.

Hedrick, Joan. *Harriet Beecher Stowe: A Life*. New York: Oxford University Press, 1994.

Hoganson, Kristin. "Garrisonian Abolitionists and the Rhetoric of Gender." *American Quarterly* 45.4 (1993): 558–95.

Honor, Hugh. *The Image of the Black in Western Art*. Vol 4, No. 1: *From the American Revolution to World War I: Slaves and Liberators*. Cambridge, MA: Harvard University Press, 1989.

Hooker, Charles E. "Mississippi." In *Confederate Military History*. Vol. 7. Atlanta: Confederate Publishing Company, 1899.

Hopkins, Vincent. *Dred Scott's Case*. New York: Russell and Russell, 1967.

Horton, James Oliver, and Stacy Flaherty. "Black Leadership in Antebellum Cincinnati." In Taylor, *Race and the City*, 70–95.

Horton, James Oliver, and Lois E. Horton. *In Hope of Liberty: Culture, Community, and Protest among Northern Free Blacks*. New York: Oxford University Press, 1997.

House, Elizabeth. "Toni Morrison's Ghost: The Beloved Who Is Not Beloved." *Studies in American Fiction* 18.1 (1990): 17–26.

Hunter, Louis C. *Steamboats on the Western Rivers: An Economic and Technological History*. Cambridge, MA: Harvard University Press, 1949.

Jillson, Willard Rouse. *Pioneer Kentucky*. Frankfort: State Journal Company, 1934.

Johnson, Michael P. "Smothered Slave Infants: Were Slave Mothers at Fault?" *Journal of Southern History* 47 (1981): 494–520.

Jones, Jacqueline. *Labor of Love, Labor of Sorrow: Black Women, Work, and the Family from Slavery to the Present*. New York: Basic Books, 1985.

Jordan, Winthrop. *White Over Black: American Attitudes toward the Negro, 1550–1812*. Chapel Hill: University of North Carolina Press, 1968.

———. *Tumult and Silence at Second Creek: An Inquiry into a Civil War Slave Conspiracy*. Baton Rouge: Louisiana State University Press, 1993.

Kaufman, Kenneth C. *Dred Scott's Advocate*. Columbia: University of Missouri Press, 1996.

Kiple, Kenneth F., and Virginia H. Kiple. "Slave Child Mortality: Some Nutritional Answers to a Perennial Puzzle." *Journal of Social History* 10 (1977): 284–309.

Kolchin, Peter. *American Slavery: 1619–1877*. New York: Hill and Wang, 1993.

Krumholz, Linda. "The Ghosts of Slavery: Historical Recovery in Toni Morrison's *Beloved*." *African American Review* 26.3 (1992): 395–408.

Kutler, Stanley, ed. *The Dred Scott Decision: Law or Politics*. Boston: Houghton Mifflin, 1967.

Lerner, Gerda. *Black Women in White America: A Documentary History*. New York: Random House, 1972.

Levine, Lawrence W. *Black Culture and Black Consciousness: Afro-American Folk Thought from Slavery to Freedom*. New York: Oxford University Press, 1978.

Levy, Andrew. "Telling *Beloved*." *Texas Studies in Literature and Language* 33.1 (1991): 114–23.

Lucas, Marion B. *A History of Blacks in Kentucky*. Vol 1: *A History of Slavery in Kentucky*. Frankfort: Kentucky Historical Society, 1992.

McDougall, Marion Gleeson. *Fugitive Slaves (1619–1865)*. Fay House Monograph No. 3. Boston: Ginn, 1891.

Middleton, Stephen. "The Fugitive Slave Crisis in Cincinnati, 1850–1860: Resistance,

Reinforcement, and Black Refugees." *Journal of Negro History* 72.1–2 (1987): 20–32.

Miller, William Lee. *Arguing about Slavery: The Great Battle in the United States Congress*. New York: Alfred A. Knopf, 1996.

Morrison, Toni. *Beloved*. New York: Alfred A. Knopf, 1987.

————. Acceptance speech. Frederick G. Melcher Book Award, Unitarian Universalist Association. Cambridge, MA: The Cambridge Forum. Broadcast WVTF, Roanoke, VA, 5 April 1991.

Myers, Robert Anson, ed. *The Children of Pride: A True Story of Georgia and the Civil War*. New Haven: Yale University Press, 1972.

Niven, John. *Salmon Portland Chase: A Biography*. New York: Oxford University Press, 1995.

Numbers, Ronald L. and Todd Savitt, eds. *Science and Medicine in the Old South*. Baton Rouge: Louisiana State University Press, 1983.

Pease, Jane H. *The Fugitive Slave Law and Anthony Burns: A Problem in Law Enforcement*. Philadelphia: J. B. Lippincott, 1975.

Potter, David. *The Impending Crisis, 1848–1861*. New York: Harper & Row, 1976.

Raboteau, Albert J. *Slave Religion*. New York: Oxford University Press, 1978.

Ripley, C. Peter, ed. *The Black Abolitionist Papers*. Vol. 4. Chapel Hill: University of North Carolina Press, 1992.

Rody, Caroline. "Toni Morrison's *Beloved*: History, 'Rememory,' and the 'Clamor for a Kiss.'" *American Literary History* 7.1 (1995): 92–119.

Roediger, David. *The Wages of Whiteness: Race and the Making of the American Working Class*. New York: Verso, 1991.

Savitt, Todd L. *Medicine and Slavery: The Diseases and Health Care of Blacks in Antebellum Virginia*. Urbana: University of Illinois Press, 1978.

Scheper-Hughes, Nancy. *Death without Weeping: The Violence of Everyday Life in Brazil*. Berkeley: University of California Press, 1992.

Scholten, Catherine M. *Childrearing in American Society: 1650–1850*. New York: New York University Press, 1985.

Scruggs, Charles. "The Beloved Community in Toni Morrison's *Beloved*." In *Sweet Home: Invisible Cities in the African American Novel*. Baltimore: Johns Hopkins University Press, 1993.

Sears, Richard D. *The Day of Small Things: Abolitionism in the Midst of Slavery—Berea, Kentucky, 1854–1864*. Lanham, MD: University Press of America, 1986.

Sernett, Milton C., ed. *Afro-American Religious History: A Documentary Witness*. Durham, NC: Duke University Press, 1985.

Siebert, Wilbur H. *The Underground Railroad from Slavery to Freedom*. New York: Russell and Russell, 1898.

Sifakis, Steward. *Compendium of the Confederate Armies: Mississippi*. New York: Facts on File, 1995.

Slaughter, Thomas R. *Bloody Dawn: The Christiana Riot and Racial Violence in the Antebellum North*. New York: Oxford University Press, 1991.

Smith, Margaret Ross. "Sandford C. Faulkner." *Arkansas Historical Quarterly* 14 (1955): 301–14.

Sobel, Mechal. *Trabelin' On: The Slave Journey to an Afro-Baptist Faith*. Westport, CT: Greenwood Press, 1979.

Stampp, Kenneth. *The Peculiar Institution: Slavery in the Antebellum South*. New York: Alfred A. Knopf, 1956.

Steckel, Richard. "Miscegenation and the American Slave Schedules." *Journal of Inter-disciplinary History* 11 (1980): 251–63.

———. *The Economics of U.S. Slave and Southern White Fertility*. New York: Garland, 1985.

Stevens, Charles Emery. *Anthony Burns: A History*. Williamstown, MA: Corner House, 1973.

Stevenson, Brenda. *Life in Black and White: Family and Community in the Slave South*. New York: Oxford University Press, 1996.

Stone, Albert E. *The Return of Nat Turner: History, Literature, and Cultural Politics in Sixties America*. Athens: University of Georgia Press, 1992.

Stuckey, Sterling. *Slave Culture: Nationalist Theory and the Foundations of Black America*. New York: Oxford University Press, 1987.

Sundquist, Eric. *To Wake the Nations: Race in the Making of American Literature*. Cambridge, MA: Harvard University Press, 1993.

Tadman, Michael. *Speculators and Slaves: Masters, Traders, and Slaves in the Old South*. Madison: University of Wisconsin Press, 1989.

Tanner, Paul. "Slavery in Boone County, Kentucky (and Its Aftermath)." 1986. Boone County (KY) Library. Typescript.

Taylor, Henry Louis, ed. *Race and the City: Work, Community, and Protest in Cincinnati, 1820–1970*. Urbana: University of Illinois Press, 1993.

———. "Spatial Organization and the Residential Experience: Black Cincinnati in 1850." *Social Science History* 10.1 (1986): 43–69.

Tragle, Henry I. *The Southampton Slave Revolt of 1831: A Compilation of Source Material*. Amherst: University of Massachusetts Press, 1971.

Trussell, James, and Richard Steckel. "The Age of Slaves at Menarche and Their First Birth." *Journal of Interdisciplinary History* 8.3 (1978): 477–506.

Tucker, Beverly Randolph. *Tales of the Tuckers*. Richmond, VA: Dietz, 1942.

Walters, Ronald G. *The Antislavery Appeal: American Abolitionism after 1830*. Baltimore: Johns Hopkins University Press, 1976.

Walz, Robert B. "Arkansas Slaveholdings and Slaveholders in 1850." *Arkansas Historical Quarterly* 12 (1953): 38–60.

Way, Frederick. *Directory of Western Rivers Packets*. Sewickley, PA: n.p., 1950.

Webber, Thomas L. *Deep Like the Rivers*. New York: W. W. Norton, 1978.

Weisenburger, Francis Phelps. *The Life of John McLean: A Politician on the United States Supreme Court*. Columbus: Ohio State University Press, 1937.

Wheeler, Leslie, ed. *Loving Warriors: Selected Letters of Lucy Stone Blackwell to Henry B. Blackwell, 1853–1893*. New York: Dial, 1981.

White, Deborah Gray. *Ar'n't I a Woman?: Female Slaves in the Plantation South*. New York: W. W. Norton, 1985.

———. "The Lives of Slave Women." In *Black Women in United States History*. Ed. Diane Clark Hine. Brooklyn: Carlson, 1990. 1–14.

Wiecek, William M. "Slavery and Abolition before the United States Supreme Court, 1820–1860." *Journal of American History* 65 (1978): 365–98.

Williams, Richard. *Hierarchical Structures and Social Value: The Creation of Black and Irish Identities in the United States*. New York: Cambridge University Press, 1990.

Wilson, Forrest. *Crusader in Crinoline: The Life of Harriet Beecher Stowe*. Philadelphia: J. B. Lippincott, 1941.

Wolff, Cynthia Griffin. " 'Margaret Garner': A Cincinnati Story." *Massachusetts Review* 32 (1991): 417–40.

Wood, Stephen E. "The Development of Arkansas Railroads." *Arkansas Historical Quarterly* 7 (1948): 103–18.

Woodson, Carter G. "The Negroes in Cincinnati Prior to the Civil War." *Journal of Negro History* 1.1 (1916): 1–22.

Woodward, W. C. "The Rise and Early History of Political Parties in Oregon." *Quarterly of the Oregon Historical Society,* 12.1 (1911): 34–43.

Wyatt-Brown, Bertram. *Honor and Violence in the Old South.* New York: Oxford University Press, 1986.

———. "Leroy Percy and Sunnyside: Planter Mentality and Peonage in the Mississippi Delta." *Arkansas Historical Quarterly* 50 (1991): 60–84.

Yanuck, Julius. "The Garner Fugitive Slave Case." *Mississippi Valley Historical Review* 40 (1953): 47–66.

Yellin, Jean Fagan. *Women and Sisters: The Antislavery Feminists in American Culture.* New Haven: Yale University Press, 1989.

INDEX

✢❧